D1475097

COOPERATION AND DISCORD
IN U.S.-SOVIET ARMS CONTROL

COOPERATION AND DISCORD IN U.S.-SOVIET ARMS CONTROL

Steve Weber

PRINCETON UNIVERSITY PRESS   PRINCETON, NEW JERSEY

Library of Congress Cataloging-in-Publication Data

Weber, Steve, 1961–
Cooperation and discord in U.S.-Soviet arms control / Steve Weber.
p.   cm.
Includes bibliographical references and index.
ISBN 0-691-07837-8
1. Nuclear arms control—United States. 2. Nuclear arms control—
Soviet Union. 3. Strategic forces—United States. 4. Strategic forces—
Soviet Union. 5. Game theory. I. Title.
JX1974.7.W39   1991
327.1'74—dc20   90-27300

This book has been composed in Linotron Sabon

Princeton University Press books are printed
on acid-free paper, and meet the guidelines
for permanence and durability of the Committee
on Production Guidelines for Book Longevity
of the Council on Library Resources

Printed in the United States of America by
Princeton University Press, Princeton, New Jersey

10   9   8   7   6   5   4   3   2   1

Contents

Abbreviations

ABM	Antiballistic Missile System
ACDA	Arms Control and Disarmament Agency
ARPA	Advanced Research Projects Agency
ASAT	Antisatellite System
BMD	Ballistic Missile Defense
CEP	Circular Error Probable
DCI	Director of Central Intelligence
DDR&E	Director, Defense Research and Engineering
DEW	Directed-Energy Weapon
DIA	Defense Intelligence Agency
DoD	Department of Defense
ERIS	Exoatmospheric Reentry Interceptor Subsystem
FOBS	Fractional Orbital Bombardment System
FY	Fiscal Year
ICBM	Intercontinental Ballistic Missile
INF	Intermediate-Range Nuclear Forces
JCS	Joint Chiefs of Staff
LEO	Low Earth Orbit
MHV	Miniature Homing Vehicle
MILSAT	Military Satellite
MIRV	Multiple Independently Targetable Reentry Vehicle
MRV	Multiple Reentry Vehicle
NCA	National Command Authority
NIE	National Intelligence Estimate
NSC	National Security Council
NSDM	National Security Decision Memorandum
NSSM	National Security Study Memorandum
NTM	National Technical Means
OSD	Office of the Secretary of Defense
OSI	On-site Inspection
PALS	Permissive Action Links
PD	Prisoner's Dilemma
PSAC	President's Scientific Advisory Committee
R&D	Research and Development
RV	Reentry Vehicle
SALT	Strategic Arms Limitation Talks
SAM	Surface-to-Air Missile

SCC	Standing Consultative Commission
SDI	Strategic Defense Initiative
SLBM	Submarine-Launched Ballistic Missile
SLCM	Sea-Launched Cruise Missile
TFT	Tit for Tat

Preface _____

THIS BOOK starts with a historical question, but the project from which it evolved has been driven by a theory. In late 1985 I first encountered Robert Axelrod's *The Evolution of Cooperation*. Like so many others, I found this book exciting and pregnant with possibilities. Here was a simple and elegant formalization of a "folk theorem" about cooperation in the Prisoner's Dilemma. Axelrod was circumspect when it came to suggesting the possible applicability of what he wrote about game theory to events in the real world, and particularly to international politics. But those possibilities cried out to be tested. The challenge came in trying to figure out where and how to do that.

The logic of Axelrod's argument brought me to a set of cases from U.S.-Soviet strategic arms control. That turns out to have been fortuitous. The 1980s have been a good time to be thinking about superpower cooperation and arms control. The 1990s will be just as good a time, if for different reasons. The basic question I ask here—why have the United States and the Soviet Union been able to achieve and sustain cooperation in certain arms control issues but not in others—is likely to be an important one for U.S.-Soviet relations and international politics generally in the coming decade. I hope that some of the findings of this book will be helpful to theorists and policymakers who have to think about and manage the new and complex problems that U.S.-Soviet security relations will no doubt hand them.

I have had an enormous amount of help in writing this book. I started it at Stanford University, with support from the Political Science Department and the Center for International Security and Arms Control. Stephen Krasner, Sidney Drell, Theodore Postol, David Holloway, Condoleeza Rice, Lynn Eden, Judith Goldstein, Coit Blacker, Jeffrey Knopf, Uri Bar-Joseph, Susan Stern, Joan Rohlfing, and others shared ideas, read drafts, and were generous with their time and thoughtful criticism. At this point, Deborah Larson and George Downs read the entire manuscript and pointed out its many flaws in a constructive way. An early version of the book followed me across the country to the Center for International Affairs at Harvard University, where an Olin Fellowship gave me needed time to think it through again. At Harvard I had the help of David Spiro, Yuen Fong-Khong, Robert Powell, Robert Art, Peter Katzenstein, Michael Desch, Ted Hopf, Nicholas Ziegler, Emmanuel Adler, Andrew Bennett, and others. An improved manuscript followed me back across the country to Berkeley, where in the final round I had help from George Breslauer, Ernst Haas, Kenneth Waltz, David Collier, and a number of special students in my graduate seminars. The Institute for Global Conflict and Cooperation provided much-needed research support at this point. Along the way, I also had help from four top-notch research assistants—Matthew Finch, Dora Lee, and especially Rudra Sil and Eileen Doherty. I also thank Malcolm De Bevoise and others at Princeton University Press who shepherded the manuscript to completion; and Ron Twisdale, a copyeditor with an unusually keen eye for clarity and precision. Some of Chapter 6 previously appeared in *U.S.-Soviet Security Cooperation: Achievements, Failures, Lessons*, edited by Alexander L. George, Philip J. Farley, and Alexander Dallin. Copyright © 1988 by Oxford University Press, Inc. Used by arrangement.

I have left out the two people to whom I owe the greatest debt. Alexander George was part of this project from its inception. He read innumerable pages with the greatest care and gave both criticism and support in near-perfect measure. He has been a consistent source of inspiration to me, both intellectually and personally. Felicia Wong stepped into the picture later. She has been the most severe, and at the same time, the most gentle critic. I want to dedicate this book to both of them.

Berkeley, California
May 1990

COOPERATION AND DISCORD
IN U.S.-SOVIET ARMS CONTROL

1

Introduction

THIS BOOK is a study of U.S.-Soviet efforts to cooperate in the limitation of strategic nuclear weapons systems. Current theory in international relations provides a powerful analysis of the many impediments to cooperation between states, but it does not yet offer an adequate explanation of why those impediments are sometimes overcome. Arms control cooperation between two adversarial superpowers would be a particularly difficult case to explain. Why have the United States and the Soviet Union achieved cooperative agreements with the goal of enhancing their mutual security in certain arms control issues, but not in others?

This is an important question, not only for international relations theorists but also for political leaders concerned with superpower arms control and the broader U.S.-Soviet relationship in which it is embedded. The success of cooperative arms control efforts has become, for better or for worse, a crucial indicator of larger trends in U.S.-Soviet relations. There is clearly some connection between the two. The Limited Test Ban Treaty concluded in 1963 was an important part of the thaw in relations that followed the Cuban Missile Crisis of 1962. The SALT I accords, signed by President Richard Nixon and General Secretary Leonid Brezhnev in May 1972, ushered in and became a symbol of the detente of the 1970s. The "new detente" of the late 1980s was similarly accompanied by the December 1987 signing of a treaty abolishing the superpowers' intermediate-range nuclear forces.

Arms control may be important in and of itself, apart from its connection to broad trends in U.S.-Soviet relations. Ideally, superpower arms control should help both states to reduce the costs of their continuing military competition. It should also serve to reduce the risks of war, and to limit damage to both sides should war somehow occur.[1] Politicians, political scientists, and strategic analysts disagree strongly over whether U.S.-Soviet arms control has achieved any of these objectives. Nor is it obvious that arms control has, on balance, contributed toward a more constructive and mutually beneficial superpower relationship. In the course of this study, I will consider these questions and set forth an alter-

---

[1] In their classic work on the theory and practice of arms control in the nuclear age, Schelling and Halperin identify these criteria as a practical definition of what constitutes arms control per se. See Schelling and Halperin, *Strategy and Arms Control*.

native perspective on the variegated history of U.S.-Soviet security cooperation. I will also prescribe an alternative approach to the practice of superpower arms control, an approach that I argue has greater potential to maximize the limited contribution that cooperation can make to the security interests and obligations of the United States and the Soviet Union. These analyses and prescriptions follow directly from the findings on the central question of this book: why have the superpowers achieved cooperation in certain arms control issues but not in others?[2]

I seek an answer to this important question by developing a theory of international cooperation that starts from, but goes beyond a formal, game-theoretic approach. In his landmark 1984 work, Robert Axelrod set forth an elegantly simple formal model of the evolution of cooperation in a Prisoner's Dilemma game.[3] This book is an attempt to explore and extend the applicability of Axelrod's model to the problem of explaining cooperation in U.S.-Soviet arms control. I will examine three historical cases—attempts to limit antiballistic missile systems, multiple independently targetable reentry vehicles, and antisatellite weapons (ABM, MIRV, and ASAT)—and I argue that each case fulfills the initial conditions for cooperation identified by Axelrod's model. The formal theory points toward a cooperative outcome in each case. But the actual outcomes do not match the prediction. Cooperation emerges in ABM but not in MIRV, and in ASAT a partially cooperative arrangement deteriorates over time.

Several conclusions are possible. Axelrod's theory could be "wrong" in and of itself. Or it could be valid, and simply not applicable to these cases. Neither of these conclusions is correct. I argue instead that the game-theoretic approach to the study of cooperation is *incomplete*. Axelrod's theory yields important insights about the evolution of cooperation, but it is not by itself sufficiently discriminating to explain the variance in outcomes among these three important cases. How can we do better?

One reason why the theory is incomplete is that it does not include an adequate analysis of *strategy*. Strategy, in game theory, is simply a decision rule—an algorithm that players use to select a course of action in a game. Axelrod shows that the simple strategy of "Tit for Tat," which

---

[2] The reader should take note of the fact that while I use the term "arms control" or "U.S.-Soviet arms control," this book concentrates on arms control issues relating to central strategic weapons systems. There are many other kinds of arms control that this book does not directly address. I discuss the reasons for limiting the scope of the book in this way in Chapter 3.

[3] Axelrod, *The Evolution of Cooperation*. Axelrod was not the first to suggest the possibility for cooperation in an iterated Prisoner's Dilemma, but his book is the most elegant exposition of the conditions under which cooperation is possible and the processes by which it may come about. I discuss the relationship between Axelrod and earlier work in formal theory in Chapter 2.

cooperates on the first round and thereafter does whatever the adversary did on the previous round, can under certain conditions elicit cooperative outcomes in the Prisoner's Dilemma. But strategy in international politics is different. Strategy is the combination of political, military, and diplomatic measures a state employs to promote desired outcomes in its interactions with other states.[4] States face a difficult challenge in developing a strategy that will elicit cooperation from a rival state. Tit for Tat may be an effective strategy in game theory but it does not translate directly into real world behavior. States can employ many different types of strategies based on reciprocity that are broadly consistent with the game-theoretic concept of Tit for Tat. And while Axelrod's "players" can change their behavior and adapt their strategies easily, neither is true of states. In U.S.-Soviet security relations, strategies shift only at critical junctures; once established, they are difficult and costly to modify.

I start with the hypothesis that the specifics of strategy make a difference. In other words, differences among strategies based on reciprocity can explain an important part of the variance in empirical outcomes that is left unexplained by the formal theory. I argue that the particular strategy of reciprocity that a state chooses at a critical juncture is a central determinant of whether cooperation does or does not occur. The basic reason for this is that influencing another state's behavior through a strategy of reciprocity is a more complex process than is captured in game-theoretic models. My hypothesis calls for an explanation of two processes: why states choose the particular strategies they do; and how different strategies bring about changes in the behavior of both states that may or may not produce cooperation.

Using the case studies as an inductive guide, I construct a typology of strategies based on reciprocity that the superpowers have used in their arms control relationship. It turns out that the range of strategies that will successfully promote cooperation in U.S.-Soviet arms control is severely circumscribed to a small subset of those that would be consistent with Tit for Tat. I will make the case that strategies based on one specific ideal type—what I call "enhanced contingent restraint"—will most successfully promote cooperation in U.S.-Soviet security relations. I explore in three case studies the conditions under which a strategy of enhanced contingent restraint can be implemented and how it operates to produce a cooperative outcome. I also consider why other types of reciprocal strategies fail.

Could we have gotten to the same point through formal theory? In principle, the answer may be "possibly"; in practice, the answer is no. The issues of interest here—how states conceive, develop, implement, and

---

[4] This definition follows from Posen, *The Sources of Military Doctrine*, p. 13.

respond to strategies of reciprocity—are not well-suited for analysis by formal game-theoretic models. And because they are issues of the first importance for theorists and policymakers, I argue that empirically based research is for many purposes a more promising way to build theories of cooperation than is the further development of highly complex formal models.

This book is in no sense a definitive "test" of Axelrod's theory. Quite the contrary: since the theory does not yet explain the variance in outcomes among important cases that fit its assumptions and initial conditions, it cannot as it stands be tested against historical evidence. The purpose of this book is more circumscribed: to extend Axelrod's work in an empirical direction that generates new insights about cooperation and U.S.-Soviet arms control, while providing an important agenda for further research.

The Problem of Cooperation

Cooperation occurs in international relations when states adjust their policies in a coordinated way, such that each state's efforts to pursue its interests facilitate rather than hinder the efforts of other states to pursue their own interests. Cooperation is not always seen as a "problem" per se. It is common to hear that we live in a world of increasing interdependence, where global issues and shared interests create strong demands for international cooperation. Even security, the basic province of sovereignty, has been invaded by interdependence. Because nuclear weapons render the superpowers utterly and equally vulnerable, cooperation in limiting the shared threat to the survival of humanity has become an "imperative." A group of authors, sometimes lumped under the rubric "liberal interdependence" thinkers, argue that though it may take some time to work out the details, the United States and the Soviet Union will learn to cooperate in arms control because they must do so in order to survive.[5]

This view is not acceptable to proponents of the more traditional, realist perspective on international relations. Realists justly criticize some of their more optimistic colleagues as being naive about power and conflict, and for underestimating the incentives for states to compete even when all stand to lose in absolute terms. But this critique can be carried too far. Joseph Grieco, among others, extends the realist view to suggest that "cooperation theory" is fundamentally wrong-headed because it adopts a liberal interdependence perspective on international relations and understates the importance of conflict.[6]

[5] For example, see Schell, *The Fate of the Earth*; idem, *The Abolition*.
[6] Grieco, "Anarchy and the Limits of Cooperation." "Liberal interdependence," like all

This is a mistake. Cooperation theory, as I develop it here, starts from the fundamental premises of realism. I assume that the international system remains fundamentally anarchic. Without an international authority capable of making and enforcing rules, there are no inherent limits on the pursuit of sovereign interests by individual states. That extends to the use of force at any time. The consequence of anarchy is that each state must observe the principle of self-help and rely primarily on its own capabilities to ensure security and well-being.

Anarchy also places a premium on the "relative" position of states, as opposed to the absolute gains that may be realized from cooperation. Cooperation may make everyone better-off, but one state will be wary if it helps another state more than itself, since the other may then "use its disproportionate gain . . . to damage or destroy" the state.[7] In a realist world, states with conflicting interests are strongly inclined to eschew potential gains from cooperation with potential rivals.

The point is that "imperatives" do not always occur under anarchy, and the most compelling shared interests and the strongest of incentives will not always produce cooperation. Even under the most auspicious circumstances, cooperation is risky. The potential for exploitation is high, and the penalty for misplaced trust can be damaging or even catastrophic. Prudent political leaders are wary of conciliatory gestures, and they take seriously the worst-case interpretation of an adversary's intentions.

The "security dilemma" is an important result. States that are engaged in military preparations, even if intended for defense, will tend to provoke responses from other states, who must always fear the threat arising from any state's enhanced capabilities, regardless of intentions. In some situations, the incentives to exploit another state or to act preemptively in the face of possible exploitation may be compelling. And if these structural factors were not by themselves sufficient to hamper security cooperation between two competing superpowers, the difficulties are enhanced by the general hostility and distrust that has characterized U.S.-Soviet relations over time. The fact that each superpower's ideology long identified the other as the major threat to international peace and progress does not make cooperation any easier.

Yet few relationships between states are characterized solely by conflicting interests. U.S. and Soviet leaders have at various times perceived a number of interests in common, including interests relating to their own

---

such labels, is a stereotype that does not capture the range and complexity of the views held by those who might be lumped into the category. All the usual caveats apply to my use of this label. Grieco uses the term "neo-liberal institutionalism" for what I call the liberal interdependence perspective.

[7] Waltz, *Theory of International Politics*, p. 105. Waltz's earlier book, *Man, the State, and War*, remains the single best exposition of the consequences of anarchy for international politics.

most fundamental security concerns. Some common interests can be achieved through unilateral actions that states can take on their own—for example, deterrence based on mutual assured destruction (MAD) can be had if both states independently deploy large arsenals of survivable nuclear weapons suitable for retaliatory attacks against cities. However, states in this position may wish to coordinate their behaviors so they can achieve the same result at lesser cost. Sometimes the incentives can be great. If Washington and Moscow agree not to deploy counterforce weapons that threaten each other's retaliatory capabilities, the problem of guaranteeing MAD can be solved more easily, less expensively and with greater confidence. There are other instances where common interests can *only* be realized through coordinated action. Either of these conditions can spawn a demand for cooperation, even between long-term adversaries.

In the starkest of realist worlds, this demand for cooperation would go unmet. But the real world is not so stark: despite the obstacles, the scope and magnitude of international cooperation have sometimes been quite extensive. International relations theory needs to account for this cooperation in some way, because it affects the character of life in the international system for all states.

Realism, by itself, has trouble explaining some forms of cooperation. A realist view can accomodate limited cooperation that occurs when states' short-term or "myopic" self-interests are identical: U.S.-Soviet cooperation that is directly tied to the superpowers' overwhelming interest in avoiding a catastrophic nuclear war is not a puzzle for realism. But superpower cooperation in arms control has at times gone beyond shared myopic self-interest. In 1972, Nixon and Brezhnev signed a treaty that severely limited the deployment of antiballistic missile systems. During the 1960s and much of the 1970s, the two sides refrained from developing and deploying antisatellite weapons. More recently, the superpowers agreed to remove a large number of medium-range missiles from Europe; and in 1990 they are on the verge of accepting substantial reductions in their strategic arsenals. None of these actions was necessary to prevent nuclear war. All involved the possibilities of cheating and relative gains. Realism can accommodate this kind of cooperation only uncomfortably. The logic of realism leads us to expect that these more elaborate forms of security cooperation will be short-lived, tenuous, and insignificant in the evolution of relations between the superpowers.[8]

These are a few "successes" of arms control. There have also been

---

[8] While "the anarchy of the [international system] strongly affects the likelihood of cooperation," Waltz notes that states do not in all circumstances "find it impossible to work with one another, to make agreements limiting arms, and to cooperate in establishing organizations." Precisely what "circumstances" would permit such cooperation to occur is left unspecified, as are its consequences. Waltz, *Theory of International Politics*, p. 115.

many failures. Washington and Moscow failed to place meaningful constraints on MIRV warheads in the early 1970s, when the arguments for doing so were at least as convincing as those favoring restraint in ABM. And although the character of U.S.-Soviet relations has changed dramatically at the beginning of the 1990s, the potential for additional costly failures in arms control remains.

It is an important weakness in the realist argument that it cannot explain why cooperation develops in some of these instances but not in others. Cooperation is not *inconsistent* with realism, but this is a much weaker statement than to say that cooperation is *explained*. Success or failure matters, and sometimes it matters greatly. Cooperation has not always been short-lived and tenuous. It has had tremendous impact on the evolution of U.S.-Soviet relations. Realist theory as it stands addresses the constraints on security cooperation, but it has little to say about how states sometimes overcome those constraints, and even less to say about the consequences of their having done so.

Cooperation theory does not deny the constraints. It does not *replace* realism. It is an addition to realism. It elaborates and supplements the theory to provide a more precise explanation: to address why, how, and under what circumstances cooperation will emerge between states in an anarchic environment. It should also deal with the consequences of cooperation.

As the first step in developing such a theory, I limit this book to explaining cooperation in U.S.-Soviet arms control. Along the way, I construct an argument about the reasons why states choose the strategies they do. I explore the processes of influence, learning, and change by which different types of strategies based on reciprocity may be more or less successful in promoting cooperation. This leads me to refine the concept of cooperation: there are different types of cooperation with distinct consequences for the development and deterioration of arms control agreements. All of these findings are additions to realism. Are the lessons generalizable to other kinds of international cooperation, beyond U.S.-Soviet arms control? Perhaps, but I make no assumptions until the necessary empirical research has been done.

Game Theory and the Problem of Cooperation

Game theory has been a subject of sustained interest among social scientists ever since the publication of Von Neumann and Morgenstern's classic work, *Theory of Games and Economic Behavior*, in 1944.[9] Game the-

---

[9] Von Neumann and Morgenstern, *Theory of Games and Economic Behavior*. The classic survey of formal game theory remains Luce and Raiffa, *Games and Decisions*.

ory attracted special attention among international relations scholars during the early 1960s, when a cadre of civilian strategists began to apply game models to the analysis of nuclear deterrence. This work was abstract and deductive, and its primary purpose was to generate prescriptions for policymakers.[10]

A separate body of work developed around attempts to use game theory for explanation. The focus here was on the actual behavior of states, particularly during international crises. There are a number of reasons why game theory seemed promising for this kind of application. Well-articulated game models had the virtues of parsimony and elegance that most studies of international relations lacked. The models were also wonderfully abstract. Precisely because it dealt with idealized actors in a generic environment, game theory seemed capable of shedding light on problems of conflict and cooperation across the spectrum of international political, security, and economic issues.

The game-theoretic model most commonly applied to the study of world politics has been the Prisoner's Dilemma (PD), because its structure seems to capture the essence of a number of classic problems in international relations. In the well-known PD, the logic of individual action defeats the logic of collective action. Both actors would receive substantial benefits if they were to cooperate, but each is tempted to defect and receive a higher payoff, leaving the adversary with less. Each player has an incentive to defect if there is reason to believe that the other may cooperate, and each knows that the other faces the same situation. It is rational for both players to defect; but by doing so, both are left worse off than they would have been had they managed to cooperate. The logic of the game is at least suggestive of one source of "nonoptimal" outcomes in world politics.[11]

The PD model leads to generally pessimistic conclusions about the prospects for international cooperation. Can states, seen as rational egoists in an anarchic environment, ever cooperate in PD-type situations? In 1984, Axelrod's *The Evolution of Cooperation* generalized and formalized the argument, which had been floating around in the game-theoretic literature for some time, that mutual defection was *not* the inevitable outcome of the PD.[12] In a disarmingly simple model, Axelrod demonstrated

[10] The classic example, of course, is Schelling, *The Strategy of Conflict.*

[11] In game theory, "nonoptimal" has a well-defined meaning in terms of the payoffs accruing to the players. In international relations, what is nonoptimal may be more difficult to define. I use the term here loosely, to suggest an outcome where all parties would have received greater benefits from mutual cooperation had they been able to achieve it.

[12] For example, the important book by Taylor, *Anarchy and Cooperation.* Axelrod's earlier work in cooperation theory focused on the question of how to "play" the PD more effectively: for example, see his "Effective Choice in the Prisoner's Dilemma." *The Evolu-*

that self-interested actors can achieve and sustain cooperation in the PD under a set of restrictive conditions. If the probability of continued inter-action between players is high, and payoffs in future rounds of the game are not heavily discounted or valued less than present payoffs, coopera-tion can be strategically rational and can emerge even in an initially hos-tile environment. It followed from Axelrod's argument that uncondi-tional defection is not always a dominant strategy for self-interested actors in the PD. But the question of what strategy players *should* use was indeterminate, because even in an iterated PD with a low discount rate, the "best" strategy—that which will maximize a player's payoffs—de-pends upon the strategies employed by others.

Are there strategies that do promote cooperation in this world? Axel-rod tried to answer this question by pitting a variety of strategies against each other in a computer tournament. He found that a surprisingly simple strategy of reciprocity—"Tit for Tat" (TFT)—can elicit a stable cooper-ative solution in a wide variety of environments. Does this damage real-ism's outlook toward cooperation? Not at all. In fact, Axelrod strength-ens the realist argument, because *The Evolution of Cooperation* suggests a more powerful way to start thinking about cooperation without ever compromising the theory's central assumptions of anarchy and "the state as rational egoist."

Building on Axelrod

The Evolution of Cooperation is only a starting point. A theory of coop-eration in the PD is not a theory of cooperation in U.S.-Soviet arms con-trol or any other real-world issue. There are reasons to be wary. I have already mentioned one: that Axelrod's theory is incomplete. Chapter 2 considers precisely how the theory is incomplete, and in Chapter 3 I fill in some of those gaps. At the outset it is important to recognize that there are two general ways to build upon an incomplete deductive theory.

One way is to construct more complex formal models that refine the theoretical constructs of the formal PD. For example, a number of theo-rists have experimented with stylized models of incomplete information and misperception to replace Axelrod's assumption that actors possess perfect information about the adversary's behavior.[13] By incorporating

---

tion of Cooperation has a similar prescriptive agenda: Axelrod notes (p. 29) that a major gap in the literature on the PD is that none of it "reveals very much about how to play the game well."

[13] See, for example, Molander, "The Optimal Level of Generosity in a Selfish, Uncertain Environment"; George W. Downs, David M. Rocke, and Randolph M. Siverson, "Arms Races and Cooperation," in Oye, *Cooperation under Anarchy*; Crawford, "Dynamic

more highly refined assumptions into the theory, it is possible to generate more complex and interesting results.

But are these refined formal models any more "realistic" than the characterizations they replace? Intuitively, one wants to answer yes. It is more plausible to start with the assumption that states sometimes misperceive important things about the behavior of other states. But intuition is a dangerous way to justify theoretical assumptions. In fact, because the refinements are by their very nature difficult and sometimes impossible to test, formal theorists rarely go beyond that. A formal model that randomly misinterprets incoming information 10% or 20% of the time has no greater prima facie empirical validity than does a model that assumes perfect information.

The point is simply that a deductive theory expanded in this direction remains deductive, regardless of the level of detail introduced into its assumptions. Such a theory can be used to deduce hypotheses about relationships between independent and dependent variables. The "truth" of these relationships can be tested mathematically because "truth" is only a question of valid reasoning within the logic of the theory itself. A deductive theory that passes this test possesses *internal* validity: it is "true" within the abstract world defined by its logical structure and assumptions. The theory gains an epistemological status equivalent to the mathematical statement, $X + Y = Z$.

However, the *external* validity of these relationships remains unproven. Put simply, deductive theories generate internally valid statements about abstract variables in a theoretical world. Bruce Bueno de Mesquita, among others, notes that deductive logic can generate an infinite set of internally valid statements, only some of which are applicable to the real world. The rest are trivial exercises in logic, art for art's sake.[14] It is impossible to distinguish by purely deductive means between what is interesting and what is merely elegant.

The other way to build upon an incomplete deductive theory is through *induction*. By forcing a simple theory to confront a set of historical cases that it ought to be able to explain, that subset of deductive statements that are powerful for understanding real world events can be isolated. Such empirical analysis can also suggest additional variables that can be added to improve a theory's applicability to a set of data. Often, these additional variables would not have emerged from purely deductive theorizing.

Neither approach is inherently "better," but they do different things.

Games and Dynamic Contract Theory"; and Kreps et al., "Rational Cooperation in the Finitely Repeated Prisoner's Dilemma."

[14] Bueno De Mesquita, *The War Trap*, p. 9.

That said, it is important to keep in mind that the purpose of theory in studying international relations is to increase our understanding of actual events in relationships among states. An internally valid deductive theory by itself may be suggestive, but students and practitioners of international relations need theories that have external validity, theories with demonstrated explanatory, predictive, and prescriptive power relevant to real-world events.

This book, unlike most of the work that has followed Axelrod, focuses on the second, inductive approach. This is not a book about game theory per se. It is an attempt to expand a relatively simple deductive theory through the use of historical case studies. What results is a political (not game-theoretic) explanation—an externally valid model of how cooperation can evolve in U.S.-Soviet arms control.

What can Axelrod's theory tell us about this empirical problem? Neither an inductive nor a deductive approach on its own can answer that question.[15] Formal game theories, as Schelling noted, are *not* empirical theories of how real world "actors"—be they individuals, firms, or states—actually behave.[16] Induction by itself would be no more satisfying. Inductively derived generalizations about relationships between so-called variables in empirical cases may be entirely spurious, or just case-specific descriptions. The most powerful possible arguments can be derived from an interactive approach, which can supply the deductive, logical framework for empirical generalizations *and* the empirical correlates of a relationship deduced in formal theory. Axelrod's theory is ripe for such an approach.

Bridging the Gap: Formal Theories and Empirical Research

The interactive approach requires transiting the gap between an abstract-deductive theory and a set of empirical cases, and that is a difficult task in any science.[17] This is the second and most important problem in build-

[15] I do not mean to underestimate either the power or the importance of the deductive approach to theory building. Formal theory has the considerable advantages of elegance and parsimony which inductive work can rarely achieve. My point here is simply that for a specific purpose, one or the other approach may be more useful. This is at once the most obvious and most convincing argument in favor of methodological pluralism in social science research. I will make the strongest possible case that an empirical approach will be more productive for the study of cooperation in U.S.-Soviet arms control, but this should not be taken to imply intolerance on my part for other methodologies. For the moment, I take these as complementary to my approach in this book.

[16] See Schelling, "What is Game Theory?" pp. 213–14.

[17] Theoretical physicists, for example, encounter a similar problem. They have the distinct advantage of being able to design and conduct experiments; but this does not solve the

ing on Axelrod, and many previous attempts to do this with game theory and international relations have been deficient. It is not enough to "stretch" formal models and impose them on complex historical situations by noting certain correspondences between relationships deduced in game theory and *possibly* analogous events in the real world. It is not enough to draw mechanistic analogies between abstract concepts and empirical data; or to make an implicit claim that if game-theoretic language can be used to *describe* a historical case,—and a formal model can be devised that produces an outcome similar along some dimension to that seen in the case,—then history has at some level been *explained.* To simply describe real events in game-theoretic language does not constitute explanation or evidence of external validity. It actually undermines the potential utility of game theory in the study of international relations.

This book develops a more complex means of transiting the gap between game theory and international politics, involving four discrete steps. The first step is to delimit a set of cases where the assumptions of Axelrod's model can be readily established. This can be a controversial step because it must confront a vast literature critiquing the many assumptions of game theory as inadequate representations of world politics.[18] Of course, all theoretical assumptions are inadequate as description. The real challenge is whether the subsequent theory can produce useful information and hypotheses rather than simply trivial statements about an unreal world. It is also a valid criticism to say that assumptions can be so highly unrepresentative of the real world that they cannot lead to a theory with external validity.

In the next section I will examine the central assumptions of Axelrod's model in the context of U.S.-Soviet arms control. I argue that the assumptions of Axelrod's theory, albeit imperfect, are not so unrepresentative of certain features of world politics that applications of the theory ought to be dismissed outright. Theories of cooperation derived from the PD model should not be expected to illuminate all issues in international relations, but there may be some issues to which such a theory can be applied. In fact, in the specific case of U.S.-Soviet arms control in an era of rough nuclear parity, the assumptions may be surprisingly close to reality.[19]

---

larger epistemological problem of linking abstract theories to the experimental evidence that their colleagues can provide. Philosophers of science have proposed means for resolving this dilemma. I will draw from their approach in my discussion of "bridge principles" in Chapter 3.

[18] For an excellent review that discusses many of the main issues, see Jervis, "Realism, Game Theory, and Cooperation."

[19] This permits me to avoid a cycle of critique and counter-critique over the *general* validity of game theory's assumptions in applications to international relations. A better way to

The second step is to link the *concepts* of game theory to real world *indicators*. Such concepts as preferences, iteration, cooperation, and defection have precise meanings in game theory but not in the real world. Chapter 3 proposes a set of "bridge principles" that forge a link between each of these concepts and suitable indicators that can be measured in the empirical realm of U.S.-Soviet arms control.[20]

The first two steps are needed to establish that ABM, MIRV, and ASAT share the initial conditions of Axelrod's model. The third step focuses on the strategies that states use in attempts to elicit cooperation. It is here that the formal theory is incomplete, leaving two critical questions: why do states choose one type of reciprocity strategy over another; and why do different types of strategy that vary only in their criteria of reciprocity produce such different outcomes?

In Chapter 3 I suggest additions to the theory that are needed to answer the first of these questions. Surveying the history of U.S.-Soviet arms control, I develop a typology of reciprocity strategies that are variants of Tit for Tat. There are three ideal types that U.S. decisionmakers have used, at different times, in their arms control dealings with the Soviet Union. They are: contingent restraint, enhanced contingent restraint, and contingent threat of escalation. Each is consistent with Tit for Tat, but each prescribes a different approach and each has different consequences for cooperation.

Why do decisionmakers choose one of these strategies over another at a given juncture? I propose five variables to explain this choice: interests and incentives, saliencies, the general political environment of U.S.-Soviet relations, strategic theory, and bureaucratic pressures. Each of these is very general, but I develop them more specifically in Chapter 3. For now, it is important to recognize where these variables come from. Clearly, they are not a part of Axelrod's model; nor could they be understood within the context of a formal theory. They emerged from an iterative process that began with candidate variables extracted from a preliminary investigation of U.S.-Soviet arms control cases. I refined the variables by applying them to increasingly more detailed data. This led to a set of questions about the impact of each variable on the type of reciprocal

---

proceed is to limit the project to a carefully delineated set of cases, exploring the utility of assumptions vis-à-vis the historical data of those particular cases. I will not try to establish that game theory's assumptions are valid in a general sense, but only that they are sufficiently realistic and are useful for developing a theory of cooperation in U.S.-Soviet arms control.

[20] I adopt the notion of "bridge principles" from Carl Hempel and other philosophers of science who have been concerned with an analagous problem of epistemology and methodology, mostly in the physical sciences. See Hempel, *Philosophy of Natural Science*, especially pp. 70–84.

strategy adopted by the United States, questions that are detailed in Chapter 3 and then posed to each of the case studies. In Chapter 7 I assess how each of the variables influenced the choice of strategy and develop these findings into a set of hypotheses that could be tested against other cases.[21]

The second critical question demands further additions. To explain why different strategies of reciprocity alter the prospects for cooperation, a more complex model of learning and strategy change needs to be added to the game-theoretic model. My starting point is a simple proposition: interstate influence, adjustment of behavior, and "learning" are complex and sensitive processes in international relations, and these complexities are not captured in a useful way by game theory. In Chapter 2, I explain why Axelrod's simplistic models of "learning" and change are inadequate for studying U.S.-Soviet arms control. Then I discuss the alternative concepts of learning and strategy change that I will add to the game-theoretic model in order to "push" it in this empirical direction. Again, I develop a set of questions that I then use to interrogate the cases. Finally, in Chapter 7 I assess the findings and formulate hypotheses about learning and change in response to different strategies of reciprocity.

The fourth and final step is to focus on the processes or causal paths through which strategies influence outcomes. If strategy does indeed make a difference, explaining cooperation requires that we understand how one of these ideal type strategies leads to cooperation and others to failure. In a fully specified formal model where we know both players' strategies, this would be a trivial problem. For example, if both players' strategies are to cooperate contingent on certain demands of the other, and those demands are compatible, then the outcome is cooperation.

But in U.S.-Soviet arms control, the problem is not at all trivial. Retrospective analysis, like the decisions of contemporary policymakers, rests on reliable data about strategy on only one side of the equation. U.S. decisionmakers may know their own strategy, but they do not know the Soviets' strategy, nor are they certain how their behavior influences Soviet choices. They develop "working hypotheses" about Soviet interests and reason from there to the impact of American strategy on Soviet behavior. They use bits and pieces of feedback, which they evaluate in the context

---

[21] There is a reason why I have chosen to present the variables in Chapter 3 linked to a set of *questions*, rather than a set of *hypotheses* that I might then claim to "test" in the case studies. Because the variables were induced from a preliminary investigation of the cases, it would be deceptive to set them up with "hypotheses" to be tested in the same cases. Where would such hypotheses come from? They could not be derived from the game theory on which this project is based. They would have to come either from a knowledge of the outcome of the cases (in which case I would be "testing" hypotheses against the same set of data from which they were derived) or from other, peripheral theories on bargaining behavior, bureaucratic politics, etc., which are not being tested in this project. It is important to remember that I am developing a new theory, not testing an already well-developed one.

of those hypotheses, to monitor and modify their strategies over time. Neither of these decisionmaking tools is open to analysis through formal theory, but understanding how they function is an essential part of explaining the success or failure of cooperation and the consequences for U.S.-Soviet relations.[22]

Applying this four-step method of linking game theory to international relations is an intricate process, but it makes it possible to harness the power of game theory more fully. It treats game theory neither as a formal model nor as mechanistic description, but rather as a heuristic or "framework for analysis" in the manner suggested by Thomas Schelling.[23] The sacrifice of parsimony is necessary to achieve my objectives.

Game Theory and U.S.-Soviet Arms Control

With all of these difficulties, why concentrate on a model of cooperation derived from game theory? *The Evolution of Cooperation* is provocative, even seductive; but why assume that an abstract theory of games will be a particularly useful tool for studying U.S.-Soviet arms control? The question can be put the other way around: why should someone who wants to explore possible applications of Axelrod's model focus their interest on the limitation of central strategic weapons systems rather than some other example of international cooperation?

There are a number of reasons for forcing these two realms to confront each other. Game theory aims at uncovering the logic of interdependent decisions: situations in which two or more actors have choices to make,

[22] Jack Levy has pointed out to me that this approach is sometimes referred to as "theoretical specification," which means delineating the causal chain linking independent and dependent variables. When brought to bear on an empirical case, it is closely related to what Alexander George calls "process-tracing." I find it interesting that theorists in other areas, particularly economics, have also complained that applications of game theory rarely devote sufficient attention to the important issue of process. Robert Wilson, in a review of theoretical models of oligopolistic competition, wrote that "the field's research is mostly a summary of what observations can be approximated by the predictions of a plausible model," and "the actual decision processes and behaviors of the firms it [game theory] purports to describe have rarely been examined closely." Robert Wilson, "Deterrence in Oligopolistic Competition," in Stern et al., *Perspectives on Deterrence*.

[23] In *The Strategy of Conflict*, Schelling demonstrated how game theory could be used as a framework for analysis of a wide variety of "situations in which there is common interest as well as conflict between adversaries," or mixed-motive games. He argued, for reasons I discuss in Chapter 2, that the results of empirical research would have to be added to the basic structure of game theory in order to render it useful. This was not simply a matter of "testing" game theory per se, but of expanding it and elaborating it so that it could serve as a framework for a more complex analysis of the actual behavior of states, firms, or anything else. See Schelling, *The Strategy of Conflict*, especially the Preface and Chapters 1, 4, and 6.

some preference regarding outcomes, and some knowledge of the possible choices and preferences of others, where the actual outcome depends upon the choices of *all*. Game models are most interesting when players' preferences describe a mixed-motive game, one in which shared and conflicting interests coexist.[24] U.S.-Soviet nuclear arms control in an era of rough nuclear parity resembles a mixed-motive game in more than superficial fashion. The elements of conflict are obvious: nuclear weapons by themselves have not transformed the anarchic structure of international politics or rival relationship between the superpowers. Each has strong incentives to pursue its own security through independent means. That said, deterrence based on the prospect of MAD constrains the means by which superpower competition can be pursued. The nuclear balance of terror is not inviolable, but it is arguably more robust than any previous balance of military capabilities. Incremental changes in force structure that can be achieved by either side in a short period of time do not threaten deterrence stability; and over the longer term, each state has demonstrated both its will and capability to take whatever unilateral actions are necessary to insure, at a minimum, the maintenance of MAD.

The underlying stability of mutual deterrence generates substantial incentives for the superpowers to cooperate, in limited ways, in the joint management of the nuclear arms race. These incentives range over military, political, and economic interests, and have at certain times been perceived by U.S. and Soviet leaders as being quite strong. They are occasionally so convincing that cooperation of a sort is nearly over-determined. Both sides, for example, have chosen not to place nuclear weapons in orbit around the earth because their unilateral reasons for not doing so are compelling. The more interesting cases are those where the balance between shared and conflicting interests is more tenuous, and the "best" decision for each side is exquisitely sensitive to what the other chooses to do. The cases I have chosen to examine—ABM, MIRV, and ASAT—fall into this category. Cooperation in these strategic arms control issues, at first glance, looks much like a mixed-motive, interdependent decision situation of game theory.

But when we probe beneath the surface, the vices of game theory start to complicate the question of whether game theory can serve as a useful tool for studying arms control. What about the assumptions that game theory makes about the actors and the world in which they live? The simple PD model, the prototype for cooperation theory, takes perfectly

[24] In some interdependent decisions, the players may have entirely shared interests and agree on the preferred outcome. In others, they are completely at odds; there is no single outcome that would please them both. The former are referred to as "games of pure coordination"; the latter are "games of pure conflict." For a discussion of such games, and empirical examples, see Schelling, *The Strategy of Conflict*, Chapter 4.

rational players with perfect information and places them in a stark environment, free of institutions, where no communication is possible.[25]

Formal theorists have long acknowledged these limitations. They have refined the simple PD model by incorporating more complex representations of decisionmaking under uncertainty, imperfect information, updating of probabilistic assessments of others' preferences, and the like. These refinements remain formal and deductive. They *seem* to be increasingly plausible representations of reality, in part because they are typically drawn from observation about how decisionmakers actually behave; but they, too, are built on a foundation of assumptions that are not tested against empirical data.[26] As the formalizations become more complex, even the idea of testing becomes prohibitively complicated. To repeat an earlier point, how would we know that states misperceive each other's actions 10% of the time? The nature of such formalizations makes them difficult and perhaps impossible to test. A note of caution is in order. If a model based on this type of assumption produces a "result" that resembles the actual outcome of a particular historical case, this does not constitute evidence that the model itself or its assumptions are valid.

Can an empirical approach do better? It is easy to criticize the assumptions of the simple PD model at a general and abstract level; but when these assumptions are brought to bear on certain specific issues in international relations, they no longer seem so absurd. Earlier I made the assertion that these assumptions are surprisingly close to a description of reality in certain U.S.-Soviet arms control cases. While I will not pretend to prove this or to settle controversy about all potentially problematic assumptions at this point, I do maintain that basic assumptions about the environment, players, and stakes of the game in the simple PD model are sufficiently representative of important characteristics of U.S.-Soviet arms control that we can proceed in a serious way with an analysis.

The Environment

Axelrod's model demonstrates possibilities for cooperation to evolve in an environment free of institutions. The international system is not en-

[25] This is only a sampling of simple game-theoretic assumptions that are, at the very least, problematic when applied to the world of international relations in general and U.S.-Soviet arms control in particular. For a concise discussion of these and other "suspicious" assumptions of game theory, see Beer, "Games and Metaphors."

[26] Herbert Simon has shown that such theories *necessarily* incorporate empirically derived modifications to the assumption or definition of rationality in a selective fashion. Some of these modifications are later incorporated into a primarily deductive theory by deriving formalizations from them. Simon, "Human Nature in Politics."

tirely free of institutions and states are not atomistic players in a feature-less vacuum. Even the basic concept of anarchy might be troubling if it were applied simplistically to certain issues in international political econ-omy where there are a variety of strong international regimes, or to re-gional security "subsystems" such as NATO where a radically uneven distribution of power generates a form of "hegemonic stability." But in the U.S.-Soviet security relationship, anarchy lies considerably closer to the surface. Cooperation, if it occurs, is not likely to be enforced by any kind of hegemonic distribution of power. And cooperation in the limita-tion of central strategic weapons systems developed during the late 1960s in the absence of substantial preexisting institutions. It is not so far-fetched to start from the assumption that U.S. and Soviet leaders ponder-ing the possibilities of cooperation in the cases of ABM, MIRV, and ASAT did so in an environment quite close to the institution-free world of the simple PD.

The Players

The players in the simple PD model are rational unitary actors. With com-plete knowledge of the game's payoff matrix, they employ strategies aimed at other players whose identity and past behavior are entirely clear. No one claims that these assumptions describe the "players" in U.S.-So-viet arms control; but as an analytic starting point they are more powerful than they are sometimes given credit for. At the level of international pol-itics, it is clear that the United States and the Soviet Union as *states* are the dominant actors in security relations. States deploy strategic weapons systems or refrain from doing so. Cooperation, when it occurs, occurs between states. Reinforcing this is the fact that the U.S.-Soviet arms con-trol relationship has remained essentially bipolar, with the attention of each superpower focused primarily upon the other. There is little doubt about the identity of the "other player," and each maintains a vigorous and wary watch to observe and interpret the behavior of its principal adversary.

This is not the same thing as making the heroic assumption that the state approximates a unitary decisionmaker at the level of domestic poli-tics. Individuals in Washington and Moscow disagree about what the state should do. Bureaucracies and domestic constituencies generate dis-sensus. The internal bargaining that follows affects what the state's be-havior will be; but there remain external actions that can be identified as actions belonging to the state.

I start, then, with a more plausible assumption: that the superpowers behave in arms control as coherent and goal-oriented actors subject to the constraints of bureaucratic desires and other domestic pressures. Bureaucracies are the channels through which external stimuli are perceived, measured, and interpreted—and in which policy alternatives and potential responses are generated.[27] This assumption, which could be called "strategic unity," is only a starting point. It rests on the claim that the arms control behavior of the superpowers is driven principally by external factors, most importantly a perceived security threat, and not principally by the internal politics of bureaucratic bargaining. Whether this claim is true or not will not be resolved by contrasting the two opposed "driving forces" at an abstract level: it is better to make it an empirical issue for the case studies to resolve. The challenge to my claim is particularly strong in this instance, because two of the cases that I use—ABM and MIRV—were instrumental in the initial development of the bureaucratic politics paradigm. In contrast to the earlier and mostly historical studies that led to this paradigm, I argue that the superpowers' behavior in these cases and in ASAT can be seen as responsive primarily to external factors, with bureaucracies playing a secondary role.

What about the rationality assumption? In a mixed-motive interdependent decision situation, to act rationally is simply to act strategically, because there is no single "best" choice independent of what others do. Strategic rationality, as it might be called, does not require perfect information or fully specified utility functions. It requires only that "actors choose courses of action based on preferences and expectations of how others will behave."[28] This is also a reasonable starting point. Precisely how the superpowers actually arrive at those preferences and expectations in arms control issues is again an empirical question.[29] But the point is that to proceed with strategic rationality as a baseline does not require heroic assumptions. For a state to employ a strategy in a rational manner does not mean that it must have a fully specified algorithm that can generate decisions under all conceivable contingencies. Rather, it

[27] Christopher Achen proposes a formal model for foreign policy decisionmaking with similar logic. He concentrates on a "focal actor" whose decision calculus is influenced by bureaucratic bargaining. The decision that emerges can be represented as that of a unitary actor whose utilities are a weighted compromise among other actors' preferences within a pluralistic decisionmaking system. See Achen, "When Is a State with Bureaucratic Politics Representable as a Unitary Rational Actor?"

[28] Duncan Snidal, "The Game *Theory* of International Politics," in Oye, *Cooperation under Anarchy*.

[29] This follows Schelling's argument that "some *essential* part of the study of mixed motive games is necessarily empirical . . . there is no way that an analyst can reproduce the whole decision process either introspectively or by an axiomatic method. There is no way to build a model for the interaction of two or more decision units, with the behavior and expectations of those decision units being derived by purely formal deduction." *The Strategy of Conflict*, p. 163.

means coherence in "a pattern of decisions" and "a general policy stance" that demonstrates a conception of the interdependent nature of decisions, as well as a capacity to forgo short-run considerations for longer-term objectives.[30] This too does not seem a misleading first approximation of U.S. and Soviet behavior in strategic arms control issues.

The Stakes

In the simple PD game, players seek to maximize their own payoffs, not the *difference* between their payoff and that of the adversary. In other words, they play for absolute, not relative, gains. This is a potential stumbling block because, as I have noted, relative gains are important in international relations and may sometimes be the most critical criteria of success.[31] If players are only interested in relative gains, Axelrod's results go away. But although states are clearly sensitive to relative gains, it is misleading to assume prima facie that states are always and only positional actors.[32] A better assumption would be that states' propensities to play for relative and absolute gains vary across time, issue, and relationship. This means that a theory of cooperation based on Axelrod's work may not be applicable to all issues of international relations, but it may be applicable to some.

Superpower arms control is again an obvious candidate. As long as decisionmakers believe that nuclear parity and mutual deterrence maintain, they will pay more attention to absolute payoffs because relative gains in nuclear forces do not translate into relative gains of any significance in security. Clearly, the United States and the Soviet Union can af-

---

[30] Snidal notes that "for any but the most trivial decisions, this conception [strategy as a fully specified decision rule for all possible contingencies] is hopelessly complicated and beyond the calculating power of any man, machine, or state bureaucracy." He then offers the more forgiving criteria of "a general policy stance," arguing that "it is meaningful to speak—on a broad level—of strategies of free versus restricted international trade without worrying about the myriad of nuances such as differential treatment of steel versus textiles." "The Game *Theory* of International Politics," p. 37. For Axelrod, the concept of strategy does not require conscious choice or sophisticated reasoning; he observes that "an organism does not need a brain to employ a strategy." *The Evolution of Cooperation*, p. 93. For a general consideration of the concept of strategic rationality, see Bruner et al., *A Study of Thinking*.

[31] Michael Taylor uses the term "game of difference" to describe a world in which players are motivated by egoism (the desire to maximize their own gains) *and* negative altruism (which is simply "envy," or the desire to maximize the difference between their own gains and that of the adversary). Negative altruism makes each player's temptation to defect even greater than it was in the original PD, and creates much higher obstacles to cooperation. See Taylor, *Anarchy and Cooperation*, pp. 93–94.

[32] As Grieco does in "Anarchy and the Limits of Cooperation," especially p. 488.

ford to play an arms control game with less attention to relative gains than would have been possible in a world without nuclear weapons.[33] There are certainly considerations that cut in the opposite direction: the demands of extended deterrence, technological uncertainties, and beliefs about the possible political impact of a quantitative imbalance in nuclear arsenals, to name a few. Determining the mixture of relative and absolute gains criteria in arms control is also not something that can be done by assumption; it is finally a subject for empirical research. But it need not be done by assumption. The point here is simple. If unique characteristics of the nuclear balance facilitate playing the arms control game with a larger emphasis on absolute gains, then game theory's assumptions about the stakes of the competition, like its other assumptions, make up a plausible foundation for a serious attempt to apply Axelrod's model.

[33] This general statement leaves out the impact of other important factors, such as geography and the nature of military technology. If a state has easily defensible borders, and military technology is such that the defense has an advantage over the offense, security may be comparatively abundant and less sensitive to changes in the relative magnitude of forces. See Jervis, "Cooperation under the Security Dilemma." Some of the effects that I ascribe to nuclear deterrence would presumably also be present in such a world.

2

Current Approaches

THE SUPERPOWERS' arms control experience is rich with potential for building theories of cooperation, but that potential has not yet been tapped. At the same time, theories about arms control have not provided the kinds of explanations of success and failure of cooperation, and the implications of each, that would be valuable to theorists and policymakers. There have been previous attempts to apply theories about cooperation, mostly drawn from international economics, to security relations, but the results have generally been disappointing. The payoff so far is limited to broad statements about why security cooperation is different from economic cooperation and is more difficult to achieve.[1]

Students and practitioners of arms control need to know more than this. A theory of arms control cooperation should focus on the interface between the superpowers' interests, their behavior, and the outcomes of cases, to explain why cooperation in arms control does or does not come about in specific instances. It should also generate useful prescriptions: at a minimum, it should offer advice on how best to promote cooperation when that is seen as being in the states' interests. A more ambitious goal would be to identify additional opportunities for mutually beneficial cooperation, or to aid in defining the scope of what cooperation can contribute to each superpower's security interests and obligations. The theory that emerges from this book is most fully developed with regard to the first of these objectives. It offers more speculative arguments about the others, connected to hypotheses that future studies can begin to test and refine.

What do current theories in arms control and in international cooperation have to say about these issues?[2]

---

[1] For a concise overview see Lipson, "International Cooperation in Economic and Security Affairs."

[2] For obvious reasons, I have not tried to construct a comprehensive review of the literature on international cooperation or arms control. What I have tried to do in this chapter is to select out the most directly relevant areas of theory that concentrate on the central question of this book and its principal theoretical focus.

Arms Control Theory

Arms Control and Preferences

Many political scientists think of arms control as an area lacking in general theory, but this is not accurate.[3] Since the first use of atomic weapons in World War II, civilian and military thinkers have struggled to understand the impact that nuclear weapons have had upon the relationship between military force, national security, and international relations. It was not until the late 1950s, however, that a theory exploring a rationale for cooperative arms control in the nuclear age began to emerge. The "golden age" of classical arms control theory centered around a series of books published in the early 1960s, most notably Schelling and Halperin's *Strategy and Arms Control*; *Arms Control, Disarmament, and National Security*, edited by Donald Brennan; and Bull's *The Control of the Arms Race*.

This body of theory defined arms control broadly, to include measures to restrain states' armaments policies and reduce the risks of war, limit damage if war should occur, and moderate the costs of the arms race.[4] The starting point was that meaningful arms control did *not* rest on a prior settlement of outstanding political conflicts, because the United States and the Soviet Union shared a number of common interests in regard to nuclear weapons regardless of the continuing political-military competition between them. The primary focus of classical arms control theory was to flesh out this complex of shared interests. As unforeseen technologies emerged in subsequent years, the classical approach expanded into a larger body of strategic theory that explored in great detail the impact of new weapons systems upon deterrence, crisis stability, and the like.

Classical arms control theory is mostly a theory about *preferences*. In other words, it identifies what kinds of weapons systems and balances are desirable by explaining how they might contribute to a state's security. The ABM case is a good example of how these theories sometimes influenced decisionmakers' conceptions of self-interest: it is not intuitively obvious that security would be enhanced by agreeing to leave cities abjectly vulnerable to destruction.

ABM is not the only example. Classical arms control theories identify a number of other areas where cooperative behavior can contribute to the

---

[3] For a balanced survey of the state of general theory in arms control, see Morgan, "Arms Control in International Politics."

[4] This "definition" is distilled from those provided by Bull and by Schelling and Halperin.

vital security interests of both superpowers. But the problem of achieving cooperation is still unresolved. In fact, much of the early arms control literature viewed possible bilateral arrangements, either implicitly or explicitly, as having a "payoff structure" and logic that resembled a mixed-motive game. Put simply, many potential arms control measures would be mutually advantageous if both sides were to subscribe to them, but each side might do better if it were able to "cheat" or take advantage of unrequited "cooperation" on the adversary's part. As with other mixed-motive games, the outcome of these arms control games were indeterminate. Classical arms control theory does not explain why cooperation is attained and sustained in some of these "games" but not in others.

Arms Control and Strategy

In the late 1950s, prior to the golden age of classical arms control theory, Thomas Schelling was experimenting with a similar set of questions about cooperation, at a more abstract level. The Strategy of Conflict was an elegant attempt to apply some new tools of game theory to a simple but important puzzle: in an interdependent decision situation with non-zero-sum payoffs, how do actors go about achieving mutually beneficial forms of cooperation? Schelling recognized that the structure of this puzzle resembled many of the interesting questions that faced international relations theorists and practitioners, and particularly those who were beginning to think about the possibilities for arms control in a world approaching nuclear parity.

But in an essay entitled "The Retarded Science of International Strategy," Schelling argued that game theory had not yet proven itself a powerful tool for answering the question of how actors could get to cooperation in ways that would be relevant to international relations, for two basic reasons. First, game theory was most fully developed in the area of zero-sum or pure conflict games, while most interesting interactions between states were probably mixed-motive games. Second, game theory remained at too high a level of abstraction. It was treated too much as if it were "solely a branch of mathematics"; the problems of applying a formal mathematical theory to historical data had not been confronted head on.[5]

These two deficiencies were closely related. Schelling recognized that while it might be possible to build a powerful theory of strategy in a zero-sum game with formal deductive methods, this was not possible for mixed-motive games. It was not possible because in a mixed-motive game

[5] Schelling, Thomas C. "The Retarded Science of International Strategy," in The Strategy of Conflict, p. 10, especially n. 4.

there is no "best" strategy for any player independent of what other players do. Players must form expectations about others' behavior in order to choose a strategy, which means that they necessarily engage in some form of mutual perception and communication between "two or more centers of consciousness." Because it is impossible to determine by purely formal means how particular real-world "players" actually do this, Schelling argued that "some essential part of the study of mixed-motive games is necessarily empirical . . . [and that] the principles relevant to *successful* play, the *strategic* principles, the propositions of a *normative* theory, cannot be derived by purely analytical means from a priori considerations."[6]

In *The Strategy of Conflict*, Schelling was able to develop intriguing formal game models by exploring the logic of strategic moves such as commitment, threat, promise, and randomization. Although the book includes an occasional empirical illustration from cases like the Korean War, the analysis remains primarily formal and deductive. It generates important *questions* about strategy, such as "what communication is required, and what means of authenticating the evidence communicated? . . . what is the need for trust, or enforcement of promises? . . . Can one threaten that he will 'probably' fulfill a threat; or must he threaten that he certainly will?" But as Schelling recognized, formal theory by itself could not provide better than abstract and overly general *answers* to these questions. Complete answers depended upon the players involved and the nature of their interaction. When it came to superpower arms control, there did not as yet exist a body of empirical evidence about how the United States and the Soviet Union would actually play the game. Schelling produced a catalog of possible strategic moves that *might* be useful in mixed-motive games, but the science of international strategy in arms control remained more or less retarded.[7]

The empirical evidence necessary to build on Schelling's preliminary arguments about strategy, cooperation, and arms control was not long in coming. By the end of the 1970s, a decade of U.S.-Soviet arms control negotiations in an era of rough parity had been captured in histories, memoirs, and analyses by insiders and outside observers alike. The memoirs of practitioners in particular tend to draw generalizations about the causes of "success" and "failure" in arms control, but these lessons often exhibit personal biases and their proponents rarely compare them to alternative interpretations or experience in other cases.[8]

---

[6] Ibid., pp. 162–63. Emphases in original.

[7] Ibid., pp. 13–14. Schelling and Halperin, in *Strategy and Arms Control*, extended this analysis and further developed the catalog of strategic moves (communication, negotiation, military deployments, domestic statements, etc.) that a state might combine in an overall strategy for influencing the adversary's expectations and incentives in order to facilitate cooperation in arms control.

[8] A comparison of the many accounts of the SALT negotiations written by participants

One area in which there have been sustained attempts to draw general lessons across cases about the process of U.S.-Soviet arms control is in the impact of domestic politics. This literature focuses on the inner workings of the Washington or Moscow bureaucracies and catalogs the many impediments to arms control negotiations that can be thrown up by domestic political actors on each side. This tells us something about the conditions for putting together "winning coalitions" to support a particular policy, which is an important part of understanding why states choose the strategies they do.[9] The bureaucratic politics approach to analyzing arms control is particularly seductive because of the high political saliency of many of the issues. But the power of this approach for explanation is limited. Historians can always tell the story of how one policy was chosen over others after the fact, by detailing who wanted what and how the necessary deals were made. But it is almost always misleading to assume that this was the only deal possible, that a winning coalition for other policies was ruled out. ABM and MIRV are particularly poignant illustrations of this problem. Both cases were important prototypes that Halperin, Allison, and others used to develop a bureaucratic politics paradigm for international relations; but as I will argue later on, U.S. strategy in ABM and MIRV was not over-determined by bureaucracies. Domestic politics made a difference, but neither the United States nor the Soviet Union appear as autonomous actors driven by internal dynamics in either of these cases. The fundamental problem with a bureaucratic politics argument here is that it ignores the interdependent logic of a mixed-motive game. Domestic politics constrain the set of strategies that are possible, but it does not explain why certain strategies work to elicit cooperation from an adversary while others do not.[10]

One approach that tried to relate the domestic politics of arms control more directly to international outcomes was Charles Osgood's GRIT pro-

---

(Kissinger, Smith, Garthoff, etc.) and highly informed observers (Newhouse, Talbott, etc.) supports this assertion. The recent book by Sloss and Davis, *A Game for High Stakes*, compiles a selection of personal anecdotes from American participants in U.S.-Soviet arms control negotiations, who were asked to evaluate their experiences and attempt to draw general lessons. This book nicely illustrates the unfulfilled promise for developing a theory of strategies to promote cooperation in U.S.-Soviet arms control. It contains a wealth of data on the sources and possible impact of various American strategies, but it lacks a theoretical framework across the cases and largely fails to develop convincing or even consistent generalizations.

[9] See, for example, Miller, "Politics over Promise."

[10] If we had better information about the internal politics of Soviet decisionmaking for defense, it would be possible and worthwhile to trace with precision the impact that one state's strategies have on the internal political coalitions of the other, deepening our understanding of how strategies in the international realm influence the distribution of power among domestic political actors. Matthew Evangelista has made some progress in trying to do this; see his "Sources of Moderation in Soviet Security Policy," in Tetlock et al., *Behavior, Society, and Nuclear War*, vol. 2.

posal, originally formulated in the 1950s as a means of reducing tensions in the Cold War. GRIT is a multifaceted strategy that Osgood believed states could use to replace "bad faith" images with a measure of mutual trust. The underlying presumption is that lack of trust in the adversary is the major source of domestic impediments to cooperation, and that when distrust is overcome, cooperative outcomes at the international level are strongly favored. This itself is a troubling assumption, but granting it does not transform GRIT into a valid theory of domestic politics. It is certainly not a theory of foreign policy or strategic interaction. GRIT by itself does not address the question of when a state is likely to adopt such a strategy; nor can it predict how or why the "target" will respond (or fail to respond) to initiatives. GRIT is marginally valuable for its attention to real-world psychological and political impediments to cooperation that are bypassed by game theory. But it is basically just a *prescriptive* agenda for what states should do. GRIT itself does not predict or explain anything; it is not a theory of strategy or outcomes in U.S.-Soviet arms control.[11]

Arms control is not atheoretical; but the kind of theory that presently exists does not say whether attempts to cooperate will succeed or fail. If strategic theories define certain interests that translate into PD-type preferences over possible outcomes concerning the destiny of a particular weapons system (Will both sides deploy it? Will there be an agreement for mutual restraint? etc.), the outcome of the "game" is indeterminate. Strategy seems to matter; but arms control theories do not explain why states choose one strategy over another. Nor do the theories explain why or how particular strategies promote cooperative outcomes. Schelling's game-theoretic experiments in *The Strategy of Conflict* offered a framework for thinking about strategy in mixed-motive games, and there is now a rich source of empirical data about U.S.-Soviet arms control, but these separate traditions have not yet been forced to confront each other. Looking at other theories of cooperation in international relations may reveal some hints about how to do so.

International Relations Theory

Beyond Realism: Reciprocity and Regimes

Realism, as discussed in Chapter 1, includes compelling arguments about why international cooperation is so difficult. Yet these impediments are

[11] The original nine-point GRIT (Graduated Reciprocation in Tension Reduction) proposal can be found in Osgood, "Suggestions for Winning the Real War with Communism." In an otherwise excellent paper, Deborah Larson makes the mistake of using GRIT as if it were a theory of strategic interaction in trying to explain the success of the Austrian State Treaty negotiations in 1955. Larson, "Crisis Prevention and the Austrian State Treaty."

sometimes overcome. Realism's efforts to explain cooperation extend in two directions: the first focuses on strategy, particularly strategies that incorporate reciprocity; and the second on institutions, or international regimes.

Reciprocity as a concept appears repeatedly in theories of bargaining, negotiation, and social exchange, as well as in international relations.[12] As a general strategic principle or guide to action, reciprocity may be particularly well suited to the harsh environment of game theory or an anarchic international system. The simple, rational egoist story about reciprocity is that told by Axelrod: states as unitary actors may reciprocate concessions because in a set of repeated interactions over time, cooperation promises the highest payoff for each individual state. Beyond Axelrod, if states are more complicated entities and domestic politics matter, then reciprocity may be an effective way of influencing public opinion so that it exerts pressure on key decisionmakers to respond in a conciliatory fashion to another state's concessions. Reciprocity may even elicit perceptions of "indebtedness" or responsibility, if we are willing to stretch the analysis even further to a world where there are strong preexisting standards of behavior between states.[13]

But reciprocity also has a number of weaknesses as a strategic principle. Concessions can be revocable, difficult to measure, and hard to compare; and reciprocal defections can engender damaging feuds. These are reasons why reciprocity does not always succeed in gaining its desired results, but they may not be the only ones. It would be useful to understand precisely why reciprocity sometimes does and sometimes does not elicit cooperation.

Robert Keohane took an important step toward answering this ques-

[12] On reciprocity as a cultural norm see Gouldner, "The Norm of Reciprocity." Elisabeth Zoller writes that some form of reciprocity is manifested in "every legal norm of international law." *Peacetime Unilateral Remedies*, p. 15. Keohane provides other examples of how the concept of reciprocity is used in different literatures for different theoretical purposes, "Reciprocity in International Relations." I see the concept employed in three general ways: reciprocity as a *norm* underlying a relationship; as a *desirable characteristic* of an agreement; and as a *strategic principle* or guide to action.

[13] For example, see Martin Greenberg, "A Theory of Indebtedness," in Gergen, Greenberg, and Wills, *Social Exchange*. Reciprocal strategies that are "nice" (that begin with a concession and call for a positive response) do not always elicit conciliatory responses in the channels of domestic politics. For example, when the Soviet Union offered a number of concessions to the West following Stalin's death in 1953, Secretary of State John Foster Dulles argued that the United States should respond with firmness, the goal being "to crowd the enemy and maybe finish him once and for all." See Larson, "Crisis Prevention and the Austrian State Treaty," p. 41. Similar logic underlay the arguments of the "squeezers" as opposed to the "dealers" on Soviet policy during the Reagan administration. See Alexander Dallin and Gail W. Lapidus, "Reagan and the Russians," in Oye, Lieber, and Rothchild, *Eagle Defiant*, pp. 191–236.

tion in a study of reciprocal strategies in international trade. Keohane started by defining reciprocity as a form of action that is contingent on others' behavior, but he soon recognized that the terms of contingency can vary. Do I return good for good, ill for ill, or both; and how long do I wait before reciprocating? Terms of equivalence can vary as well: states might demand strictly equivalent concessions; they might accept rough equivalence spread among a basket of commodities; or they might agree to unbalanced trades, with the understanding that current assymetries would be compensated for at some point in the future.[14] On this basis, Keohane distinguished between two ideal types of reciprocity, "specific" and "diffuse." In specific reciprocity, the terms of exchange are precisely defined. The partners trade items of equivalent value in strictly defined sequence. Diffuse reciprocity is based on flexible criteria of equivalence and more permissive timing of exchanges. The terms of contingency are loosely defined, and obligations are implicit.[15]

The distinction is useful because it leads to a more detailed analysis of the logic behind the strengths and weaknesses of reciprocity. Specific reciprocity is good at protecting a state against exploitation, but it may promote "hoarding" of potential concessions to be used as bargaining chips, and can engender cycles of feuding. Diffuse reciprocity expands the number and scope of potential bargains that can be made, but it is vulnerable to exploitation and can leave too much room for disagreement over criteria of rough equivalence, impeding the completion of agreements. Is one strategy somehow better than another for international trade? Keohane is notably pessimistic about the efficacy of diffuse reciprocity and only slightly more favorable toward specific reciprocity. While arguing that "stable patterns of specific reciprocity are often the most one can expect in world politics," he also notes that "neither diffuse nor specific reciprocity has provided a fully satisfactory principle of behavior."[16]

What does this analysis of reciprocity suggest about strategy in U.S.-

[14] Keohane, "Reciprocity in International Relations." In practice, economists distinguish among several different kinds of reciprocity, including overall reciprocity, sectoral reciprocity, and national-treatment reciprocity.

[15] Ibid. Keohane's definition of diffuse reciprocity incorporates the idea that the partners in such a relationship may be viewed as a group rather than as particular actors, and may not even be clearly specified. I see no logical reason why diffuse reciprocity must be limited to multilateral relationships; the concept could theoretically be applied with equal force to a bilateral relationship between two specific actors, such as the United States and Soviet Union in their arms control relationship.

[16] Ibid., pp. 23, 25. Keohane adds the observation that stable patterns of specific reciprocity can sometimes generate shared expectations and norms that may develop into international institutions, which in turn facilitate diffuse reciprocity. While this may have happened to a considerable degree in issues of trade and money between the advanced industrial countries, the same cannot be said of superpower arms control.

Soviet arms control? Several things, at least in principle. Keohane's research and other work on reciprocity suggests that we should expect to see specific reciprocity almost exlusively in superpower arms control, because the strong norms of obligation and interdependence that make diffuse reciprocity a viable strategic principle in some social relationships are least likely to be found in security relations between rival states. Yet when we examine the history of ABM, MIRV, and ASAT, we find that strategies of specific reciprocity are *not* the only ones employed by the United States in arms control—elements approximating diffuse reciprocity are also present. This is an interesting puzzle.

A related consideration is whether diffuse reciprocity can produce cooperation in arms control while it fails in international trade; or would specific reciprocity be more effective? These are, of course, rhetorical questions. Both logic and history suggest that different strategies are more effective under different conditions; the real challenge is to determine under what conditions and in what issue-areas specific or diffuse reciprocity is more likely to succeed. Some things are clear. If the environment is highly forgiving, the costs of unrequited cooperation are low and retrievable, and other players are not by nature exploitative, diffuse reciprocity is logically favored. But history suggests how hard it is to transform these general statements into particular arguments. It has only been done effectively in studies of specific relationships bounded closely in time, such as the U.S.-Japan trade relationship in the 1980s.[17]

This is another reason for focusing on specific historical cases instead of general, abstract theories. But in U.S.-Soviet arms control, the particular typology Keohane developed for studying international trade is not very helpful. Superpower arms control strategies typically have mixed elements of diffuse and specific reciprocity, and neither seems to be clearly associated with cooperative outcomes.[18] Consider the case of SALT I. Washington sought something quite close to specific reciprocity on defensive systems and gained cooperation, while a much more diffuse reciprocity strategy for offensive systems failed. Yet an even more highly diffuse reciprocity resulted in sustained cooperation in ASAT weapons during the 1960s and much of the 1970s. This suggests that we should look for

[17] See, for example, Krasner, *Assymetries in Japanese-American Trade*. It is certainly possible that we could discover more general (and nontrivial) rules that will apply across cases, but it seems that the best way to specify such rules will be to start by constructing theory from specific subsets of cases.

[18] In fact, there is reason to suspect that this typology may not even be very well suited to studying trade. State strategies in trade typically use elements from both ideal types; Keohane provides several interesting examples of how the GATT is set up to facilitate strategies that combine principles of specific and diffuse reciprocity in order to maximize the strengths of each while compensating for their defects. "Reciprocity in International Relations," p. 25.

an alternative typology. In Chapter 3 I propose such a typology, focusing on the form and timing of reciprocal punishments for defection.

Strategies of reciprocity, of course, do not always exist in an institutional vacuum. In international issues where regimes are strong, where institutions embody norms, principles, rules, and decisionmaking procedures that are the shared expectations of states, strategies of reciprocity should be generally more successful. Regime institutions typically reduce the costs of monitoring behavior and responding to defection; if they also reduce states' uncertainty about other states' propensity to exploit cooperation, regimes should favor strategies approximating diffuse reciprocity in particular. On the other hand, when states try to cooperate outside the bounds of a regime, strategies should tend more toward specific reciprocity.

A body of research in international trade and finance generally supports these hypotheses, but they do not seem to explain the pattern of U.S.-Soviet efforts at arms control cooperation.[19] The basic reason is because security regimes are so rare. It is important to remember that cooperation and institutions are not the same thing: when cooperation is limited to the obvious intersection of myopic self-interest between two states, that is hardly an institution. The two states are doing what they would have done on their own; the putative "institution" has no autonomous effect on their behavior. This comes close to characterizing the environment facing U.S. and Soviet leaders as they contemplated the prospects of cooperation in ABM, MIRV, and ASAT. What arms control cooperation there was between the superpowers prior to the SALT agreements is better seen as intersections of myopic self-interest than as reflecting any institution or regime.[20] If institutions were going to aid the emergence of cooperation in these three cases, they would have to be created de novo by the cooperating states.

There are good theoretical reasons to believe that constructing institu-

[19] See Krasner, "Structural Causes and Regime Consequences," in *International Regimes*, pp. 1–23, and the case studies in this volume.

[20] Regime theory uses the term "institution" in a broad sense, to mean stable and valued patterns of behavior that have an autonomous impact upon actors' expectations and behavior. See March and Olsen, "The New Institutionalism." On the issue of institutions and regimes in U.S.-Soviet arms control, Jervis doubts that even the SALT agreements qualify as regime institutions. "Security Regimes," in Krasner, *International Regimes*, p. 173. Caldwell, *American-Soviet Relations*, and Nye, "Nuclear Learning," disagree. Both see "partial regimes" evolving in delimited subsets of the superpower security relationship, such as nonproliferation, crisis management, and perhaps in arms control as well. Condoleeza Rice also sees a partial regime evolving out of SALT. "SALT and the Search for a Security Regime," in George, Farley, and Dallin, *U.S.-Soviet Security Cooperation*, pp. 293–306. None of these authors or any other that I am aware of argues that a U.S.-Soviet security regime of any importance existed *prior* to the cases that I examine in this book.

tions in this setting would be extremely difficult. That security regimes have been so rare is no accident; the stakes of security are generally higher than those of economics, because the costs of sacrificing self-reliance may irreversibly risk the continued autonomy of the state. Regime theorists point out that these constraints were in fact overcome for a short period of time in the early 19th-century Concert of Europe, but that regime rested on a broad convergence of interests between great powers that shared a cultural homogeneity rarely matched among subsequent rivals.[21] It was clearly not matched in the U.S.-Soviet relationship of the 1960s– 70s.

But what about the sequelae of U.S.-Soviet arms control cooperation in the early 1970s? It is here that regime theory is potentially most interesting. SALT was not a full-fledged security regime, but arms control during this period did extend beyond myopic self-interests in avoiding nuclear war.[22] The superpowers agreed to limit some of their most central strategic weapons systems, in part to save money, enhance military stability, and facilitate a broader improvement in political relations. None of these things was necessary to prevent nuclear war. SALT also included rules and decisionmaking procedures to back up these objectives. And as I discuss in Chapter 7, SALT had an important set of "domestic reflections": the international institutions of SALT affected the decisionmaking systems of both superpowers and substantially changed the means by which expectations about the future of the strategic environment would be developed in both Washington and Moscow.

Regime theory does not explain cooperation in U.S.-Soviet arms control, but it may have something to say about the consequences. We know that regime institutions, *once in place*, can have an autonomous impact on behavior by modulating transaction costs: the institutions of SALT did this for the United States and the Soviet Union in a way that influenced how decisionmakers calculated the costs and benefits of further cooperation. Institutions affect the strategies that actors can use with their predetermined preferences.

But can regimes do more than this? Ernst Haas, for example, believes that international institutions can have a more fundamental effect upon conceptions of self-interest, influencing decisionmakers' basic understandings of the relationship between objective features of the interna-

[21] Paul Gordon Lauren, "Crisis Prevention in Nineteenth Century Diplomacy," in George, *Managing U.S.-Soviet Rivalry*; Holbraad, *The Concert of Europe*. Jervis, in "Security Regimes," attributes cooperation under the Concert primarily to a shared fear of domestic instability and interstate conflict after the experience of the Napoleonic wars, and only secondarily to broader common interests outside the context of the regime.

[22] Jervis, "Security Regimes," disagrees. For alternative perspectives closer to my own, see Caldwell, *American-Soviet Relations*; and Nye, "Nuclear Learning."

tional environment and their states' interests in it.[23] As I discuss in Chapter 7, there are reasons to believe that this effect has been and will continue to be more pronounced in nuclear security questions than in other international issues. There are several implications for U.S.-Soviet arms control. The most important follow from the fact that the arms control institutions set up in the 1970s were not historically absolute, necessary, or optimal in any sense. SALT was contingent on the unique set of circumstances under which cooperation developed. Cooperation of a certain kind came at a critical juncture in the evolution of U.S.-Soviet relations; and in contrast to the realist argument, it has had a long-standing impact on the subsequent development of the relationship. The form and content of SALT institutions continue to have a profound effect on decisionmakers' conceptions of self-interest in nuclear security, and this effect has not always contributed positively to U.S.-Soviet security and political relations. Whether a different set of institutions was possible and might have had more positive sequelae is also discussed in Chapter 7.

A Return to Game Theory

In 1984, Robert Axelrod took another look at the problem of mixed-motive games and cooperation, paring down the complex models and theories that had been built up in the interim back to the minimal essentials of the simple PD. The power of *The Evolution of Cooperation* lies in its resulting elegance. In the starkest of game-theoretic worlds, where there are no mechanisms for communication or threats, no misinformation or misperception, and no inequalities of power, a set of featureless players meet over time in a series of PD games. If they can recognize each other and recall the result of their last meeting, and if they do not heavily discount the value of payoffs in future rounds of the game, defection is no longer a dominant strategy. Instead, Tit for Tat becomes strategically rational and can lead to a stable cooperative solution.

By taking a step back from complexity, Axelrod clarified the most central elements affecting cooperation in the PD and maximized the generalizability of his argument. At the same time, his book crystallized the problem of applying such an argument to real-world events. Without claiming that he had done so successfully, Axelrod suggested that his model could in principle be made "relevant to many of the central issues of international politics."[24] This led to a series of critiques pointing out the many pitfalls along the way. Many of these critiques were excellent

---

[23] Haas, "Why Collaborate?"; idem, *When Knowledge Is Power*.
[24] Axelrod, *The Evolution of Cooperation*, p. 4.

and insightful, but they did not demolish Axelrod's challenge.[25] The question of whether Axelrod's model can tell us anything about cooperation in international relations, or is merely an interesting but trivial exercise in logic, cannot be settled by abstract reasoning alone. The first step lay in finding a set of cases where the assumptions of Axelrod's model can be reasonably established. U.S.-Soviet arms control under nuclear parity comes close. The challenge now is to develop a means for transiting the gap between the simple game model and the much more complex real world.

Axelrod himself tried to forge a path through this problem. It is easier to understand his effort if we divide *The Evolution of Cooperation* into two separate books: the first develops the formal model of cooperation in the PD, and the second grapples with possible applications to two settings: cooperation between microorganisms and cooperation between trench-warfare soldiers during World War I.

The first book is certainly the more elegant of the two. It defines a simple set of conditions under which the Tit for Tat strategy can elicit cooperation in an iterated PD game. But it is critical to note that these conditions are neither necessary nor sufficient conditions for cooperation, even within the confines of Axelrod's game-theoretic world. Consider what is missing. For these conditions to be truly *necessary*, it would have to be the case that there are no alternative routes to a cooperative outcome other than the one that Axelrod elucidates. Neither Axelrod nor any of his critics has demonstrated this. There may be many different paths to cooperation in game theory, and there are almost certainly other paths in the real world. Apart from successful reciprocity, decisions based on altruism, empathy, misunderstanding, or stupidity could all lead to cooperation via a different route that might not require the presence of Axelrod's conditions.

But even if Axelrod's route were the only one leading to cooperation, the conditions attached to it are clearly not *sufficient* ones, either in game theory or in the real world. In order for cooperation to get started, TFT must somehow be introduced into an inhospitable environment, and other players must respond. If no one ever starts playing TFT, or if other players do not or cannot respond, cooperation will not occur. For both these reasons, *The Evolution of Cooperation* is incomplete even as a deductive theory. It demonstrates that cooperation can occur in the PD, but it does not predict that cooperation must or will occur. There is a revealing convergence here with Schelling's argument. Strategic interaction in

[25] Two of the most interesting critiques that focus specifically on the utility of Axelrod's work for international relations research are Gowa, "Anarchy, Egoism, and Third Images"; and Beer, "Games and Metaphors."

mixed-motive games is not deterministic, but it is a key factor in explaining cooperation.

This by itself is no great insight, but it points to two critical questions that together capture the most important reasons why Axelrod's theory must be considered incomplete. The questions are: Where does TFT come from? And how does it elicit cooperation from other players? Within the confines of game theory, the answers are simple. TFT is introduced through a computer program—it enters the game because Anatol Rapaport suggested it to Axelrod. TFT interacts with the strategies suggested by others who also hoped to win Axelrod's tournament. The terms of the interaction are, again, defined by Axelrod through a computer program. The computer imposes simple definitions of how players change their behavior in response to what is going on around them. In the first round, players change their strategies according to an *ecological* model: the entire set of potential strategies from which players can choose is defined at the start of the tournament, and the probability that players will switch from their current strategy to another one is a function of the relative "success" of the two. The second round uses an *evolutionary* model: now all potential strategies that could conceivably exist are free to enter the environment, and players will switch to their neighbor's strategy if that strategy is scoring higher than their own. In both cases, players change strategies effortlessly and without cost. If others are doing better, they receive this information instantaneously and without distortion, painlessly adapting their own behavior to take advantage of changes in the environment and what they can learn from the strategies of others.

While these "solutions" may be acceptable as the starting point for a formal theory, they complicate any attempt to apply the theory to the real world. States do not develop strategies as do game theorists for a computer tournament; nor do states change behavior smoothly when other strategies are more successful. Axelrod recognized these problems. In setting the stage for the transition to the "second" book, he imports modifications that focus on the question of how players might actually assess their environment and choose or modify their strategies. But without specific empirical referents, without focusing the analysis on a particular set of players in a specific relationship, the modifications are as general and as abstract as were Schelling's in *The Strategy of Conflict*. For example, Axelrod tells us that if the environment is forgiving and other players are not prone to exploitation, returning "9/10ths of a Tit For A Tat" might be a better strategy than straight TFT. But he does not specify how players evaluate the environment or the propensity of others to defect. These and other such variations are familiar to formal game theorists.[26] But neither

[26] See Axelrod, *The Evolution of Cooperation*, p. 120. There are several formal algo-

Axelrod's work nor the more complex formal theories have any immediate claim to external validity. There is no reason to believe that they capture how U.S. and Soviet decisionmakers formulate and modify strategies for arms control. Some 25 years later, the science of game theory and international strategy remains retarded when it comes to arms control.

The first book cannot by itself get past this roadblock. What it can do is offer a powerful heuristic—a guide to new formulations, models, and experiments that stand in their own right independent of their origins. *The Evolution of Cooperation* demonstrates a particularly interesting route to a cooperative outcome that can operate under inauspicious circumstances. It is neither necessary nor sufficient to produce cooperation. But if Axelrod's world constitutes something of a least-likely case for cooperation to succeed, the "discovery" of a simple route to cooperation in this world is important and should be taken seriously. It may turn out to have empirical analogues in more complex environments.

The second book takes up this possibility. There are two preliminary case studies, the first of which examines a primitive biological system where the players are bacteria or other nonsentient organisms. In the environment of a primordial soup, the evolutionary mechanism for strategy choice is quite plausible: bacterial "strategies" are introduced through random genetic variation and are modified en masse through natural selection.[27] This is intriguing, but not very helpful when it comes to the strategies of states. The source of variation in state strategies, whatever it may be, is clearly not random genetic variation. There may be selective pressure in the international system, but natural selection in the classic Darwinian sense cannot be an important mechanism for change. States do not exist in anything approaching the large numbers that are needed for natural selection, and states that are marginally less successful in in-

---

rithms for updating beliefs about preferences. For a discussion of Bayes' rule, see Ordeshook, *Game Theory and Political Theory*, p. 457; and the classic treatment by Harsanyi, *Rational Behavior and Bargaining Equilibrium in Games and Social Situations*. The well-known Kreps/Wilson equilibrium, which shows cooperation to be possible in a finitely repeated PD game, follows from a more complex but still entirely axiomatic updating rule that is applied to the "chain-store paradox." See Kreps et al., "Rational Cooperation in the Finitely Repeated Prisoner's Dilemma"; and the two articles that follow in the same journal issue, by subsets of these authors: "Reputation and Imperfect Information," and "Predation, Reputation, and Entry Deterrence." These models are compelling as formal theory, but there is a danger of reasoning backward from outcome to assumptions. As I noted previously, the fact that a formal theory produces an outcome similar to that seen in a historical case does not necessarily mean that the theory's assumptions about how actors assess their environment are correct. Nor does it mean that the independent variables of the theory are the relevant ones in the case, or that the causal path leading to outcomes in the theory is related to historical processes.

[27] This reinforces an important point about strategy: players do not need to be intelligent or even conscious of what they are doing in order to employ a strategy per se.

ternational politics rarely die off or disappear. In fact, marginal differences in gains from arms control are nearly irrelevant for survival value:
within the bounds set by MAD and deterrence, relative gains by one side
do not translate into comparative advantages. Nor does the success or
failure of any particular bilateral arms control effort have a determining
impact on the positions of the superpowers relative to other states in the
system. The biological model of strategy choice and change is interesting
but ultimately no more appropriate to international politics than was the
computer-generated model of the first book.

The second case study is potentially more compelling. Here Axelrod
takes up the story of the "live and let live" system that developed between
trench warfare soldiers during World War I. The payoff structure of opposing battalions, according to Axelrod, can be described as a PD matrix;
in addition, the game is iterated and future payoffs should not be heavily
discounted.[28] This sets up the initial conditions for the evolution of cooperation, as in the biological case; but now the players are more like
states in the international system than bacteria in the primordial soup.
Groups of soldiers are not mechanistic "responders"; they can use fore-
sight and some form of collective intelligence to develop and modify strategies. Their environment is rich in contextual detail and opportunities for
communication. How did cooperation get started and how was it sustained?

Axelrod's answers are fragmentary. He has no explanation for the ini-
tiation of strategies of reciprocity, apart from the observation that restraint seems to have evolved "spontaneously" at certain times of the day
easily recognized by both sides (such as the serving of meals). And although Axelrod recognizes that soldiers rely "on thought as well as experience . . . and deliberate rather than blind adaptation" when deciding
how to respond to a bid for reciprocal restraint, there is no argument
about how a collective body makes the difficult transition from a strategy
of unconditional defection to some kind of reciprocal restraint.[29] But
when Axelrod goes on to discuss the ways in which cooperation was sustained, the fragments become much more intriguing. The story is one of
the development of a primitive social structure of cooperation that resembles in interesting ways the concept of a regime. Cooperation that began

[28] Gowa, "Anarchy, Egoism, and Third Images," questions Axelrod's assessment of the
payoff matrix for trench warfare, arguing that the game is closer to one of pure collaboration than PD, in which case cooperation is hardly surprising. This kind of critique points up
the weakness of relying on "objective" analytic assessments of the payoff matrix facing
decisionmakers. The argument is better justified by looking at how the decisionmakers
themselves perceived their payoff matrices. This is what I refer to in the next chapter as a
"subjective" assessment of the payoff matrix.

[29] Axelrod, *The Evolution of Cooperation*, Chapter 4, especially p. 84.

in a world without institutions bred its own institutions that in turn reinforced cooperation. The institutions did so in part by affecting transaction costs, but also by fostering changes in the players' conceptions of their self-interests that lay behind their preferences.[30] Institutions did more than just affect the strategies that actors could choose with predetermined preferences; they deeply affected the preferences themselves. This is an important departure from the simple PD model. It opens up the game to the notion that the success or failure of cooperation can have an important legacy for conceptions of self-interest and for an evolving relationship between long-term rivals. But how cooperation does this, and the question of whether institutions always reinforce cooperation or whether they can actually undermine it, is left open.

In sum, the evolution that takes place within *The Evolution of Cooperation* is perhaps its most tantalizing feature. Axelrod started by taking a step backward from Schelling and from more complex game theory, to demonstrate that even in the most inhospitable world of the simple PD game cooperation could be achieved and sustained. But in trying to apply this model to the real world, Axelrod brought back perceptions, communication, and other elements of social structure that went beyond his formal theory. The next step seems almost obvious: to make these empirical features, those that were accentuated by the formal theory, *primary* in a follow-on project. How do these perceptions, communication channels, and institutions work? How do they affect the prospects for and legacy of cooperation in a set of real-world cases? Curiously, cooperation theory did not continue in this direction.

Cooperation under Anarchy

The most extensive application of Axelrod's theory to international relations thus far was the fall 1985 special edition of *World Politics*, reprinted with the title *Cooperation under Anarchy*.[31] This project began with the now-familiar gap in the realist argument about cooperation: if the common condition of anarchy "gives rise to diverse outcomes" of both cooperation and conflict, "why does cooperation emerge in some cases and not in others?"[32] Oye and his coauthors set out to answer this question

---

[30] In Axelrod's words, "not only did preferences affect behavior and outcomes, but behavior and outcomes also affected preferences." *The Evolution of Cooperation*, p. 85. He even suggests that a shared "ethic of cooperation," what Keohane might call "empathetic interdependence," in some cases seems to have emerged across the trenches. Ibid; Keohane, *After Hegemony*, p. 123.

[31] Oye, *Cooperation under Anarchy*.

[32] Ibid., p. 1.

by extracting a "unified analytical framework" from Axelrod's formal model and applying it to six historical cases spanning security and political economy. To understand their effort, it is important to look more closely at the origins and consequences of this research strategy.

The analytic framework set out in Oye's introduction is made up of three relatively simple hypotheses that he derives directly from *The Evolution of Cooperation*. Each hypothesis takes a key independent variable from Axelrod's theory and links it to the prospects for international cooperation; this results in a set of predictions for the case studies to test. The predictions are that international cooperation is more likely to succeed when:

> 1. The temptation to defect and the sucker's payoff for unrequited cooperation are small relative to the rewards for mutual cooperation.
>
> 2. The shadow of the future is long (the game is played repeatedly, and the value of payoffs in future rounds is not highly discounted).
>
> 3. The number of players is low.[33]

Notice that this analytic framework rests on a "structural foundation." Mutuality of interests (short for hypothesis 1), the shadow of the future, and the number of players are all treated here as objective features of the environment. This strategy of starting with structural variables as the primary engine for constructing an explanation has obvious virtues of parsimony and simplicity. But it rests on two implicit assumptions that, curiously, run counter to the learning experience of Axelrod's book. The first assumption is that it is in fact possible to construct a theory that can explain cooperation on the basis of structural variables alone, or more realistically, by taking structural variables as its primary focus. The second assumption is that a single general theory of cooperation, if sufficiently abstract, can explain cooperation in both security and economic affairs across time periods and interstate relationships.

Both of these assumptions are troubling. The first entails a decision to "black-box" perceptions, the formation of preferences, "communication" of expectations, and other decisionmaking factors that might influence the effective value of each of the structural variables. It is crucial to understand that this decision is more than just a bow to parsimony. It is a direct challenge to Schelling's argument that a theory of cooperation in mixed-motive games must of necessity include elements of perception and communication in its basic formulation. If Schelling is correct, the task as Oye *initially* frames it is an impossible one.

The second assumption accepts the risk that a theory abstract enough

---

[33] Kenneth A. Oye, "Explaining Cooperation under Anarchy," in *Cooperation under Anarchy*, pp. 1–24.

to encompass such a diversity of cases will end up so general as to seem trivial. It also increases the risks of falling into the trap that lies between a deductive theory and an externally valid explanation of real world events. If mutuality of interests, shadow of the future, and the number of players each do affect the prospects for cooperation, it is still important to uncover how they do so and to show that this process bears some relation to the process that links independent and dependent variables in the formal theory. Demonstrating that causation in the real world is similar at some level to the causal chain between independent and dependent variables in formal theory is always difficult. But it is an essential part of demonstrating external validity. It is surely harder to do this in a broad and general set of cases than in a tightly delineated sample.

Oye recognizes these points and some of the implications in his introduction to *Cooperation under Anarchy*. After offering up the three hypotheses, he engages in theoretical specification: that is, he tries to fill in the putative causal pathways between independent and dependent variables. Exactly how do mutuality of interests, shadow of the future, and the number of players affect the prospects for cooperation?

What he uses to fill in these pathways is most interesting. Starting from the level of logical argument, before applying the framework to any case study, Oye recognizes that perceptions and misperceptions, decisionmaking biases, and the players' basic understandings of their environment can radically change the effective value of any of the variables. In fact, intelligent and active players (like states) often need not take the condition of these variables as a parameter at all: if the objective values of the variables do act as constraints, they are unusually plastic. States typically engage in what Oye calls "higher order strategies" that aim to change the basic structure of the environment, including the number of players and the effective shadow of the future. States can even try to influence mutuality of interests by working to convince other states that the basic terms in which they understand their interests and the potential benefits of cooperation should be revised.[34]

This raises a crucial issue. If each of the "structural" variables is subject to willful manipulation by states, how much can one explain by taking those variables as primary? We now expect that the impact of each variable will be mediated through some complex web of perceptions and other processes that are not a part of the formal theory and are not easily captured within it. Not surprisingly, the case studies in *Cooperation under Anarchy* bear out this expectation.[35] Starting with the unified analytic

[34] Oye, "Explaining Cooperation under Anarchy," pp. 2, 5.

[35] Stephen Van Evera, "Why Cooperation Failed in 1914," in Oye, *Cooperation under Anarchy*, pp. 80–117, is the most dramatic, but each of the other case studies tends in the same direction.

framework, each case study soon gets drawn beyond it into perceptions and decisionmaking, particularly into the development and modification of individual decisionmakers' preferences and state strategies. In fact, most of the interesting material in the cases focuses on these issues and not on the three hypotheses set out in the introduction. Each case produces interesting and potentially important findings about the impact of nonstructural factors on cooperation, but the findings are hard to compare across cases. In the end, they do not cumulate toward a theory of cooperation or even into discrete hypotheses about how nonstructural processes influence cooperation.

Cooperation under Anarchy fails in this regard as a direct consequence of its research strategy. If structural variables are the primary focus, it makes sense to look at cases that differ in structure. That was the genesis of the decision to select six cases across time and issue area. The approach is well suited for "testing" the three hypotheses of the unified analytic framework, but it is not as good for trying to look beyond structure.

What if nonstructural processes are primary? What if cooperation is most sensitive to perceptions, communication, and strategies? In that event, the case studies will struggle against the premises of the introduction. Each case will end up concentrating, if reluctantly, on the processes that modulate the impact of the original variables on the outcome of the case. From a larger perspective, the research strategy starts to look unnaturally restrictive. It might not be so, if those nonstructural processes turn out to be similar across cases; but there is no reason to believe a priori that they will. In *Cooperation under Anarchy* they do not. The lesson is quite simple. There seems to be no general theory of cooperation sufficiently abstract to capture the impact of changing preferences, decisionmaking, communication, and the like, across the security/political economy and other divides that separate the case studies. The attempt to elaborate Axelrod's model into a general theory of cooperation and to work from that general theory toward more specific manifestations in particular cases fails. It fails because the principal weight of explanation in the kinds of interesting and complex cases the book takes on rests not within differences of structure, but within strategies, decisionmaking, and perception.

In the final chapter of *Cooperation under Anarchy*, Axelrod and Keohane come to similar conclusions. They note that "the three dimensions discussed in the introduction—mutuality of interest, the shadow of the future, and the number of players—help us to understand the success and failure of attempts at cooperation." The "tests" of the hypotheses are complete. But Axelrod and Keohane also register frustration with how little they are ultimately able to say about cooperation with these completed tests in hand. They write that "the importance of perceptions has kept asserting itself." At a more general level, they conclude that the impact of the structural variables on the prospects for cooperation can finally not be understood except with regard to something called "the context of interaction."[36]

What is this "context of interaction"? In principle, it could include almost anything that is black-boxed by the formal theory and its descendent unified analytic framework. It is obviously not an easy task to sort out what is significant here, but Keohane and Axelrod do recognize that because "context" means different things in different relationships, the best way to approach the problem is to start with specific sets of empirical cases. For example, they suggest that in political economy among the advanced industrial states after World War II, "deep norms" of embedded liberalism and international institutions have been essential features of the context and have had an important role in cooperation.[37] But norms and institutions are not part of the relevant context for other sets of cases; most obviously not for U.S.-Soviet arms control in ABM, MIRV, and ASAT.

What is left? Axelrod and Keohane's presumptive answer to this question takes an additional hint from Axelrod's earlier argument about Tit for Tat. *The Evolution of Cooperation* proved the ability of TFT to promote cooperation in a stark environment lacking in deep norms and institutions. The strength of TFT lies precisely in the fact that it remains robust in the face of differing contexts of interaction; that is, it does relatively well regardless of the environment. But it does not do equally well in all.

In international relations and in U.S.-Soviet arms control, strategies based on reciprocity do not always succeed in eliciting cooperation. Without deep norms and institutions, understanding the context of interaction reduces to understanding what affects the viability of strategies of reciprocity and their ability to promote cooperation. Axelrod and Keohane note that reciprocity in international relations practice encounters many of the difficulties that are predicted for it in theory. They find that "actors in world politics seek to deal with problems of reciprocity in part through the exercise of power," and also through "international regimes."[38] Both aid reciprocity and facilitate cooperation in the case studies of *Cooperation under Anarchy*. But when power resources are roughly matched and

[36] Robert Axelrod and Robert Keohane, "Achieving Cooperation under Anarchy," in Oye, *Cooperation under Anarchy*, pp. 227, 247, 238.

[37] Ibid., p. 238; John Ruggie, "International Regimes, Transactions, and Change: Embedded Liberalism in the Postwar Economic Order," in Krasner, *International Regimes*, pp. 195–231.

[38] Axelrod and Keohane, "Achieving Cooperation under Anarchy," p. 249.

institutions are negligible, as is the case in ABM, MIRV, and ASAT, how do strategies of reciprocity function?

An obvious way out of this impasse is to shift from a "telescopic" research agenda to a "microscopic" one. *Cooperation under Anarchy* is telescopic in its quest for a general theory of cooperation. It treats structural variables as primary and compares cases that vary in structure.

The microscopic alternative is to focus on a specific set of cases that hold structural variables nearly constant. ABM, MIRV, and ASAT share the structural variables that are the initial conditions for cooperation according to Axelrod's theory. Mutuality of interests, shadow of the future, and number of players are similar; but the outcomes of the three cases are different. The explanation for that difference lies in the processes that intercede between structural variables and cooperation.

In the next chapter I propose an argument that focuses on strategy as a central feature of these processes. Why should strategy play such a critical role? There is a revealing convergence here between the several lines of argument I have discussed, from game theory to regimes and beyond. Remember that in Axelrod's formal theory, the introduction and propagation of TFT is the critical intervention between structure and cooperative outcome. If no one starts playing TFT or if other players do not respond, the structural preconditions can go on ad infinitum without ever spawning cooperation. Strategy is also a critical element of cooperation in the context of international regimes: regimes are usually conceived of as being composed of institutions that modulate transaction costs in a way that affects the range of strategies that actors can pursue with predetermined preferences.

Finally, strategy captures the critical elements of interaction between players that Schelling saw as the essential gap in the theory of mixed-motive games. For that reason, a research agenda that focuses on strategy as its primary engine of explanation is less limiting than it might seem at first glance. It opens up what *Cooperation under Anarchy* tried to keep in a black box: perceptions of interests, assessments of the preferences of other players, the development and implementation of strategies of reciprocity appropriate for a particular relationship, and the means by which players evaluate the success or failure of a strategy and attempt to modify it. It pushes research backward, to explain why states adopt one or another variant of strategies of reciprocity when all are consistent with game theory's TFT. It also pushes research forward, to explain why strategies differ in their ability to elicit cooperation.

Lastly, focusing on strategy hints at the possible legacies of different kinds of cooperation that are arrived at through different routes. The experiences and institutions that follow from the success or failure of reci-

procity in U.S.-Soviet arms control matter for future efforts at cooperation and, more broadly, for the superpower relationship in general.

Summary

This chapter began with the central problem of explaining the variance
in outcomes among critical cases in U.S.-Soviet arms control. Classical
arms control theory and its descendents provided the prerequisites, explaining how states' security interests could sometimes be enhanced by
arms control measures that require active cooperation between rivals.
These theories did not explain how such cooperation could be attained
and sustained in an environment lacking central authority, while incentives to "defect" remained. Schelling's work recognized that the logical
structure of this problem resembled that of the economists' mixed-motive
games. His explorations of game theory raised important issues about
how real-world players like states, rather than game-theoretic actors, actually behave in such games. But without a body of empirical evidence
about how the game would be played in U.S.-Soviet arms control, the
science of international strategy remained retarded or at least underde-
veloped.

Theories of international cooperation provide an alternative perspective on the problem. Realism offers convincing arguments about the for-
bidding impediments to cooperation, but it does not discriminate between cases where the impediments are overcome and those where they
are not. Reciprocity seems to be a principle of strategic behavior relatively
well suited to elicit cooperation in a "realist" world, but it is not perfect;
and different types of reciprocity have their own strengths and weaknesses whose impact upon the prospects for cooperation are difficult to
predict at an abstract level. If international regimes were strong in security issues, this might facilitate some strategies of reciprocity and promote
cooperation; but regimes were at most a marginal factor in the early evolution of U.S.-Soviet arms control cooperation. Regime theory turns out
to be more interesting for what it suggests about the consequences and
legacy of cooperation.

What seemed a theoretical impasse was broken by turning back to
game theory. Axelrod's *The Evolution of Cooperation* advanced an elegant and powerful formal model of a route to cooperation in the PD that
could operate in a most inhospitable environment. *Cooperation under
Anarchy* tried to establish the external validity of Axelrod's theory in international politics by transforming the formal model into a general theory of international cooperation that would be applicable across the se-
curity/economy divide. It succeeded at some level in doing this, but was

frustrating in its success. *Cooperation under Anarchy* points toward an alternative approach better suited to explain success and failure in U.S.-Soviet arms control.

The next chapter takes up that agenda. It brings Axelrod's work into direct contact with the problem of U.S.-Soviet arms control, driving the game-theoretic model of cooperation in the PD toward a more comprehensive argument about cooperation in U.S.-Soviet arms control. The new approach that emerges will concentrate on the development and operation of strategies of reciprocity. This brings the discussion full circle. It brings us back to the project that Schelling started but could not complete in *The Strategy of Conflict*: to add the necessary empirical content to a primarily deductive theory of cooperation by examining a small set of real-world, mixed-motive games: ABM, MIRV, and ASAT.

3

Cooperation: A New Approach

THIS CHAPTER proposes a new argument about cooperation in U.S.-Soviet arms control. Because I start with Axelrod's model, my argument sits within the genre of "cooperation theory," a term that has been bandied about frequently in the international relations literature in recent years. Of course, there is no "cooperation theory" per se, but only a diverse body of theoretically oriented research that focuses on the question of why states sometimes cooperate and sometimes do not. There are obviously many different ways of thinking about this problem. Thus far, I have drawn a sharp distinction between formal, deductive methods and empirical methods of studying cooperation based on case studies. Much of the research in cooperation theory preserves that distinction. This chapter proposes one way of breaking it down.

The interactive approach I offer here forces a head-on confrontation between a formal mathematical theory and historical case studies. It bridges the gap between the game-theoretic model and real-world cases, and then adds certain additional concepts that are needed to "push" the theory further in an empirical direction. Notice from the beginning that these additional concepts were not deduced from the formal theory, but arise instead from empirical generalizations. That has an extremely important consequence. It is proper to treat these additions as *variables*, not as *assumptions*. The variables are then developed into *questions* and not into *hypotheses* per se. Variables and questions that are induced from historical cases are subject to modification as we learn more from history. These modifications do not damage the basic structure of the theory to which the new, empirically derived concepts are being added. On the contrary, they enrich it.

This strategy follows logically from the conclusion of the previous chapters that Axelrod's theory remains incomplete. It cannot as it stands generate hypotheses that are specific enough to make predictions about the variance in outcome among U.S.-Soviet arms control cases. The theory cannot yet be "tested" in the traditional sense, or in the closely related sense that has recently become popular in international relations research.[1] Thus I have not deduced a set of hypotheses from Axelrod's

---

[1] That is, take two or more theories, deduce hypotheses from them that make differential predictions about empirical cases, and then test the hypotheses against the cases to see which

theory and then tested them against U.S.-Soviet arms control. My ambitions here are more circumscribed.

This chapter uses Axelrod's theory as a heuristic and expands upon it, adding empirically derived concepts when that is necessary to explain important variance that the formal theory does not. From Chapters 1 and 2 we know that we need to supplement the theory with some additional notions about the development of strategies and the relationship between strategies and outcomes. Why do states choose the strategies they do? And how do states modify their strategies in response to changes in the environment and particularly to changes in the strategies of other states? We also need to tease out whether and how the "causal path" that is operating in the empirical cases is analogous to that which links independent and dependent variables in Axelrod's theory. This must be true both of cases where cooperation occurs and of those where it does not occur. Put differently, the mechanism behind Axelrod's model should be operating both in ABM and in MIRV, but we would expect to see it diverted at some critical juncture in the latter case.

The heuristic use of theories leads to new formulations, models, and experiments that stand in their own right, independent of their origins. The results are typically less simple and parsimonious than the predecessor. That is why this chapter is not about game theory per se. The empirical approach to building on Axelrod's theory is clearly less elegant than deductive refinement, but it can coexist with and complement the formal approach.

PD Games and the Prospects for Cooperation

Cooperation occurs in international relations when states adjust their policies so that their behaviors contribute to the realization of shared goals. If they fail to do so, and instead follow policies based on myopic self-interest that damage the interests of others, the outcome is discord. Sometimes cooperation may be preferable to discord but still difficult to achieve. That is particularly true when each state believes that it could do even better if it were to stick to its own most preferred policy while the other state gave in.

The PD captures the basic mechanism behind a mixed-motive game in which the logic of individual action confounds states' or any other play-

---

are most nearly correct. Such "tests" provide confirming or disconfirming arguments for alternative theories. For an excellent example, see Posen, *The Sources of Military Doctrine*. Posen contrasts two theories or theoretical traditions that are adequately developed so that he can deduce differential predictions about his cases from them—that is the sine qua non of theory testing by this method.

ers' efforts to achieve cooperation. Although both players would do better if they were able to cooperate, in a single-shot PD game defection is a dominant strategy for each individual. Thus under the very stark conditions of the simple PD, mutual defection or discord is certain. Loosening up the conditions, by permitting some limited forms of communication or side-payments, makes cooperation possible, but generally still difficult to achieve. Another way to make cooperation possible is to extend the PD to an iterated game, where a set of players meet in repeated rounds over time. If the players have a long shadow of the future and a low discount rate for prospective payoffs, cooperation once again becomes a feasible outcome. Most real-world analogues of the PD probably fit one or both of the latter categories, where the conditions of play are not so stark and cooperation is indeed a possible outcome.

But how likely is it that in any given PD game, cooperation will actually come about? Game theory is one way to answer that question. The simple PD model provides an obvious first cut, which requires only that we know something about the players' preferences. The PD is defined by a unique relationship among ordinal preferences: in the game-theoretic terminology of Figure 1, $T > R > P > S$, and $R > (T + S)/2$. If preferences fall outside these boundaries the game is no longer the PD but something else (such as "Chicken"), and it is not clear that Axelrod's theory can be applied.[2] But *within* the bounds of the PD there can still be considerable differences in the relative magnitude of preferences. These relative magnitudes make a difference in the likelihood that players may in fact find their way to cooperation. Put simply in the language of international relations, arms control or other cases that resemble the PD will vary in the degree to which they are inherently conducive to a cooperative solution, or tend strongly toward discord. As in game theory, if the potential payoff for exploiting an adversary is only slightly more tempting than the payoff for cooperation, and the costs of mutual defection are large, international cooperation is more likely to emerge and to be sustained.[3]

This may seem an obvious point, but it is also an extremely useful one. When it is brought into contact with a set of real-world cases from U.S.-

[2] Keohane presents a similar argument in political, not game-theoretic terms. *After Hegemony*, Chapter 4. The PD is clearly not the only game in town; much of international relations is not properly thought of even as mixed-motive games. For example, if two states' interests in a particular issue are entirely compatible, *harmony* results—and the simple coordination of behavior that may be necessary to achieve the interests is not properly thought of as cooperation. Conversely, if interests are entirely incompatible, such that each state's policies must necessarily hinder the attainment of the other state's goals, then there is pure *conflict*: cooperation is irrelevant in this case as well, because there is nothing to cooperate about. Between these two extremes lie mixed-motive games, with possibilities for *cooperation* and *discord*. I discuss these in the text.

[3] For the classic treatment, see Jervis, "Cooperation under the Security Dilemma."

Player Two

	cooperate	defect
cooperate	R = 3, R = 3 reward for mutual cooperation	S = 0, T = 5 sucker's payoff, and temptation to defect
defect	T = 5, S = 0 temptation to defect, and sucker's payoff	P = 1, P = 1 punishment for mutual defection

Player One

Figure 1. The Prisoner's Dilemma

Soviet arms control, it suggests a very useful way of categorizing the variance in outcomes. We can expand the cooperation-discord distinction to take account of the impact that differences in the relative magnitude of "payoffs" have on the probability of cooperation. If states' interests and the resulting preference structures are heavily skewed in favor of cooperation, it is more likely that impediments will be overcome and cooperation will in fact result. I label this kind of outcome an "expected success." Conversely, if the relative magnitude of payoffs is heavily skewed toward competition, an outcome of mutual defection would be an "expected failure." A prominent example of an expected success in U.S.-Soviet arms control is the 1963 agreement to construct a "hot line" between Washington and Moscow; an expected failure would be the general and comprehensive disarmament negotiations of the 1950s.[4]

---

[4] I provide these examples only as illustrations; I do not claim to have demonstrated that either case fulfills the requirements for analysis as a mixed-motive game or particularly as the PD. Both cases, however, do combine shared and conflicting interests, in very different relative magnitudes. The disarmament negotiations are an obvious case of mostly conflicting interests. And the hot line agreement was not a case of pure harmony: some American strategic analysts and decisionmakers feared that the establishment of a hot line would dam-

In between these two extremes lie the majority of interesting U.S.-Soviet arms control issues. They are interesting precisely because their outcome is most highly indeterminate. The mixture of shared and conflicting interests is not radically skewed; the relative magnitudes of the payoffs for cooperation, exploitation, and other behaviors do not convincingly prejudice the outcome in one or another direction. What can we say about the likely outcome in such cases? Realism suggests that most if not all will end in discord, particularly when the subject is security cooperation between rival superpowers in a bipolar international system. Axelrod's work suggests that realism may be unnecessarily pessimistic. *The Evolution of Cooperation* provides a possible route to cooperation in a small subset of these cases, where certain initial conditions are fulfilled. I label cooperation that emerges in such cases a "surprising success." If discord or mutual defection occurs, I label this outcome a "missed opportunity."

This book concentrates on cases of surprising success and missed opportunity. Leave aside, for a moment, the important question of how I will demonstrate that my case studies belong in these categories, and consider the rationale behind this approach. Axelrod tells us that cooperation in the PD is possible under certain conditions, but his theory does not differentiate between a surprising success and a missed opportunity. Both outcomes are consistent with its predictions. The most obvious way to extend the theory and improve its discriminatory power is to compare cases from these two categories, aiming to isolate what *intervenes* to "push" the outcome in one direction or the other.

This approach makes equal sense from a practical standpoint. Missed opportunities and surprising successes are the cases that hold promise to generate findings about cooperation that are most interesting and relevant to policymakers. Some of what intervenes, the so-called *intervening variables* that favor cooperation or discord, may be subject to control by governments. If that turns out to be the case, a more detailed understanding of what causes an indeterminate U.S.-Soviet arms control case to "lean" toward cooperation would be of particular value to policymakers as well as to theorists.

Strategies of Reciprocity: The Intervening Variable

Assume once again that we can identify surprising successes and missed opportunities in U.S.-Soviet arms control. The immediate problem in try-

age the credibility of extended deterrence. See Nye, "Nuclear Learning," p. 390; and Ury, *Beyond the Hotline.*

ing to devise a more discriminating explanation is that a large number of additional factors might account for the difference between them, and it is not immediately clear where to look. *The Evolution of Cooperation* provides an important hint.[5] In the game-theoretic model, the introduction and propagation of TFT is a critical intervention without which cooperation would not occur, regardless of the presence of initial conditions. A logical direction for extending Axelrod's model into the real-world, then, would be to focus on the importance of strategy, to see whether a more fine-grained analysis can improve the specificity of the theory.

The meaning of "strategy" in game theory is unambiguous: strategy is a decision rule or an algorithm that determines a player's choice of action. TFT is a particularly simple decision rule. But the meaning of strategy in international relations is considerably more complex.[6] It is not at all obvious how TFT could be directly "translated" into a real-world strategy that a state could employ to seek cooperation in arms control. In relations between states, there are in principle *many* different strategies based on different conceptions of reciprocity that would be more or less consistent with TFT. Why would a state choose a strategy based on one particular conception of reciprocity over others? This is a critical question if, as I have proposed, the type of strategy chosen makes a significant difference in the likelihood that cooperation will occur.

The history of U.S.-Soviet arms control suggests that strategies of reciprocity do vary in their ability to promote cooperation. Developing an appropriate typology of these strategies is the first step toward understanding why. I argued in Chapter 2, however, that Keohane's distinction between diffuse and specific reciprocity is not particularly helpful in arms control. From where would one derive an alternative and more useful typology?

There are always two ways to develop typologies: through deduction and through induction. Deductive typologies are typically comprehensive. One could pick different aspects of reciprocity and generate an exhaustive typology that captured all possible variants of reciprocity strategies in all their conceivable permutations. But it is likely that only a subset of those strategies would actually appear in the historical record. In fact, because my set of cases is closely circumscribed in time and content, that subset may be relatively small. In this setting, there are obvious

---

[5] The most interesting parsimonious theories also suggest the most fruitful places to look for more detailed explanations that would "fill in the gaps" when the predictions of the original theory are no longer considered adequately specific. One strength of Axelrod's theory is that it does precisely this.

[6] Strategy, as noted earlier, refers to the combination of diplomatic, political, and military methods that the state employs to promote its goals vis-à-vis other states.

advantages to developing a typology through induction. The most important advantage is that the ensuing typology focuses on the strategies of reciprocity that the superpowers actually use in arms control.[7]

On this basis, I propose an alternative typology based on a dimension of reciprocity that does seem to vary in the historical record of U.S.-Soviet arms control. My typology concentrates on the criteria of *contingency* that delineate when and what kind of retaliation is to be delivered in response to a "defection" on the part of the adversary.[8] It consists of three ideal type strategies: contingent restraint, enhanced contingent restraint, and contingent threat of escalation.

Contingent restraint is based on relatively permissive criteria of contingency. A state adopting a strategy of contingent restraint declares that it will not take action in a certain area as long as its rival maintains acceptable behavior, usually of a specified nature. For example, Washington might assert that as long as the Soviets refrain from deploying additional heavy ICBMs, it would not be necessary for the United States to deploy new strategic weapons. What if the Soviets did not refrain? Contingent restraint does not commit the United States to a specific response, or indeed to any response at all, should the Soviets choose to deploy more ICBMs. It only suggests that continued U.S. restraint would be reevaluated at that time, and that some form of reciprocal retaliation might be delivered if it were then deemed necessary.

To achieve a cooperative outcome when one state is playing a strategy of contingent restraint demands comparatively little from the adversary. The other state need not take any specific, positive action; it need only refrain from doing what was proscribed. This strategy is also relatively permissive because the state playing it does not identify precisely what it would do if the other state defects: it maintains the option to do nothing or to wait for an unspecified period of time before responding with some reciprocal move. Another important feature of contingent restraint is that any retaliation that is in fact delivered would be carefully limited to steps that only match or compensate for the rival's transgressions. There is a

---

[7] This makes the task of comparison much more tractable by leaving aside the many empty or sparsely populated cells that would populate a deductively derived, comprehensive, Weberian typology. It may, of course, harm the potential generalizability of the results. That is, the resulting theory of cooperation in arms control may not be immediately applicable in other areas. It is also important to remember that the explanations I develop may not fully capture the complexity of possible variance *within* each ideal type strategy. Finally, note that there may be other strategies, *not* based on reciprocity, that the superpowers use in attempts to elicit arms control cooperation. These do not belong in my typology, but it is important to remain aware of their possible significance in these and other cases.

[8] The typology presented here bears some resemblance to that developed by Schelling in "A Framework for the Evaluation of Arms Control Proposals."

clear intention to avoid further escalation that could trigger a "conflict spiral" or feud.

Enhanced contingent restraint is based on a somewhat less permissive conception of contingency. It differs from the previous ideal type in that the state adopting a strategy of enhanced contingent restraint will take special steps to emphasize that it has the capability and political will to respond to a defection, should it so choose. The precise character of the response would again not be specified; nor would the state declare that the response was necessarily forthcoming within a certain period of time. But the state playing enhanced contingent restraint would take serious and highly visible steps to expand its range of options and improve its ability to mount a response to the adversary's defection in the near future. This enhances the credibility of a possible response, while preserving the state's choice among the available options (one of which is to do nothing). Returning to the previous example, the U.S. Congress might allocate funds to construct new production facilities for various strategic delivery systems to underline the credibility of a possible response should the Soviets continue to deploy heavy ICBMs. With production lines in place, restraint could be reversed relatively easily, when and if decisionmakers concluded that Soviet behavior had indeed made some concrete reciprocal action necessary.

Contingent threat of escalation, the third ideal type, is based on much more precise and demanding criteria of contingency. A strategy of contingent threat rests on a specific and highly credible commitment to abstain from a provocative action *if and only if* the adversary state forgoes certain specific activities of its own. The state playing contingent threat declares that it will certainly defect and will take a set of clearly defined actions unless the rival state responds with specific concessions prior to an established deadline.

The "default position" for contingent threat, unlike the previous two strategies, is to compete. Cooperation is gained only if the rival state stops doing something it is currently doing or takes other specific actions that are defined by the state playing contingent threat. In the previous example, the United States would threaten to begin deployment of specific new weapons (such as the MX ICBM) within a defined time period unless the Soviets explicitly agreed not to deploy any new ICBMs of their own. There are two additional features that are important aspects of strategies of contingent threat. First, successful cooperation will usually require some type of formal agreement that spells out the obligations of both sides in fairly precise terms. (In the previous two strategies, cooperation could readily take the form of a tacit agreement where commitments and the terms of restraint are not so precisely specified.) Second, contingent threat implies that the state's competitive response will, by design, do more than simply compensate for the behavior of the adversary. Instead, the state retaliates with the express intention of escalating and exacerbating the competition in a manner that will cause damage to the target state's interests greater than any suffered by the state carrying out the threat.

Abstract typologies and their ideal types do not do justice to the nuances and details of reality in superpower arms control or elsewhere. They are not supposed to. What this typology does is reflect the most important features that differentiate the kinds of strategies of reciprocity that appear in the historical record of U.S.-Soviet arms control. The proper "test" of the typology is whether it can be used to construct a theory that explains cooperation in U.S.-Soviet arms control.

There is a key obstacle, which I just point to now and will take up in detail later. The three ideal type strategies include within their definitions game-theoretic concepts whose meaning in the real world I have not yet defined in a rigorous way. The most obvious and important of these are the concepts "cooperation" and "defection." What is a cooperative move, or a defection, in an arms control strategy? This raises larger questions about how to use the typology; for example, what kind of reciprocity is being offered if the United States deploys medium-range missiles as a bargaining chip, with the express intention of trading them away for Soviet weapons of a similar kind?

Without answering these questions now, it is important to note that they point again toward a fundamental issue that I have raised repeatedly from several different directions. Constructing an externally valid model of cooperation in arms control requires a precise and explicit means of bridging the gap between the concepts of formal theory and historical events. Later in this chapter I discuss some general epistemological problems that come up in this task, and then go on to develop specific bridge principles that can underlie a theory of U.S.-Soviet arms control cooperation. This should solve the problem of mapping behavior in arms control onto the three ideal type strategies. But before turning to bridge principles, it is helpful to take a step back and expand on how strategy will play a central role in explaining cooperation within the model.

Explaining Cooperation: Strategy and Outcomes

The central argument of this book is that game theory's TFT is consistent with several different strategies of reciprocity in the real world, and that these different strategies vary critically in their ability to promote cooperation in the U.S.-Soviet arms control relationship. The logic of this argument rests on two components: the strategies states choose, and the relationship between strategies and outcomes. If the difference between a surprising success and a missed opportunity in U.S.-Soviet arms control cases that fulfill Axelrod's initial conditions for cooperation can indeed be explained on the basis of differences among strategies of reciprocity, then the prior issue becomes explaining the choice of strategy. Why does a state choose one particular ideal type strategy over others?

The most promising way to answer this question for U.S.-Soviet arms control is again through empirical, not deductive analysis. Looking at the histories of ABM, ASAT, and MIRV, I ask why U.S. decisionmakers did or did not choose strategies based on particular conceptions of reciprocity at different points in time. This is not the same thing as defining a preference structure, which I will also do as a prerequisite to the argument in each case. Preferences are part of the initial conditions for cooperation, but a certain preference structure does not in and of itself explain what strategy the United States will pursue. There must be additional factors influencing decisions about strategy, and these factors are not a part of the formal PD model. Nor can they be deduced from it.[9]

The history of U.S.-Soviet arms control suggests five variables that appear most important in predisposing U.S. decisionmakers to choose strategies related to one or another of the ideal types. The variables are: changes in interests and incentives, saliencies, the general political environment, strategic theory, and bureaucratic politics. These variables describe the most important features of the milieu within which decisionmakers choose strategies, and the impact of the variables is sensitive to the beliefs and perceptions of these key individuals. These effects cannot be studied through deductive analysis alone. It makes sense, therefore, to build these variables into my model primarily as a set of questions and not as a set of hypotheses. The case studies provide preliminary answers to these questions, answers that can then be properly developed into hy-

---

[9] Formal theories work through this problem by incorporating additional assumptions about how idealized actors choose strategies. The simplest approach is to adopt the expected utility model for decisionmaking under risk. According to this model, the player estimates the probability that each possible action will lead to each possible outcome. Multiplying the utility of the outcome by the probability that it will result, and summing for each potential action, yields a set of expected utilities attached to each action. Strategy is simply a matter of choosing the action with the highest expected utility. Keep in mind, however, that "expected utility" is based on auxiliary assumptions, again not necessarily derived from empirical evidence, and that these are simply imported for the sake of building the model. In addition, there would be obvious problems in trying to apply this model to strategies in U.S.-Soviet arms control, and it is not clear how expected utility could distinguish among the three ideal types. An inductive approach to constructing the argument about strategies will be less general, but more powerful in the specific set of cases I am interested in here.

potheses about the impact of each of these variables upon the likelihood that one or another type of strategy will be chosen.

After accounting for the particular type of strategy that decisionmakers choose, the second component of the argument examines the relationship between strategy and outcomes. This would be easy, even trivial, if we were to have perfect information about the strategies being played by *both* sides. Game theory generates the outcome. Even within my expanded approach, it is no great insight to say that if two players choose strategies of contingent restraint and make compatible demands, the outcome will be cooperation. But the real problem in explaining U.S.-Soviet arms control is not at all trivial. This is because retrospective analysis, like the decisions of contemporary policymakers, rests on reliable data about strategy on only one side of the equation. That is, I can make reasonably well-supported arguments about strategies, underlying preferences, and the links between the two only for the U.S. side. Similar arguments on the Soviet side remain speculative. Is it possible to get past this impasse? It certainly presents serious problems for a purely deductive, game-theoretic argument. An empirical approach offers a more promising alternative.

I begin by making some assumptions, based on available information and secondary sources, about Soviet preferences and strategies. My task in doing this is similar to that which faced contemporary U.S. decisionmakers in ABM, MIRV, and ASAT. Despite a lack of reliable information from Moscow, decisionmakers in each of these cases had to formulate and then act on assumptions about Soviet preferences and strategies. American decisionmakers did this by developing "working hypotheses" about the interests of the Soviet leadership and the possible impact of American strategy upon their behavior.

These working hypotheses serve a number of purposes for decisionmakers. They reinforce decisions to seek cooperation in the first place. They strongly influence the type of strategy that is chosen as the most effective means to promote that outcome. And they also define what type of information decisionmakers seek out as *feedback*. In other words, what kinds of Soviet actions would signal that a strategy was having its intended impact, or that it was failing and would have to be modified? Teasing these working hypotheses out of the historical record is one way to get past the roadblock. By tracing how decisionmakers on one side actually implement, evaluate, and modify their state's strategy in response to changes in perceptions of the other's behavior, it becomes possible to construct a persuasive argument about the relationship between strategies and outcomes in carefully selected cases.

With the logical path of the argument settled, I now return to an earlier impasse: the gap between game-theoretic concepts and the real-world events that this argument tries to explain. How can we effectively bridge this gap?

Building the Model: Linking the Theory to Case Studies

An analogy from physics is helpful at this point. The field of modern high energy physics is divided into two distinct areas of theory and experiment. This division is both sociological and intellectual, so that experimental physicists and theoretical physicists make up two nearly discrete scientific communities.[10] Contemporary theorists of international relations are likely to find this a familiar story. Those who by temperament or expertise prefer deductive theory or formal models in international relations have trouble convincing others that their theories have any relevance to what happens in the real world. Those who prefer detailed historical research and choose to rely primarily on inductive methods have trouble convincing their colleagues that the findings of case studies can be generalized beyond the cases from which they were drawn, or sometimes that they are valid at all in light of other possible interpretations.[11]

They might disagree about the best way to do so, but proponents of both approaches would agree that to explain or make predictions about real-world events, formal theories must always be given some kind of empirical interpretation. Forcing a formal theory of cooperation to confront a set of cases from U.S.-Soviet arms control requires a carefully specified means of linking game theory to historical events. The experience of the physicists, who confront an analogous problem in bridging the gap between theory and experiment, may throw some light on how to deal with this problem.

Some theoretical physicists do "pure theory," by which I mean the abstract elaboration of mathematical formulations divorced from empirical observation. Others do what is called "phenomenology," which involves trying to apply less dignified models to the analysis of data and as a guide to further experiments. The latter is more like using game theory as a heuristic to develop a theory of cooperation in U.S.-Soviet arms control. But even phenomenology faces the challenge of linking its models to the experimenters' world. That is because in physics as elsewhere, philosophers of science recognize that "no deductively formulated theory or any propositions in that theory are ever *directly* testable [in the real world]."[12] This is part of the problem of evaluating external validity; and the proper

[10] See Pickering, *Constructing Quarks*, pp. 21–45.

[11] See, for example, the five articles comprising a "Roundtable on Rational Deterrence Theory," *World Politics* 41, no. 2 (1989): 143–237.

[12] Blalock and Blalock, *Methodology in Social Research*, p. 11. Emphasis is mine.

lesson from the philosophy of science is simply that the relevance of a deductive theory to empirical events cannot be evaluated on its own.

The basic reason for this is that theories and empirical phenomena are described by two separate "languages" that exist at different levels of abstraction. The language of theory consists of abstract *concepts*: for example, iteration, preferences, and cooperation are concepts within game theory. Remember that a deductive theory is internally valid if the statements it makes about relationships between concepts within the theory can be proven by logical arguments.

The language of history, however, is not one of concepts. It is made up instead of people, events, and other empirical phenomena. The central challenge in linking a deductive theory to history lies in specifying the relationship between theoretical concepts and empirical phenomena. That relationship is usually not a simple, one-to-one translation. This is an important part of what physicists call the "measurement problem": what empirical phenomena should be used as "indicators" to correspond to the concepts of theory? No one has ever seen a quark, but physicists agree that certain scattering patterns detected in particle collidors are indicative of their presence. The analogy to game theory and arms control is apparent. What would we have to see in history to claim an "iterated game"? How do we distinguish in practice between a policy decision to "cooperate" and a decision to "defect"? Until we answer these questions, there is no way to know if the logical relationships between concepts in a deductive theory are in fact reproduced in any way in the real world.[13]

One need not look to the esoteric world of particle physics for a possible answer from the philosophy of science. Consider the problem from the standpoint of classical mechanics. A physicist wants to test a simple theory, like Force = Mass × Acceleration. *Mass* is a theoretical concept that refers to the quantity of matter in an object; but the scales that experimental physicists typically use do not measure mass. They measure *weight*, which is the force that gravity exerts upon an object. Experiments can go forward only because physicists have agreed, *prior* to carrying out the experiment, that when testing F = MA, weight can be treated as an empirical indicator that corresponds to mass.

Where does this agreement come from? It rests on a set of auxiliary theories that deal with the predictable effect of gravity on mass. Because these auxiliary theories are previously agreed upon within the commu-

---

[13] Lebow and Stein make an analogous point but carry it too far when they describe rational deterrence theories as internally valid but empirically irrelevant arguments "about nonexistent decisionmakers operating in nonexistent environments." "Rational Deterrence Theory," p. 224. The key lies in understanding the relationship between the game-theoretic concept of rationality and the ways in which real-world decisionmakers act when confronted with deterrent threats.

nity, the physicists can also agree that at a particular elevation above sea level the masses of different objects can be compared by measuring their weights. It is these auxiliary theories that make it possible to test the external validity of F = MA, by applying a force to several different objects and measuring their acceleration. In the terminology of philosophy of science, the auxiliary theories constitute *bridge principles* for this particular research design.[14]

Bridge principles could play an analogous role in linking a formal PD theory to historical cases in U.S.-Soviet arms control. But the bridge principles here (as in most social sciences) are not likely to be as firmly established and noncontroversial as those that link weight to mass. To get past this dilemma, I turn back to the analogy with physics. It is important to remember that physicists construct bridge principles in order to test a theory in a *particular* empirical setting. They do this because there are often many empirical indicators of the same theoretical concept; the translation between languages is not one-to-one. The most easily measured indicators can be different in different experimental situations. For example, current flowing through a wire can be measured by the magnetic field it induces in one experiment; or it could be measured by the brightness of a light it illuminates in another. The bridge principles that underlie these two experiments must be different. The point is that bridge principles should be thought of as an integral part of a specific research project that aims to test the external validity of a theory within a particular class of events, making best use of the indicators that can be measured within that setting.

There is another reason to think about bridge principles in this way. When they are confined to a particular research design, the necessary bridge principles can more readily be established as valid by prior agreement, before conducting experiments. The bridge principles that I propose for this project have no "absolute" epistemological status, and I do not have to claim that they would be relevant in some other empirical setting. I do have to claim that they have the virtues of simplicity, clarity, and intuitive plausibility for linking Axelrod's theory to U.S.-Soviet arms control.

There is one further point about bridge principles that is critical. Once the bridge principles command a consensus that they are valid for the specific project at hand, scientists treat the bridge principles themselves as *not* subject to falsification within the context of a single research project. By common agreement, what is being tested in the experiment is the theory itself, not the previously established bridge principles. The reasons for taking this step are obvious. If it were not agreed, and the bridge princi-

---

[14] Hempel, *Philosophy of Natural Science*, pp. 72–73.

ples were also open to question, empirical tests could never provide evidence to confirm or disconfirm a theory.[15] Every experiment would be one in which there were "too many variables, too few equations."

The next step is to propose a set of bridge principles that link the concepts of game theory to U.S.-Soviet arms control. I start with the two most central concepts, cooperation and defection.

Bridging Key Concepts: Cooperation and Defection

In game theory, cooperation and defection can refer to game *moves*, as in a "cooperative move" or a "competitive move" (which I use interchangeably with the term "defection"), and to *outcomes*, as in an outcome of cooperation or discord. To avoid confusion, I will discuss these separately. The bridge principles that I use to link cooperative and competitive *moves* to policy options in arms control rest on a well-known auxiliary theory about the security dilemma and its consequences for states. The security dilemma explains how certain actions a state takes to enhance its own security will have the effect of reducing the security of others, who respond in ways that in turn reduce the security of the state taking the first action. I "bridge" the concept of a cooperative move to policy options that do not exacerbate the security dilemma; that is, options that deal with a security threat to one state without decreasing the security of the other side. Defections or competitive moves are policy options that make the security dilemma worse. They immediately enhance one state's security, but in posing new threats to the adversary, competitive moves tend to incite a response that can lead to "conflict spirals" or feuds and an increase in the overall level of competition.

In arms control, as in other issues, there are different kinds of cooperative moves that states can take. A state may sometimes have options that it can carry out on its own, that will improve its position and not harm others *regardless* of what others do. I will call these options "unilateral cooperative moves" because they do not require any coordination with rival states to be effective. There are often alternative policy options that

[15] This is not to say that the auxiliary theories making up bridge principles are never subject to falsification. Rather, an attempt to test these theories would require a different research project designed to make them the principal subject of investigation. The kind of criticism I allude to here is a common critique of game-theoretic applications in international relations. Duncan Snidal notes, properly in my view, that too much time is spent in such critiques "sorting out whether the Cuban missile crisis was really Chicken or Prisoner's Dilemma." "The Game *Theory* of International Politics," p. 26. It is the responsibility of the researcher who wants to use one of these models to establish the bridge principles that validate its use in a project *prior* to beginning. If this is done successfully, then a critic is at fault who raises questions about the bridge principles after seeing the results.

also would not exacerbate the security dilemma, but differ in the important respect that they will not contribute to the security of the state unless the rivals can coordinate their actions effectively. These I call "bilateral cooperative moves."[16]

The first general task for each case study is to establish that these bridge principles are valid for the project. I do this for the security dilemma by exploring the historical background that leads to critical choices about each weapons system. Decisions about the future of ABM, MIRV, and ASAT are brought to the fore because policymakers perceive the development of a threat to which they feel compelled to respond. In each instance, there are a range of options available. What is interesting about these three cases is that decisionmakers perceive options as "resolving" themselves into two sets, which can be labeled "cooperative" and "competitive" according to the bridge principles outlined above. That is, they perceive a dyadic choice between responses that are likely to exacerbate the security dilemma and those that will not. It is important to recognize that while the latter category includes some unilateral cooperative moves, in none of these three cases do decisionmakers believe that such measures can by themselves deal adequately with the threat. Thus, the issues connected to ABM, MIRV, and ASAT all involve truly interdependent decisions where one state cannot on its own initiative "escape" the PD.

It may seem strangely oversimplified to argue that decisionmakers act as if they face a dyadic choice between cooperative and competitive moves in these or any other arms control cases. In ABM, for example, Washington's deployment options included a heavy defense of key cities, a light area defense covering much of the country, point-defenses to protect missile silos, and others. It is not surprising that in ABM and the other cases, decisionmakers at a certain point in time come to believe that they have reached a "key decisional point" where they are forced to make critical decisions about the future of the weapons system. What is striking is that at these critical junctures, political and technological circum-

---

[16] An example of a unilateral cooperative move would be the installation of permissive action links (PALS) on certain nuclear weapons systems. When one state installs PALS, this increases the security of both sides regardless of whether the adversary takes similar actions. An example of a simple bilateral cooperative move would be the establishment of a direct communications link (hot line). It would not increase the security of one state to establish a line of communication with the other's capital, unless the other agrees to do the same in reverse. The distinction is important. If there were unilateral moves available in a particular issue that could by themselves acceptably deal with the security threat, then the states would not be "condemned" to interdependent decision but could choose to act on their own. Cooperation, which we normally think of as involving coordination and adjustment of policies between two actors in an interdependent decision situation, *might* be irrelevant (bilateral cooperation might still have certain attractions if unilateral options produced a clearly suboptimal outcome).

stances coalesced in ways that caused the range of options to "collapse" into what decisionmakers perceived as an essentially dyadic choice between cooperative and competitive moves. In ABM, MIRV, and ASAT, decisionmakers believed and acted as if they faced a branching point between discrete pathways, not unlike the choice facing game-theoretic actors in the PD. These are the critical junctures at which I focus on how they developed and implemented strategies of reciprocity.

Game theory uses cooperation and defection to refer also to *outcomes*. I draw on Keohane's work, again, for a useful way of bridging these concepts to my cases. In *After Hegemony*, Keohane defines cooperation as an outcome where governments adjust their policies in a coordinated way so that the new policies facilitate the attainment of each other's goals. Discord, or mutual defection, occurs when attempts to adjust policies in this way are either not made or are not successful.[17] With these definitions, the outcome of each case can be coded with relatively little ambiguity: the ABM case yields cooperation; the MIRV case, discord; and the ASAT case varies from cooperation to discord over the course of time.

The details of the cases, however, will suggest that these bridge principles are barely adequate and should be treated only as a starting point. This is one area where cooperation theory needs additional concepts to bring it into full contact with history. Put differently, we need to add more specific conceptions of what cooperation can mean in U.S.-Soviet arms control. Obviously, cooperation varies in *form*: in ABM, cooperation is based on a formal treaty, while in ASAT cooperation manifests itself in tacit arrangements that are not always explicit. Cooperation also seems to vary in *substance*. Arms control cooperation can make different types of contributions to security: for example, the superpowers may agree to entirely close off an area of potential competition, or to devise only limited rules that constrain but permit or even facilitate further competitive efforts. Finally, I will argue that cooperation varies according to the kinds of *intersecting interests* from which it arises. All of these differences matter greatly, both for theories of cooperation and for the scope and stability of arms control, particularly for its bearing on the broader U.S.-Soviet relationship.

These comments foreshadow several elaborations to the concept of cooperation that will emerge from this study. I bring them up here to underscore my point that constructing bridge principles from Axelrod's theory to the world of arms control will not, by itself, fulfill the objectives of this project. It is necessary to go further and add new concepts that are

---

[17] I draw these definitions, in paraphrase, from Keohane, *After Hegemony*, p. 53. I leave out, for reasons stated earlier, the outcomes of harmony and conflict— these are not relevant to a study focusing on mixed-motive games. The auxiliary theories that lie behind bridge principles here should be obvious.

not a part of game theory and would not have come out of a purely formal model.

Setting Up the Cases

The case studies that follow in Chapters 4–6 are constructed along a common framework that consists of four analytic sections: (1) historical background, (2) payoff analysis, (3) strategy development, and (4) strategic interaction.[18] I consider each in turn.

Historical Background

How do U.S. decisionmakers arrive at a key decisional point for the future of a weapons system? ABM, MIRV, and ASAT systems have long histories. Each was conceived as a response to a perceived threat and as a possible source of some opportunity for advantage in the arms race. As research and development progressed, these original justifications sometimes changed, while the interests of bureaucratic players became intertwined with the proposed weapon. Both can happen for several reasons: alternative means of responding to a threat may arise, or the threat itself may diminish; and incentives to pursue opportunities can change over time. Together, these "legacies" constitute the technological and political background against which critical decisions about the future of the system will be made.

The purpose of the historical background is to uncover precisely how contemporary decisionmakers viewed a particular weapons system in its relation to broad perceptions about the evolving strategic environment. This requires adding a new concept to the analysis because decisionmakers in Washington and Moscow are not armed with a full and concrete understanding of the "nuclear environment" that the new weapon will enter. In the world of strategic weapons, the criteria for a net gain in security are highly ambiguous. What constitutes a threat or an opportunity for advantage can rarely be understood in objective or absolute terms. For instance, is it an advantage or a threat to American interests if the Soviets deploy missiles on a relatively invulnerable submarine, as opposed to silos?

The answers to such questions depend on theories. Put differently, the

---

[18] The ABM and MIRV cases follow this framework explicitly. The ASAT case uses the framework in a less formal way in order to facilitate looking at the historical progression from cooperation to discord in this case.

relationship between many strategic weapons issues and conceptions of national interest depends on auxiliary theories that are not derived from concrete or experiential criteria. They come instead from sets of ideas, abstract arguments, and intellectual constructs. In other contexts, Ernst Haas refers to such a set of ideas as *consensual knowledge*: a "body of beliefs about cause-effect and ends-means relationships among variables (activities, aspirations, values, demands) that is widely accepted by the actors, irrespective of the absolute or final truth of these beliefs."[19] To understand the historical background for critical decisions about a particular weapons system, it is essential to grasp the consensual knowledge criteria that decisionmakers use to evaluate the risks and opportunities of proceeding.

In the historical background then, I am primarily interested in describing the consensual knowledge that underlies American decisionmakers' perceptions of developments in the strategic environment. Like consensual knowledge in other issues, this set of ideas serves to shape preferences and will influence how states develop and modify strategies. But the cases will suggest that consensual knowledge in strategic nuclear issues differs in fundamental ways from its analogue in political economy and other areas. At this point I speculate that those differences will have important implications for U.S.-Soviet cooperation in arms control.

In sum, the primary questions of the historical background are:

1. What is the consensual knowledge that defines the threat to which a particular weapons system is designed to respond? Do the arguments change over time, and do perceptions of the threat change accordingly? Does this affect the progression of the weapons system toward its key decisional point?

2. What are the important technological, political, and bureaucratic legacies of research and development behind the weapons system? Are there alternative means of managing the perceived threat, and for what reasons are these thought to be less attractive? How do these factors mesh with the developing threat to produce a widespread perception that a critical decisional point for the future of the weapons system is at hand?

Payoff Analysis

Can ABM, MIRV, and ASAT each be modeled as iterated PD games with a long shadow of the future? Bridging the concepts of preferences, iteration, and shadow of the future to U.S.-Soviet arms control are the main

---

[19] See Haas, "Why Collaborate?"; Rothstein, "Consensual Knowledge and International Collaboration"; and Nye, "Nuclear Learning."

tasks of this section. I begin by expanding on the argument that there exist critical decisional points where policy options are perceived to resolve into cooperative and competitive moves. At these junctures, American decisionmakers choose strategies subject to their preferences over alternative "outcomes." I propose that game-theoretic outcomes correspond to decisionmakers' conceptions of alternative potential futures or scenarios for the strategic environment. Preferences emerge as decisionmakers compare how these alternatives fit within their conceptions of self-interest. I say "preferences emerge" because in analyzing preferences, I treat this as an active process of evaluation, persuasion, and argumentation in a political realm, not an objective comparison among static or preexisting utilities. In each case, I argue that U.S. decisionmakers come to hold PD preferences and to view their predicament as an iterated game with a long shadow of the future.

The first step in making this argument is to disassemble the concept of preferences. In game theory, preferences follow simply from a comparison of the utilities that actors attach to various outcomes. The historical background took a preliminary step toward bridging this concept to the world of arms control by establishing that the superpowers confront an interdependent decision in which policymakers face a choice between cooperative and competitive moves. This generates a "two by two matrix" with four potential outcomes. Each outcome corresponds to a scenario for a potential future state of the strategic environment. For example, decisionmakers can imagine alternative worlds in which both, neither, or only one of the superpowers possess MIRV warheads. I analyze preferences as the state's comparative evaluations of these alternative worlds.

Assessing state preferences in a particular case, and demonstrating that they match the PD, is the next step in the argument. This involves two parts. First, assume that the consensual knowledge that states use to make sense of the strategic environment provides straightforward criteria for evaluating alternative "worlds." Because this is true for ABM, MIRV, and ASAT, it is possible for an analyst standing outside the history of the cases to logically derive a preference order over those worlds. This generates what I call an *objective* analysis of preferences, which is just a hypothetical specification of preferences consistent with prevailing conceptions of self-interest. This is exactly what political economy theorists do when they use trade theory to generate a set of hypothetical state preferences for open markets or protection.

But the actual preferences of states, in arms control or in trade, may not match this objective analysis. Perceptions and misperceptions, extraneous beliefs, bureaucratic pressures, and a large number of other factors affect the preferences of real-world decisionmakers. The objective analysis is only a point of reference. The weight of my argument about cooperation must rest on the second part, which I call a *subjective* analysis. This is an assessment of the actual preferences of contemporary decision-makers as they viewed the possible alternative worlds in which they might later find themselves.

The subjective analysis itself demands additional bridge principles. The utilities, or in this case the subjective expected utilities, that define preferences in game theory are not reproduced, or at least are not easily recognized, in the world of U.S.-Soviet arms control. Decisionmakers here do not deal in utility functions. Instead, they deal in *arguments*. History shows them formulating and comparing sets of arguments about the relative desirability of alternative outcomes. Seen in this light, the development of a preference structure is indeed a creative and constructive process, not a static comparison of preexisting utility functions. Choice is a matter of conflict resolution more than utility maximization; preferences emerge in the context of making difficult decisions.

The bridge principle here is a theory of "argument-based choice." Developed by Amos Tversky and his colleagues as a competitor to the traditional view of choice as utility maximization, argument-based choice pictures decisionmakers favoring qualitative over quantitative criteria; and it sees choices as sensitive to the framing of and response to the particular arguments that are elicited in support of one or another option at a given time.[20] Using argument-based choice as a bridge principle is more intuitively plausible than the traditional utility approach for studying preferences in nuclear security issues. It also facilitates a more finely textured analysis of the range of decisionmakers' preferences in each case. What arguments did decisionmakers bring forth about the political and military costs and benefits attached to each of the four outcomes? How did they go about comparing expected short and long-term implications of each for the state's security, as well as for the superpower relationship and the state's position in international politics generally?

In any significant arms control case there is going to be a fair diversity of views on these questions within the American decisionmaking elite. In Chapters 4–6 I reconstruct the range of opinion for ABM, MIRV, and ASAT by surveying a wide variety of historical evidence, including primary sources such as contemporary writings and statements, journals, newspaper reports, transcripts of Congressional hearings, and interviews,

---

[20] Apart from picturing the *process* of decisionmaking differently, argument-based choice generates predictions that contradict utility maximization. For example, arguments can have interference or enhancement effects upon each other that are sensitive to context and framing; both effects violate transitivity and other principles central to utility maximization. Amos Tversky, personal communication, February 1988; Kahneman, Slovic, and Tversky, *Judgement under Uncertainty*; Tversky and Kahneman, "Rational Choice and the Framing of Decisions."

and secondary sources, particularly the sometimes excellent histories of U.S.-Soviet arms control. I develop for each case a summary picture of the range of American decisionmakers' preferences. It is no surprise that the U.S. decisionmaking system never approximates the unitary actor of game theory. But as decisionmakers compare arguments for different potential outcomes, the history of these three cases shows preferences converging around what I call a "working consensus" that commands sufficient power to guide the behavior of the state. This makes it possible to focus on the *state* as the principal actor, and to proceed with the argument about cooperation with the assumption that the state's strategy reflects a set of preferences derived from a broad consensus among its decisionmaking elite.[21]

PD preferences do not by themselves constitute the initial conditions for cooperation in Axelrod's model: the game must also be an iterated one in which players do not markedly discount payoffs that will come in future rounds. A priori, the U.S.-Soviet nuclear relationship in general seems to fulfill these criteria. From an objective standpoint, rough nuclear parity and the resulting condition of MAD would seem to imply that the superpowers' nuclear security "game" would be expected to continue, perhaps indefinitely. Substantial lead times for the development of weapons systems should insure that decisionmakers maintain a long-term perspective on "payoffs." Because both states monitor the other's actions closely, and have demonstrated the capability to respond to new developments that might threaten interests in maintaining the nuclear balance, it is very unlikely that any short-term gain in relative nuclear capability would give one side sufficient power to fundamentally restructure the strategic environment, or otherwise bring the game to an end.

A subjective analysis, however, has to take account of the historical

---

[21] Although I sometimes use the term "American decisionmakers" or "the decisionmaking elite" in shorthand as if it were a coherent entity with full agreement on preferences, the reader should appreciate that the meaning discussed here applies. Arrow's impossibility theorem raises a potential objection to this approach. In general terms, Arrow's theorem shows that social institutions do not always aggregate individual preferences in a way that preserves the essential properties of the latter. If decisionmakers' preferences are not homogenous, it may be misleading to postulate a priori a set of preferences for the United States. Arrow, *Social Choice and Individual Values*. The empirical research on which my argument rests, however, does not have to rely on a priori postulates. I deal with the concerns of Arrow's theorem by telling a detailed story of decisionmaking that includes analysis of the inner workings of the institutions and processes that intervene between individual preferences and social decision. How do policymakers formulate their preferences in a particular setting, and how is the creative process of developing the working consensus modified by decisionmaking institutions? I answer these questions by focusing on the key individuals and institutions that control decisionmaking for the future of each weapons system, and considering how these central figures and decisionmaking organizations guide the formulation of the working consensus about preferences that then guides the choices of the state.

observation that decisionmakers' *beliefs* about "iteration" and "the shadow of the future" seem to have varied over time. In assessing these beliefs, I focus on how American elites perceive central political and military aspects of the superpower relationship at the key decisional points in each case. Politically, do the Americans view the Soviet government as a stable and predictable competitor?[22] Do decisionmakers sense opportunities for faits accomplis or other short-term actions that could significantly change the balance of the political competition? If so, was the international system thought to be sufficiently stable to support a "dynamic equilibrium," where such gains by one side would be balanced by gains for the other; or were disturbances and instabilities likely to multiply?[23]

From the military perspective, American decisionmakers' beliefs about the stability of nuclear deterrence are most important for perceptions of an iterated game. Was the balance of terror believed to be robust or delicate? Was parity considered sufficient to support the U.S. commitment to extended deterrence in Europe? Beliefs about the role of a presumed American advantage in military technology are also important. Was the technological edge something to be capitalized upon as a source of possible superiority; was it seen as a reserve that could be called upon to compensate for other Soviet advantages; or was it something that the United States was compelled to exploit to its fullest merely to maintain parity? The answers to these questions will establish that at the critical junctures in each case study, American decisionmakers' perceptions of their environment and interests were in fact compatible with Axelrod's concept of an iterated PD game with a long shadow of the future.

The central questions of the payoff analysis are:

1. Can the historical case be represented as a PD game? How do decisionmakers conceive of alternative potential futures for the strategic environment and develop a set of preferences among them? How do key individuals and the state's decisionmaking institutions aggregate the preferences of the elite into a working consensus to guide the state's action?

2. If the state's preferences are in fact those of the PD, are decisions that have to be made concerning the destiny of a particular weapons system seen as part of an iterated game with a long shadow of the future?

[22] By "stable competitor" I mean one whose policies follow a generally consistent line, without radical changes in fundamental objectives. I do not mean to imply that during the time period covered by my cases, Americans doubted the ability of the Soviet government to sustain itself.

[23] The contrast between these two images of the international system is similar to Walt's distinction between systems where states tend to balance and systems where states bandwagon. In the former, small gains by one side are damped and counter-balanced; the system tends toward equilibrium. In the latter, small gains are multiplied through positive feedback; the system is highly unstable and short-term gains may be far more important. Walt, *The Origins of Alliances*, Chapters 1 and 3.

Strategy Development

Payoff matrices do not by themselves determine strategy in the iterated PD game. Where do strategies of reciprocity in arms control come from? Why do decisionmakers choose one particular type of reciprocal strategy over others?

Answering these questions requires two more additions to the game-theoretic model. The first concerns the issue of how decisionmakers acquire expectations about the rival state's behavior in future rounds of the game. Formal theory, of course, recognizes that the choice of an "optimal" strategy depends in part upon these expectations; and different formal theories incorporate elaborate algorithms for their development and updating. But these formalizations are not immediately useful for explaining cooperation in U.S.-Soviet arms control for the same reasons that weaken other abstract refinements to simple game models. Bayesian updating and other such algorithms do not necessarily capture how real-world actors like states actually develop expectations about other states' behavior: they may be normative constructs, but they are not descriptive. The content and impact of expectations will not be deduced effectively from abstract formulations alone.

Induction is a more direct approach. How do U.S. decisionmakers actually develop and modify expectations about Soviet behavior in ABM, MIRV, and ASAT? I posit that this process has two distinct components. The first and most obvious starts with an assessment of Soviet *preferences*. In what order do the Soviets rank alternative future scenarios for the strategic environment when it comes to the impact of a particular weapons system upon it? Key American policymakers guide the construction of a consensus in Washington on this score. Frequently, this is not so difficult to do. For example, by 1970 or 1971 most of the relevent community in Washington agreed that Moscow preferred cooperation over competition when it came to ABM.

Axelrod's model stops with an assessment of preferences. But a theory of arms control cooperation has to go further, and look *behind* preferences. This is because the development of strategies of reciprocity by states depends as much on perceptions of *interests* that lie behind preferences. ABM is again the obvious example. Soviet preferences were by 1971 quite clear: Moscow wanted mutual restraint that would limit ABM deployments to insignificant levels on both sides. What was not clear was *why*.

In 1971, American decisionmakers disagreed over what they thought were the underlying interests that had brought Moscow to its apparent preferences over ABM outcomes. Some Americans argued that the Soviets were trying to slow down American progress in defense technologies and were willing to give up their own ABM to do so, but were still committed to building the kinds of weapons that were needed for nuclear war-fighting. Others argued that Moscow's interests were to move toward a broad arrangement for joint management of deterrence based on the American concept of MAD. These differing assessments of underlying interests led to conflicting arguments about an appropriate U.S. strategy. ABM is not unique in this regard. In MIRV and ASAT as well, assessments of underlying interests mattered greatly for the kind of reciprocal strategy that decisionmakers believed would best promote cooperation. And forging a consensus around one or another of these assessments was an essential precondition for the state to attempt reciprocal strategies at all.

The simple lesson is that if preferences are sometimes transparent, interests are not. But judgments about interests are a crucial part of developing reciprocal strategies to elicit cooperation. It is necessary to ask how key decisionmakers formulate their working hypotheses about Soviet interests; what "data" do they use and how do they put it together? How does the decisionmaking system manage the uncertainties and disagreements among policymakers and forge a consensus strong enough to underwrite a strategy of reciprocity?

Adding interests to the model in this way stimulates other important findings about the development of strategies. To foreshadow what turns out to be a complicated story: U.S. decisionmakers thinking about Soviet interests in ABM, MIRV, and ASAT tended to focus on a small set of peculiar "indicators" that may not have been representative of actual Soviet interests in any sense. For reasons I discuss later, these indicators were nonetheless established as key guides to interpreting interests; and the partial success of arms control cooperation during the 1970s institutionalized their importance in a manner that had broad consequences for future arms control endeavors. Throughout, decisionmakers paid greater attention to change in the indicators than they did to fundamental consistencies. Using the resultant data, decisionmakers developed working hypotheses about Soviet interests that could accommodate observed Soviet preferences. When American leaders succeeded in forging a consensus around a set of hypotheses, they were then able to develop and implement reciprocal strategies aimed at eliciting cooperation. Without consensus, similar attempts were stillborn.

The importance of interests drives a second addition to the game-theoretic model, an addition that was also recognized as essential by Oye and his colleagues in *Cooperation under Anarchy*. States, unlike the actors in the PD, are not constrained to take other states' preferences as immutable. They can and do engage in what Oye calls "higher order strategies" to alter rival states' preferences. In U.S.-Soviet arms control, higher-order strategies would logically be directed at trying to modify the consensual knowledge that decisionmakers on one side believe is guiding the other side's basic understanding of the game. I will call such efforts "meta-strategy," by which I mean attempts to alter the rival state's preferences by changing basic conceptions of self-interest.[24]

Adding the concept of meta-strategy opens new questions and possibilities for a theory of arms control cooperation, some of which I again foreshadow. States do not always attempt meta-strategies, and they are not always successful. When and how did U.S. decisionmakers try to alter Soviet conceptions of self-interest in ABM, MIRV, and ASAT? How did they evaluate the results? The experience of these cases also prompts the question of whether this is a viable route to cooperation in U.S.-Soviet arms control. Put differently, can consensual knowledge that is modified through meta-strategy serve as a foundation for nuclear security cooperation between rival superpowers?

To repeat the distinction, *meta-strategies* seek to alter conceptions of self-interest and preferences, while *strategies* are aimed at influencing the adversary's behavior *given* existent preferences. The game-theoretic model has more to say about the latter issue, the traditional notion of strategy, to which I now return. Assume that U.S. decisionmakers believe that both sides' preferences match the PD. They might then develop a strategy based on reciprocity as a means of eliciting cooperation. In the course of the ABM, MIRV, and ASAT cases, we will see representations of three ideal type strategies of reciprocity: contingent restraint, enhanced contingent restraint, and contingent threat of escalation.

Since all are consistent with game theory's TFT, we need to understand why decisionmakers favor one of these reciprocal strategies over others in particular instances. Earlier, I proposed five additional variables that explain the choice of strategies, both within each case and across the cases: changes in interests and incentives, saliencies, the general political environment, strategic theory, and bureaucratic politics. I now develop each of these variables into a set of questions to be directed at ABM, MIRV, and ASAT. The reasoning behind this approach should be clear: Axelrod's theory does not specify any means of deducing specific hypotheses about why states choose the strategies they do; and to arbitrarily add

---

[24] Meta-strategy is thus related but not identical to Oye's notion of "higher order strategies." *Cooperation under Anarchy*, p. 2. Oye emphasizes other means of altering the dynamics of a game, but does not extend his discussion to the possibility of changes in the basic payoff structure. An example of Oye's higher-order strategies would be enhancing iteration and the shadow of the future by decomposing a single interaction into a set of smaller games. Such efforts do not fundamentally change the consensual knowledge that underlies actors' preferences over alternative outcomes, and are not meta-strategy as I have defined it.

auxiliary theories that can do this would defeat the logic of both my argument and my methodology.[25]

In the course of developing these questions, I will present some preliminary hypotheses about the impact of each of the variables on the state's choice of strategy. Keep in mind that these also are not logical deductions; they are inductive hypotheses drawn from preliminary investigation of a wide variety of cases in U.S.-Soviet arms control. These hypotheses are not being "tested" and the external validity of Axelrod's theory does not depend upon their veracity. I present them here only to clarify my argument and to focus the investigation on the most important aspects of the case studies in Chapters 4–6. In Chapter 7, I use the evidence from these cases to flesh out the logic that underlies the preliminary hypotheses or undermines them should they fail. This method focuses on whether the preliminary hypotheses hold up under more intense investigation, and most importantly, *why*. The logic that I finally attach to the more detailed hypotheses in Chapter 7 is thus based not on deduction from an incomplete formal theory or some arbitrary supplement, but rather on the empirical evidence of history.[26]

CHANGES IN INTERESTS AND INCENTIVES

Interests and incentives are obviously a primary source of preferences. The *rate* at which interests and incentives change in response to technology affects decisionmakers' choice of strategy, even while they retain PD preferences.[27] The central question is whether existing consensual knowledge can incorporate new technological possibilities into a state's conception of self-interest. When rapid technological change engenders possibilities whose potential impact on interests cannot be readily interpreted

[25] To repeat the point, which auxiliary theories would one add? Without some logical link between Axelrod and a particular supplemental theory that talked about the development of strategy, we could pick almost randomly and generate almost any hypothesis about strategy. All of those hypotheses would be equally legitimate "deductions"; testing and falsifying any number of them would not test, falsify, or improve Axelrod's theory at all.

[26] My approach recalls one of Herbert Simon's most important critiques of the use of rational actor models in political science. Simon notes that political theories based on the rationality principle always incorporate auxiliary assumptions (for example, assumptions about actors' goals) to explain behavior. These auxiliary assumptions come from additional theories that are most often based on empirical observation of the way people, firms, or states actually behave. Simon, "Human Nature in Politics." What I am doing here is simply forcing the empirical derivation up front.

[27] Of course, this argument applies only when changes in technology do not so drastically alter the strategic environment or the interests of the states that they no longer perceive themselves as playing the PD. Such changes are rare. In ABM, MIRV, and at least prior to the 1980s in ASAT, changes in U.S. strategy cannot be explained simply by large corresponding changes in preferences that alter the fundamental structure of the game.

with current consensual knowledge, *radical uncertainty* results. Decision-makers find themselves unable to envision what the strategic environment will look like if certain technological innovations go forward. Preferences become extremely difficult to evaluate because alternative future scenarios are hard to envision. Radical uncertainty is rare, but it did afflict American decisionmaking in the ASAT case during the 1960s; third-generation strategic defense systems such as X-ray lasers may present similar uncertainties in the 1990s.

Technological change is usually less disruptive of conceptions of self-interest. Typically, new technological possibilities fall within the bounds of consensual knowledge, resulting in what I call *moderate uncertainty*. Decisionmakers operating under moderate uncertainty are able to comprehend the general shape of possible future strategic environments. In principle, information is plentiful. While precise calculations are always difficult, decisionmakers can and do estimate how various scenarios would impact upon their interests. Moderate uncertainty, for example, characterized the ABM case during the late 1960s.

These two kinds of uncertainty appear to predispose decisionmakers toward different types of reciprocal strategies. Radical uncertainty favors strategies with permissive criteria of contingency such as contingent restraint, while moderate uncertainty tends to yield more stringent criteria of reciprocity. The case studies here also suggest that the substance of cooperative agreements that emerge under radical and moderate uncertainty may differ. Radical uncertainty presents opportunities to close off entire areas of competition; agreements under moderate uncertainty tend to be more circumscribed in scope. The two types of cooperation also raise different problems when technologies change so that uncertainties are reduced or resolved. I consider the impact of declining uncertainty and transitions from radical to moderate uncertainty on the evolution of cooperative agreements in Chapter 7.

SALIENCIES

Saliencies are conspicuous discontinuities in the environment that states recognize as focal points around which they can coordinate their behavior. In arms control, the existence of saliencies depends mostly upon the technical characteristics of weapons systems and verification capabilities, which together can be used to define the terms of an international agreement. For example, any particular number of silos might serve as a saliency for an agreement limiting ICBM deployments, while the only recognizable saliency for sea-launched cruise missiles (SLCMs) might be a total ban on deployment or testing.

All three ideal type reciprocal strategies depend upon the existence of saliencies as a nexus for cooperation. But must the cooperating states recognize the same saliencies, and must they do so for the same reasons? There may be an important relationship here with consensual knowledge. If the two sides look at the strategic environment with similar interpretive frameworks, they are more likely to perceive the same saliencies; but the former is neither a necessary nor a sufficient condition for the latter. I postpone discussion of these complicating factors until Chapter 7, and ask simply: if the two states can agree that the environment lacks saliencies recognized by both, is it then possible to "construct" new shared saliencies as a target for reciprocal strategies?

Apart from the existence of saliencies, beliefs about the *number* of potential saliencies influence the type of reciprocal strategies that decisionmakers favor. Large numbers of saliencies favor strategies of contingent restraint. Criteria of contingency tend to be sharpened as the number of saliencies is believed to decline. But this effect does not seem to proceed linearly, and it certainly does not extrapolate to the limiting case where there is only one saliency. How do decisionmakers react when they believe that the "last" significant saliency is about to be breached?

GENERAL POLITICAL ENVIRONMENT

Two components of the general political environment of superpower relations have a powerful influence on the development of reciprocal strategies. The first concerns the images that American decisionmakers hold of the Soviet Union as an adversary. The most important element of that image seems to be American beliefs about Soviet conceptions of the relationship between military power and political competition. Do American decisionmakers believe that their Soviet counterparts see cooperation in military issues (at least at the level of strategic nuclear weapons) as facilitating constructive developments in U.S.-Soviet relations generally, thereby enhancing Moscow's status? Or does Washington suspect that Kremlin leaders see unremitting competition in military and particularly nuclear affairs as a productive or even a necessary means of enhancing the international capabilities and position of the Soviet Union? Arms control has been possible in either case. Strategies for achieving cooperation should, however, be different. In the latter case, well-defined and highly credible threats of escalation might be deemed necessary to elicit cooperation, under the assumption that Moscow would be apt to exploit a less demanding approach. If decisionmakers saw a less aggressive Soviet Union seemingly interested in a moderation of the military competition as a means of improving superpower relations and supporting other political goals, then Washington would have reason to adopt strategies tending more toward contingent restraint.

The second component of the general political environment that affects strategies of reciprocity concerns U.S. decisionmakers' beliefs about the nature of the superpower competition. The most important distinction here seems to be between the image of a full-fledged struggle in which one of the two states must eventually prevail, and the alternative picture of a mixed "competitive-collaborative" relationship that, properly managed, could further the interests of both states over the long term.[28] If the latter image were strong, it would make sense to assume that neither side was prone to exploit the other's restraint for small or short-term gains; the major risk in a reciprocal strategy would be the possibility of provoking conflict spirals that lead to missed opportunities for mutual benefit. This should favor strategies that tend toward contingent restraint. However, if the competition were viewed instead as a struggle for hegemony, the risks would lie in tempting the Soviet Union to take advantage of American restraint. It is not obvious that either side would then pursue cooperation at all. Do American decisionmakers ever seek arms control cooperation with the Soviets under such circumstances? If so, it seems that American strategy would reflect this image of the competition and tend toward contingent threat. I speculate further that the substance and sequelae of cooperation that emerge will differ in important ways from those achieved under the more benign image.

Beliefs about the nature of "equilibrium" in the international system are also an important part of how U.S. decisionmakers view the superpower competition. Is the balance of power between the United States and Soviet Union a dynamic but *robust* equilibrium, where gains for one side tend to be counterbalanced by gains for the other elsewhere? Or do decisionmakers suspect that equilibrium may be more *volatile*, and that small advantages for one side tend to "snowball" and multiply? The former image would support strategies based on permissive criteria of reciprocity. The latter image would seem to require that cooperation be based on precisely balanced concessions in order to prevent either side from gaining advantages in power that might prove difficult to redress.

STRATEGIC THEORY

I have already considered American strategic theory as part of the consensual knowledge that underlies Washington's preferences in arms control. I return to it here because beliefs about the *congruence* or lack of congruence between American and Soviet strategic theory directly affect the development of reciprocal strategies. The most important elements here are

[28] George Breslauer, "Why Detente Failed," in George, *Managing US-Soviet Rivalry*, pp. 319–40.

prevalent beliefs about parity and the military requirements of strategic stability, and perceptions of whether the superpowers share those beliefs. Do the two sides have a common perception of the boundaries beyond which assymetrical concessions might erode strategic stability? When American decisionmakers believe that U.S. and Soviet strategic theories are congruent or at least compatible on this score, they should be more likely to favor strategies with permissive criteria of contingency.

Congruence of strategic theory on the political significance of the nuclear balance is a second important factor. Do decisionmakers view nuclear weapons as a critical source of political power in the U.S.-Soviet relationship, and in each superpower's relations with other states? If both superpowers seem willing to place a lesser emphasis on the nuclear balance in their conceptions of power, arms control strategies with more permissive criteria of reciprocity should be favored. But decisionmakers in Washington may sometimes suspect that Soviet leaders view an "optical" imbalance of nuclear weapons as a source of political power, or they may come to believe this themselves.[29] To what extent do these beliefs promote strategies based on more stringent criteria of reciprocity?

Finally, strategic theory influences decisionmakers' views about the role of technology in promoting cooperation. If American technology can compensate for numerical or other advantages that favor the Soviet Union, decisionmakers are more likely to view strategies tending toward contingent restraint as an effective means to promote cooperation. An offer to hold back on certain technologies may be a powerful incentive or a useful concession to trade for other forms of Soviet restraint. But when strategic theories see the resources of technology as incapable of compensating for Soviet strengths, decisionmakers are likely to consider such restraint only with much more stringent criteria of reciprocity.

BUREAUCRATIC POLITICS

Sustained attempts to cooperate with the Soviet Union on arms control matters require the consistent attention of the president. Government bureaucracies and other domestic actors with disparate interests have to be brought into line so that a reciprocal strategy can be implemented with some consistency in behavior and rhetoric. Strategies that are based on less specific and exacting criteria of reciprocity leave more room for dis-

[29] By "optical" imbalance I mean a situation in which there is a considerable numerical inequality between the strategic weapons systems of the two sides. An optical imbalance is not necessarily significant in strictly military terms: optical imbalance may be entirely compatible with what I earlier called "functional parity," where both sides fulfill what they believe to be the requirements of deterrence with different combinations of weapons systems.

satisfied domestic players to express their concerns in ways that harm consistent implementation. Strategies of contingent restraint are likely to be particularly demanding of the president's ability to manage bureaucratic politics. To what extent are American presidents willing to assume the political risks that such a strategy entails; is it possible to maintain domestic support for assymetrical concessions? Do limits on a president's ability to absorb the political costs of temporarily unrequited restraint tightly restrict how permissive a reciprocal strategy can be chosen and put in place?

In sum, and going back to the discussion that preceded consideration of these five additional variables, the central questions of strategy development are:

1. How do American decisionmakers evaluate what they believe to be Soviet preferences? When do they engage in meta-strategies aimed at altering preferences, and how do they measure success?

2. If decisionmakers come to believe that both sides are facing an iterated PD with a long shadow of the future, how do they develop strategies of reciprocity aimed at promoting cooperation? How do the five additional variables influence the type of strategy they choose to adopt?

Strategic Interaction

Reciprocal strategies depend upon the give-and-take between actors. In the PD, an actor playing TFT responds to cooperation with cooperation and defection with defection. This presumes that the TFT player receives and reacts to information about what the rival actor does; in Axelrod's world such information is cost-free, unambiguous, and without error. The concept is simply one of "stimulus-response"—there is incoming information to which the game-theoretic actor responds. Linking this concept to the world of U.S.-Soviet arms control again necessitates bridge principles and the addition of a new concept.

How do states adapt? That is, given an established strategy of reciprocity, how does a state decide that the other state's actions merit a cooperative or a competitive move in response? Two bridge principles are necessary. The first captures the information that decisionmakers on one side intentionally try to transfer to the other. This I call *communication*, and it can range from blatant weapons deployments to nuanced off-the-record statements by unnamed individuals. What do U.S. decisionmakers see as the most important impediments to effective communication and what efforts do they take to surmount these difficulties? How does communication differ when states choose relatively conciliatory strategies as opposed to strategies based on contingent threat?

Intended communication is usually only a small part of the wealth of incoming information to which a state might respond. What additional elements from that larger set of information actually drive adaptation? A second bridge principle, the notion of *feedback*, is needed here. Feedback, in this instance, encompasses the kinds of information that U.S. decisionmakers focus on and use to evaluate how Soviet behavior might be responding to American strategy. Do decisionmakers tend to look at a wide or a relatively narrow range of data? Are the criteria for what constitutes relevant feedback closely linked to the consensual knowledge that defines interests, or do the criteria reflect other considerations, such as domestic political demands?[30]

Communication and feedback are the immediate sources of adaptation. Together they can be used to explain how a state playing a particular reciprocal strategy reacts to a stimulus; for example, how the United States, having adopted a strategy of contingent restraint, chooses to defect in response to Soviet actions. But strategic interaction goes beyond simply responding according to the dictates of an established strategy. States, like game-theoretic actors, sometimes change their strategies. How and why do they do so? As discussed in Chapter 2, Axelrod's model is incomplete on this score. To fill in the gap, I add a new concept of *learning*.[31]

Learning involves a redefinition of self-interest that in turn drives a change in strategy. Such redefinitions can come about through several routes. Learning could follow a major change in the image of the adversary—decisionmakers might then come to believe that entirely different kinds of incentives are needed to elicit cooperation, or that cooperation was inherently less valuable (or more so) because of the kind of state they were cooperating with. More dramatically, learning could follow a

[30] The auxiliary theories that lie behind this bridge principle could be drawn from neurobiology, cybernetics, or organization theory. The basic notion is the same. Receptive systems that respond to environmental stimuli are set up to receive and amplify particular kinds of signals and to ignore others. The former are relevant data or in this case feedback; the latter are noise. Note that abstract models do not predict what subset of incoming information will be taken as relevant feedback. That depends on the receptive system itself. There are formal models in the area of decision analysis that specify how a "rational" actor operating under information processing constraints might make optimal use of feedback; but these models are once again normative and not descriptive.

[31] Learning is a complex concept that has recently undergone an explicit revival in international relations research. For examples of how the concept is currently being used, see Haas, *When Knowledge Is Power*; and Breslauer and Tetlock, *Learning in US and Soviet Foreign Policy*. I, among others, have used this term in different ways over time. See Steve Weber, "Interactive Learning in US-Soviet Arms Control," in Breslauer and Tetlock, *Learning in US and Soviet Foreign Policy*; and idem, "Realism, Detente, and Nuclear Weapons." At the start of this project I restrict learning to its meaning as defined in the text; I will expand on it some in Chapter 7.

change in the body of consensual knowledge that decisionmakers use to interpret the environment. At a minimum, this would force a shift in preferences among previously foreseen alternative outcomes. More broadly, decisionmakers might envision new potential outcomes in the strategic environment. Both kinds of learning do appear in the case studies, but they are remarkably rare in contrast to adaptation.

This is an important puzzle for cooperation theory because the consequences of learning and strategy change are vital. Why do strategies so rarely change? To foreshadow once again, recall the previous discussion of strategy development where I argued that U.S. reciprocal strategies rest on a foundation of working hypotheses about Soviet interests. The five additional variables explain more specific characteristics of the reciprocal strategy that decisionmakers choose. But these strategies, once put into place, turn out to be resistant to change. Shifts in the state of the five variables become less important. So also, to a surprising extent, does Soviet behavior. Strategies change when the working hypotheses change, but this takes place unevenly in a way that appears at least partially disconnected from both. Because Axelrod's model has no way to capture this dynamic, I go back to an inductive approach with an analogy from cybernetics.[32]

Picture the U.S. decisionmaking system as a receptor and Soviet actions as a set of stimuli. The first part of the story is adaptation, a change in U.S. behavior according to a preestablished strategy. Adaptation happens when a new stimulus exceeds the threshold of the receptor. The receptor itself is passive: its receptive field (the kinds of events to which it is attuned to respond), its threshold, and the repertoire of possible responses are fixed. This is the typical cybernetic model, where stimuli change but the receptor itself does not. For example, a thermostat (the receptor and servomechanism) always responds to changes in temperature (the stimulus), but never to humidity or wind speed.

Learning is the second part to the story. Learning occurs in U.S.-Soviet arms control because the "receptor" is not always passive. In contrast to the cybernetic model, I posit that the receptive field, sensitivity, and repertoire of the receptor also change. In ABM, MIRV, and ASAT, working hypotheses about Soviet interests—once established within the U.S. decisionmaking system—were more than just a fixed blackboard onto which subsequent Soviet behavior was written. American leaders often constructed partial "tests" of the hypotheses by predicting the direction in which selected indicators should change in response to an American strategy. Interestingly, these tests were sometimes spelled out before the Sovi-

<hr>

[32] The classic and still relevant discussion of the "cybernetic paradigm" for decisionmaking is Steinbruner, *The Cybernetic Theory of Decision*, Chapter 3.

ets in explicit terms. In ABM, for example, Washington clearly signaled that it expected Moscow to voluntarily slow its deployment of offensive nuclear delivery systems, and that this would be taken as a test of deeper Soviet interests in cooperation.

But learning, or changes in strategy based on changes in the working hypotheses, did not always follow. American reactions to failed or equivocal "test results" were strikingly uneven. There were sharply delimited windows of time during which hypotheses were volatile, interspersed among much longer periods of stasis in which incoming information about Soviet interests had much less demonstrable impact upon American behavior. These mark off the critical periods or junctures during which the receptor itself goes from passive to active. Strategies change during these critical junctures. In Chapter 7, I discuss possible explanations for critical periods; how the windows might open and close; and the possible implications for the evolution of cooperation in U.S.-Soviet arms control over the long term.

The central questions of strategic interaction are:

1. What elements of communication and feedback do decisionmakers use to monitor the interaction of their strategy with the adversary's behavior?

2. If both suggest that American strategy is failing to elicit desired responses, how do decisionmakers modify state behavior? When does the state simply adapt, and when does learning produce a change in strategy?

Summary

The central argument of this chapter is that different strategies of reciprocity explain the variance in outcomes among arms control cases that fulfill Axelrod's conditions for cooperation in the PD. I will make the case that strategies of enhanced contingent restraint promote cooperation, while others do not. Particularly because the argument is based on only three cases, it is important to do more than simply note a correlation between strategies of enhanced contingent restraint and cooperative outcomes; the case studies and Chapter 7 focus on *why* enhanced contingent restraint succeeds while other strategies fail to elicit cooperation.

The "experiment," of course, is far from perfectly controlled. There are many other factors that could contribute in significant ways to the outcome. The logic of Axelrod's theory points to strategies of reciprocity as a particularly important intervening variable. The case studies assess its causal weight in arms control cooperation. If strategies had been different, would outcomes have been different as well?

If strategies of reciprocity are a central determinant of cooperation, explaining the choice of one type of strategy over others is a crucial step, and I proposed five variables to do that. Combining these two elements should lead to a better understanding of the differences between surprising successes and missed opportunities in U.S.-Soviet arms control.

Using game theory as a heuristic should also lead to new formulations and theories that stand on their own. The payoffs here come from the additional concepts introduced in this chapter to bring a formal model of cooperation up against historical cases whose logic it should be able to capture. One of the messages is that the historical experience of superpower arms control can be used to build on nascent theories of cooperation. But cooperation theory also has important implications for superpower arms control, despite my earlier warning that the game-theoretic concept of cooperation does not capture some important aspects of cooperation in the real world. Chapter 7 elaborates the concept of cooperation along several lines suggested by the analysis in this chapter and the data of the next three. I will distinguish among types of cooperation that are arrived at by different routes and that are based on different kinds of intersecting interests. They also have very different sequelae. Besides shedding important new light on the variegated history of arms control and U.S.-Soviet relations in a general sense, this has significant implications for future efforts at cooperation.

A final note on why I selected ABM, MIRV, and ASAT as the principal cases closes out this chapter. Recall that Chapters 1 and 2 brought into conjunction a theoretical problem and an historical puzzle: the problem of expanding on Axelrod's theory of cooperation in the PD and the puzzle of why the superpowers succeed in attempts to cooperate in some arms control cases, and fail in others. Chapter 1 also explained why U.S.-Soviet arms control in an era of functional nuclear parity is a bounded set of cases well suited to an application of Axelrod's theory. I could in principle have drawn from many other cases that make up this "universe," but there are theoretical and practical justifications for focusing at present on ABM, MIRV, and ASAT.[33]

From the standpoint of theory, these cases provide control over the "structural" variables that are the linchpin of my argument here in Chap-

[33] The logic of my approach most closely resembles Alexander George's method of "structured, focused comparison" for developing theory from case studies. For a detailed discussion see Alexander George, "Case Studies and Theory Development," in Lauren, *Diplomacy: New Approaches in History, Theory, and Policy*; and Alexander L. George and Timothy J. McKeown, "Case Studies and Theories of Organization Decisionmaking," in *Advances in Informational Processing in Organizations* (Greenwich, Conn.: JAI, 1985), pp. 21–58.

ter 3. Recall that *Cooperation under Anarchy* looked at cases that *vary* along the dimensions of payoff structure, shadow of the future, and number of players, to explain differences in outcomes. ABM, MIRV, and ASAT are *similar* along these dimensions. They share Axelrod's conditions for cooperation, but they differ in outcome. Controlling for structural factors in this way isolates the impact of other variables that can explain the differences in outcomes. My argument is that reciprocal strategies make up the critical intervening variable. ABM, MIRV, and ASAT include different types of reciprocal strategies, both across the cases and within each case. Finally, the outcomes of these cases can be fairly easily "coded"; not only by objective analysis, but also according to the subjective assessments of contemporary decisionmakers, and the two largely agree. ABM stands out as a surprising success; MIRV as a missed opportunity; and ASAT as a surprising success that deteriorates over time into a missed opportunity.

The practical reasons for selecting these cases have mostly to do with the availability of data. Each case has already been the subject of at least one detailed history, and many of the primary sources bearing on the analysis are available for further scrutiny. Another practical reason is that ABM, MIRV, and ASAT are critically important cases in the history of U.S.-Soviet arms control. What happened in each continues to have a great bearing on the strategic nuclear environment. Even as relations between the United States and the Soviet Union change in the 1990s, the legacy of these cases will continue to have a powerful impact on their security. To a great extent, the sequelae of these cases define the major nuclear security threats that Washington and Moscow will have to manage in the coming decade. Their most important legacy may lie in the effects on how decisionmakers in both capitals think about the prospects and processes of arms control cooperation. I acknowledge that the use of new theoretical tools to rework cases that have already been studied may not break fundamentally new historical ground. But my purposes here are clearly different than that.

One final caveat: it is important to note that ABM, MIRV, and ASAT are not independent cases in some ideal or statistical sense. They are linked most obviously by "strategic logic," and also by the fact that they involve the same two states within a relatively short time frame. We fully expect to see decisionmakers transferring lessons and beliefs between cases. No relationship between states is made up of discrete acts of cooperation and noncooperation. But it should also be clear how the argument of this chapter allows for connections between the cases. In fact, the links between them are an integral part of the story I will try to tell.

The next chapters are histories of three attempts to control a particular weapons system within the larger context of the superpower political and military relationship. I compare missed opportunities to surprising successes. What are the critical factors that push the outcome in one or another direction? This chapter used the logic of Axelrod's theory to generate the proper questions; the following chapters should provide some answers.

4

Antiballistic Missile Systems

THE 1972 Treaty on the Limitation of Anti-Ballistic Missile Systems
stands out as a "surprising success" of cooperation. This agreement,
which placed substantial constraints on what otherwise promised to develop into a vigorous competition in missile defenses, was in no sense
historically over-determined. It is true that the technology needed to build
highly effective ABM systems was not available in 1972. Yet states often
compete to develop and deploy even less promising weapons technology
if the payoffs for success might be substantial. Similarly, there was nothing intuitive or inevitable about strategic theories that portrayed a competition in defenses as mutually undesirable.

Technology, strategic beliefs, and domestic politics are all part of the
story that leads to the ABM treaty, but they do not by themselves explain
cooperation. Axelrod's model suggests a different focus, aimed at the interactive processes between the United States and the Soviet Union that
led to that outcome, but is also by itself insufficient to explain cooperation. A critical additional factor was American strategy, which resembled
the ideal type enhanced contingent restraint. Had the strategy been different, the short-term outcome and the longer-term sequelae of ABM would
probably also have been different. To explain cooperation it is necessary
to account for the development of strategy. The five variables discussed
in Chapter 3 are a starting point; but it is also necessary to understand
how U.S. decisionmakers assessed and used feedback to modify strategy
over time, reflecting changing conceptions of how to successfully influence Soviet beliefs and behavior.

Historical Background

Research in ABM systems began in both the United States and the Soviet
Union in the late 1940s, long before ICBMs were first deployed. In the
United States, ABM research proceeded in parallel to the missile program,
constrained only by technology until about 1964. As the technology began to show increasing promise in the mid-1960s, evolving strategic theories prompted some American decisionmakers to question the desirability of defense on doctrinal grounds. The Soviets, on the other hand,

seemed determined to press ahead with development and deployment of ABM systems. From Washington's perspective, meta-strategy aimed at changing the Kremlin's conception of self-interest appeared to be a necessary prerequisite to any demarche for cooperative restraint in ABM.

Both the Army and the Air Force became interested in ABM systems soon after World War II. The technological problems of defending against ICBMs were thought to be serious but not unconquerable: by the mid-1950s Air Force Projects Thumper and Wizard had demonstrated rudimentary capabilities in the central components of a defensive system.[1] The Army's parallel program to upgrade its Nike-Hercules air defense system to ballistic missile defense (BMD) capability showed similar promise. In 1958, the Eisenhower Defense Department awarded the BMD mission to the Army's system (renamed Nike-Zeus) and budgeted $600 million for further R & D over the next two years. The administration's commitment to defense was a logical complement to the strategic doctrine of massive retaliation, which placed a premium on counterforce *and* defense as two ways to limit vulnerability and retain a "usable" American nuclear superiority. The Army became a powerful bureaucratic proponent of ABM, and in 1959 and 1960 requested $1.3 billion for moving ahead to production and deployment. Congress was mostly in favor, and in fact added funds for that purpose to Eisenhower's budget, but the president demurred. Troubled by the prospect of committing at least $15 billion to a weapons system with as yet questionable capabilities, Eisenhower chose to restrict spending to continued research and development. This was an interim decision taken on technological and economic grounds. From the standpoint of strategic doctrine, Washington's fundamental commitment to ABM remained strong.[2]

Doctrinal arguments continued to favor the ABM program during the first several years of the 1960s. The Kennedy administration's efforts to increase the cost-effectiveness of American security policy and to replace the marginally credible massive retaliation doctrine gave greater attention to conventional forces, but also implied an effort to retain a degree of

[1] See David N. Schwartz, "Past and Present: The Historical Legacy," in Carter and Schwartz, *Ballistic Missile Defense*, pp. 330–33. The two essential components of a first-generation ABM system were powerful radars and interceptor missiles that linked together could acquire, track, and destroy incoming warheads.

[2] See Yanarella, *The Missile Defense Controversy*, p. 137. The 1957 Gaither Report noted that upgraded air defense systems would have limited capabilities against ballistic missiles, but that new systems capable of intercepting warheads at higher altitudes might do better and "the importance of providing active defense of cities or other critical areas demands the development and installation of the basic elements of a system at an early date. . . . Active defense is an essential part of the national military posture." *Deterrence and Survival in the Nuclear Age*, Report to the President by the Security Resources Panel of the Scientific Advisory Board, November 1957, declassified 1973.

nuclear superiority. Both were seen as necessary prerequisites for Kennedy's internationalist activism and his expansive conception of American national interest: Paul Nitze, then assistant secretary of defense, noted in 1961 that the American arsenal "gives the West a definite nuclear superiority we believe . . . to be strategically important in the equations of deterrence and strategy."[3] The administration's nuclear doctrine was shaped so as to maximize that superiority and its impact: Secretary of Defense Robert McNamara's famous 1962 "Ann Arbor speech" outlined a war-fighting stance that emphasized the ability to limit damage through a combination of intra-war deterrence, counterforce strikes, and defense. The cost-effectiveness of current technology remained the primary constraint on ABM: McNamara judged quite directly that civil defense and other passive measures would buy more defense per dollar than a Nike-Zeus deployment. In ABM, the administration placed its bets on more advanced technologies (such as phased array radars) that showed potential to overcome the problem of discriminating between warheads and decoys that was the major infirmity of Nike-Zeus.[4]

The Kennedy administration's early commitment to superiority was not, however, immune to the rapid expansion of Soviet capabilities and the new intellectual ferment in strategic thought and planning in the early 1960s. A 1961 RAND study of the best prospects for a damage-limitation strategy that combined counterforce, civil defense, and optimistic projections about the capabilities of ABM technology still concluded that attempts to protect American cities in the event of nuclear war would most likely fail catastrophically.[5] Although the Soviet threat did not reach the levels predicted earlier in the decade, it was clear by 1964 that the military rationale for strategic superiority based on the ability to limit damage had become a weakening reed on which to base American nuclear policy.

The Johnson administration found, in fact, that a majority of the defense scientists who had been brought into key advisory positions under Kennedy were now in agreement with a prominent group of civilian analysts that usable nuclear superiority was a chimera, and that the United States ought instead to seek a balance of mutual deterrence based on assured destruction.[6] "Official" strategic doctrine was not at first affected

[3] Speech to the International Institute of Strategic Studies, London, December 11, 1961, cited in Gaddis, *Strategies of Containment*, p. 218.

[4] For the text of the June 1962 Ann Arbor speech, see *New York Times*, 17 June 1962, p. 26. McNamara continued to deny the Army's requests for funds to produce and deploy Nike-Zeus, but the Pentagon budget for FY 1963 included $350 million for R & D in Project Defender (renamed Nike-X in 1962), the technological follow-on to Nike-Zeus. See Adams, "McNamara's ABM Policy 1961–1967," pp. 218–19.

[5] See Newhouse, *Cold Dawn*, p. 68.

[6] See Gilpin, *American Scientists and Nuclear Weapons Policy*. Prominent among these scientists were Jerome Wiesner, top science advisor to President Kennedy; Herbert York,

in any substantial way by these arguments, but McNamara in particular demonstrated increasing sensitivity to the logic on which they were based. McNamara was also impressed by models of arms race action-reaction patterns that had been developed by operations analysts at the Department of Defense (DoD). If "action-reaction" was an important impetus to arms competition, selective *inaction* or restraint might produce a corresponding reaction of its own and slow the drive toward what were now seen as possibly redundant nuclear capabilities.

It is true that the new strategic theories, still in their infancy, were not yet fully developed to the point where they offered operational criteria for identifying precisely what kinds of restraint, in numbers or particular types of weapons, would contribute to security. However, the two interrelated concepts of nuclear parity and strategic stability were beginning to move in this direction. This logic called for *functional* as opposed to *numerical* equivalence of nuclear forces, on the argument that mutual deterrence would be stable so long as both sides had high confidence in their respective abilities to destroy the population centers and industrial resources of the other. This had serious implications for ABM systems.

Those implications began to be explored in a number of different forums. At the 1960 International Pugwash meeting, Jerome Wiesner argued that ABM technology could destabilize a developing strategic equilibrium based on MAD and should be limited by U.S.-Soviet agreement. A 1963 study commissioned by the Office of the Secretary of Defense (OSD; the "Betts Report") expanded on Wiesner's reasoning that ABM systems would probably spur new offensive deployments as both sides struggled to maintain confidence in their assured destruction capabilities. In 1964, Jack Ruina and Murray Gell-man together developed a comprehensive analysis of the strategic impact of ABM systems, entitled "BMD and the Arms Race," which predicted that ABM deployments would spawn a new, extremely expensive action-reaction arms race cycle that would kill off possibilities for arms control and raise substantial new tensions in East-West relations.[7] By 1964, these arguments had had a substantial impact on McNamara's thinking. This was the last year in which the secretary's posture statement claimed that damage limitation was a fundamental objective of American strategic policy. The FY 1966 statement went further, explicitly adopting assured destruction as the "overriding objective for American strategic forces." The revised declaratory doctrine was not matched by equally dramatic shifts in targeting policy,

---

DDR&E; George Kistiakowsky, an important member of PSAC; and George Rathjens, head scientist at ACDA.

[7] Jerome Wiesner, personal communication, January 1990; Wiesner, *Where Science and Politics Meet*, pp. 209–40; Yanarella, *The Missile Defense Controversy*, p. 104; Schwartz, "Past and Present," p. 335.

but the revision did reflect a fundamental change in the character of American strategic thought.[8] After 1964, American decisionmakers were seriously concerned about the doctrinal and strategic implications of ABM deployments, and were at least willing to consider possible arrangements for limiting an imminent defensive race with the Soviet Union.

Washington's embryonic interest in an arms control arrangement for ABM, however, did not appear to be matched by similar interests in the Soviet Union. Moscow too had begun efforts in strategic defense soon after World War II, concentrating on the development and rapid deployment of a sophisticated air defense network.[9] Research in defense against ballistic missiles was from its inception closely linked to the air defense program, making efforts in the two areas difficult to distinguish; but by the mid-1950s American analysts were convinced that at least one strand of Soviet research was specifically committed to BMD. By April 1960, when U.S. officials first publicly disclosed their knowledge of Soviet BMD programs, the scope of the effort had led many American intelligence analysts to conclude that Moscow was committed to and capable of deploying a large scale operational ABM system in the near future, possibly by 1963.[10]

Moscow did not disappoint. Spectacular claims about the Soviet Union's putative BMD capabilities began to appear frequently in military and political writings—Marshal Malinkowsky's famous pronouncement that "the problem of destroying enemy missiles in flight has been successfully solved" and Khrushchev's claim that Soviet interceptors could "hit a fly in outer space" were only the most dramatic.[11] More seriously troubling to American observers was a series of high altitude nuclear tests that the Soviets carried out in late 1961. Certain characteristics of these tests suggested that Moscow might be developing an enhanced X-ray warhead for use in an ABM interceptor.[12] It was also in 1961 that U.S. intelligence

---

[8] *DoD Appropriations for FY 66*, part 3, pp. 33–57; see especially pp. 33–40. For discussions of the relationship between changes in declaratory policy and operational war plans, see Rosenberg, "The Origins of Overkill"; Sagan, *Moving Targets*, pp. 26–39.

[9] With the help of captured German scientists, the Soviets built their first SAM system in 1952, and in 1956 began an extensive deployment of the SA-1 air defense system around Moscow. Stevens, "The Soviet BMD Program," in Carter and Schwartz, *Ballistic Missile Defense*, pp. 190–91.

[10] Max S. Johnson, "Danger: Anti-Missile Gap," *U.S. News & World Report*, 14 November 1960, p. 67. For details on the early Soviet BMD program, see Graybeal and Goure, "Soviet Ballistic Missile Defense Objectives"; and Prados, *The Soviet Estimate*.

[11] See *Pravda*, 25 October 1961; and Deane, *The Role of Strategic Defense*, p. 26.

[12] Freedman, *US Intelligence*, pp. 87, 91, 157. In addition, U.S. intelligence sources detected construction of several additional "hen house" radars across Soviet territory that would be useful for setting up a nationwide defense. Several ICBM test launches from the Kapustin Yar range were also reported to have taken place in conjunction with BMD test activities downrange at Sary Shagan.

reported the first deployment of what appeared to be a rudimentary ABM system, named Griffon, around Leningrad.[13] Early in 1962 the Soviets began to deploy what was clearly a dedicated ABM system (named Galosh) around Moscow, using what was then state-of-the-art technology. U.S. analysts believed that Galosh was slated for a final deployment of at least 8 missile complexes with a total of 128 interceptors, making it a viable threat against penetration of at least the less-sophisticated first-generation reentry vehicles (RVs).[14] Capabilities aside, the fact that the Soviets had moved so quickly to deploy this system was taken as another indication of the depth of Soviet leaders' commitment to defense. In 1964, few in Washington doubted the seriousness of Soviet efforts in ABM.

This appraisal was cemented into the perception of the American strategic community by a 1964 article in the Soviet journal *International Affairs*. In "Anti-Missile Systems and Disarmament," retired Major General Nicolai Talensky argued that defense of the homeland remained a primary responsibility of the Soviet military. Nuclear weapons made that task more difficult but not impossible. ABM systems, like any other weapons constructed by a peaceful state, were intended for defense and would *enhance* deterrence of potential aggressors. Thus it made sense for the Soviet Union to deploy strategic defenses and to do so in conjunction with offensive forces, because "powerful deterrent forces and an effective antimissile defense system, when taken together, substantially *increase* the stability of mutual deterrence." This logic was fully consistent with general American understandings of Soviet strategic thought during the early 1960s, particularly its notion that the most reliable means to deter war was to be prepared to fight and win should war occur.[15] Given this reasoning, the Soviets seemed bound to reject American arguments about the possible destabilizing effects of ABM; on the contrary, anything that contributed to Moscow's military might relative to the United States would

[13] Although construction was slowed through 1962 and the system was mostly dismantled in 1963, the Griffon deployment did much to frame American perceptions of the Soviet ABM program at the outset. Later in the decade, the majority of U.S. analysts concluded that Griffon was essentially an upgraded SAM system, substantially less sophisticated than the American Nike-Zeus, and probably had very little capability against ballistic missiles.

[14] Galosh relied on megaton-range exoatmospheric interceptors that would be guided by three large phased-array radars then under construction. See Freedman, *US Intelligence*, pp. 88–89. For a contending view see Whalen, "The Shifting Equation of Nuclear Defense," *Fortune* 1 (1967): 176.

[15] Nicolai Talensky, "Anti-missile Systems and Disarmament," *International Affairs* 10 (1964): 15–19. Quote from p. 17, emphasis added. I will use the term "Talensky doctrine" to refer to the American school of interpretation that perceives Soviet views on ABM in this vein. For a general discussion of American perceptions of Soviet military thought in the 1960s, see Holloway, *The Soviet Union and the Arms Race*, particularly Chapter 3, where he quotes at length from the influential 1962 *Military Strategy* volume, authored by a group under the direction of Marshal V. D. Sokolovskii, a former chief of the general staff.

serve to enhance deterrence. Vigilant pursuit of military power, both offensive and defensive, was believed consistent with Soviet thought; to engage in cooperation or mutual restraint with an opportunistic and aggressive United States was not.

Under these circumstances, the prospects for limiting ABM systems
seemed bleak. Cooperation depended first upon convincing Soviet leaders
of a different logic through which to comprehend self-interest with regard
to defense. Accordingly, a core of U.S. strategic thinkers, defense scientists, and government officials began an active, multifaceted, and not always coordinated meta-strategy. The goal, diffuse as it might seem, was
to set in motion a learning process that would " 'educate' Soviet strategic
planners in the requirements of deterrence strategy, which according to
American strategic thought, meant abandoning its defense strategy . . .
and embracing ours."[16]

The stubborn Soviet commitment to ABM did not give way, although
it probably had a greater direct impact on American *offensive* programs
and particularly on MIRV, as we shall see in the next chapter, than on the
American ABM program. But the period 1964 to 1967 also saw the lines
of ABM controversy congeal in Washington. As opposition to ABM on
doctrinal grounds mounted among prominent scientists, civilian strategists, and many of McNamara's closest advisors, the uniformed military
and a significant part of the Congress pushed hard for an American deployment. The Joint Chiefs of Staff (JCS), citing technological success in
the Nike-X development program, in 1965 unanimously called for the
production of long lead-time components as a foundation for deploying
over the next several years an anti-Soviet area defense system that would
cost about $20 billion. Congress balked at the projected cost, but broad
support for moving forward incrementally toward deployment led the
Armed Services Committees in both the House and Senate to recommend
that substantial funds be spent in 1965 for "pre-engineering" of an operational Nike-X system.[17]

[16] Yanarella, *The Missile Defense Controversy*, pp. 197–98. While there were at this time
no formal, intergovernmental institutions available to facilitate American meta-strategy,
there were a number of informal and quasi-official channels that were used for this purpose.
Contacts between defense scientists were particularly important: forums such as Pugwash
came to focus increasingly on the ABM problem during the course of the mid-1960s. Raymond Garthoff reports that "several senior Soviet officials have privately referred to an
unofficial meeting of US and Soviet scientists . . . in 1967 as especially useful and significant
in influencing Soviet thinking away from the [Talensky doctrine] on BMD and arms control." "BMD and East-West Relations," in Carter and Schwartz, *Ballistic Missile Defense*,
p. 298 n. 44.

[17] The JCS plan is detailed in *DoD Appropriations for FY 67*, part 1, p. 531; and part 5,
p. 156. On the reaction of the Congress, see Wilson, "Senate May Force New Anti-Missile
Policy," *Aviation Week and Space Technology*, 2 May 1965, p. 28.

McNamara, supported by a strong and growing consensus among civilian analysts and scientists at DoD, held firm against these pressures through much of 1966. In arguing against a U.S. deployment, he focused primarily on the issue of cost-effectiveness for the United States, claiming that Nike-Zeus could be defeated by offensive countermeasures significantly less expensive than the system itself. Whether or not the Soviets were interested in mutual restraint, it made sense for the United States to continue its research program and to delay any decision on deployment.[18] His position came under attack from a variety of directions. A September 1966 report of the Defense Science Board Task Force, chaired by Richard Latter of RAND, argued that an American ABM system based on current technology could substantially degrade a Soviet attack and should be deployed rapidly, before Soviet scientists had time to develop effective penetration measures.[19] The Army, the JCS, the Director of Defense Research and Engineering (DDR&E), and the Advanced Research Projects Agency (ARPA) all favored deployment, as did a number of influential senators with close ties to the president, including Richard Russell, Henry Jackson, and John Stennis.

In December 1966, McNamara reluctantly agreed to restore to the Pentagon's budget request $375 million in ABM procurement funds that he had chosen to delete, although the money was to be held in escrow pending State Department efforts to explore Soviet interest in negotiations.[20] The Soviets offered little in return, and the domestic political pressures on President Johnson were growing apace.[21] In January of 1967, McNa-

[18] See William Beecher, "Soviet Increases Build Up of Missiles and Deploys a Defensive System," *New York Times*, 13 November 1966, p. 84. McNamara argued that even worst-case scenario forecasts of Soviet offensive deployments did not warrant deployment of active defenses prior to the mid-1970s; hence, there was no reason to commit to a system configuration (and particularly one with as many imperfections as Nike-X) at this time. See *DoD Appropriations for FY 67*, part 1, pp. 49–62.

[19] *Ballistic Missile Defense*, Report of the Defense Science Board Task Force, 15 September 1966, NHP Box 16. This report went so far as to argue that if budget constraints forced a choice between an ABM deployment and additional deployments of offensive countermeasures to defeat Soviet defenses, the United States should favor the former.

[20] Newhouse, *Cold Dawn*, p. 86. In late December, Secretary of State Dean Rusk in an open statement called on Soviet leaders to join with the United States in strategic arms negotiations with particular attention to ABM systems. See John Finney, "Rusk Seeks Curb in Missile Race," *New York Times*, 22 December 1966, pp. 1, 19.

[21] A putative "ABM gap" began to appear as a potential campaign issue for 1968 when Michigan's Governor George Romney, who in 1966 was believed to be the Republicans' favored presidential candidate, came out in strong support of U.S. deployment. While Johnson claimed that both strategic and domestic considerations were important in forming his opinion, Kissinger argues that Johnson was influenced primarily by the latter. See Kissinger, *White House Years*, p. 197; Johnson, *The Vantage Point*, pp. 479–80. For general assessments see Lapp, *Arms Beyond Doubt*, p. 48; and Halperin, "The Decision to Deploy the ABM."

mara arranged for the president to meet with a group of prominent defense scientists, all of whom were opposed on technological and doctrinal grounds to the deployment of an ABM system aimed at defending against a Soviet attack.[22] Johnson listened to these arguments with care, but he was equally interested in a new JCS plan for immediate deployment of a light area and hard site defense based on Nike-X that would be upgraded over time to heavy area defense. Sensitive as always to the political context of the issue, Johnson must have been particularly affected by the Chiefs' argument that failing to respond to Galosh with an American ABM deployment "could lead to Soviet and allied belief . . . that our technology is deficient or that we will not pay to maintain [the strategic balance]."[23]

The Soviets, meanwhile, were beginning to show hints of flexibility on the question of limiting ABMs. Through 1966, the official line maintained that defensive systems were *not* a source of strategic or arms race instability.[24] But in a December 1966 response to discussions between American ambassador Llewellyn Thompson and Soviet ambassador Anatoly Dobrynin, Moscow stated in an official exchange of notes that offense and defense were in fact interdependent, and that limits on both would have to be part of a strategic arms accord.[25] In February 1967, *Pravda's* political commentator Fedor Burlatsky wrote that "the Soviet government is ready to discuss the question of the prevention of a further arms race both in the fields of offensive and defensive arms."[26] This flurry of activity was interpreted by at least some American decisionmakers as signaling a possible shift in Soviet strategic thought about ABM systems.[27]

---

[22] The group of scientists included the current as well as past holders of the office of Special Assistant to the President for Science and Technology (James Killian, George Kistiakowsky, Jerome Wiesner, Donald Hornig), and the current and past directors of DDR&E (Herbert York, Harold Brown, John Foster). The scientists were divided over the issue of whether the United States should at some point consider the alternative of a thin defense against a less-than-massive attack, but the consensus was that there was no urgent reason to proceed with any such deployment at the present time. See Newhouse, *Cold Dawn*, p. 89.

[23] *DoD Appropriations for FY 68*, part 1, pp. 178–79. There was a general expectation within the executive branch that the Congress would respond to the Joint Chiefs by pressuring Johnson if he did not include funds for ABM in his budget; see *Washington Post*, 24 November 1966.

[24] See the account of Kosygin's press conference in *Pravda*, 11 February 1967. Garthoff notes that *Pravda* amended Kosygin's actual remarks so as to render the official line more definitive in its opposition to limiting defenses. "BMD and East-West Relations," pp. 295–96.

[25] See Garthoff, "SALT I: An Evaluation."

[26] *Pravda*, 15 February 1967.

[27] See "Soviet Hints Shift on a Missile Pact," *New York Times*, 17 February 1967.

Within just a few days, denials in the Soviet press presented unusual signals that the controversy over Soviet interests in ABM had not been settled behind the walls of the Kremlin. "Un-named Soviet authorities," claiming that Burlatsky's article had been mistaken, quickly proclaimed that there had been "no change in the Kremlin's position" against limitations on strategic defense.[28] Thompson's efforts to clarify Dobrynin's demarche were unsatisfying, as was a long conversation on the subject between McNamara and the Soviet ambassador.[29] But evidence pointing to a heated internal debate in Moscow continued to surface, and there were new indications that Soviet military leaders as well were deeply divided over the ABM issue.[30]

Washington's interest was certainly piqued by the Soviet debate, but the inconsistent feedback came as too little and too late. By the beginning of 1967, Johnson seems to have concluded that it was no longer sensible to resist pressures for an American deployment. McNamara too recognized that his opposition was increasingly a rear-guard action, bringing him into conflict with the JCS and other influential officials in OSD who supported their plan. The consensus that the time had come for Washington to make some concrete move ran so deep, according to Assistant Secretary of Defense Phil Goulding, that "our choice in the Pentagon . . . was not a small ABM versus none at all, but rather a small ABM versus a big one."[31] I will consider what the United States chose to do in the subsequent discussion of strategy development; first, I analyze the payoff structure on ABM as perceived by decisionmakers in the late 1960s.

Payoff Analysis

Can the ABM issue facing American decisionmakers at the end of the 1960s be modeled as an iterated PD game with a long shadow of the future? Using the methods of Chapter 3, the following discussion establishes that U.S. policymakers at this juncture faced a critical decisional

[28] "Soviet ABM Shift Denied," *Washington Post*, 18 February 1967.

[29] Newhouse, *Cold Dawn*, p. 94.

[30] For examples of this debate, see Marshal R. Malinovsky, *Pravda*, 23 February 1967; Marshal V. I. Chuikov, Radio Moscow, translated in *FBIS Daily Report*, Soviet Union, 23 February 1967, p. CC11; Army General P. A. Kurochkin, interview, Radio Moscow, *FBIS Daily Report*, Soviet Union, 21 February 1967, p. CC3. Malinovsky, Minister of Defense at the time, argued that BMD could never be highly effective, while his colleagues (generals with close ties to the Air Defense Forces) saw Galosh as the first phase of a system that would "reliably protect the territory of the country against ballistic missile attack."

[31] Goulding, *Confirm or Deny*, p. 233. Prominent supporters of the JCS plan in OSD included Air Force Secretary Harold Brown, Navy Secretary Paul Nitze, DDR&E Director John Foster, and ARPA Director Charles Herzfeld.

point for the future of strategic defense. The U.S. decisionmaking system developed a consensus around PD preferences over alternative future scenarios for the strategic environment as it might be affected by ABMs. Decisionmakers also viewed their predicament as an iterated game with a long shadow of the future. Together, these conditions fulfill the prerequisites for bringing Axelrod's model to bear.

Threats, Opportunities, and a Critical Decisional Point

By the end of the 1960s, most American strategists and decisionmakers believed that the Soviet Union was on the verge of attaining rough parity with U.S. strategic nuclear forces. Chapter 5 will consider the implications of offensive parity in greater detail; for the moment, it is enough to note that both sides' current ability to carry out threats of "assured destruction" was barely questioned. In the short term, deterrence based on offense dominance seemed remarkably stable. Two sets of developments threatened to degrade this stability in the longer term: a growing threat from counterforce-capable ICBMs, which had the potential to attack the other sides' forces in a preemptive strike and thus prevent a full-fledged retaliation; and ABM systems, which promised to protect cities from incoming warheads.

By 1969, the Soviets had in fact deployed a fairly sophisticated ABM system around their capital, while the Americans had not. Galosh, however, was not thought to pose any immediate difficulty for a dedicated American nuclear attack on Moscow. U.S. researchers had devoted much energy to designing a repertoire of countermeasures against Soviet ABM systems—as we shall see in the next chapter, MIRV was only one of these. Galosh was in any case limited by its reliance on a three-tiered radar infrastructure including mechanically steered radars that were themselves highly vulnerable to attack, and by the fact that the less than 100 deployed Galosh interceptors were relatively slow accelerators. In a 1968 assessment of Galosh, McNamara reassured Congress that it was "the consensus of the intelligence community that this system could provide a limited defense of the Moscow area but that it could be seriously degraded by sophisticated penetration aids, precursor bursts, and the vulnerability of the radars to nuclear explosions."[32]

[32] Secretary of Defense Robert S. McNamara, *FY 1969–73 Defense Program and FY 1969 Defense Budget*, January 1968, p. 63. (This annual *Statement of the Secretary of Defense on the Five Year Defense Program and Annual Defense Budget* is hereinafter cited in the footnotes as the *Military Posture Statement* of the Secretary of Defense.) Other contemporary assessments echoed McNamara's conclusions; see "Soviet's Antimissile Steps Spur Study of U.S. Needs," *New York Times*, 8 December 1966, p. 1; "Russia and the ABM,"

There were, however, both objective and subjective arguments that made the long-term prognosis on Soviet defenses much less sanguine. On technical grounds, Galosh did provide basic infrastructure that could be expanded over time into a larger area defense, offering some protection to a large percentage of Soviet population centers and ICBM silos. If the Kremlin were fully commited to strategic defense, as it then seemed to be, the United States could expect to face incremental upgrades of Galosh combined with other active and passive defenses that together might come to degrade the American assured destruction threat. At the very least, the United States would be compelled to devote large technological and economic resources toward insuring that its offensive systems always remained a step ahead of Soviet defenses, and that the Soviets were fully aware of this fact.

More troubling was the prospect that Soviet defenses would continue to grow in conjunction with the further expansion of the counterforce threat. With the new strategic theories' concentration on the determinants of crisis stability in their heads, American war planners naturally worried about the potential synergism between imperfect defenses like Galosh and offensive systems that seemed to be dedicated to preemptive attack. It was possible to imagine a war scenario in which Moscow would mount a first strike against American forces and then rely upon a combination of active BMD, air defense, and passive civilian defense to protect the Soviet homeland against a degraded American retaliation. While this scenario was dismissed as fanciful by some American decisionmakers, it had to be thought through even by the most skeptical because the fact that the Soviets were spending a considerable sum of money to deploy highly imperfect defenses did make greater sense in the context of expanding counterforce capabilities.

The technical and strategic challenges posed by Soviet ABMs were compounded for Washington by a perceived political threat. The option of responding to Galosh only with compensatory penetration measures and not with an American ABM deployment might have made sense to strategic analysts, but it was increasingly unacceptable to politicians and particularly to President Johnson. The idea of an "ABM gap" focused decisionmakers' attention on the notion that it would be difficult for an American president to explain to his own country, U.S. allies, and the world at large why a self-proclaimed peaceful state was concentrating on designing new offensive nuclear systems while its adversary (the supposed aggressor) was building defenses. Apart from issues of propaganda and

---

Ordnance, 1972, p. 374; *Scope, Magnitude, and Implications of the United States Antiballistic Missile Program*, 1967, p. 66. For details on the limited capabilities and vulnerability of Galosh's radar infrastructure, see Freedman, *US Intelligence*, pp. 88–90; and Stevens, "The Soviet BMD Program," p. 200.

electoral appeal, there might be serious concern among allies that America's resolve to compete in all facets of the arms race was slipping, just at the time that "flexible response" was being put into place as official NATO doctrine. At the same time, engaging in a full-fledged defense race with the Soviets would complicate whatever prospects existed for a political rapprochement or detente between the superpowers in the immediate future.

Threats and dangers notwithstanding, ABM also offered certain attractive opportunities for American strategists and war planners. The promise of rendering Soviet nuclear forces "impotent and obsolete" should the United States achieve unforeseen success or a technological breakthrough in area defense, always loomed in the background. More immediately, ABM systems based on current technology seemed capable of providing significant point or hard site defense, an attractive means of responding to the increasing vulnerability of silos to preemptive attack.[33] At the very least, an American ABM system would complicate the Soviet targeters' tasks and thus might enhance the stability of mutual deterrence.

These strategic, technological, and political considerations coalesced in the late 1960s and early 1970s, so that U.S. decision makers came to believe they were facing a key decisional point for the future of ABM. Reinforcing this was the fact that the American strategic triad of offensive forces was essentially complete and in a de facto state of freeze by 1969.[34] The presumption was that offensive forces would be incrementally modernized and improved, but a decision to embark on a new competition in defenses would mark a qualitative escalation of the arms race that would make a (still dynamic) equilibrium based on this "mature" force posture difficult to establish.

Politics reinforced this strategic calculus. At the same time that U.S. and Soviet nuclear forces were approaching parity, political relations between the superpowers were on a moderate upswing. Arms control, and particularly agreements to constrain the superpowers' central strategic weapons systems, would do much to reinforce further rapprochement and moves toward detente. The domestic political scene in the West was highly favorable to such developments. The incoming Nixon administration would have the advantage of impeccable anticommunist credentials that would allow a shift toward "an era of negotiation" with the Soviet Union. The American public, widely skeptical of the Vietnam War and increasingly concerned about the economic impact of mounting defense budgets, would probably be supportive of careful but serious attempts to

---

[33] Hard site defense is the protection of small, hardened targets like missile silos or command posts. This is to be distinguished from area defense, which involves protecting cities and other "soft" targets spread over a wide area.

[34] For details, see discussion in Chapter 5.

slow the arms race. Alliance politics were also pushing toward detente, with West German Chancellor Willy Brandt's Ostpolitik leading the way. In 1966, the Harmel Report had commited the NATO alliance to a similar if less ambitious policy stance of combining deterrence with detente as the best means for conducting relations with the East.[35]

Technological considerations, however, were probably most important in bringing the ABM issue to a key decisional point. After a decade of progress, the Army was optimistic about the prospects of Nike-Zeus and wished to move rapidly toward deployment, "having spent several billion dollars in R and D money to develop an ABM system that looked as though it would actually work."[36] Indeed, all but the most vigorous opponents of ABM conceded that it was now possible on strict technological grounds to deploy a system with at least some capability to defend silos or to protect cities against a small-scale attack.[37] The pressure to do so was of course enhanced by the fact that the Soviets, facing similar technological constraints, had chosen to invest considerable resources in deploying an ABM system that would in the short run offer less protection than a comparable American system.

As we shall see in detail later, U.S. weapons scientists offered alternatives for potential deployment ranging from pure hard site systems to "thick" area defenses that promised significant protection of cities. For political decisionmakers, however, this range of alternatives collapsed into an esentially dyadic choice. Pure hard site defense was seen in Washington as politically difficult—strategic logic aside, the voting public would balk at the prospect of protecting missiles while leaving cities open to attack. A "thick" area system to defend silos and cities was more plausible on political grounds, but this would be a full-fledged competitive move that would challenge Soviet assured destruction capabilities and incite an escalated arms race. A technologically viable intermediate option

---

[35] "The Future Tasks of the Alliance" (the Harmel Report) is summarized in a final communique excerpted in Kaplan, *NATO and the United States*, pp. 223–25. For general impressions of a political "window of opportunity" in U.S.-Soviet relations and arms control at this time, see York, *Race to Oblivion*, pp. 160–64; and Garthoff, *Detente and Confrontation*, Chapter 4. Also revealing is the Congressional testimony of George Rathjens in *The Economics of National Priorities*, 1971, pp. 404–5. For a summary of perceptions of a parallel Soviet interest, see the 1969 Senate Hearings before the Subcommittee on International Organization and Disarmament, *Strategic and Foreign Policy Implications of ABM Systems*, p. 345.

[36] See Schwartz, "Past and Present," pp. 336–37.

[37] A common argument was that continued progress in ABM now required moving out of the laboratory and into at least preliminary deployment of an operational prototype in order to gain experience in operating the system. The view that such experience can make a significant contribution has since been questioned by a number of scientists, particularly Jack Ruina (personal communication), but at the time it seemed to carry considerable weight among a large number of decisionmakers.

was to deploy a system dedicated primarily to hard site defense, with some capability for a thin defense of populations against an inadvertent launch or a small attack. While this might seem to ease Soviet worries on an objective level, U.S. decisionmakers did not believe that perceptions could be quite so discriminating. Most strategic analysts agreed that the Kremlin would be compelled to respond to almost *any* significant ABM deployment as if it posed a threat to Soviet assured destruction capabilities. Given the long lead times for strategic weapons and the Soviets' uncertainty over current and future political intentions of their American adversary, Moscow would be driven to respond to projected worst-case scenarios and would most likely move toward an offensive posture capable of defeating thick area defenses. Indeed, many Americans thought that Washington should behave the same way toward Galosh, regardless of its present capabilities.[38] The action-reaction theory had had its impact in Washington; U.S. decisionmakers had become highly sensitive to the interdependent nature of the two sides' decisions about ABM. The perceived range of alternatives thus resolved into essentially two: the cooperative option of tight mutual restraint and the competitive option of moving forward with ABM deployments and a new phase of the arms race.

But if the late 1960s held a "window of opportunity" for cooperative restraint, many Americans also believed it to be fleeting. Unrestrained technological momentum threatened to undermine the strategic balance that had developed between U.S. and Soviet nuclear forces, and a political environment conducive to cooperation could not be expected to last. The medium to long-term prospects for stability would diminish considerably if the present opportunity were not seized; according to Princeton's Carl Kaysen:

> We are now in a situation in which we understand each other's deployments in both a quantitative and a qualitative sense. Deterrence . . . rests on the perception and interpretation of the military situation by political decision makers. This inevitably marks it with a certain elusiveness. . . . Constant or slowly

---

[38] These arguments were most vehemently expressed in the debate over Safeguard during 1969. Opponents reasoned that the Soviets would not and could not respond to even the early phases of Safeguard as if it were solely a hard site defense system. For example, Jerome Wiesner argued that Soviet planners looking at Safeguard would have to conclude "that a number of sites have been selected not because they will protect minuteman, but because they will protect something else." *Strategic and Foreign Policy Implications of ABM Systems*, p. 528. Asked to compare projected Soviet responses to the likely American response in a similar situation, George Rathjens argued that "without verification arrangements that would be unacceptably intrusive, I doubt whether we could ever have adequate confidence that a nationwide Soviet ABM system was of such limited capability that we could accept a lengthy freeze on our strategic offensive capabilities." *Ibid.*, p. 362.

changing force structures, whose technical performance characteristics are reasonably well understood . . . provide a much more stable basis for mutual reliance on and acceptance of deterrence than a rapidly moving process of qualitative and quantitative competition.[39]

An Iterated Game, With a Long Shadow of the Future

The "objective conditions" that render the superpower competition like an iterated game were strongly reflected in the "subjective" perceptions and strategic arguments about ABM of American decisionmakers. From a political perspective, a broad consensus in Washington had by the late 1960s come to accept as inevitable a long-term competition with the Soviet Union across the military, economic, and political spheres. But the competition was no longer seen as zero-sum. At a minimum, the superpower relationship held potential for some collaboration to moderate the level of hostility and costs of competition, as well as reduce the risk of war. Most important in this perception was the stability of the de facto postwar settlement in Europe, where memories of the last serious crisis were almost a decade old.[40]

The superpower nuclear relationship had reached a comparable state of potential stability that rendered it, too, like an iterated game. Rough parity in offensive forces with large retaliatory capabilities on both sides made the central deterrent balance appear far more robust than in the 1950s. Importantly, NATO's recent formal adoption of MC 14/3, the "flexible response" doctrine, seemed to adequately reconcile strategic parity with extended deterrence in Europe. Long lead times for new systems and the sturdiness of offense dominance meant that this condition could be expected to persist, which in turn meant that decisionmakers had to maintain a longer time frame and not discount future payoffs for short-term temptations of nuclear "advantage." The most prominent strategic theories of the time linked these developments to mutual vulnerability; and because vulnerability seemed nearly impossible to erase, deterrence took on something of an "existential" quality in the minds of many strategic thinkers. In this world, the United States was not compelled to vigorously exploit its technological edge, but could rely upon it to compensate for perceived Soviet advantages if need be.[41] Because

[39] *Strategic and Foreign Policy Implications of ABM Systems*, p. 160.

[40] Washington's relatively moderate reaction to the Soviet invasion of Czechoslovakia in 1968 was a good indication of this prevailing belief.

[41] To quote McNamara in 1967, "with any numerical superiority realistically attainable, the blunt, inescapable fact remains that the Soviet Union could still . . . effectively destroy the US even after absorbing the full weight of an American first strike . . . [thus] the corner-

maintenance of an appropriately structured offensive nuclear arsenal was sufficient to insure MAD, and deterrence based on MAD was regarded as an acceptable means of protecting central national security interests, the nuclear balance had the potential to achieve a long-term, dynamic, but managed and therefore predictable equilibrium.

PD Preferences

Faced with what was perceived as a dyadic choice between cooperative moves (refraining from any significant deployment) and competitive moves (deploying outside the context of any agreement), and assuming that the Soviets faced a comparable choice, American decisionmakers confronted a "2 × 2 matrix" with four potential outcome "cells" for ABM, as shown in Figure 2.

In Chapter 3, I defined preferences as comparative evaluations of the

USSR

	cooperate	defect
U.S. cooperate	C, C mutual restraint	C, D U.S. refrains; USSR deploys
U.S. defect	D, C U.S. deploys; USSR refrains	D, D both sides deploy

Figure 2. Anti-Ballistic Missile Systems

stone of our strategic policy continues to be to deter deliberate nuclear attack . . . by main-taining . . . our 'assured destruction capability.' " See text of McNamara's speech before the editors of United Press International, San Francisco, 18 September 1967, reprinted in Art and Waltz, *The Use of Force*, pp. 503–16.

strategic scenarios attached to each of these cells. These evaluations are based not on static utilities, but on comparisons of alternative arguments about the military, strategic, and political aspects of each "outcome." The following sections examine these preferences, with a particular focus on how key individuals and the state decisionmaking apparatus play a constructive role, aggregating the heterogeneous preferences of a divided and uncertain elite into a working consensus to guide the actions of the state.

D,C THE TEMPTATION TO DEFECT

The D,C outcome represents a scenario in which the United States chooses full-fledged competition in ABM, and in time achieves some significant advantage over the Soviets in defensive capabilities. The "temptations to defect" attached to this scenario were not readily dismissed in the late 1960s: the lure of protecting American cities and industrial centers, possible gains in the credibility of extended deterrence, and the promise of diffuse political and even military advantages that might accrue to a superpower possessing a meaningful degree of strategic superiority.

Although most Americans would ideally have preferred this outcome, the magnitude of the potential payoff was sharply reduced in the perception of contemporary decisionmakers by a number of factors. Domestic politics was one of the most important: even the strongest advocates of ABM, in the uniformed military and elsewhere, recognized that growing public opposition to nuclear warheads deployed in heavily populated areas would hamper Washington's ability to sustain its "defection," particularly if the Soviets showed interest in cooperative restraint.[42] There were also significant technical constraints on how much defense the United States could realistically hope to achieve in the near term. While many American elites shared Nixon and Kissinger's reluctance to forgo competition in a high-technology weapons system, most defense scientists were doubtful as to whether even a massive commitment of American resources would succeed in producing a viable ABM system capable of protecting cities.[43] It is clear that most of Washington accepted the

[42] Particularly influential were large public protests against the initial Safeguard deployments that were held in Boston and Chicago during 1968. Antimilitary sentiment directed primarily at the Vietnam War was also important; public opposition could easily be redirected at a new strategic weapons program whose level of visibility would be matched only by its price tag.

[43] According to Henry Kissinger, "all of Nixon's instincts were against unilaterally giving up a weapons program—especially one approved by his predecessor. I shared his view; I considered it highly dangerous to stop programs in the area of our traditional superiority—advanced technology." *White House Years*, p. 205.

boundaries of this technological consensus, if reluctantly. For example, the Congressional hearings on ABM show almost a complete absence of any discussion about "strategic superiority" in the traditional sense as a realistic option for the United States, or as a goal to which ABM might contribute.[44] Rather, the debate was framed within the bounds of mutual deterrence, the primary question being "will technologically foreseeable ABM systems enhance or weaken mutual deterrence?" Within these bounds, the magnitude of the temptation to defect was considerably lessened.

But even if the United States were to achieve a breakthrough and attain a significant advantage in strategic defense, the political payoffs seemed at best uncertain. Anything less than a near-perfect defense of population centers would leave U.S. cities unacceptably vulnerable to Soviet attack. In the late 1960s, the political and military concomitants of vulnerability seemed decisive and inescapable.[45] Carl Kaysen expressed a common perception when he argued that "it is clear to me, and I think to every other careful observer, that strategic striking power cannot now, has not in the recent past, and will not in the foreseeable future, offer the kind of military threat . . . that is translatable into useful political power."[46] The D,C payoff, tempting in the abstract, was thus reduced in the perception of contemporary decisionmakers by political and technological constraints, and by related beliefs about the diminishing value of nuclear weapons as a source of power in U.S.-Soviet relations.

C,D THE SUCKER'S PAYOFF FOR UNREQUITED COOPERATION

The C,D outcome represents the scenario in which the United States assumes a position of unilateral restraint in ABM, while the Soviets continue to compete vigorously. Military and political arguments alike identified this as the least acceptable outcome for the United States. Most

---

[44] President Johnson's accession to this view was apparently secured at the previously described "ABM meeting" of January 23, 1967, in which he was told by the nation's most prominent defense scientists and engineers that current technology could not protect American cities from devastation by a determined Soviet attack. See Herbert York, "Military Technology and National Security," *Scientific American* 222, no. 2 (1969): 17–29, especially p. 18.

[45] The United States had enjoyed a degree of nuclear "superiority" and a considerably lower level of vulnerability through the early 1960s, but decisionmakers at the end of that decade did not for the most part favor the argument that this had played a decisive role in U.S.-Soviet competition. For a detailed discussion that emphasizes the experience of the Cuban Missile Crisis as a source of American beliefs, and the implications thereof for detente, arms control, and nuclear weapons strategy, see Weber, "Interactive Learning in U.S.-Soviet Arms Control," in Breslauer and Tetlock, *Learning in US and Soviet Foreign Policy.*

[46] *Strategic and Foreign Policy Implications of ABM Systems*, p. 137.

American decisionmakers did not fear the short-term military costs of unrequited restraint: the prospects that the Soviets would achieve technological breakthroughs seemed slim, and McNamara was reassuring in repeated messages to the effect that the United States maintained "both the lead time and the technology available to [compensate such that] their expensive defensive efforts will give them no edge in the nuclear balance whatever."[47] By 1969, some Pentagon officials (including McNamara's successor Melvin Laird) argued that the United States needed to take action on ABM almost immediately to insure stable deterrence, but this remained a distinctly minority view.[48] The long-term military threat was seen as a more serious problem. Absent any significant arms control, incremental upgrades of Soviet defensive capabilities combined with a growing counterforce arsenal might lead to a situation where Soviet leaders could suspect that they held a significant advantage in the ability to limit damage from a nuclear exchange. American decisionmakers naturally viewed this as entirely unacceptable. Washington's immediate military problem was thus to guard against being "lulled" by technological complacence into a long-term C,D scenario.

Of greater immediate importance than the military problem were the perceived political ramifications of a failure to compete with the Soviets in a high-visibility, high-technology weapons system like ABM. Some American ABM opponents believed that Moscow's commitment to defense was driven largely by a fear of American technological superiority, but this was a minority view.[49] Far more common was the belief that Moscow, as an opportunistic competitor, would pocket unilateral American "concessions" while interpreting U.S. restraint as weakness and lack of will to compete. Allowing this perception to develop would be a dangerous mistake: according to one prominent ABM supporter, even a postponement of the ABM program "might be considered by potential op-

[47] See McNamara speech before UPI in San Francisco, 18 September 1967, in Art and Waltz, *The Use of Force*, pp. 503–16.

[48] Scientists and strategists outside the Pentagon were in almost unanimous agreement that it would pose no military risk to the United States to defer a decision on ABM deployment for at least several years. Even a number of officials who cited the "greater than expected threat" forecasts as a planning tool agreed that the risk was not imminent and that from a military perspective, the United States could afford to wait. For examples, see testimony by York, Killian, Kistiakowsky, Bethe, Ruina, and Daniel J. Fink (former DDR&E) in *Strategic and Foreign Policy Implications of ABM Systems*, especially pp. 56, 105.

[49] Proponents of this view argued that Galosh represented Moscow's attempt to position itself for a race with the United States that it desperately feared losing—a result of the Soviets' perception of American technological superiority. Accordingly, if the United States were to take unilateral steps to demonstrate its willingness to moderate the military competition (particularly in the area of high-technology weaponry), the Soviets would respond with reciprocal restraint, leading to a "spiraling down" of the arms race.

ponents of this country as a sign of unwillingness of this country to defend itself."[50] Kissinger suspected that even in the short run, the perception of "an eroding strategic equilibrium was bound to have geopolitical consequences"; specifically, a diminished level of confidence within the NATO alliance and an increased Soviet willingness to take risks and exploit opportunities in turbulent regions of the Third World.[51]

American decisionmakers largely agreed that the short-term military risks were small, but held differing views about the immediate political ramifications that might attach to unrequited restraint in ABM. Washington was thus divided over whether temporary American restraint would increase or decrease Soviet propensity to negotiate mutual limitations on ABM. Later, I discuss how beliefs about the Soviet Union as an adversary and about the stability of the superpower balance of power played an important role in mediating these perceptions. But looking past short-term restraint, American decisionmakers largely accepted Kissinger's argument that "the USSR would accept a stabilization of the arms race only if convinced that it would not be allowed to achieve superiority."[52] The C,D outcome was thus over the long term the worst of the four potential scenarios.

C,C THE REWARD FOR MUTUAL COOPERATION

The C,C outcome represents a situation in which the United States and the Soviet Union agree to ban or limit ABM deployments to militarily insignificant levels. This scenario, which would mean codified mutual vulnerability among other things, is for U.S. decisionmakers a compromise from the possibilities of the D,C outcome, but it is clearly preferable to C,D. Importantly, it is also preferable to a full-fledged competition in ABM, the D,D scenario to be considered next.

The major reward for cooperative restraint in ABM lay in the improved stability of the strategic balance that American decisionmakers expected to result. By 1969, the most widely accepted tenets of contemporary strategic theory pointed to BMD as the major short-term impediment to gaining a strategic equilibrium based on offense dominance and functional parity, where neither side would have anything to gain by striking first. ABM cooperation thus meant greater crisis stability.[53] Mutual restraint

[50] See the testimony of Donald Wigner, *Strategic and Foreign Policy Implications of ABM Systems*, part 2, p. 559.

[51] See Kissinger, *White House Years*, p. 203.

[52] Ibid.

[53] This was particularly valuable in so far as contemporary strategic theory focused heavily on crisis instability as the most probable route to nuclear war. I thank Marc Trachtenburg for this point.

in defense would contribute equally to arms race stability by removing an important impetus for further expansion of offensive forces, and this would add a measure of predictability to the nuclear balance that would facilitate further arms control measures. Limiting defenses would also preserve the value of currently deployed U.S. offensive systems, which were not slated to undergo expansion in the immediate future.[54] The only possible downside to cooperation in terms of the central strategic balance lay in the continuing threat of counterforce. Limiting ABMs meant giving up hard site defense of silos, and Washington would have to consider alternative means of dealing with the possible counterforce threat; but as we shall see in this chapter and the next, decisionmakers believed they had attractive alternative options and a fairly long time frame in which to act.

Another important payoff from avoiding an ABM race were the potential economic benefits. Estimates for the cost of a heavy BMD system ranged upwards of $100 billion, depending on its presumed architecture and capabilities. These figures did not, of course, include the additional resources that strategic analysts believed would have to be spent developing and deploying countermeasures to defeat Soviet ABMs. In an era of fiscal restraint, and with public attention particularly focused on the military as a result of growing opposition to the Vietnam War, ABM became a symbol of high military budgets. Even strong supporters of military spending in the Congress worried that money spent on ABM would be money not spent for what were seen as more important needs elsewhere in the DoD budget.[55]

Reinforcing these "objective" considerations were the important political benefits that U.S. decisionmakers expected to follow from mutual restraint. For Nixon and particularly for Kissinger, and for many in the legislative branch as well, some form of cooperation in managing the superpower military competition was judged a necessary prerequisite to political detente.[56] An agreement to sharply limit strategic defenses would

---

[54] Except for the critical addition of MIRV warheads, which I consider in the next chapter. Although MIRV was originally conceived for other purposes, by the early 1970s the Pentagon wanted to use MIRVs primarily to "cover" an expanding set of targets in the Soviet Union. In this context, an agreement on ABM would actually enhance the strategic value of MIRV, since the warheads would not have to be "wasted" in saturating or otherwise defeating strategic defenses.

[55] John Stennis, Chairman of the Senate Committee on Armed Services, was particularly vehement on the issue of these opportunity costs. Following hearings on Safeguard, Stennis wrote of ABM systems that "if the geometric cost increase for these strategic weapons systems is not sharply reversed, then even significant increases in the defense budget may not insure the force levels required for our national security." *DoD Authorizations for FY 1972—Safeguard*, p. 17.

[56] For details see Weber, "Realism, Detente, and Nuclear Weapons," pp. 66–68.

be compelling evidence that Soviet leaders had truly amended their traditional commitment to the pursuit of absolute, autarkic security—and had given up ambitions to overturn American power by force of arms in a quest for Soviet hegemony. Arms control thus took on the role of a quasi-test of Soviet willingness to share in implementing the American conception of international system stability. It would also play an important legitimating role in American domestic politics, providing Nixon and Kissinger with a concrete and highly visible achievement that they could claim as the first fruits of detente.[57]

There were at the same time several factors that for some American decisionmakers seemed to reduce the payoff for cooperation. The most important was the perceived risk that the Soviets would cheat on any agreement; even strong advocates of cooperation recognized that there were valid reasons to be skeptical about the Kremlin's reliability. They also argued, however, that the risks could be reduced by prudent American behavior, and that the remaining risks had to be weighed against the costs of no agreement. Herbert York spoke for a wide consensus in Washington when he noted that "there is always going to be some residual risk, but that risk has to be compared with the obviously great risks of the arms race itself."[58] Many American elites were also particularly reluctant to restrain the arms race in an area of high technology, a perceived American strength. That Washington was ready in the end to forgo this type of competition is strong evidence of the positive value that decisionmakers attached to cooperative restraint in ABM. In fact, the open record of the negotiations supports the assertion that it was the United States that pushed hardest for tight constraints on the development and deployment of "exotic" defensive technologies.[59] Finally, some Americans were troubled by the possible political implications of acknowledging mutual vulnerability and elevating it to the level of a principle for the future conduct of U.S.-Soviet military relations. Nonetheless, while no one knew precisely what the effects on Soviet behavior were going to be, the experience

[57] See Alexander George, "Domestic Constraints on Regime Change in US Foreign Policy," in Holsti et al., *Change in the International System*, pp. 233–62.

[58] *Strategic and Foreign Policy Implications of ABM Systems*, p. 113. Regarding early worries about Soviet compliance, Gerard Smith believes that many American decisionmakers were troubled by a perceived "legacy from our bad experience with the Yalta and other post-war agreements . . . [in addition], many officials believed that the informal nuclear testing moratorium of 1958–60 had been breached by the Soviets." *Doubletalk*, p. 122.

[59] This became a political issue during the mid-1980s when the Reagan administration opened a debate over whether the ABM treaty actually covered the deployment of defensive systems based on so-called new physical principles. For details of how the exotic technologies issue was treated during the negotiations, see Smith's account in *Doubletalk*, particularly pp. 344–46, 367–69; and Newhouse, *Cold Dawn*, particularly pp. 231, 237–39. This was confirmed in an interview with Ambassador Smith, April 1987.

of the previous decade had been for the most part reassuring on that score.[60] The Nixon-Kissinger plan for detente also addressed this concern: by engaging the Kremlin in a web of cooperative arrangements, including arms control, it would be possible to dampen the potential instabilities that might otherwise have followed from the Soviet accession to nuclear parity.

With this strong case for cooperation, why did the C,C outcome become powerfully associated in U.S. decisionmakers' minds with a formal negotiated agreement and not with alternatives, such as tacit mutual restraint? Insofar as cooperation on ABM was seen as a prerequisite to political detente, a highly visible, precedent-setting formal agreement would obviously be more valuable. But technological saliencies seem to have been most important. Any current generation ABM system would require an infrastructure of large and conspicuous radar installations that took a long time to build and were easily detected through national technical means of verification. Neither side had yet deployed such a network; if this saliency could be preserved, the possibilities for short-term "breakout" from an agreement would be small.[61] This had to be reinforced by limiting development of lasers and other exotic technologies, because the current saliencies could disappear rapidly if extensive development work on these types of systems were to continue. The publicity that the ABM issue had attracted in the United States by 1969 reinforced each of these reasons. If there was to be cooperation with the Soviets, a formal agreement with precisely specified obligations for each side seemed necessary.

D,D THE PUNISHMENT FOR MUTUAL DEFECTION

The outcome of mutual defection represents a scenario in which the United States and the Soviet Union engage in unrestrained competition in

[60] That is, the last major crisis in U.S.-Soviet relations had come in Cuba, when the United States had a large advantage in strategic weapons—in fact, many Americans suspected that the strategic advantage itself had been a major cause for Soviet actions leading to crisis. Over the course of the decade, as Moscow inched toward nuclear parity, U.S.-Soviet relations actually improved, apparently weakening the earlier predictions of Herman Kahn and others, who had argued that parity would bring a new Soviet aggressiveness.

[61] ACDA's Assistant Director for Science and Technology Herbert Scoville noted that "ABMs . . . are complicated and large systems. They require large radars which have a high visibility, have a long lead time for construction. . . . All of these factors greatly facilitate verification." See his 1970 testimony before the Senate Subcommittee on Arms Control, International Law and Organization, *ABM, MIRV, SALT, and the Nuclear Arms Race*, pp. 227–31. On the other hand, if either side were to deploy a nationwide radar infrastructure, it might then be possible to secretly produce and stockpile a large number of interceptor missiles that could be rapidly deployed in a breakout scenario.

strategic defense. The payoff for D,D will clearly be less preferred than mutual cooperation; ABM is not a game of "deadlock." At the same time, mutual defection is preferred to unrequited cooperation (C,D); this is also not a game where one side prefers to cooperate regardless of what the other does.

The principal punishment for mutual defection would come in the military area. The vast majority of American decisionmakers accepted the argument from current strategic theory that "defense breeds offense": ABM deployments were expected to incite further proliferation of offensive systems on both sides. Arms race stability would be an immediate and expensive casualty: estimates were that the United States would spend a minimum additional $5 to $10 billion on offensive countermeasures over the next few years in an effort just to keep up, which would "raise the level of equilibrium, but with no more security for either side."[62] Even more serious was the potential impact on crisis stability: in a world of partial defenses, where either state lacked confidence in both sides' ability to fulfill the threat of retaliatory destruction, the pressures to strike first in a crisis might tempt or even compel acts of boldness or desperation.[63]

But if Washington was willing to spend the money and bear the risks of crisis instability, was it possible that the United States would emerge "victorious" with a significant strategic advantage in a full-fledged ABM competition? Despite the fact that a race in high-technology weapons seemed to play to U.S. strengths, few American decisionmakers thought so. Economic constraints on U.S. expenditures, bolstered by growing public opposition to the Vietnam War, were thought to be prohibitive. The Soviets might start with an inferior technological base, but they had the advantage of being able to extract greater resources from their population. The United States was also handicapped by a geographical asymmetry. American cities, clustered and mainly on the coasts, would be inherently harder to protect than Soviet cities, which were more widely dispersed around the interior of the country. To make matters worse, the Soviets already had a headstart in Galosh and in their expanding arsenal of large ICBMs.[64] At least for the foreseeable future, mutual defection might be even worse for the United States than for the Soviet Union.

[62] The cost estimate was cited by Gerard Smith, *Strategic and Foreign Policy Implications of ABM Systems*, p. 4. The quote is from the testimony of Jack Ruina, p. 54.

[63] For a particularly vivid statement of this problem, and the sympathetic response of key congressmen, see the testimony of Carl Kaysen, *Ibid.*, p. 138.

[64] In the immediate future, MIRV technology would favor the United States in countermeasures to ABM defenses. As we shall see in Chapter 5, decisionmakers believed that this advantage would be short-lived. It was expected that Moscow would in just a few years be in a position to deploy their own MIRVs and other penetration aids on a large and expand-

The political costs of mutual defection were also expected to be substantial. As ABM took on the mantle of a test case for a fledgling detente, the prospects for constructive development of the superpower political relationship became even more closely tied to nuclear arms control than it otherwise might have been. Failing cooperative restraint in the military competition, Washington would be thrown back on its own resources and the "grand design" for detente would be more or less moribund.

American decisionmakers were not prepared to wait much past the early 1970s; if the Soviets went forward with ABM, the United States would be compelled to respond with defenses of its own. Mutual defection, despite its costs, was still preferred to unrequited cooperation; for the reasons cited earlier, unilateral restraint was seen as militarily dangerous and politically unacceptable. But while Washington held PD preferences over potential outcomes in ABM, it was not at all clear that the Soviets shared a similar conception of self-interest. How American decisionmakers developed a strategy to elicit cooperation in this case is the subject of the next section.

Strategy Development

In the winter of 1967, President Johnson chose to finesse and in effect temporarily delay a decision on ABM deployment. Less than a year later, his secretary of defense announced a plan to deploy Sentinel, a light area defense against the "Chinese threat." In 1969 a new administration would announce still another plan with different objectives, named Safeguard. American preferences over outcomes in ABM did not change during this time. Why, then, the change in American strategy? And what was its impact on Soviet behavior and the outcome of the case?

Early 1967—Contingent Restraint

In his January 1967 budget message, Johnson requested that Congress allocate $440 million for continued R&D on Nike-X, as well as an additional $375 million in preliminary production and deployment funds to be held in escrow pending further efforts to engage the Soviet Union in negotiations.[65] This was a strategy of contingent restraint. It had the ef-

---

ing arsenal of modern, heavy ICBMs—a capability the United States would not be able to match for some time thereafter.

[65] For details, see text of the president's 1967 State of the Union Message, *New York Times*, 11 January 1967, p. 16; and "The President's Message to Congress," 24 January 1967, *Weekly Compilation of Presidential Documents*, vol. 3, 1967, p. 893.

fect of defusing for a time domestic pressures for immediate deployment and the NATO allies' growing concerns about American impassiveness.[66] But it did not pose new threats to Soviet security that would impel escalation of the competition. Johnson did not specify what Moscow would have to do in order to forestall deployment, nor did he set a deadline or ultimatum for a positive response. The scope of the possible American "defection" was similarly vague: the plan did not include specific details about what the United States would do in ABM in the absence of agreement. In conjunction with this approach, Washington kept up the pressure on the Soviet leadership and tried to explore the "cracks" in Moscow's consensus on defense that continued to surface in the spring of 1967. In a series of letters between Johnson and Kosygin, the Soviets expressed general interest in strategic arms talks but remained noncommittal on the subject of defenses. The American response was surprisingly hopeful, as Johnson and his advisors seem to have believed that Soviet leaders were stalling for time while a debate about the merits of strategic defense was being settled behind the Kremlin walls.[67]

This working hypothesis did not go untested. When Kosygin announced that he would attend a UN session in New York on the Arab-Israeli War in June, Johnson's advisors seized the opportunity to elicit additional feedback about evolving Soviet interests in ABM. Under pressure from Washington, the reluctant Soviet premier agreed to meet Johnson for a mini-summit at Glassboro, where the president proceeded to push the agenda away from Kosygin's preferred topics (the Middle East and Vietnam) and toward arms control. McNamara engaged Kosygin along with Gromyko and Dobrynin in a long seminar on current American strategic theory, with exhaustive details about the dangers of strategic defense. Apparently, the Soviets showed no sign of flexibility in their beliefs about ABM. After listening to McNamara with "some astonishment," Kosygin reportedly argued that "giving up defensive weapons was the most absurd proposition." The Soviets maintained that arms control should deal first and foremost with offensive systems; as for ABM, Mos-

---

[66] On domestic considerations, see Kahan, *Security in the Nuclear Age*, pp. 123ff.; and Halperin, *Bureaucratic Politics and Foreign Policy*, p. 301. On NATO concerns, see *Background Paper for NATO Ministerial Meeting in Luxembourg*, 13–15 June 1967, NHP Box 17.

[67] The exchange of letters took place during January, February, and May 1967. For American interpretations, see Yanarella, *The Missile Defense Controversy*, p. 138; Garthoff, "BMD and East-West Relations," p. 297; and Johnson, *The Vantage Point*, p. 480. Also see *Background Paper for NATO Ministerial Meeting in Luxembourg*, 13–15 June 1967, p. 2, which shows guarded optimism about the possibility of changing Soviet preferences on ABM: "the Soviets have a strong bias for defense, but we believe that there are some in the Soviet Union who recognize the high cost of a large-scale ABM program."

cow's position remained that "the anti-missile system is not a weapon of aggression, of attack; it is a defensive system."[68]

Taken at face value, the Glassboro experience seemed to indicate that American meta-strategy had had no substantial impact on Soviet interests, and that Soviet preferences in ABM remained basically unchanged.[69] The working hypotheses that underlay Johnson's demarche were weakened by this feedback; at the same time, public pressure was growing for the United States to do something visible in ABM. Immediately after Glassboro, there was a strong renewal of public and Congressional pressures for an immediate American deployment. In August, the Joint Congressional Atomic Energy Committee and the Senate Appropriations Committee asked that new funds for ABM deployment be included in the 1968 budget on a noncontingent basis. Believing that he could no longer bear the political costs of unilateral restraint, Johnson instructed Secretary of State Rusk to make one final demarche to the Soviets on ABM.[70] When it failed to elicit any positive response, the administration brought forward a revised ABM policy, the Sentinel Plan, which was based on a new strategy of enhanced contingent restraint.

Prelude to Sentinel: Working Hypotheses about Soviet Interests

Johnson's 1967 plan was at best an interim solution. Without any positive response from the Soviets, the administration was soon left facing a difficult dilemma: what to do with the contingency funds from the 1967 budget, and what provisions for ABM to include in the January 1968 budget request, which would be Johnson's last prior to the presidential elections. Broad support within Congress for some action on strategic defense was making contingent restraint increasingly infeasible to maintain on the domestic front without signals of interest in cooperation from

[68] *Izvestia*, 27 June 1967, p. 1; "Johnson, Kosygin End 'Useful' Talks with No Gain on Mideast or Vietnam," *New York Times*, 26 June 1967, p. 1. Also see Kissinger, *White House Years*, p. 208; Rostow, *The Diffusion of Power*, pp. 384–90; Johnson, *The Vantage Point*, especially pp. 483–84; and Weihmiller and Doder, *US-Soviet Summits*, pp. 48–53. For a provocative account by a Soviet defector, see Shevchenko, *Breaking with Moscow*.

[69] Andrei Kokoshin (Institute of USA and Canada Studies) claims that Kosygin's reaction was at least in part "that of a politician," driven by the format and style of McNamara's presentation. He suggests that Kosygin was not so unreceptive to the arguments about ABM and that had the discussions taken place more subtly and in a private forum, the response of the Soviet side might have been different. Private communication, January 1990. This could hardly have been known to the Americans at the time, however.

[70] On Congressional action during summer 1967, see Yanarella, *The Missile Defense Controversy*, p. 138. On the Secretary of State's gesture, see "Rusk Urges Speed on Missile Defense," *New York Times*, 9 September 1967, p. 1.

Moscow. But in trying to develop a new strategy for ABM, the U.S. decisionmaking system was hampered by a high level of uncertainty and resulting lack of consensus about general Soviet beliefs and interests in the strategic competition, and the relationship between these and Soviet preferences in ABM. Did the Soviets share American views of parity and strategic stability as compatible and mutually desirable goals? Did Moscow accept American theories about how to achieve these goals? The tentative "answers" Americans gave to these questions divided the decisionmaking elite into two general schools of thought, which differed primarily in their assessments of the Soviet Union as an adversary and of Soviet beliefs about the nature of the superpower military competition. These differences had clear and definite implications for developing an American strategy to elicit cooperation in ABM.[71] The two schools also differed in the type of feedback they relied upon for assessing and updating their beliefs about Soviet preferences and behavior.

The first school of thought, at once the most conciliatory view of the Soviet perspective and the most widespread within the American elite, I will label the "Garthoff doctrine." This school of thought argued that Soviet leaders, at least partly in response to American meta-strategy, had undergone a sweeping reevaluation of their conceptions of self-interest in the nuclear arms race and consequently in ABM. Having come to accept the basic logic of American strategic theory, Moscow now saw MAD based on functional offensive parity as a sufficient and desirable means of assuring security. The central element of the Garthoff doctrine was thus the belief that the Soviets' strategic buildup aimed only at achieving a survivable second-strike capability and not a first-strike or damage-limiting force. Moscow had given up any aspirations to nuclear "superiority." This had obvious implications for the Kremlin's preferences on ABM, much as a similar shift in strategic theory had had for Washington several years earlier. It also had implications for American strategy: if the Soviets now held PD preferences with a large reward for cooperation and a small temptation to defect, mutual restraint would be relatively easy to elicit with a strategy based on permissive criteria of contingency.[72]

[71] These schools of thought represent highly stylized and simplified interpretations, best thought of as ideal types. The boundaries between them were not so sharply defined as I portray them here. Contemporary documents show that decisionmakers tended to indentify strongly with one of the schools; but when pressed by proponents of a different interpretation, most were quick to admit to a high degree of uncertainty and to accept the need to hedge against the possibility that their interpretation would prove mistaken. The titles I have chosen to apply to these schools are a matter of convenience only.

[72] After Raymond Garthoff, whose writings on Soviet political and defense affairs at the time and since have consistently expressed this set of beliefs. Secretary of Defense McNamara was a chief spokesman for this school, and it was supported by a sizable majority of

How did adherents of the Garthoff doctrine use feedback from Soviet behavior to support their arguments? Much of the available evidence was filtered through a prior belief that American meta-strategy, and particularly the informal contacts among the two states' scientific communities, had led to a substantial change in the fundamentals of Soviet strategic theory. The inconsistencies about ABM preferences that surfaced in the Soviet press and in Kremlin leaders' statements were explained as evidence of the time it took for new ideas to diffuse through the decision-making system. Not surprisingly, this diffusion appeared to be taking place more rapidly and more completely within political than in military circles. There were certainly changes in the tone of both. By the end of 1968, statements from the Soviet political leadership almost unanimously supported the idea of limiting defenses in the context of strategic arms talks. There was a similar if less dramatic shift of tone evident in Soviet military writings as well. *Military Thought*, which had often argued in favor of defenses through 1967, by 1969 was populated with articles that at least acknowledged the possible detrimental aspects of an ABM race.[73] The most common interpretation of these shifts was expressed by the influential scientist George Kistiakowsky, who claimed that the logic of American strategic theory had diffused first through the Soviet scientific community and then up to the political leadership, and that this process was now complete: he saw "a substantial change of attitude in the sense that until a few years ago, [the Soviets'] position was that defense against missiles is not only possible but is also essential and is . . . an automatic right. . . . That attitude, I am quite sure, has disappeared."[74]

Other facts and observations were similarly cast to support the basic tenets of the Garthoff doctrine interpretation. Some American observers believed that slowdowns and cutbacks in the Galosh deployment were intended to signal Washington that the Soviet leadership was now seriously interested in moving toward an ABM accord. This was coupled

---

top DoD officials as well. See testimony by Deputy Secretary of Defense Alain Enthoven, *US Tactical Air Power Program*, 6 June 1968, p. 238.

[73] For representative arguments see "Commentary," *Izvestia*, 13 March 1969, which reflected the Kremlin's new line that it was now an imperative to "limit and curtail both offensive *and* defensive weapons" (emphasis added). For an example of the Soviet military's earlier position in favor of strategic defenses, see A. I. Zimin, "PVO Strany Troops in the Great War," in excerpts from 1965 *Military Thought* article in *CIA Foreign Press Digest* 949, 5 November 1966, p. 116. For a representative statement of the Soviet military's revised position, see Semyon P. Ivanov, "Soviet Military Doctrine and Strategy," *Military Thought* 5 (1969): 47; V. I. Zemskov, "Wars of the Contemporary Era," *Military Thought* 5 (1969): especially p. 59. Both of these authors argued that ABMs could not effectively defend cities and that attempts to do so would plunge both sides into a new round of arms competition more dangerous than any in the past.

[74] *Strategic and Foreign Policy Implications of ABM Systems*, p. 103.

with a new argument that the continuing large share of Soviet GNP devoted to defense should be seen as evidence that Moscow viewed itself as actually struggling to maintain parity with the United States, not bidding for some kind of military superiority. Even Nixon's secretary of defense Melvin Laird, who as a congressman had been highly skeptical of this argument, suggested that the fact that the Soviets were spending three times as much as the United States on defense could now be seen as a sign that Moscow would be interested in an agreement to limit ABMs, and not as evidence that the USSR was committed to superiority.[75]

There was a contending school of interpretation that rejected most if not all of these arguments. The "Talensky doctrine," as I will call it, maintained that Soviet strategic thought had *not* undergone any fundamental revision and that Moscow's current behavior and preferences in ABM were still being driven by the older, dual beliefs about defense and superiority. On this interpretation, American meta-strategy might have helped to convince the Kremlin that functional parity and MAD was a current reality, but had not convinced Soviet leaders to accept either for the long term. The Soviets' shift on ABM policy was viewed principally as a tactical maneuver by this school. Because the Soviets respected superior U.S. defensive technologies, they feared an American breakthrough that might throw the Soviet Union back to a position of strategic inferiority—something the leadership had worked hard to escape from in the 1960s. Preventing this scenario was naturally the principal goal of Soviet strategic nuclear policy. Thus to block progress in American ABM programs, the Soviets were reluctantly willing to arrest their own. This preference did not stem from a reevaluation of interests and did not reflect any reduction in Moscow's long-term commitment to strategic superiority. It was simply an effort to rechannel the competition away from weapons systems where the Americans could most effectively capitalize on their technological edge. Although the Talensky doctrine was a distinctly minority viewpoint in the late 1960s in Washington, it did have some influential proponents within the Pentagon and in the scientific community whose voices forced many political decisionmakers to at least take the arguments under serious consideration.[76]

[75] Ibid., p. 216. On Galosh, Senator Claiborne Pell argued that the tentative pace of construction, highly atypical of Soviet defense projects, indicated at the very least that Moscow was ambivalent about moving toward full-scale competition with the United States in defense (p. 102). York, Killian, and Kistiakowsky explicitly endorsed his interpretation in subsequent testimony. On Soviet economic incentives and ABM, see the testimony of Marshal Schulman, p. 126.

[76] Secretary of Defense Melvin Laird often expressed this view, particularly when representing the services and the JCS. Gordon MacDonald of the University of California and the Institute for Defense Analysis was a key proponent within the scientific community.

Adherents of the Talensky doctrine focused on the continuing buildup of Soviet offensive forces as the most important source of feedback to support their reasoning.[77] In the next chapter, I discuss why some American analysts in 1969 were already projecting that Moscow's ICBM program would expand far beyond the requirements of mutual deterrence according to the American criteria. This in itself was troubling; but when put beside a large commitment to deploying defensive systems that could only be partially effective, the possibilities seemed insidious to some. On this logic, the entire Soviet program was most easily understood as a two-pronged effort to gain strategic superiority based on the ability to limit damage by striking first. Gordon MacDonald, a prominent advocate of this interpretation, struggled to convince the Congress that "the primary thrust of the Soviet strategic deployment has been toward development of an offense-defense system that will guarantee the survival of the Soviet Union as a nation in the case of nuclear war."[78]

The perplexing problem for most American decisionmakers was that the Talensky and Garthoff doctrines both could be fully consistent with what was known about Soviet preferences for cooperation in ABM. The major difference between how the two schools viewed Soviet preferences lay principally in the presumed relative magnitude of the temptation to defect. On the logic of the Talensky doctrine, Moscow's perceived temptation to defect if there were even a small chance that the Americans would not respond would be substantial. This had important implications for American strategy: any efforts to elicit cooperation from the Soviets would have to include highly credible threats to reciprocate defection, and would thus have to be based on extremely stringent criteria of reciprocity.

In the political and technological context of the late 1960s and early 1970s, two very different interpretations of Soviet interests both translated into assessments of Soviet preferences that resembled the PD. Because American preferences for mutual restraint in ABM remained strong, both schools believed that the Soviets could and should be brought to a cooperative solution; and although they disagreed on the precise kinds of incentives that would be needed, there were in fact several

---

[77] Laird, for example, cited the ongoing SS-9 program as evidence that "they are going for our missiles and they are going for a first strike capability. There is no question about that." His interpretation was, however, criticized by a wide spectrum of subsequent witnesses and was described by Senator Fulbright in the conclusion to the hearings as being a personal view having "little basis" and lacking support elsewhere. See *Strategic and Foreign Policy Implications of ABM Systems*, especially pp. 196, 174; and part 2, p. 568.

[78] Ibid., part 2, p. 545. MacDonald recognized that his was a minority viewpoint; he began his testimony with the disclaimer that his argument was a highly controversial one, based on relatively thin evidence, and "at variance with that usually presented."

important points of consensus around which most American decision-makers could agree. These constituted the working hypotheses that would serve as a foundation for the new American strategy in ABM.

The first point of consensus was that Moscow's understanding of its self-interest in ABM was currently in flux. Albeit for different reasons, both schools reasoned that Washington had an opportunity to substantially influence Moscow's behavior in the arms race through some combination of meta- and traditional strategies. The second point was that Soviet political leaders and at least some of the military had given up on previous technological optimism about defenses. They now feared falling behind the Americans in ABM capabilities. Technology was thus a potential source of bargaining leverage for the United States, but one that had to be used with care. In 1969, the notion that the United States should first try to establish superiority in ABM systems "on the ground" and then negotiate an agreement was generally rejected, principally on the belief that the Soviet leadership would balk at negotiating with the United States from an overt position of weakness.[79] The third point was that Soviet leaders were now seriously concerned about the expanding economic, technological, and political costs of the arms race. So long as fundamental strategic and security goals could be fulfilled at lesser cost in all these areas, both sides seemed ready to consider the possibilities of cooperative restraint.

Most importantly, both schools viewed Soviet preferences in ABM as matching the PD, although their respective logics depicted different sets of interests underlying those preferences. This was, again, the principal reason why American decisionmakers disagreed about the relative magnitudes among Soviet preferences and particularly about the "size" of the temptation to defect. This presented a fundamental problem for developing an American strategy that would at once prod the Soviets toward cooperation and at the same time protect American interests should attempts to cooperate fail. Should the United States seek a cooperative outcome in ABM on its own, as the Garthoff doctrine logic seemed to indicate; or should limits on defenses depend on a broader arrangement designed to avert Soviet efforts to achieve an advantage in other areas, as the Talensky logic seemed to prescribe? In the short term, the problem jelled around what the United States was going to do when it came to an ABM deployment decision. The Sentinel Plan, announced by McNamara

---

[79] See Ibid., particularly the comments of Senator Pell on p. 245. Most American decisionmakers agreed that the Soviets would simply not agree to negotiate from a position of inferiority but would seek to "catch up" first, for fear of freezing any asymmetry. Also see Smith, *Doubletalk*, p. 31.

in the fall of 1967, was a careful, almost artful finesse between the consensus on working hypotheses and these unsettled disagreements.

September 1967—The Sentinel Decision

On September 18, 1967, McNamara delivered a lengthy public speech on superpower military relations, claiming that the United States and the Soviet Union stood on the brink of a new arms race in defensive systems and countermeasures. This, he argued, would be costly, dangerous, and ultimately futile. Yet he ended the speech by announcing that the United States would immediately begin production of a light area defense system designed to protect U.S. cities against a limited ICBM attack, presumably from China, at an eventual cost of about $5 billion. Most historians of the "Sentinel decision" agree that the decision to deploy *some* ABM system at this juncture was dictated principally by domestic and bureaucratic pressures in Washington.[80] Both were important factors behind the American policy shift. It was certainly clear by the end of 1967 that U.S. ABM policy as it stood had achieved almost none of its objectives on either the domestic or international stages and would have to be reworked. But while domestic and bureaucratic pressures drove a change in American policy, neither determined its precise shape or scope. The Sentinel Plan was more than just a reluctant answer to domestic politics; it was also part of a broader shift to a new American strategy of enhanced contingent restraint for ABM.

Enhanced contingent restraint differs from contingent restraint in the degree to which the state demonstrates that it has the will and capability to respond to defection, should it choose to do so. Sentinel was an improvement over Johnson's 1967 budget plan in this regard, because it included a definite commitment to go forward with some deployment of ABM. If Soviet leaders had thought that Johnson would not spend the 1967 deployment funds held in escrow, the Sentinel Plan would have caused them to revise their expectations. But in contrast with a more demanding strategy of contingent threat, the Sentinel Plan was consciously designed and presented so as to minimize the threat posed to Soviet interests in the short term. While offering suggestions about the U.S. potential

[80] Halperin, *Bureaucratic Politics and Foreign Policy*; idem, "The Decision to Deploy the ABM." For contemporary public reaction, see "McNamara Warns Soviet on Adding to ICBM Defense," *New York Times*, 19 September 1967, p. 1. For the text of McNamara's speech, delivered to the editors of UPI in San Francisco, see Art and Waltz, *The Use of Force*, pp. 503–16. Speaking of the potential that Chinese leaders might act irrationally or miscalculate American intentions, McNamara argued that "there are marginal grounds for concluding that a light deployment of US ABMs against this possibility is prudent."

to escalate the ABM competition in the future, McNamara did not issue an ultimatum or set specific criteria for a positive Soviet response to prevent such escalation.

Washington could have done more in ABM at this juncture, even in the context of McNamara's reluctance to engage the United States in a full-fledged defensive race. But instead of presenting the Soviet Union with an effective ultimatum backed up by the threat of American technology, the United States took the least provocative step possible that would satisfy domestic pressures. It is well known that this approach was further complicated by technical constraints making it difficult to design and deploy a light area defense that would be readily distinguishable from a prelude to heavy anti-Soviet defense, and there were substantial bureaucratic pressures that still wanted the latter.[81] But McNamara went against both technology and bureaucracy in a series of attempts to communicate to Soviet leaders that Sentinel was only a change of strategy, and that the central American objective—to forestall a U.S.-Soviet competition in defenses—had not changed. One aspect of this effort was to emphasize repeatedly, in private and public channels, that the fundamental precepts of American strategic theory on ABM had not changed and that Washington's preferred way to achieve its principal goal of deterrence would be to avoid ABM deployments altogether. In an additional step, the Pentagon was ordered to establish a separate bureaucratic command for Sentinel, to differentiate it from Nike-X and other R & D programs dedicated to heavy defense. McNamara also tried to limit, to the extent that this was possible, the technological "overlap" between Sentinel and a heavy anti-Soviet ABM system in developing detailed plans for deployment. The most obvious constraints came in the area of funding. While estimates of the cost of a heavy anti-Soviet system started at $40 billion, Sentinel's proposed budget was limited to about one-tenth that amount.[82]

At the same time, Sentinel did represent a substantial tightening of the

[81] Halperin argues that technology and bureaucratic politics conspired with geography to make it appear, from imputed Soviet perspectives, that Sentinel "was designed as if its purpose was to protect American cities against a large Soviet attack." *Bureaucratic Politics and Foreign Policy*, p. 304.

[82] The Sentinel speech stressed that "the cornerstone of our strategic policy continues to be to deter deliberate nuclear attack . . . by maintaining 'assured destruction capability' . . . [because this] is the very essence of the whole deterrence concept." Administration spokesmen repeated this argument many times during the next few months. For examples see Newhouse, *Cold Dawn*, p. 96; and Yanarella, *The Missile Defense Controversy*, p. 141. It is clear that some Pentagon officials with responsibility for detailed implementation of the Sentinel Plan, notably John Foster and less clearly Paul Nitze, did favor keeping the heavy defense option open, at the very least. See Talbott, *Master of the Game*, p. 103. For a revealing discussion of McNamara's efforts to undermine this option, see Goulding, *Confirm or Deny*, Chapter 7, especially pp. 224–32, 239–44.

criteria of reciprocity in American strategy for ABM. While McNamara did not set any deadline for an agreement to limit defenses or demand specific concessions from the Kremlin, he did maintain that "should these talks fail, we are fully prepared to take the appropriate measures such a failure would make necessary." The implied threat to move toward some as yet unspecified competitive options in ABM had now gained additional credibility. The Sentinel Plan called for an eventual deployment of ABM interceptors at 15 sites, 10 of which were near major metropolitan areas. Within several years, this would have furnished the rudimentary infrastructure for moving toward heavy defenses if future Soviet actions prompted it. McNamara also stressed that the current budgetary constraints on the program could be lifted if need be. The limits placed on Sentinel were thus presented to the Soviets as part of a conscious, strategic decision to forestall escalation of a race in defenses; a decision that could and would be reversed if necessary. To underscore the point, McNamara warned Moscow of the bureaucratic forces in Washington pressing the administration to move forward more decisively, and essentially asked the Soviet leaders to provide some kind of positive feedback as additional evidence of Soviet interest in cooperative restraint. On balance, Sentinel did not as yet threaten vital Soviet interests, but it did underscore American determination not to tolerate unrequited restraint for an indefinite length of time. In McNamara's words, "if the only way to prevent the Soviet Union [from achieving asymmetrical capabilities in defense] is to engage in such a race, the US possesses in ample abundance the resources, the technology and the will to run faster in that race . . . [but] what we would much prefer to do is to come to a realistic and reasonably riskless agreement with the Soviet Union which would effectively prevent such an arms race."[83]

The administration took the first concrete steps toward implementing Sentinel in January 1968 when it requested $1.2 billion in production and deployment funds for the current fiscal year. This was followed almost immediately by a new series of formal and informal American demarches that stressed Washington's continued preference for forestalling any deployment through formal agreement.[84] The Soviet leadership offered no official response to Sentinel at first, beyond the obligatory condemnations. But in a rather sudden move in May, Deputy Foreign Minister Kuznetsov announced in front of the United Nations that Moscow was now

[83] McNamara, in Art and Waltz, *The Use of Force*, pp. 503–16.

[84] See, for example, the comments of Assistant Secretary of Defense Paul Warnke, quoted by Newhouse, *Cold Dawn*, p. 99. The signals coming out of Washington were, however, somewhat inconsistent: the Joint Chiefs and some important senators (notably Richard Russell, Chairman of the Senate Armed Services Committee) continued to speak of Sentinel as the first step toward a heavy anti-Soviet system.

ready to reach a formal agreement on strategic arms with the United States. Foreign Minister Gromyko clarified his government's position the following month when he stated that such an agreement would logically include "strategic means of delivery of nuclear weapons, both offensive and defensive, *including* anti-ballistic missiles."[85] This was the first official statement of the Soviet government's willingness to negotiate limits on ABM, and it was soon followed by other indications of a new consensus in Moscow that together seemed to spell a significant change in the character of Soviet preferences for cooperation on strategic defense.[86]

The Johnson administration moved quickly to follow up on these signals. During the summer of 1968, Soviet and American officials engaged in a series of private contacts that led to a broad understanding on a set of general principles for strategic arms talks. These principles explicitly included the idea that the integral relationships between strategic stability and arms race stability, and between offense and defense in the overall balance, made it necessary to work toward limiting weapons of both types.[87] This was the key piece of feedback necessary to cement Washington's working hypotheses about Soviet preferences for cooperation in ABM. The next step, to which a broadened consensus of American decisionmakers could now agree, was to move directly to formal negotiations with the Soviet Union.[88] A public announcement that the two sides had agreed to begin formal SALT talks was scheduled for August 21, but it was canceled in the wake of the Soviet invasion of Czechoslovakia and the talks were indefinitely postponed. This did not, however, spell the end

[85] Kuznetsov's speech and Gromyko's clarification are excerpted in Newhouse, *Cold Dawn*, pp. 102–3. Emphasis added.

[86] American observers noted positively that the number of references to BMD in the Soviet press dropped sharply in 1968. More importantly, it was noted that Moscow's annual military parade did not (for the first time since 1963) include displays of an ABM interceptor. This was seen by some American decisionmakers as signaling the effective end of the Soviet military's resistance to cooperation in ABM. Garthoff himself interpreted this feedback as evidence that "views such as those of General Talensky favoring ABM active defenses . . . had been superceded by concern over the 'arms race stability' of an ABM-offensive missile . . . interaction and arms race." "BMD and East-West Relations," pp. 301–2.

[87] For an account of the private discussions, see Garthoff, "BMD and East-West Relations," pp. 301–2, and especially n. 59.

[88] There were a few holdouts. The most ardent proponents of the Talensky doctrine did not accept the idea that the United States should enter into even exploratory talks on ABM with the Soviet Union, but this was an extreme minority view. More common was the notion that Washington could afford a careful demarche, if for no other purpose than to put the other interpretations of Soviet intentions to a more demanding test. For example, Princeton's Eugene Wigner argued that a serious bid for a broad agreement could be launched; and if it were in fact accepted, he and others should and would "consider it as a sign that [the Soviets] have largely given up the hope to impose their will on us or to conquer us." *Strategic and Foreign Policy Implications of ABM Systems*, part 2, p. 555.

of the U.S. administration's hopes for achieving some progress before the November elections. Private, exploratory discussions continued between the two sides through the remainder of the summer and into the fall, although without any further concrete progress.

The signals of interest from Moscow continued to be more auspicious than they had been only several months earlier. From Washington's perspective, the Soviets were exhibiting a new-found seriousness of purpose in the question of ABM restraints. But what is interesting about the period from the fall of 1967 to the election of 1968 is the degree to which the Johnson administration acted as if the Sentinel strategy had been a critical factor in moving the Soviet Union toward a seemingly more cooperative stance on ABM. Soviet behavior did not in any way compel this interpretation. There had been signals of Soviet preferences for cooperation before Sentinel; and there were plausible explanations for the change in Soviet behavior after the beginning of 1968 apart from American strategy. For example, the technological roadblocks in Sentinel's way must have been looming equally large before the Soviet military.[89] What's more, the "results" of the new pressure brought to bear by U.S. strategy could still be explained according to the logic of the Talensky doctrine as well as that of the Garthoff doctrine. Nonetheless, the latter school of interpretation set the tone for American strategy. The problem for the incoming administration was established as one of maintaining the new momentum toward cooperation that Sentinel had presumably triggered.

Strategic Interaction

Safeguard and Enhanced Contingent Restraint

On entering office in January 1969, the Nixon administration almost immediately suspended the Sentinel program pending the results of a broad review of American strategic policy under NSSM-3.[90] In March, the new

[89] Kokoshin reports that a special commission of the Ministry of Defense was set up in Moscow to examine the problem once again in 1968. It came to the conclusion that it would be "impossible to provide defense without nuclear warheads on top of the interceptors"; and that the first nuclear explosion near the defense radars would disable them and render the system blind and useless. Personal communication, January 1990. This Soviet position could not have been known to decisionmakers in the United States, but it is surprising that this kind of explanation for the change in Moscow's attitude did not receive more serious consideration at the time.

[90] The National Security Study Memorandum (NSSM-3) and its results are reported in *New York Times*, 22 January, and 1–2 May 1969. Sentinel deployment was suspended on February 6, 1969. Nixon also turned aside repeated Soviet requests, relayed through Dobrynin,

president would cancel Sentinel entirely and announce a new American ABM program, Safeguard. Safeguard was part of a modified American strategy that shared basic elements of enhanced contingent restraint with its predecessor, but also differed from the Sentinel Plan in important ways. How did Safeguard modify American ABM strategy, and what accounts for the change?

A draft Presidential Memorandum, prepared by Johnson administration DoD officials in early January as briefing notes for the new president, spells out in a revealing way the continuing rationale behind American preferences in ABM, stressing the action-reaction logic between offense and defense that the United States still wished to avoid.[91] Nixon's strategic review, completed in early March, echoed the essence of this argument. Strategic defense was portrayed as an interdependent decision where both sides would benefit from limiting competition, but there remained substantial temptations to defect. The United States had to demonstrate that it would not accept a C,D outcome (unrequited restraint); but it was equally important that the Soviets not misperceive American strategy as itself seeking unilateral advantage (the D,C outcome).[92] Holding it up to close examination, the new administration found Sentinel to be inappropriate for these purposes in a number of respects. Because Sentinel was designed principally as a light area defense, it actually contributed very little to deterrence as viewed through the lens of current American strategic doctrine. For this reason, the new administration concluded that Moscow would be more apt to interpret Sentinel as the first step toward a heavy anti-Soviet defense, regardless of its current limitations. Sentinel also ran against the logic of American domestic politics. Johnson's scheme called for placing large numbers of nuclear-tipped interceptors near major urban centers during the first stages of deployment, a plan that had already begun to raise vehement public opposition. Finally, the vague nature of the medium and long-term plans for Sentinel did not demonstrate in what Nixon administration officials thought was a sufficiently explicit way how the future of the system would be contingent on Soviet behavior. Sentinel was a useful improvement over Johnson's earlier strategy of contingent restraint, but overall it remained a flawed program

to begin SALT negotiations; he preferred to remain aloof until the strategic review was complete. See the president's news conference of January 27, 1969, in *New York Times*, 28 January 1969.

[91] This memorandum argued that as ABMs engendered offensive countermeasures, each side would "view each other's buildup in forces as an increased threat, each side would take counteracting steps, generating a costly arms race with no net gain in security for either side." *Draft Presidential Memorandum on Strategic Offensive and Defensive Forces*, DoD, 9 January 1969, NHP Box 17.

[92] See the report in *New York Times*, 1–2 May 1969.

for influencing Kremlin decisionmakers toward a cooperative solution in ABM.

Responding to these concerns, the Pentagon developed several new alternative plans for the U.S. ABM program. These were reduced to four principal options: a heavy area defense of 25 cities, a lighter area defense of 15 cities, no defense at all, and "Plan I-69"—which called for reorienting current Sentinel hardware toward hard site defense of missile silos while preserving some potential for later upgrading to area defense.[93] The new Secretary of Defense Melvin Laird and Arms Control and Disarmament Agency (ACDA) director Gerard Smith joined forces in a strong endorsement of I-69, promoting it as a useful compromise that would provide a greater incentive for the Soviets to negotiate limits on area defenses, while not posing any immediate threat to Soviet assured destruction capabilities. Because the intermediate stages of I-69 would enhance rather than detract from deterrence stability according to American reasoning, the Soviets were thought more likely to see the plan for what it was—and not to misinterpret it as a signal of changed American preferences in ABM. Nixon too favored I-69 for these reasons, as well as for the fact that it was a more flexible approach that would allow Washington to expand or reduce the scope of ABM efforts relatively easily in response to Soviet deployments and progress on SALT.[94]

On March 14, 1969, Nixon publicly announced his decision to proceed with a new ABM program, now renamed Safeguard. Safeguard was designed for a series of phased deployments that could be postponed or accelerated depending on Soviet actions. In the short-term, Safeguard's primary mission was defense of American missile silos, not cities. Phase 1 of the program, in fact, was limited to covering two Minuteman bases and was explicitly designed to minimize any degradation of Soviet assured destruction capability against American cities.[95] These stringent limits could be lifted, however, as the subsequent phases of Safeguard were slated to include as many as 12 deployment sites for defense of cities. Nixon's conditions for proceeding toward city defense were left vague—while arguing that continued American restraint was contingent on Soviet reciprocity, he offered no deadlines, ultimatums, or specific concessions

[93] Yanarella, *The Missile Defense Controversy*, p. 171. Deputy Secretary of Defense David Packard presented these four options to the president at an NSC meeting of March 5, 1969.

[94] Ibid., p. 172.

[95] Nixon emphasized that Sentinel had been unacceptably ambiguous in this regard: "moving to a massive city defense system even starting with a thin system and then going to a heavy system, tends to be more provocative in terms of making credible a first strike capability against the Soviet Union. I want no provocation which might deter arms talks." See the transcript of the president's news conference in *New York Times*, 15 March 1969, p. 16.

that the Soviets would have to fulfill in order to forestall the move toward heavy area defense. This left the terms of reciprocity rather loose: in Nixon's words, "on an annual basis, the new Safeguard will be reviewed. And the review *may* bring about changes in the system based on our evaluation . . . of what our intelligence shows us with regard to the magnitude of the threat . . . and in terms of our evaluation of any talks that we are having by that time or may be having with regard to arms control."[96]

Safeguard, like Sentinel, was thus a strategy of enhanced contingent restraint. It was, however, a more carefully designed plan that showed greater sensitivity to the impact of the security dilemma on Soviet calculations by seeking to minimize unnecessarily provocative aspects of Sentinel. Again, top administration officials underscored continued American preferences for cooperation in a series of carefully constructed statements pitched as elaborations of Nixon's decision. These emphasized the logic of deterrence underlying Safeguard's shift to hard site defense and its consistency with Nixon's professed goals of "strategic sufficiency," stable deterrence based on parity, and a negotiated agreement to limit ABM deployments to insignificant levels.[97] At the same time, Safeguard hedged against a failure of cooperation by providing a long-term potential for upgrade to area defense. It finessed the constraints of public opinion by avoiding the necessity for immediate deployment of nuclear interceptors near cities, while promising that an American ABM would eventually defend more than just missile silos. Finally, Safeguard was offered up as a rudimentary test of the different interpretations of Soviet interests. Because it seemed so well designed to demonstrate American commitment while not provoking the Soviet Union in the short term, Laird was able to argue that Safeguard "offered the Soviet Union added incentive for productive arms control talks . . . while requiring no [military] reaction at all from the Soviet Union—provided the Soviet Union has a responsible, *deterrent* nuclear war policy."[98]

[96] Ibid. Secretary Laird later reemphasized the possibilities for restraint contingent on Soviet behavior, saying "should Soviet efforts suddenly cease, because of successful arms talks or for any other reason, the options for phased and measured deployment of the Safeguard ABM system would not have to be exercised." *Strategic and Foreign Policy Implications of ABM Systems*, p. 178.

[97] Secretary of State William Rogers, for example, commented that "if the Soviet Union indicates that they want to get out of the defensive missile business, we can get out of it very quickly." *New York Times*, 28 March 1969, pp. 1, 15. The Soviets seem to have recognized these efforts. See "Pravda Briefly Reports Nixon Sentinel Decision," *New York Times*, 16 March 1969, p. 7, paraphrasing a Tass dispatch that "emphasized Mr. Nixon's remarks that the Sentinel decision should not affect American-Soviet arms limitation talks and quoted the President as saying the US was ready to discuss limiting defensive as well as offensive weapons."

[98] See testimony of Secretary of Defense Melvin Laird, *Strategic and Foreign Policy Implications of ABM Systems*, pp. 168, 178. Emphasis in original.

Explaining Safeguard

Once in agreement on U.S. preferences in ABM, the Nixon administration faced the problem of designing a new strategy of reciprocity to replace what it saw as the flawed Sentinel Plan. The first step in this process was to try to assess the impact that Johnson's earlier approaches had had on Soviet conceptions of self-interests and on Soviet policy. In this, the new administration followed the leads established by its predecessor. Discreet contact between government officials continued to suggest that the Soviet leadership was strongly inclined toward a cooperative agreement on ABM. American confidence in these apparent preferences was reinforced by intelligence data showing that work on the Galosh deployment had now been suspended for over a year. Nixon and Kissinger were thus apt to make the same assumptions that Johnson and his top advisors had made in assessing the impact of American strategy. The key assumption was that Soviet behavior reflected a change in conceptions of self-interest regarding defense that was more consistent with the Garthoff than with the Talensky doctrine. On this logic, the earlier U.S. strategy of contingent restraint had not worked principally because the Soviets suspected they could still pursue a unilateral advantage in defense. But their motivation to do so, the temptation to defect, was relatively weak and could be easily overcome. The shift to enhanced contingent restraint and the Sentinel deployment had then played an important role in eliciting more cooperative moves from the Soviet leadership. The working hypotheses that underlay American strategy seemed to be reinforced by Soviet behavior. There was little cause to do anything more than improve on the strategy of enhanced contingent restraint.

The five additional variables that I proposed as a means of explaining strategy choice favored enhanced contingent restraint in this case; and Safeguard fit the ideal type more closely than did Sentinel. By 1969, American interests and incentives in ABM were relatively stable. The possibilities for deploying a partially effective defense had been clarified, and the uncertainties were moderate. Current technology also offered relatively clear saliencies for cooperation, which Safeguard was better designed to emphasize. American images of the Soviet Union and of the superpower competition in the era of a budding detente were beginning to favor more open-ended and less stringent criteria of reciprocity than had seemed viable in the past. Instead of viewing superpower relations as something approximating a zero-sum competition, with the Soviets apt to press for any immediate advantage, U.S. decisionmakers in the early 1970s were more confident that their Soviet counterparts shared some conception of joint superpower interests and positive-sum possibilities in the arms race. There was also greater optimism about the robust character of the U.S.-Soviet balance: gains for one superpower in one area were thought likely to be met with gains for the other somewhere else. The strategic theory of the Nixon administration reinforced this belief. Because the United States now placed greater emphasis on the notions of "sufficiency" and rough parity as the guarantors of stable deterrence, strategic theory in principle allowed for greater asymmetries in force posture between the two sides.[99] On balance, the first four variables strongly favored a strategy tending toward permissive criteria of reciprocity.

What worked against the administration's preferred strategy of enhanced contingent restraint was the fifth variable, bureaucratic politics. Even before Nixon came to office, opponents of ABM both in Congress and in the public at large were gaining strength. An important demonstration of that strength came in the summer of 1968, when the Senate considered a proposal to unilaterally postpone Sentinel deployment for one year. This amendment was defeated soundly in a 52–34 vote, but the heated week-long debate that preceded the vote foreshadowed greater opposition during the Nixon administration.[100] Public opinion, which had largely supported at least the idea of an American ABM through much of the 1960s, was also undergoing a shift toward opposition in late 1968, particularly after it became clear that Sentinel would require deployment of nuclear interceptors near major cities. By 1969, several strong public coalitions had formed against the ABM. An influential group of defense scientists joined with grass-roots anti-Vietnam War activists to organize a vocal campaign of public opposition to ABM that gained new prominence during the spring of 1969.[101] In the Congress, liberal senators who had fought ABM on economic and ideological grounds were gaining new support from powerful, centrist, pro-defense senators of both parties, who questioned the desirability of ABM on strategic doctrinal grounds as well. Less than four months after Nixon's inauguration, the opposition to ABM could claim the votes of 47 or more senators for at least a delay and possibly even outright cancellation of the new president's Safeguard plan.[102]

[99] I consider the Nixon administration's declaratory doctrine of "strategic sufficiency" in greater detail in the following chapter.

[100] For the debate over the proposed amendment to postpone Sentinel, see Senate *Congressional Record*, 90th Cong., 2d sess. 1968, especially pp. 9638–50.

[101] Particularly noteworthy was the "New England Citizens' Committee on ABM" led by Abram Chayes. This group organized a two-day university strike in March as a protest against what it called misuse of technology for military ends. See Allen, *March 4: Scientists, Students, and Society.*

[102] An important convert to the forces opposing ABM in the Senate was the powerful Republican John Sherman Cooper. Other key opponents included majority leader Mike Mansfield, Philip Hart, Frank Church, Stuart Symington, and Charles Percy.

During the summer of 1969, Senator William Fulbright and the Committee on Foreign Relations broke precedent by convening a series of hearings on the ABM issue—thus challenging the traditional primacy of the Armed Services Committee.[103] These hearings were filled with contention, some of which was quite bitter; but they were critically important in forging a consensus among the various arguments about U.S. preferences and strategy, given continuing disagreements between the two principal interpretations of Soviet interests. The information and the arguments presented at these hearings, not surprisingly, reflected and reinforced American decisionmakers' continuing preferences for cooperation in ABM restraint. What is more interesting is the way in which the controversy contributed to a stronger consensus on working hypotheses to support a reciprocal strategy, between American officials who favored the Garthoff or Talensky doctrine interpretations of Soviet interests. Proponents of each school confronted each other's arguments and were forced to make concessions to them. Safeguard opponents argued, for example, that the system would not work or would be easily defeated by Soviet countermeasures, but mostly acknowledged that it would be difficult (for political if not strategic reasons) to permit the Soviets to go ahead unilaterally with ABM deployments. At the same time, Safeguard proponents conceded that bureaucratic forces would push to expand the system toward thick area defense in ways that would threaten to defeat American objectives. Almost all the witnesses and senators agreed that Safeguard had some potential to be interpreted by Soviet leaders not as a bid for cooperative restraint, but as a signal that the United States now intended to engage in full-fledged competition in defense. Given the technological constraints and the acknowledged difficulty in communicating the nature of American strategy, it was generally agreed that any U.S. reciprocal strategy would have to give priority to minimizing the potential for such misinterpretation, even at the cost of significantly reducing the effectiveness of the defense to be provided.[104]

---

[103] See "Missile Hearing Slated," *New York Times*, 1 March 1969, p. 17. One of the unusual and important aspects of these hearings was that a number of prominent scientists from *outside* the administration were called upon to testify about the technological possibilities and strategic implications of ABM systems.

[104] A small minority (including some Army officials and several scientists, notably Edward Teller) continued to favor a full-fledged effort in strategic defense irrespective of Soviet actions. Most decisionmakers held a more moderate position and demonstrated acute sensitivity to the possible detrimental impact of the security dilemma in this interdependent decision. Physicist Hans Bethe, who opposed area defense but expressed qualified support for hard site defense, argued that it was an *imperative* to design a system for the latter purpose that would "give the Russians better assurance that we are not seeking to deny them their second strike capability." Marshal Shulman agreed that without serious efforts to reassure Soviet leaders about American preferences for cooperation, Safeguard would "strengthen

This agreement, that it was principally Washington's responsibility to worry about the possible security dilemma repercussions of its actions in ABM, was a crucial part of the cement that held the consensus on working hypotheses together. The acrimonious debates of August 1969 ended with the full Senate defeating three separate amendments to reduce funding or otherwise constrain the Safeguard program.[105] This was a critical victory for the Nixon administration, which had in June publicly declared its readiness to begin SALT negotiations. Most importantly, it was a signal that a consensus on working hypotheses sufficient to support a strategy of reciprocity on ABM had been forged within the U.S. decisionmaking system. By the end of the summer, Washington was ready to begin SALT.[106]

The SALT Negotiations—To the May 20 Accord

Moscow, however, did not respond to Nixon's invitation until late October. This puzzled many American decisionmakers, who remembered the Kremlin's impatience to begin talks soon after Nixon's inauguration. It may be that border clashes with the Chinese during this period preoccupied the Kremlin, giving adequate cause for delay. Nixon and Kissinger, however, preferred an alternative interpretation: that the Soviet leadership was stalling for a resolution of the Safeguard controversy in

---

the position of those on the Soviet side who are only too ready to argue that the US is too committed . . . to an arms race to be seriously interested in its abatement." *Strategic and Foreign Policy Implications of ABM Systems*, pp. 40, 63, 128. These arguments were widely accepted by both supporters and opponents of Safeguard.

[105] A proposal to delete all funds for Safeguard (including research and development funds) was decisively defeated, 11-89. A second amendment, to ban deployment but permit continued R & D work, was barely defeated in a dramatic 50-51 vote, with the tie broken by Vice President Spiro Agnew. A final attempt to postpone deployment for one year was then defeated 49-51. See "Nixon Missile Plan Wins in Senate by a 51-50 Vote; House Approval Likely," *New York Times*, 7 August 1969, pp. 1, 22.

[106] See statement by President Nixon, *Documents on Disarmament 1969*, p. 255. In July the White House established a Verification Panel chaired by Kissinger to serve as the formal nexus of decisionmaking for SALT. Smith reports that the most important decisions on SALT were typically made by Nixon and Kissinger, and then agreed to by the Verification Panel, whose members included Smith, David Packard (Deputy Secretary of Defense), Admiral Thomas Moorer (Chairman, JCS), Elliot Richardson (Undersecretary of State), and later, John Irwin (Undersecretary of State), Richard Helms (Director of Central Intelligence), and John Mitchell (Attorney General). The Verification Panel was backstopped by a Verification Working Group, chaired first by Lawrence E. Lynn, Kissinger's assistant and the senior White House staffer for SALT, and later by K. Wayne Smith, Kissinger's NSC Staff Deputy for Analysis. See Newhouse, *Cold Dawn*, p. 162; and Smith, *Doubletalk*, p. 108.

Washington.[107] This was a useful argument on the domestic front, but it also reflected deeper assumptions about the relationship between American strategy and Soviet behavior. Nixon clearly believed that the approval of Safeguard at this critical juncture was absolutely necessary to demonstrate that the United States could in fact carry out a strategy of reciprocity on ABM, and that this was the key to successful cooperation. In his words, "the vote on ABM would reverberate around the world as a measure of American resolve" and would have a direct impact on the prospects for SALT.[108] The timing of the Soviet acceptance of talks reinforced these beliefs.

The strategic arms limitations talks (SALT) formally began in Helsinki on November 17, 1969. The initial U.S. position was a cautious one, treating the discussions as an opportunity to "ferret out the coincident and conflicting interests of the United States and the Soviet Union."[109] Still, the first round of talks produced a striking reinforcement of the American delegation's confidence in Soviet preferences for cooperation, and tilted the consensus on working hypotheses about Soviet interests further toward the Garthoff doctrine interpretation. In fact, principal negotiator Gerard Smith reports that while he and his colleagues had embarked on the trip to Helsinki with guarded optimism, they returned to the United States several weeks later nearly unanimous in the belief that the Soviets were strongly inclined toward a cooperative solution for ABM for similar reasons as were the Americans.[110] Central to this evolution of American views was the opening speech of chief Soviet negotiator Vladimir S. Semenov. Semenov here made an explicit plea for mutual restraint in ABM, arguing that the deployment of defensive systems by either side could destabilize the current state of mutual deterrence. The Americans reacted strongly to Semenov's exposition, which showed a clear understanding of the arguments and terminology of U.S. strategic theory. According to Smith, this was strong evidence that the Soviets "had changed their minds. . . . The Soviet Union now realized that ABMs could destabilize the strategic balance." On its return to Washington, the delegation reported its judgment that the two sides now shared conceptual agreement on the need to limit ABM. The problem for the negotiators would be "only" one of working out the details.[111]

[107] "Some See Vote Spurring Arms Talks," *New York Times*, 8 August 1969, p. 12. Nixon and Kissinger's interpretation was shared by some but not all top officials in the State Department and at the Pentagon. For the alternative arguments see Newhouse, *Cold Dawn*, pp. 163–65; and Kahan, *Security in the Nuclear Age*, p. 170.

[108] Nixon, *R.N.*, p. 416.

[109] See Smith's report of National Security Decision Memorandum no. 33 (NSDM-33) in *Doubletalk*, p. 107.

[110] Gerard Smith, personal communication, April 1987.

[111] Smith, *Doubletalk*, pp. 93–94.

Nixon, Kissinger, and the top SALT decisionmakers of the Verification Committee remained comparatively cautious. This was the source of some disagreement in the winter of 1970, when the time came to make a decision about whether and how to proceed with the planned second phase of Safeguard deployment. Some members of the SALT delegation went beyond the administration's general consensus to argue that further U.S. deployment was unnecessary to bring about cooperation and might in fact be counterproductive. Nixon disagreed: in accordance with the working hypotheses that lay behind U.S. strategy he thought it important to maintain the Safeguard program as a source of pressure on Soviet decisionmakers. But he did make some concessions to the more optimistic position. In late February, Secretary Laird announced that the United States would proceed with a scaled-down version of the Safeguard Phase 2 plan. This would include preliminary work on a second hard site defense system for Minuteman fields in Wyoming, budgeting of funds for a third site to be constructed later at Whiteman Air Force Base, and acquisition of land for four additional light area defense sites, with no precise date set for construction to begin.[112] At the same time, the president agreed to support an ambitious bid for a comprehensive agreement that would cover both offensive and defensive systems, an agreement seen by Smith and others on the delegation as a maximally desirable and now realistic negotiating objective.[113]

In line with this approach, Kissinger directed the preparation of four potential negotiating alternatives for the second round of SALT, three of which included either severe constraints or a total ban on ABM deployments. In April, the White House instructed the delegation to propose to the Soviets a comprehensive package that would limit defensive systems to one ABM site each (to defend National Command Authorities, or NCA), with accompanying strict limits on offensive systems.[114] Early in the second round of talks the Soviets rejected the idea of a comprehensive

[112] See William Beecher, "Expansion of ABM to Third Missile Site Is Sought by Laird," *New York Times*, 25 February 1970, pp. 1, 30. Laird described the scaled-down plan, which would further stretch out possible deployment of the full 12-site system by at least one to two years, as "the minimum we can do and must do."

[113] See Smith, *Doubletalk*, p. 116. After returning from Helsinki, Smith lobbied Kissinger hard for carte blanche to "fully test the nature and depth of Soviet interest" in a long-term, comprehensive agreement. This reflected the delegation's new confidence that Soviet interests made such an agreement realistically attainable.

[114] The details of the four negotiating options—and the process by which they were developed—are treated at greater length in the next chapter. The "fallback" position from NCA defense, which Kissinger seems actually to have preferred for strategic reasons, was a total ban on ABM. The fourth negotiating option, which would have permitted each side to maintain 12 ABM sites, was rejected as insufficiently constraining to warrant being formalized in a treaty.

agreement out of hand. They did, however, latch on to the notion of limiting ABMs to one site on each side, defending NCA. This was rebuffed by the Americans as highly asymmetrical if taken on its own: it would have left the Soviets with a substantial advantage in defense, not least because they had already begun ABM deployments around Moscow.[115]

This was the first concrete example of what would soon become a pattern in the negotiations: concerted Soviet efforts to avoid the issue of limiting offenses, combined with repeated attempts to capitalize on small opportunities to secure marginal advantages in an agreement on ABM. Despite this, the Soviets' response was taken by the American negotiating team as supporting evidence for its developing consensus around the Garthoff doctrine. On this reasoning, the Soviets' rejection of a proposal allowing each side 12 ABM sites and their expressed willingness to consider a complete ABM ban were thought more significant. The American negotiators also stressed the fact that their Soviet counterparts had become unusually flexible with regard to details, and in an unprecedented move had agreed to accept in principle the idea that verification could take place by national technical means with a mutual pledge of noninterference. The Soviets also supported the idea of establishing a bilateral commission to deal with issues of compliance. There were additional hints of conceptual convergence that reinforced these signals. Private discussions among the delegates brought forth further evidence that the Soviets now at least understood essential elements of American strategic thought about the destabilizing consequences of defense. By early 1970, Soviet academic publications were also consistent on this score.[116] None of these indicators was by itself fully convincing. What is notable is the degree to which discrepant signals that might have pushed interpretations of Soviet interests in another direction were dismissed or recast. For example, U.S. negotiators viewed the Soviets' attempts to hold on to the Galosh system as signaling a simple reluctance to dismantle a recently deployed and expensive weapons system, a reluctance derived from ordinary political concerns and not from any fundamental strategic interests. When the second round of talks came to an end, the two sides remained far from an agreement on basic conceptual issues of how to limit defense, to say nothing of the details. At the same time, the consensus of working hypotheses

---

[115] Geography would have been another Soviet advantage in such a deal. Because the Soviets had deployed as many as 300 ICBMs in close proximity to Moscow, Galosh could provide some protection of these silos as well as defense of NCA. The United States obviously had no plans to deploy ICBMs in the vicinity of Washington, D.C. In any event, Nixon and Kissinger recognized how politically awkward it would be to propose deploying an area defense around Washington while leaving the rest of the country unprotected.

[116] See Myers and Simes, *Soviet Decision Making, Strategic Policy, and SALT*, pp. 48–54.

among the SALT negotiators had been tilted further toward the Garthoff doctrine interpretation of Soviet interests.

There were other discrepant signals that might have given additional pause. Chief among these was Moscow's continuing rejection of the principle of a comprehensive agreement that would limit offensive systems at the same time as ABMs. Here there were more definite reasons to suspect that the logic of the Soviet position might reflect some serious discrepancies between the two sides' strategic thought. One indication came up in discussions between the delegations about the conditions of crisis stability. As a result of his accounts of a rather confused exchange between the two sides on the possible dangers of adopting "launch on warning" policies for ICBMs, Smith reports that some SALT decisionmakers came to suspect that the Soviets might "not share our deep concern about the future vulnerability of ICBMs."[117] If this were correct, it should have raised serious questions about the Garthoff doctrine interpretation of Soviet interests. In any case, the Soviet position might have prompted a reassessment of the working hypotheses that were at the basis of American strategy on SALT.

The Soviets gave Nixon and Kissinger, who were consistently more skeptical than Smith, further reasons to reexamine the foundations of American strategy. During the second round of talks the Kremlin sidestepped the negotiating teams and made a private demarche to Nixon, proposing that the two sides conclude an ABM agreement immediately and not hold defensive limitations hostage to an agreement on offense. Nixon summarily rejected this feeler, but the fact that it was made at all raised new concerns in the White House about what the Soviets hoped to accomplish at SALT. Limiting ABMs while permitting unconstrained modernization and expansion of offensive forces was at a minimum more consistent with the Talensky doctrine than with the still-favored Garthoff doctrine.[118] This did not in itself scuttle the consensus on working hypotheses behind U.S. strategy. Instead it led Nixon and Kissinger to the conclusion (which they favored in any case) that proceeding with Safeguard was now more essential than ever. The most important working hypothesis was that Soviet preferences in ABM matched the PD; in this light, Moscow's moves made sense as a limited probe for unilateral advantage, a test to ascertain if U.S. restraint was actually contingent on Soviet actions. This meant that the second phase of Safeguard, like the

---

[117] See Smith, *Doubletalk*, p. 125; and pp. 134–35 for details of the exchange about launch on warning.

[118] Ibid., p. 125; and personal communication. Smith admits that he and other members of the delegation were concerned by the Soviet approach, but it seems to have had a more decisive impact upon decisionmakers in Washington. The negotiators remained, for the most part, ardent proponents of the Garthoff doctrine interpretation.

first, would be a crucial demonstration of Washington's ability to maintain a reciprocal strategy for ABM.

The White House's reasoning was not widely shared elsewhere in Washington. In fact, the context of the policy debate had shifted in the opposite direction. Nixon and Kissinger soon found themselves battling a revitalized coalition that sought an *end* to Safeguard as a result of what had transpired at SALT. The old ABM opponents in the Senate were now joined by a coterie of State Department and ACDA officials who together argued that demonstrated Soviet interest in limiting defenses was sufficient evidence to justify at least a temporary unilateral moratorium on Safeguard.[119] Kissinger viewed this as a potential disaster for American strategy. Nixon too argued that Safeguard, as a concrete demonstration of American will to compete in defense, had been and would continue to be instrumental in Soviet calculations—with a warning that unilateral restraint on Washington's part would lead to Soviet intransigence similar to that met by Johnson in 1967.[120] With an intensive lobbying campaign backed by a supportive telegram to the Congress from Gerard Smith, this proved a winning argument. The Senate approved funds for Safeguard Phase 2 by a vote of 52-47 in August.[121]

On the logic of American strategy, this should have elicited new conciliatory moves from Moscow. But the Soviets continued to push for an ABM-only agreement during the third round of talks while continually raising roadblocks about the details of offensive limitations. In a move that was clearly intended to increase the pressure on Nixon by undercutting his domestic position, the Soviet negotiators in Helsinki formally proposed the "solution" of an ABM-only agreement that Nixon had already privately but firmly rejected. This proposal was leaked to the *New York Times*, which responded with an editorial arguing that "it would be

[119] Key Senate figures included John Sherman Cooper and Philip Hart. See "Expansion of ABM Backed by Senate by 52–47 Vote," *New York Times*, 13 August 1970, p. 1.

[120] An additional consideration for Congress was growing pressure to trim the defense budget, and Safeguard was a vulnerable target. Kissinger notes that budgetary arguments strongly influenced important erstwhile proponents of defenses, including Senator John Pastore (Chairman of the Joint Atomic Energy Committee) and Representative Mendel Rivers (Chairman of the House Armed Services Committee). In his memoirs, Kissinger states bluntly his belief that "the Soviets' attitudes toward missile defense had been reversed by the start of our program." He did not accept the contending idea that a more permissive strategy with a short-term unilateral moratorium would gain cooperation from the Soviets at lesser cost, because he believed that the threat to lift the moratorium would not be taken seriously in Moscow. *White House Years*, p. 535.

[121] Smith's argument (which he reports having made only after some cajoling by White House officials), that "the success of the negotiations rests almost exclusively on our not remaining 'static' in our ABM posture," played a key role in influencing the votes of several uncommited senators, most notably Thomas McIntyre. *New York Times*, 24 July 1970, p. 1; and 13 August 1970, pp. 1, 12.

self-defeating to endanger a possible ABM agreement by insisting that offensive weapons limitations must be linked to it."[122] The influential Federation of American Scientists followed with a well-publicized proposal that the United States accept an agreement on ABM, with the weak caveat that compliance beyond a specific future date would remain obligatory only if an agreement on offensive systems had been concluded by that time. Reflecting widespread public interest, Senator Hubert Humphrey soon thereafter introduced a resolution on Capitol Hill calling on the president to adopt this proposal as a negotiating stance for the U.S. side.

Nixon stood firm. In his 1971 State of the World Message and the accompanying Foreign Policy Report to Congress, he reiterated the strategic and political reasons why the United States could not accept an ABM-only agreement. Raising the ante, he called on Congress to provide funds for a fourth Safeguard site that would reinforce U.S. strategy by sending further concrete evidence to Moscow that domestic constraints notwithstanding, American restraint in ABM remained contingent on Soviet behavior. Finally, the president set out a rudimentary test of the Garthoff doctrine, calling on the Soviets to stop or at least slow further ICBM deployments while the negotiations continued, as a demonstration of Moscow's "good faith" and more importantly its commitment to American conceptions of managed deterrence.[123]

Soviet behavior in this area had in fact been inconsistent and troubling to American decisionmakers, and particularly to the military. After a short lull in deployment of the "heavy" SS-9 ICBM in late 1969, the Soviets began work on 24 new SS-9 silos in May of 1970. In October 1970, U.S. intelligence reported that construction on these silos had stopped and was in some cases being dismantled; by December there was evidence that the SS-9 deployment program had come to a halt. Just a few months later, however, expectations of Soviet restraint were dashed by new evidence that construction was beginning on about 90 additional silos that seemed dedicated to hold a new large ICBM.[124]

The raising and then disappointing of expectations about restraint in offensive systems temporarily reversed the trend toward greater confidence in the Garthoff doctrine.[125] The Soviets had more or less failed Nixon's putative test. The weight of feedback about Soviet interests was at least as consistent with the Talensky doctrine, and it even gave some reason to doubt the continuing promise of using reciprocal strategies to elicit

---

[122] *New York Times*, 17 January 1971.

[123] Nixon, *US Foreign Policy for the 1970s: Building for Peace.*

[124] *International Herald Tribune*, 19 July 1970; *Newsweek*, 27 April 1970; *Washington Post*, 7 July 1970; and 8 May 1971. For an interpretation, see Garthoff, "SALT and the Soviet Military," *Problems of Communism* 24 (January–February 1975): 30.

[125] See Newhouse, *Cold Dawn*, p. 201.

cooperation.[126] But the negative impact of this feedback on the consensus of working hypotheses behind American strategy would prove surprisingly weak, as it was soon overturned by minimal Soviet concessions.

In the spring of 1971, the American negotiating team concentrated on pushing the Soviets toward some acceptable linkage between an ABM treaty and limitations on offense, but with no meaningful success. At the official negotiations in Vienna, Moscow continued to reject anything other than an informal pledge to continue negotiations on offense. But while that impasse continued, Kissinger and Dobrynin were making better progress within the so-called SALT backchannel that had been set up in Washington (unbeknownst to Smith and his negotiating team). Kissinger provides few specific details about the backchannel negotiations, but he does note that Dobrynin signaled a new flexibility on the precise form that the link between offensive limitations and an ABM agreement could take. By late spring, the two plenipotentiaries had worked out a compromise that was later enshrined as the May 20 Accord. This pact committed both sides to "concentrate this year on working out an agreement for the limitation of the deployment of anti-ballistic missile systems. They have also agreed that, together with concluding an agreement to limit ABMs, they will agree on certain measures with respect to the limitation of offensive strategic weapons."[127]

Both Washington and Moscow made concessions in order to reach this accord. While the United States de facto gave up claim to numerical equality in offensive systems, the Soviets formally acknowledged the link between offense and defense in a way that they had so far shied away from. But did the May 20 Accord represent any further evidence in support of Washington's working hypotheses about Soviet interests? Kissinger skirts the question, defending the accord instead as the best that Washington could do given the Soviet lead in number of deployed ICBMs and smoldering public opposition to Safeguard at home.[128]

It is true that the American leadership was watching its negotiating leverage deteriorate as the talks dragged on, and that this produced a certain sense of urgency in Washington that contributed to a greater willingness

---

[126] This was reflected in the growing influence of several anti-SALT lobbying groups outside the administration. The Committee to Maintain a Prudent Defense Policy, with principals Nitze, Acheson, and Albert Wohlstetter, was a particularly vocal and increasingly influential advocate of the argument that the United States should eschew negotiations on ABM and deploy heavy, anti-Soviet ABM defenses as quickly as possible. See Talbott, *Master of the Game*, p. 112.

[127] "US and Russians to Stress ABM's at Arms Parley," *New York Times*, 21 May 1971, p. 1; and text of accord on p. 2.

[128] Kissinger, *White House Years*, pp. 820–23. For public reactions, which were generally more optimistic, see "The Joint Statement on SALT," *Washington Post*, 23 May 1971, p. B6. For a report of Moscow's reaction, see "Moscow Gives Little Prominence to Arms Move," *New York Times*, 21 May 1971, pp. 1–2.

to make concessions. But did that same urgency drive the United States back to more optimistic assumptions about Soviet interests? It seems that Kissinger must have received some reassurance from Dobrynin on Moscow's future plans for deployment of new offensive systems in order to accept such imprecise terms as were present in the May 20 Accord. "Agreeing to agree" was hardly a concrete commitment, and the issue of timing between an ABM agreement and "certain measures" on offensive systems remained unclear. Nor did Kissinger and Dobrynin settle whether "certain measures" would extend to modernization of existing ballistic missiles or a freeze on new deployments.

In substance, the May 20 Accord did not go far beyond the previous Soviet position. For the United States to have taken this as the basis for continuing negotiations as it did indicates the resilience of the working hypotheses on Soviet interests. The core consensus was maintained: the Americans continued to assume that Soviet interests were in flux, technological pessimism and fiscal conservatism had infected Soviet military planning, and preferences for ABM matched the PD. SALT recommenced with a new, derivative belief that Moscow would restrain the growth of its counterforce-capable ICBM arsenal as part of a broader military accommodation with the United States. This belief was strongest in the U.S. negotiating team, which continued to press the Verification Committee for more conciliatory approaches to the Soviet side as a result.[129]

The trend in American reasoning as the talks progressed was thus to increasingly interpret Soviet behavior according to the logic of American strategic doctrine. This trend was usually stronger within ACDA, the State Department, and the SALT delegation than in the White House, but it gradually transformed the context of the policy debate in the United States. Simple confusion arising from apparent contradictions in Soviet behavior was one reason for this tendency. But the more important reason lay in the degree to which the working hypotheses about Soviet interests had become institutionalized within the American decisionmaking system. Discrepant evidence that might have made a difference in 1969 made much less difference in 1971. Hints that Soviet leaders might not hold the structure of interests ascribed to them by American strategic thought were either discounted or recast, while evidence to support the working hypotheses was almost systematically amplified.

To the Moscow Summit

The latter sort of evidence was not long in coming after the May 20 Accord. American intelligence in June reported that the Soviets had halted

[129] Smith, *Doubletalk*, pp. 247, 255.

new silo construction and had also apparently curtailed Galosh deployments at about half the system's projected strength. These signals revived U.S. confidence as the formal negotiations resumed in July.[130] At the talks, the Soviets quickly conceded several American concerns on the details of ABM limitations, agreeing in principle to work out strict constraints on radars and the application of "futuristic" technologies to defense. Two other signals were seen as particularly significant. First, the Soviets expressed new sensitivity to American arguments about the possible role of hard site defenses for enhancing offense-based deterrence. Second, Moscow accepted two small accords dealing with nuclear accidents and hot line modernization. Both of these were aimed at technical sources of crisis instability, an issue of great concern to the American side that the Soviets had previously deemphasized. Did this change in Soviet behavior further reinforce the basic working hypotheses behind American strategy, or differentiate between the Garthoff and Talensky doctrine interpretations of Soviet interests? Smith apparently thought so, as did other members of the negotiating team, where the Garthoff doctrine quickly reasserted itself. The sense in the summer of 1971 was that Moscow's behavior "augured well for the prospect of an ABM treaty" based on a convergence between Soviet and American conceptions of "managed deterrence."[131]

Feedback from negotiations on offensive systems was much less encouraging, with no real progress on either basic concepts or details.[132] But this had less impact on U.S. assessments of Soviet interests. In fact, the working hypotheses that lay behind U.S. strategy in ABM were now transferred in a surprising way to the problem of cooperation in offensive systems, where they were even less well supported by evidence. Facing continued Soviet recalcitrance on offenses at SALT, Nixon bucked continuing budgetary pressures and in his budget request for FY 1973 asked Congress to provide nearly a billion dollars for accelerating research and development of Trident, an advanced strategic submarine that was not slated for deployment until the end of the decade. Domestic political pressures were important in pushing the administration to act at this juncture, as a growing contingent of Washington elites inside and outside the administration became increasingly critical of the government's "conciliatory" stance on offensive systems.[133] But domestic politics did not pre-

[130] Ibid.

[131] Ibid., p. 269; and personal communication, April 1987.

[132] The Soviets continued to reject even the procedural demand that negotiations on offense proceed in parallel to those on defense and lead to simultaneous agreement. Ibid., p. 271.

[133] Again, private lobbying groups like the increasingly vocal and influential American Security Council were an important part of this trend. Secretary of Defense Laird became a spokesman for this position within the administration; by late 1971 he was calling for a

scribe Trident. The obvious alternative—to quickly deploy additional Poseidon submarines—was rejected in favor of research and development of Trident on the logic that the latter option posed less of an immediate threat to the Soviet Union while presenting a more credible demonstration of American commitment in the longer term. This was the logic of enhanced contingent restraint, and it was particularly for Kissinger a winning argument in favor of the Trident alternative.[134]

In Vienna, Smith followed up on the new American approach by informing Semenov privately that "the US will estimate USSR intentions about the overall SALT negotiations by its willingness now to engage in serious exchanges about the full coverage of offensive measures referred to in the May 20th understanding."[135] The Soviets responded with a minor concession on sequence, announcing that they would now agree to conduct parallel discussions on offensive and defensive systems leading to simultaneous accords. There was also additional movement on details of the emerging ABM agreement. The Soviets gave up some previous objections to ABM radar constraints, and advanced a general pledge to eschew defenses except "as specifically provided by treaty," which seemed to once again signal Moscow's acceptance of the principle of mutual vulnerability. Reporting these events back to Washington, the SALT delegation portrayed the movement on defense as substantive evidence in support of the Garthoff doctrine, and the former concession on procedure as an indication that American strategy had succeeded in bringing the Soviet Union toward a more cooperative stance on both ABM *and* offensive systems.[136]

Moscow's continuing recalcitrance on basic issues relating to offense did not justify this assessment. While now offering an informal commitment not to convert so-called "light" into "heavy" ICBM launchers, the Soviets staunchly avoided any explicit definition of the distinction. They

---

broad revitalization of American strategic programs in response to the Soviet threat. Laird's position gained tentative support from policymakers across a wide spectrum of the American elite; even such staunch supporters of SALT on Capitol Hill as Senators Humphrey and Cooper were becoming increasingly sympathetic.

[134] The administration's FY 1973 budget called for $942 million to accelerate Trident R & D, six times the Trident budget for the previous year. Kissinger was instrumental in the decision not to buy additional Poseidon submarines for near-term deployment, arguing that such a strategy would probably incite the Soviets to escalate their own SSBN deployments and would thus be "counterproductive, politically and diplomatically." *White House Years*, p. 1130.

[135] Smith, quoting a statement given to him by Nixon for transmittal to the Soviets. *Doubletalk*, p. 327.

[136] See Ibid., p. 336. Smith notes the American delegation's reaction to the Soviet statement: "this willingness explicitly to forbid a nationwide defense against missile attack seemed to reflect acceptance of the 'assured destruction' strategy."

also refused to accept American demands to include submarine-launched ballistic missiles (SLBMs) in a deployment freeze, at most offering hints that some other, loose provisions for limiting SLBMs might be made. In retrospect, it is clear that Moscow was simply trying to protect a series of planned deployments, the extent of which were not known to American decisionmakers at the time. Nonetheless, the Americans might have questioned more deeply than they did the degree to which Soviet responses to U.S. strategy fell out along the lines anticipated by the Garthoff doctrine. They might also have asked whether this evidence ran against the working hypotheses about Soviet interests that had now come to guide American strategy for achieving cooperation in offensive systems as well.

Kissinger, at least, does not seem to have asked these questions in a penetrating way. Meeting privately with Brezhnev and Gromyko in Moscow in April 1972, he secured a concession to include SLBMs in an offensive freeze. More important than the concession itself was Kissinger's assessment of why the Soviet leaders made it: he tied it directly to the acceleration of the Trident program, arguing that the "expanded strategic submarine program, highly visible to the Soviets," had had a decisive impact upon Soviet calculations.[137] The agreement, however, actually allowed Moscow to deploy the maximum number of submarines that U.S. intelligence projected the Soviets could deploy over the next five years.[138] What was striking about Soviet behavior, in fact, was its fundamental *consistency* in the face of American pressure. But when American decisionmakers looked for feedback they seem to have emphasized the *changes* in Moscow's position, which were often only marginal. The tendency was uneven: the U.S. SALT delegation was most inclined, while Nixon and Kissinger were somewhat less so. But together their assessments and decisions reflect a strong pattern of stressing changes over consistency in Soviet behavior, and a definite bias toward tying those changes in a causal way to American strategy. With regard to offensive systems in particular, the evidence that American strategy had been effectual was remarkably weak.[139]

[137] Kissinger, *White House Years*, pp. 1129ff.

[138] The current intelligence estimate gave a "high end" projection on the Soviet SSBN fleet as comprising 62 submarines with 950 launchers by 1977; the agreement limited the Soviets to exactly these numbers. See Smith, *Doubletalk*, p. 372. According to Smith (personal communication), the substance of the Soviet "concession" was only to include SLBMs in the freeze on a nominal basis.

[139] There were dissenting voices, including Secretary of State Rogers (who balked at accepting codified inferiority for the United States in numbers of both ICBMs and SLBMs). In contrast, Nixon and Kissinger were reportedly "elated" by what they saw as a success of American strategy. For Kissinger's and others' reactions, see *White House Years*, pp. 1129, 1151; Smith, *Doubletalk*, p. 372; and Zumwalt, *On Watch*, pp. 153–62. The White House on May 1 instructed the SALT delegation to proceed on terms essentially as developed be-

In ABM, the evidence for conceptual convergence and the impact of American strategy on Soviet behavior was moderately stronger. After some last-minute disagreements on details, Nixon and Brezhnev in May 1972 signed a historic agreement that limited ABM systems to the militarily insignificant level of two sites apiece, with additional provisions to enhance verification and guard against rapid breakout. This was the first substantial success for superpower cooperation under SALT. It was greeted by many American elites as the first and most important step toward a more elaborate regime for shared management of the U.S.-Soviet military relationship.[140]

But the relationship between the success of cooperation in ABM and the much less substantial Interim Agreement on Offensive Systems remained ambiguous. What is clear is that Washington was ready to extend working hypotheses about Soviet interests developed in ABM to offenses, while the weight of the evidence was elsewhere. Just several weeks before the Moscow summit, the Americans were informed that the Soviets were soon to test a new large ICBM.[141] Late attempts to clarify Soviet intentions in this area produced further confusion.[142] The two sides settled finally on a weak proviso to the Interim Agreement that proscribed modernization involving a "significant" increase in silo dimensions, which the United States insisted in a unilateral statement meant not more than "ten to fifteen percent." Another unilateral statement emphasized the importance Washington placed on future measures to "constrain and reduce on a long term basis threats to the survivability of our respective strategic retaliatory forces," but no such measures were concluded at SALT I. Nonetheless, Gerard Smith was able to claim a "commitment on [the Soviets'] part not to build any more of these ICBMs that have concerned us," reflecting a supposed "recognition that the deterrent forces of both sides are not going to be challenged."[143]

---

tween Kissinger and Brezhnev in Moscow. Smith, personal communication, April 1987, referring to NSDM-164 and a discussion with Kissinger.

[140] That there was a broad consensus on this score is evidenced by the testimonies and statements made during ratification hearings held by the Senate Foreign Affairs and Armed Services Committees in July of 1972.

[141] This came first through informal comments from members of the Soviet delegation; it was later confirmed by CIA reports, according to *New York Times*, 23 April 1972, p. 1.

[142] In a muddled exchange at the Moscow summit, Brezhnev first offered and then withdrew a plan to freeze silo dimensions and missile volume, which would have in effect precluded deployment of new-generation Soviet missiles. Washington in any case rejected the proposal, as it would also have prevented the United States from replacing Minuteman I with its MIRVed successor, Minuteman III.

[143] From Smith's comments at the Moscow news conference immediately after the treaty-signing ceremony. White House Press Release, 26 May 1972, in *Documents on Disarmament 1972*, pp. 210, 212.

While the Soviets had in fact made some concessions to the American notion of cooperative restraints on offense, these changes were less significant than the underlying consistencies in Soviet behavior. The Americans returned from Moscow with an ABM agreement, but without a solution to the larger problem that SALT had intended to address. The ABM treaty stood as a success for cooperation of a sort, but it was not the kind of cooperation that the Americans had expected to achieve when they set out on that path nearly a decade before.

Conclusion

The ABM story presents several challenges for a theory of cooperation. Chapter 7 considers precisely what cooperation meant in this particular case, and the implications for U.S.-Soviet arms control and cooperation theory more generally. The simpler challenge, which can be addressed now, is to explain the development of American strategies and to explore how those strategies encouraged a cooperative outcome.

Each of the five variables that I use to explain strategy choice favored an American strategy for ABM based on relatively permissive criteria of contingency. Because the range of technical possibilities for BMD was fairly well understood, both sides could predict in rough terms what future strategic environments would look like with or without defenses. Interests and incentives were thus fundamentally stable. Technology also offered clear saliencies for cooperation that could be monitored easily and without intrusion. After the mid-1960s revision of U.S. strategic theory, Washington had less reason to worry about short-term optical imbalances that were likely to develop if the United States were to pursue a less demanding contingent strategy. And bureaucratic politics, which often seemed to work at cross purposes with the goals of central decisionmakers, had the effect of pushing both the Johnson and Nixon administrations toward a moderate strategy of enhanced contingent restraint.

The foundation for an American strategy of reciprocity for ABM lay in a broad consensus of working hypotheses about Soviet interests. Although the American decisionmaking elite was divided in its assessment of those interests, the major players reached consensus around four essential points: Moscow's conceptions of self-interest were in flux; the leadership was beset with technological pessimism, and that as a result the Soviets would be open to measures that would reduce the costs and risks of the arms race; and Soviet leaders' preferences for ABM matched the PD, although there were disagreements about the source and relative magnitudes of those preferences.

At the start of SALT, Soviet behavior seemed to reinforce the central arguments of the Garthoff doctrine, that the Soviets' conceptions of self-interest in nuclear security had converged on the basic tenets of American strategic theory. If this were so, both sides' preferences on ABM would strongly favor cooperation, and the "best" reciprocal strategy would be a permissive one. Sentinel had been designed to promote cooperation by capitalizing on this opportunity. Safeguard modified the plan, making the American ABM more credible as a long-term program and less provocative in the short term. The Soviets responded with concessions on basic concepts necessary to agreement on defense, and with other moves that seemed to offer some additional support for the Garthoff doctrine interpretation. But the feedback on Soviet interests was by no means consistent. Surprises came when Moscow repeatedly probed the U.S. commitment, pushed unexpectedly hard for small advantages on defense, and refused to accept logically concomitant restraints on offense. The strength of the Garthoff and Talensky doctrine interpretations of Soviet interests fluctuated over time in response to that feedback. But there was little damage done to the broader consensus on working hypotheses between the two schools. The essential elements of the consensus were preserved, and American strategy for ABM remained one of enhanced contingent restraint.

This strategy seems to have contributed to successful cooperation in ABM, but was it a critical contribution? Contemporary decisionmakers certainly thought so. Nixon and Kissinger stressed the importance of Safeguard as a credible commitment to compete in ABM if the Soviets so chose; Nixon reports being "absolutely convinced" that without Safeguard, "we would not have been able to negotiate the first nuclear arms control agreement in Moscow in 1972."[144] The Senate Foreign Relations Committee, reporting in favor of ratification of the treaty, seconded the argument that Safeguard had been essential, because it had demonstrated an American commitment while avoiding unnecessary exacerbation of the security dilemma, minimizing the "risk that the Soviet Union will be incited into endeavors it might not otherwise undertake."[145] Even decisionmakers highly skeptical of the Garthoff doctrine seemed to agree that American strategy had been a critical factor in forging an agreement.[146]

[144] Nixon, R.N., p. 418. Kissinger generalized the argument, claiming that a properly designed "on-going program is no obstacle to an agreement, and, on the contrary, may accelerate it." "Nixon Sees Peril Unless Congress Votes Arm Fund," New York Times, 23 June 1972, p. 1. Nixon claimed that "in the event that the US does not have ongoing programs, however, there will be no chance that the Soviet Union will negotiate Phase Two of an arms limitation accord." "Transcript of Presidential News Conference," New York Times, 23 June 1972, p. 14.

[145] Report of the Senate Foreign Relations Committee, 21 July 1972, cited in Documents on Disarmament 1972, pp. 497–514.

[146] Paul Nitze, in particular, was convinced that the Safeguard program had been essential

Would a less demanding American strategy—contingent restraint—have been equally successful? Technological pessimism in and of itself might have limited Moscow's propensity to defect, but there still would have been incentives to proceed, if only incrementally, with Galosh and other defensive systems. As Soviet capabilities mounted, public opposition to ABM systems in the United States would probably have diminished. And in a continuing U.S.-Soviet arms race untouched by SALT, the technological infancy of ABM would probably have come to be viewed by American leaders more as an opportunity for the United States to exploit its technological edge than as a constraint per se. The outcome of the case might then have been mutual defection.

What of the final ideal type strategy—contingent threat of escalation? Again, there is reason to suspect that the Soviet Union would have responded in a less cooperative manner. When the SALT negotiations faltered toward the end of 1970, Moscow informed Washington in no uncertain terms that "an initiative to deploy an expansive ABM system would be an indicator that the side taking it wanted to accelerate the arms race."[147] This was more than simply a negotiating ploy. Moscow certainly had valid grounds for concern that in a high-technology ABM race the Soviet Union might lag behind. From the vantage point of the Kremlin, it would have been difficult to take the lull in U.S. strategic weapons deployments and Washington's interest in arms control as a given: past experience could not have made Moscow sanguine about the durability of Washington's (and particularly Richard Nixon's) professed commitment to joint management of the military competition. Had the United States adopted a more provocative strategy on ABM, threatening the Soviet Union with near-term deployment of heavy area defenses unless a treaty were concluded, Moscow would have been more likely to respond by putting greater immediate effort into its own strategic weapons programs than by agreeing to cooperate on Washington's terms.

Enhanced contingent restraint played an important role in setting off a cycle of reciprocity that led to cooperation in ABM. But the patterns of reciprocal interaction between the United States and the Soviet Union did not resemble the smooth patterns of adjustment associated with Tit for Tat in Axelrod's model. Why was reciprocity so irregular in this case? Meta-strategy and the difficulties decisionmakers have in evaluating its impact on state learning is the most important source of this pattern. During the mid-1960s the United States aimed to alter Moscow's conceptions

---

in securing an ABM treaty. As late as 1977 he argued in Congressional testimony that had the United States not moved forward with an ABM deployment program under Nixon, "we could not possibly have succeeded in obtaining a prudent ABM treaty." See Talbott, *Master of the Game*, p. 152.

[147] Semenov, quoted by Smith, *Doubletalk*, p. 192.

of self-interest in defense by influencing the evolution of basic Soviet be-liefs about nuclear weapons. American decisionmakers, however, found it extremely difficult to understand what impact their meta-strategy had actually had on Soviet beliefs. By 1969, the Kremlin had clearly become proficient in the language of American strategic theory and had under-gone a profound shift in its preferences on defenses. Still, the logic joining Soviet interests to Soviet preferences remained obscure. Feedback on this link, taken from public statements and private communications between negotiators, articles in military and political journals, and observed weap-ons programs was always too weak and contradictory to confirm or dis-confirm the arguments of the two major schools of interpretation. The American elite retained discrepant views of Soviet interests. When reci-procity appeared to falter, American leaders tried to construct rudimen-tary "tests" that would elicit more discriminating feedback. None of these tests was decisive; but when Soviet actions came close to failing even relatively "easy" tests of conceptual convergence along the lines of the Garthoff doctrine, U.S. decisionmakers were apt to interpret the evi-dence so as to make it at least minimally compatible with American de-signs for cooperation.

This tendency actually grew stronger over the course of the negotia-tions. The reason for this is that the criteria for evaluating feedback changed over time. American decisionmakers seem to have focused on and responded to changes in certain indicators of Soviet behavior, while underemphasizing the importance of consistency in others. They were in-creasingly apt to tie those changes to the presumed effects of American strategy. These biases further reinforced the working hypotheses on which American strategy rested. Over time, this fed a closely related ten-dency to interpret Soviet behavior according to the logic of American strategic thought. This was neither the smooth adjustment of a game-theoretic actor nor the patterned response of a cybernetic decisionmaking system.

The irregular patterns of reciprocity that led to cooperation in ABM reflect my earlier point about formal models of strategy change and learn-ing. These models do not capture fundamental aspects of the processes that intervene between initial conditions and cooperation. I say "funda-mental" because the disjuncture goes beyond simply the issue of process. It goes to the character of the outcome itself. Both the immediate nature and longer-term consequences of cooperation in ABM reflect the process by which cooperation was arrived at. Similar disjunctures will appear in MIRV and ASAT. This suggests a need for distinguishing among types of cooperation in a way that Axelrod's theory does not. Chapter 7 takes up this task as well.

5

Multiple Independently Targetable Reentry Vehicles

LESS THAN two years after the SALT I accords were signed, Henry Kissinger remarked in retrospect that "I wish I had thought through the implications of a MIRVed world more thoughtfully in 1969 and 1970 than I did."[1] The failure of the United States and the Soviet Union to place limits on MIRV warheads during the early years of SALT stands out as a critically important "missed opportunity" in U.S.-Soviet arms control cooperation, one that has had substantial and mostly detrimental repercussions for subsequent arms control efforts and the general progress of superpower relations. Can Axelrod's model help to explain this significant failure of cooperation?

Previous explanations tend to view the noncooperative outcome in MIRV as having been over-determined by some combination of technology and bureaucratic politics. Jerome H. Kahan, for example, argues that it was not until 1968 that U.S. decisionmakers began to think about the MIRV issue as an interdependent decision, and that "by that time the momentum behind MIRVs proved too great for these systems to be controlled." That momentum, according to Ted Greenwood, came principally from MIRV's multifaceted technological appeal: MIRV worked, it was relatively cheap, and most importantly it could fulfill a variety of missions consistent with the strategic and political objectives of military and civilian bureaucracies alike. Ralph Lapp and Herbert York go further, arguing that there was a full-fledged technological imperative behind MIRV. By their account, U.S. decisionmakers rejected the idea of limiting MIRV for the same reasons that they would have rejected limits on any weapons system where the United States was perceived as having a substantial technological lead.[2]

None of these arguments is fully convincing. If technological "hauteur" explains MIRV, why does the argument not apply to ABM, where the United States had at least as great and probably a greater relative edge in

---

[1] "Kissinger, after Senate Briefing, Calls Criticism of Arms Accord Surprising," *New York Times*, 5 December 1974, p. 1.

[2] Kahan, *Security in the Nuclear Age*, especially p. 139; Greenwood, *Making the MIRV*; York, "Multiple Warhead Missiles"; and Lapp, *Arms Beyond Doubt*. See also Tammen, *MIRV and the Arms Race*; and Kurth, "A Widening Gyre."

the relevant technologies? MIRV had certainly proven itself feasible, but it was only "cost-effective" in an extremely short time frame. Other technologically feasible systems were not purchased and deployed for exactly this reason.[3] But the United States went forward with MIRV, and within just a few years Washington would begin spending many billions of dollars in an ongoing struggle to compensate for the results of Soviet MIRV deployments. The problems engendered by MIRV remain unsolved today and costs continue to mount for both sides.

Can MIRV be explained simply as a mistake of short-term thinking? It is true that MIRV offered immediate "solutions" to several military missions of nuclear forces in the 1970s—most importantly, target coverage and ABM penetration. But it was not the only possible solution to either of these problems, and MIRV ran counter to other, equally important tenets of contemporary strategic theory. It was as much at odds with the goal of moving toward long-term stabilization of the strategic arms race as was ABM. All these negative features were known in Washington and recognized by the SALT policymaking elite much earlier than 1968. In this context, the momentum of bureaucratic interests behind MIRV seems somewhat less than irreversible. As always, there were choices and trade-offs. To consider MIRV as an over-determined outcome was and is a mistake. Seen in this light, MIRV stands out as a puzzle for cooperation theory. This chapter demonstrates that the initial conditions of Axelrod's model were present in MIRV, as in ABM. The five variables that I use to explain strategy choice favored reciprocal strategies with relatively permissive criteria of contingency. The United States did develop several plans for a MIRV strategy that fit the ideal type of enhanced contingent restraint. The puzzle is that none of these strategies was fully implemented. The problem, then, is to explain how the processes that Axelrod's model foresees as leading to cooperation were diverted in MIRV, leading instead to a missed opportunity.

Historical Background

MIRV stands for multiple independently targetable reentry vehicle. A MIRVed missile carries more than one warhead, each of which can be delivered to separate targets on its own distinct trajectory. This differentiates MIRV from MRV, the simple multiple reentry vehicle system, which carries several warheads that *cannot* be independently targeted.

[3] The B-70 bomber is an outstanding example. See McNamara, *The Essence of Security*, pp. 91–92.

MIRVed missiles can do things that single warhead missiles and MRVs cannot. One MIRVed missile can deliver warheads to targets that are separated by hundreds of miles. MIRVs are also much more effective at overcoming ballistic missile defenses than are MRVs. Finally, highly accurate MIRVs can provide a prompt hard target kill capability that could be used to attack an adversary's strategic forces in a preemptive strike.

Unilateral Decisions

Prior to about 1964, defense planners in the United States viewed the multiple-warhead concept almost exclusively in the context of unilateral American interests. Their first concern was with the problem of penetrating ABM systems, and as early as 1958 the Pentagon's Re-entry Body Identification Group envisioned a simple multiple-warhead system (MRV) as one way to defeat any first-generation ABM that Moscow might deploy. Multiple warheads first became a standard feature of new missile designs for this reason. By 1960, MRV systems had been conceived for both Minuteman and Polaris. Four years later the United States deployed its first Polaris A-3 warhead, a triplet MRV that could separate its RVs by a sufficient distance to defeat current-generation ABM interceptors.[4]

Building MRVs was a relatively straightforward engineering problem. MIRV, in contrast, required a qualitative jump in technological sophistication, but there were strong reasons to pursue it. MIRVs would have a great advantage over MRVs for penetrating second-generation defenses, which would incorporate powerful phased array radars and high acceleration interceptors. Just as such defensive systems were coming into the realm of technological reality, American strategic doctrine was changing in ways that suggested important *offensive* missions for MIRV as well. The "no cities" doctrine of 1962, with its stress on damage limitation, placed new demands for accuracy, flexibility, and counterforce target coverage on the American strategic arsenal. According to DDR&E John Foster, "in 1961–62 planning for targeting the Minuteman force, it was found that the total number of aim points exceeded the number of Min-

---

[4] The Re-entry Body Identification Group, also known as the "Bradley group" after its chairman William Bradley, is discussed in Jayne, *The ABM Debate*, p. 42; and York, "Multiple Warhead Missiles," p. 21. The separation between RVs on Polaris A-3 was said to be about one mile, sufficient to insure that not all three RVs could be destroyed by a single Zeus type missile, the current state-of-the-art American ABM interceptor. International Institute for Strategic Studies (hereinafter IISS), *The Military Balance 1972–73*, p. 65.

uteman missiles."[5] The Air Force responded by demanding a very large Minuteman arsenal and a new manned bomber. At about the same time, the technological foundations for MIRV were being developed by the aeronautics industry. For Secretary of Defense McNamara and many others, MIRV looked like an extremely attractive alternative to the Air Force's demands. MIRV promised a technically elegant means of fulfilling the same mission requirements at lower cost, and without unduly enlarging the number of deployed delivery vehicles.[6] By the end of 1962 the rationale behind MIRV had grown from simple ABM penetration toward a greater emphasis on expanding the number and accuracy of deployed warheads.

Although revisions of American strategic theory over the next several years would downgrade the priority of counterforce, both rationales for MIRV remained strong. As ABM-buster, MIRV would be useful in assured-destruction type retaliation; as offensive weapon, it might be capable of counterforce strikes against Soviet military assets. Technological advances soon put both capabilities within reach. In 1964, Lockheed satellite engineers demonstrated the ability of "Transtage," an operational "bus" mechanism, to launch RVs on independent trajectories with unprecedented accuracy.[7] This was the key engineering development needed to prove the feasibility of MIRV. With demonstrated technology, a multifaceted doctrinal rationale, and widespread bureaucratic support from the services in hand, McNamara in 1964 approved proposals to develop the Mark 12 MIRV system for the Minuteman ICBM and a comparable MIRVed "front end" for the new Poseidon SLBM.[8]

[5] Quoted in Lapp, *Arms Beyond Doubt*, p. 21.

[6] See John F. Loosbrock, "Counterforce and Mr. McNamara," and "History and Mr. McNamara"; in *Air Force Magazine*, September 1962, p. 8, and October 1962, p. 32. There were many reasons to want to keep the number of deployed delivery vehicles low, notably the domestic political costs of digging up vast areas of the Midwestern plains for thousand(s) of Minuteman silos. Some early advocates of arms control actually favored MIRV for similar reasons, because they expected that the number of delivery vehicles would turn out to be the "unit of account" in any future negotiations and that MIRV would help to keep those numbers low in the meantime. Talbott, *Master of the Game*, p. 98; Kahan, *Security in the Nuclear Age*, p. 91.

[7] Stockholm International Peace Research Institute (hereinafter SIPRI), *The Origins of MIRV*, pp. 14–19. "Bus" refers to the post-boost vehicle, a unit that carries and releases RVs at precise times and directions during the mid-course component of ballistic flight. It is the key engineering development necessary for MIRV systems. The possibilities for using MIRVs to mount controlled counterforce strikes were not lost on the Pentagon and least of all on the Air Force. See Sturm, *The USAF Scientific Advisory Board*, p. 174.

[8] This was not a final or irreversible decision to deploy either missile with MIRVs; McNamara also funded a large single warhead system (the Mark 17) as an option for both Minuteman and Poseidon. Irwin Stambler, "The Next ICBMs," *Space/Aeronautics* (1966):

Interdependent Decisions

The first serious reservations about MIRV had been raised by the JASON group of defense scientists about two years earlier.[9] A 1963 JASON report discussed the possible impact of MIRV on "exchange ratios" (the number of an opponent's missiles that could be destroyed by each missile fired at them) and concluded that MIRV technology could be profoundly destabilizing because it would render exchange ratios favorable to whichever side struck first. This argument was thought sufficiently important that JASON scientists decided to bring it before officials at ACDA and in the Pentagon during the summer of 1964. In a letter to ARPA, Jack Ruina (himself a former director of the agency) named MIRV the "foremost new development" in nuclear systems and called for "a systematic study of the implications of MIRV under various limiting conditions for the US and SU arsenals."[10]

These concerns found a receptive audience in ACDA, where the new arms control theories of the early 1960s were receiving the most serious attention. One important implication of these theories was that as the superpowers approached parity in nuclear forces, strategic stability would depend in large part precisely on avoiding situations where either side might have an incentive to shoot first. Counterforce-capable MIRV systems seemed to run straight up against this logic.[11] MIRV also raised serious potential problems for arms control. By 1964, ACDA was working on the assumption that the limiting factor for U.S.-Soviet arms control would be each side's ability to verify compliance with the terms of an agreement, and that on-site inspection schemes were not going to be very useful. Satellite reconnaissance was the most promising alternative, but satellites could only monitor the number of deployed missiles and could not determine how many warheads were on top. Once tested and de-

---

62; "The Text of President Johnson's Defense Message Presented to the 89th Congress," *New York Times*, 19 January 1965, p. 16.

[9] JASON refers to a group of scientists mostly from the private sector and the universities, who meet annually to act as consultants to the government on issues relating to military technology.

[10] Greenwood, *Making the MIRV*, p. 110. The letter was sent to Charles Herzfeld, deputy director of ARPA, in September of 1964.

[11] The dynamic seemed likely to work both ways, even if only one side had MIRV. A 1964 ACDA study using Pentagon computer models of strategic exchange demonstrated, for example, that Soviet forces could be vulnerable to a disarming first strike if the United States deployed MIRVs, and that this would give Moscow incentives to use its missiles preemptively out of fear of surprise attack.

ployed in large numbers, MIRV threatened to bury the prospects for substantial arms control agreements.[12]

Concerns about MIRV were also present in the Pentagon. In 1965,
Martin McGuire of the Office of Systems Analysis advanced the first serious proposal to temporarily delay U.S. MIRV programs. His primary
argument reflected unilateral assessments of U.S. interests: the United
States did not need MIRV in the short-term because the Soviet ABM systems it was supposed to penetrate were less effective than expected. But
his secondary arguments showed that the logic of interdependent decision
had penetrated as well. According to McGuire, deploying MIRV as a
counterforce weapon would be positively undesirable from a bilateral
perspective because it would incite the Soviets to further expand their
offensive forces, leading to an unstable situation where both sides would
be tempted to strike first in a crisis. For both reasons, McGuire proposed
that the United States adopt a unilateral moratorium on MIRV development and promise to continue it for as long as the Soviets refrained from
any similar activities.[13]

This was a proposal for contingent restraint. It envisioned a possible
tacit cooperation in which neither side would fully develop and deploy
MIRV. While McGuire's plan was quickly rejected, the arguments it con-
tained were given a serious hearing. By 1965, the technological charms of
MIRV were beginning to be balanced and judged against its potential
impact on newly conceived joint U.S.-Soviet interests in strategic stability
and arms control. For the short term at least, the outcome of that balance
was thoroughly in favor of going forward with MIRV. The military bureaucracy adored MIRV for a multiplicity of reasons. Chief among them
was technology: MIRV was a premier example of how American technology could make weapons more sophisticated, cost-effective, and capable than those of the Soviet Union. MIRV also fit neatly with the parochial interests of the services. Once the Air Force recognized that giving
up large warheads for smaller warheads with greater accuracies would
actually facilitate counterforce missions, and that the Minuteman force
would in fact be limited to about 1,000 launchers, it became an unalloyed
supporter of MIRV. The Navy supported MIRV from the beginning.[14]
And within OSD, MIRV was still seen as an elegant way of getting counterforce, war-fighting capabilities, and ABM penetration insurance in one
relatively inexpensive package. Arms control concerns gave little real
pause; to the extent that high officials outside of ACDA were thinking
about arms control, their interests were focused primarily on ABM and

[12] Newhouse, *Cold Dawn*, p. 70; Krass, *Verification*, pp. 103, 120, 218; Greenwood,
Making the MIRV, p. 112.

[13] Ibid., p. 113.

[14] Ibid., pp. 37–49.

not on MIRV.[15] MIRV opponents in ACDA had even less impact on pol-icymaking, mainly because they had no access. And Congress was not yet an active player: through 1965, the Armed Services Committees regularly voted support for the administration's MIRV program requests without substantial dissent, and the whole Congress passively concurred.[16]

These closely held discussions did, however, raise Pentagon officials' consciousness of the possible future consequences of MIRV for both sides. Pentagon documents from late 1965 display a new concern about what MIRV would mean for *Soviet* deterrent forces, as well as the poten-tial threat to American land-based missiles that would be posed by a heavily MIRVed Soviet ICBM arsenal. A November 1965 memorandum that was also circulated to the White House explained that if the Soviets were to retrofit their existing missiles with MIRVs, they could "wipe out our land-based missile forces regardless of whether Minuteman hardness deficiencies are corrected." In that case, "the fact that our Minuteman were MIRVed would not reduce their vulnerability." The options for dealing with this potential threat were at best unappealing: two that were mentioned were to change the firing doctrine for Minuteman "so that they would be automatically launched in the face of an attack," or to build active point defense systems to protect the silos.[17] The Pentagon remained set against any delay in the American MIRV program on this basis, but both DoD officials and the White House were certainly becom-ing aware of the troubling consequences for U.S. strategic forces should the Soviets MIRV as well.

The Controversy Begins

At the end of 1965 the decision was made in DoD to deploy MIRVed front ends on both Poseidon and Minuteman. Development work on

---

[15] Except to the extent that MIRVs were likely to be a highly effective penetrator that could render ABM defenses obsolete. MIRV could thus be viewed as a potential boon to the principal objective of arms control as it was seen at the time.

[16] Congressional attention during 1965 was focused principally on the future of the stra-tegic bomber force. MIRV was still officially a secret system and would remain so until 1967; the FY 1967 Posture Statement hardly mentions the existence of the program.

[17] "Memorandum for the President, FY 67–71 Strategic Offensive and Defensive Forces," Secretary of Defense Robert McNamara, 1 November 1965, pp. 28–29, NHP Box 19; Memo on Minuteman, Polaris, and Poseidon, DOD 1967 Budget, 8 November 1965, pp. 2–2a, NHP Box 19; "Memorandum for Mr. Bundy" on meeting with Secretary McNamara on the DoD FY 1967 Budget, Spurgeon Keeny, 9 November 1965, p. 1, NHP Box 18. These calculations were based on worst-case projections for Soviet MIRV accuracies, but none-theless demonstrate an early recognition of what would come to be known as the "Minute-man vulnerability problem."

both missiles proceeded sufficiently rapidly through 1966 so that the Pentagon set MIRV's initial operational date for 1969.[18] But while technology moved forward almost without a glitch, the opposition to MIRV on strategic and political grounds was beginning to jell. An important barrier to that opposition was broken when McNamara first officially disclosed the program in a *Life* magazine interview of September 1967. This did not immediately distract public attention away from ABM as the primary strategic weapons issue, but it did generate a substantial level of controversy about MIRV among a larger group that now included scientists, newspaper correspondents, and at least part of the attentive public.[19]

The Pentagon and the Congress remained for the most part solidly attached to MIRV.[20] But the pressures for restraint were growing here as well. As assessments of the Soviet ABM threat were revised downward, the justification for a rapid deployment of MIRVs to penetrate defenses shrunk. MIRV still made sense as an offensive weapon, particularly in the context of NATO's new flexible response doctrine; but strategic analysts both inside and outside the Pentagon were at the same time increasingly troubled by the accompanying dangers of moving into a world where both sides' retaliatory forces might be highly vulnerable to preemption. Similar concerns were already well established within ACDA, which was at the same time becoming more directly involved in the decisionmaking process as planning for SALT got underway in 1967. ACDA representatives took advantage of new-found access during interagency deliberations to present a number of policy papers focusing on the destabilizing aspects of MIRV. Some went so far as to argue that MIRV was *the* key issue in strategic weapons talks and that the United States should offer to ban the system early in the negotiations.[21]

---

[18] See *DoD Appropriations for FY 67*, part 1, p. 585 (testimony of Secretary of the Navy Paul Nitze); *DoD Appropriations for FY 68*, part 2, p. 499.

[19] See "Defense Fantasy Now Come True," *Life*, 29 September 1967, pp. 28A–28C. In an important editorial several weeks later, Robert Kleiman discussed possible strategic consequences of a U.S.-Soviet competition in MIRVs; "MIRV and the Offensive Missile Race," *New York Times*, 9 October 1967, p. 36. Greenwood notes that MIRV's impact on strategic stability was a prominent topic for both U.S. and Soviet participants at the International Pugwash Conference of December 1967. *Making the MIRV*, p. 114.

[20] It is notable that during the first open-session Congressional hearings in which MIRV was mentioned, and in a subcommittee predisposed to question a new program championed by DoD (the Subcommitee on Disarmament of the Committee on Foreign Relations), the focus of discussion remained squarely on ABM. There was almost no consideration of the strategic or arms control implications of MIRV. See *United States Armament and Disarmament Problems*, in particular pp. 7, 88.

[21] See Greenwood, *Making the MIRV*, pp. 118–19; Greenwood makes the interesting suggestion that ACDA officials may later have been willing to delete a proposed MIRV ban from the basic American negotiating posture in part because they expected the *Soviets* to raise the issue early in the negotiations.

As planning for SALT proceeded in 1968, high officials in both Defense and State began to push their own case for delaying the start of U.S. MIRV tests. Morton Halperin, at this time deputy assistant secretary of defense, took the position that Washington ought to delay testing MIRV until the Soviets' stand on offensive arms limitations could be ferreted out. He thought it possible that the Soviets might be worried about MIRV, in part because the United States was ahead in this technology, but also because of the strategic consequences that might come later when both sides had MIRV. Halperin, who was in charge of putting together the negotiating proposals for SALT within DoD, argued further that a decision to test at this point would effectively kill off the possibilities for controlling MIRV deployments, and that the issue was of such critical importance to long-term U.S. security concerns that the possibility of doing something with the Soviets had to be immediately explored. Halperin was not alone in this. Similar arguments were made on the editorial pages of the *New York Times* and in a group statement that was circulated among influential members of the defense science community and forwarded to the Pentagon in August.[22] But the military services, with support from DDR&E, continued to reject the idea of delaying MIRV tests. The Air Force was particularly reluctant to slow the only substantial offensive program that it had coming on line as it faced a steady Soviet ICBM buildup. The reasoning behind this position was that delaying MIRV might have the opposite effect from what Halperin intended and reduce Moscow's incentive to bargain. What's more, it would certainly harm the American military position should the SALT talks fail.

The services' opposition did not silence the arguments within DoD. Together with Ivan Selin from the Office of Systems Analysis, Halperin's staff proceeded to draft a plan for a six-month delay in full-scale flight tests that would permit continued testing of components and thus not delay the ultimate deployment of MIRV. This proposal was forwarded to Paul Nitze, now deputy secretary of defense, who passed it on to Secretary of Defense Clark Clifford with a negative recommendation. Nitze's principal argument against the plan was that a so-called temporary moratorium would end up being permanent, and was not likely in any case to be reciprocated by the Soviet Union.

The Halperin-Selin proposal still set off a major internal debate within DoD at the highest levels.[23] In the end, Clifford rejected the proposal. The

---

[22] See Robert Kleiman, "Delay the MIRV Tests," *New York Times*, 5 August 1968, p. 38. For an account of the genesis of Halperin's proposals to delay MIRV testing, see Greenwood, *Making the MIRV*, pp. 124–26.

[23] For an account of the controversy within DoD, see Talbott, *Master of the Game*, pp. 102–20. Selin was at the time deputy assistant secretary of defense (Systems Analysis) for strategic programs.

winning arguments against restraint came once again from the services, claiming that it would be naive or worse to delay MIRV in the vain hope of getting the Soviets to do the same. Clifford announced in a September press conference that his decision had been based on two assumptions: that "a position of substantial strength is essential and is the best position from which we can negotiate agreements . . . [and that] tests of our MIRV principle do not prejudice the prospects that such talks [SALT] would be fruitful."[24]

The Halperin-Selin proposal was a strategy that came closer to enhanced contingent restraint. It fit logically with the basic American objective on offensive forces at SALT, which was to deal with an emerging Soviet advantage in throw-weight and the possible consequences for American ICBMs. Both Halperin and Clifford seem to have thought that MIRV would give the United States bargaining leverage against the throw-weight of Soviet missiles.[25] But it was well understood that Soviet throw-weight would turn out to be a much greater threat to the United States if the Soviets were later to deploy MIRV, and in that case the fact that the United States had deployed MIRV first would be no recompense! If mutual restraint of MIRV would have been a reasonable solution, why is it that Washington chose not to even attempt a strategy of reciprocity at this juncture?

The answer to this question at one level lies in the Americans' assumptions about Soviet interests in MIRV. The working hypotheses that supported a reciprocal strategy for ABM were not matched in MIRV during 1968. Few U.S. decisionmakers expected that the Soviets might respond positively to a moratorium on MIRV tests: those who did, like Halperin, had little evidence to support their position. This argument could not contend with the more widely held assumption that Moscow would simply take advantage of American restraint to bring its own MIRV program up to speed with the American one. The failure of the United States to implement a reciprocal strategy for MIRV at this time was nearly preordained by the force of those assumptions within the bureaucracy, and particularly within the military services.[26] To overcome the momentum behind MIRV, it seemed necessary to convince at least Clifford and President

[24] Peter Grose, "Clifford Exempts Missile Defense from Budget Cuts," *New York Times*, 6 September 1968, p. 1. For reports of the debate on the Halperin-Selin proposal within DoD, see Robert Kleiman, "MIRV's First Test and the Missile Freeze," *New York Times*, 5 August 1968; and John Wilford, "A Fateful Step in the Arms Race," *New York Times*, 18 August 1968, sec. 4, p. 12.

[25] See Kahan, *Security in the Nuclear Age*, p. 128, and particularly n. 102.

[26] Greenwood argues that MIRV opponents could not convince either Johnson or Clifford that the promise of restraint, with only the weak possibility that the Soviets might respond positively, was sufficient cause to resist the military on MIRV. *Making the MIRV*, p. 127.

Johnson as well that a reciprocal strategy had a reasonable chance of eliciting a positive Soviet response, and that if it failed this would not do irreparable harm to American interests. The latter proposition was actually more acceptable to both men than was the first. While U.S. decisionmakers had come to recognize the interdependent nature of the issue and the possible long-term costs to American interests of an unrestrained MIRV competition with Moscow, there seemed no viable path to cooperation through reciprocal restraint. The working hypotheses about Soviet interests to support such a strategy were simply not present.

The MIRV flight tests were successfully completed on schedule during August of 1968. SALT fell temporary victim to the invasion of Czechoslovakia less than a week later. A few days hence, U.S. intelligence reported that the Soviet Union had tested its own multiple warhead, although the Soviet system appeared to be a MRV and not a MIRV. This issue would figure prominently in renewed controversy over MIRV during the coming years, but it had little short-term impact. The U.S. MIRV program proceeded steadily toward its next major test series scheduled for the following summer and a projected deployment on Minuteman III in early 1970.

Payoff Analysis

The year 1969 would be one of pivotal decisions for the future of MIRV. As with ABM, the American decisionmaking system approached this critical juncture with a set of preferences over alternative future scenarios for MIRV that fulfilled the initial conditions for cooperation in Axelrod's model.

Threats, Options, and Critical Decisions

The United States and the Soviet Union reached a state of rough parity in strategic nuclear forces during the late 1960s and early 1970s. Parity at this stage was viewed in Washington as having two distinct components: *functional* and *optical*. Optical parity was based on a rough equivalence in gross numbers of delivery systems. Functional parity was an operational concept, meaning that both sides had deployed large arsenals with survivable forces capable of retaliating against the adversary's homeland after absorbing a preemptive attack. By the end of the 1960s the sides were close to optical parity, and most American analysts agreed that a condition of functional parity where both sides faced a retaliatory threat of assured destruction had also been reached.[27]

According to contemporary American strategic theory, assured destruction meant mutual deterrence, since neither side could hope to gain from or even survive nuclear war. Because functional parity could not be overturned by small gains in capabilities, this in principle lent considerable stability to the nuclear relationship in the short to medium term. The long-term prospects for stability to continue on this basis were not, however, so bright. ABM systems were one important threat to that stability, and we shall see that ABM had a substantial impact on decisionmakers' calculations about MIRV. Each side had several options for counteracting ABMs, but MIRV promised to be such an effective ABM-buster that it would probably make the next generation of defenses obsolete before they were ever deployed. On this logic, MIRV promised to make a positive contribution to strategic stability by reinforcing the condition of offense-dominance that lay behind MAD.

But MIRV was also part of the growing counterforce potential of ICBMs, which posed a second serious threat to functional parity. New-generation missiles on both sides promised a combination of accuracy and throw-weight that would make preemptive counterforce strikes against the other side's missiles possible. With MIRV warheads, the counterforce threat would be multiplied manyfold. That was by no means the end of central deterrence, since partial vulnerability of land-based missiles did not in the short-term render the threat of assured destruction less convincing. Washington's SLBM arsenal could by itself mount a devastating strike against Soviet cities in return for any attack on the United States. But the possibility that U.S. ICBMs might become much more vulnerable than Soviet missiles did pose a more immediate problem for extended deterrence in Europe based on flexible response. The argument was that U.S. forces had to be capable of limited and discriminate counterforce strikes against Soviet forces in response to a conflict in Europe, and that only land-based ICBMs were suited to this mission.

While the counterforce issue never attained political prominence comparable to ABM in the 1960s, American strategic planners quite early recognized that a potentially serious "Minuteman vulnerability problem"

[27] The Soviet Union remained behind the United States in numbers of heavy bombers, but by 1969 the Soviets had deployed just over 1,000 ICBMs as part of a steady program that would bring their force to approximately 1,600 launchers in 1972. Moscow's new-generation missiles were deployed in hardened silos. They used storable liquid fuel and had cold-launch capability. The sea-based leg of the Soviet triad was undergoing comparable operational improvements: the modern "Yankee" class nuclear submarine, carrying the 2,400 km. range SS-N-6 SLBM, was first deployed in 1968. See IISS, *The Military Balance 1971–72.*

might be emerging toward the end of the decade. Pentagon analysts developed a number of different options for responding to this threat, which ranged along a theoretical continuum from unilateral cooperative measures to highly competitive options that would pose serious new threats to Soviet security interests. MIRV was just one of these options; but as we shall see in a few pages, it was neither the most efficient nor the most stabilizing, and it had recognized potential to be extremely provocative to the Soviet Union.

These emerging threats to the stability of mutual deterrence coalesced with political factors to make the late 1960s and early 1970s a period of critical decisions for the future of MIRV. Because MIRV was the only major U.S. offensive weapons program near deployment at the time, it took on symbolic value vis-à-vis the Soviets as a demonstration of U.S. determination not to fall victim to complacency during SALT. A similar argument pitched at the domestic level saw MIRV as a way of gaining the Pentagon's support for any agreements that might come out of negotiations. Finally, decisionmakers who focused principally on strategic defense as *the* threat to stability were reluctant to risk squandering the possibility of an ABM agreement over the seemingly less important and less tractable issue of MIRV.

Technological factors were, however, most important in bringing MIRV to a key decisional point. Verification was the central issue: no one knew how the number of deployed MIRV warheads could be monitored, short of intrusive on-site inspection measures that neither side was ready to consider. American analysts believed that verification was ultimately going to depend upon national technical means and particularly on satellites, and as a result argued that "only if the MIRV programs were stopped before extensive *testing* had been done was there any hope of including them in any future arms control agreements."[28] This relationship between testing, deployment, and arms control became a matter of increasing public controversy as Washington and Moscow inched toward SALT. In June 1969 a *New York Times* editorial calling for a delay in the test program argued that "MIRV can only be headed off in the test stage, since tests can be detected with relative assurance. Once deployed, MIRV can only be detected by on-site inspection more intrusive than even the United States, not to mention the Soviet Union, would be likely to accept."[29] Some congressmen believed that MIRV deployment would place limitations on offensive systems entirely out of reach and undermine the prospects for any SALT accord at all. This was an extreme position, but it was widely understood in Washington that a decision to continue the

[28] Greenwood, *Making the MIRV*, p. 193.
[29] *New York Times*, 12 June 1969, p. 14.

test series was equivalent to a decision to deploy, and that the two together would probably foreclose the option of limiting MIRV in the context of SALT.[30]

An Iterated Game, With a Long Shadow of the Future

As in ABM, the "objective conditions" that made the superpower competition like an iterated game were strongly reflected in decisionmakers' arguments about MIRV. The Nixon administration's efforts to incorporate the implications of nuclear parity into a new plan for managing the superpower relationship illustrate one aspect of this perception as it evolved around the turn of the decade. President Nixon was the first U.S. leader to openly acknowledge and accept the concept of nuclear parity: his doctrine of "strategic sufficiency" rested on the case that functional parity was a condition consistent with American security interests.[31] To be sure, strategic sufficiency was not always well defined in operational terms. When it was equated with offensive parity and deterrence based on mutual vulnerability, sufficiency was consistent with cooperative management of the nuclear competition through SALT. Almost by necessity, this would have extended to constraints on MIRV. But the need to shore up the credibility of extended deterrence, a persistent problem for American strategic doctrine, at times generated strong pressures against accepting this definition of sufficiency. Sufficiency, in operational terms, could also mean "the maintenance of forces adequate to prevent us *and our allies* from being coerced."[32]

In this light, MIRV could have been seen as offering an immediate advantage to U.S. strategic forces that would have reinforced the credibility of extended deterrence. That might have been decisive had the Soviet threat to Europe seemed urgent and American decisionmakers' shadow of the future correspondingly short. At the turn of the decade, however, the "extended deterrence dilemma" was at a nadir. The politics of emerging detente had taken precedence over nuclear strategy. Particularly im-

[30] In support of the more extreme argument, Congressman Jonathan Bingham quoted administration officials "who consider the development of MIRV, of an operational MIRV, as a kind of point of no return in terms of the feasibility of achieving agreement in the SALT talks." *Diplomatic and Strategic Impact of Multiple Warhead Missiles*, p. 15.

[31] "The President's News Conference of January 27, 1969," *Presidential Documents*, vol. 5 (February 3, 1969), p. 178.

[32] See Freedman, *The Evolution of Nuclear Strategy*, p. 31 (emphasis added). Nixon described the principle behind strategic sufficiency differently, as the recognition by both sides that "there is a point in arms development at which each nation has the capacity to destroy the other. Beyond that point, the most important consideration is not continued escalation of the number of arms but maintenance of the strategic equilibrium." Nixon, *R.N.*, p. 415.

portant in this was a set of multilateral agreements completed during the early 1970s, including the Berlin Quadripartite Agreement and later the Helsinki Accords, which in effect codified the postwar settlement and pushed the specter of conflict in Europe further into the background. To be sure, nuclear strategists continued to struggle with abstract arguments about the credibility of extended deterrence; but for political decision-makers the action was elsewhere. Detente presupposed a willingness to engage the Soviet Union in a long-term relationship of managed competition and coexistence in military, political, and economic spheres. Because American decisionmakers did not believe that political detente could coexist with unregulated military competition, SALT became a linchpin for detente.[33] Both rested on a long-term view of the superpowers' nuclear relationship comparable to an iterated game with a long shadow of the future.

PD Preferences

MIRV technology and constraints on verification combined to confront decisionmakers with what was in essence a dyadic choice for the future of this weapons system. The cooperative option was to refrain from further tests of MIRV that would make widespread deployment a nearly inevitable conclusion. The competitive option was to move forward with MIRV and hasten its deployment. Assuming that the Soviets would soon face a comparable choice, American decisionmakers again confronted a 2×2 matrix with four potential outcomes for MIRV. Comparing strategic, military, and political arguments about the desirability of each of these outcomes, Washington developed a consensus on preferences for MIRV that matched the PD.

D,C THE TEMPTATION TO DEFECT

In this scenario the United States proceeds to deploy MIRV while the Soviets do not. If this outcome could have been sustained as a result of a deliberate choice by the Kremlin not to deploy MIRV or more likely of the inability of Soviet scientists to provide the technology, it would have been the most desirable from Washington's perspective. American MIRVs would answer the challenge of current Soviet defenses and promote the resolution of an ABM treaty to limit further efforts. MIRV would also satisfy the demands of American war planners for covering an expanding target list with smaller and more accurate warheads. While

[33] Weber, "Realism, Detente, and Nuclear Weapons," pp. 66–67.

MIRV would do nothing to reduce the vulnerability of American ICBMs per se, missiles armed with MIRV that survived a preemptive strike would carry a much more potent retaliatory punch.

These strategic considerations were reinforced in the minds of some American decisionmakers by a perceptual link between MIRV and evolving concepts of nuclear "superiority." MIRV, much more so than ABM, was a symbol of the United States' technological edge; and that qualitative advantage seemed progressively more important as the Soviets caught up and passed the Americans in one after another quantitative measure of the strategic balance. Apart from arguments about optical parity, this was an important consideration because of the possible connections between extended deterrence and measures of "relative vulnerability," or the comparative damage that U.S. and Soviet nuclear forces could do to each other's societies at any point during a nuclear war. Because this balance *might* make a difference in the way decisionmakers would behave in a crisis, it could hardly hurt the United States, with its greater demands of extended deterrence, to "use" MIRV to come out on top.[34]

The magnitude of the temptation was, however, sharply reduced in contemporary decisionmakers' perceptions by a number of cross-cutting factors. Chief among these were the steps toward superpower detente and the ongoing stabilization of the security situation in Europe. Another was changing perceptions of the efficacy of nuclear forces: American decisionmakers were at this time becoming more united in the belief that nuclear weapons were useful for deterrence and not much more, so that nuclear "superiority" promised little in the way of political payoffs.[35] Finally, there was a growing recognition in Washington that "action-reaction" patterns in previous rounds of the U.S.-Soviet arms race had led to undesirable outcomes in the past, and might do so again in MIRV. A common argument was that the ABM and counterforce "gaps" of the late 1960s would turn out to be as illusory as the "missile gap" of a decade earlier, and that the present American response of pushing forward with MIRV would prove to be unnecessarily hasty. Any advantage to the United States of a leading position in MIRV that might come in the interim years before the Soviets deployed comparable systems, was likely to be ephemeral.[36]

[34] Paul Nitze later wrote the most elegant exposition of the argument; see "Assuring Stability in an Era of Detente," *Foreign Affairs* 54 (1976): 207–32.

[35] For an equally eloquent exposition of this argument, see the testimony of Herbert York before the Senate Committee on Armed Services in *DoD Authorization for Appropriations for FY 70*, part 1, p. 1119.

[36] In his opening statement to the June 1969 hearings, *Diplomatic and Strategic Impact of Multiple Warhead Systems*, Congressman Jonathan Bingham argued that MIRV had been conceived as a response to "the *now obsolete* Soviet Galosh system" (emphasis added), and should therefore be postponed if not canceled. This sentiment was echoed in the popular press. The *Washington Post* in particular stressed that previous action-reaction cycles had

C,D THE SUCKER'S PAYOFF FOR UNREQUITED COOPERATION

The C,D outcome represents a scenario in which the United States post-pones or halts its MIRV program, while the Soviets move ahead toward deployment. For both military and political reasons, American decision-makers pictured this outcome as least desirable. Arguments about the short-term military costs of unrequited restraint emphasized the problem of extended deterrence: how could the United States credibly threaten to use nuclear weapons if the Soviet arsenal were larger, more capable, and more flexible? Some military officials went further than this to suggest that the increasing vulnerability of U.S. ICBMs would pose an immediate problem for central deterrence in the event of a crisis. If left without MIRV, the United States would have difficulty mounting a retaliatory strike against remaining Soviet forces in the wake of a partial counter-force attack.[37] This would leave the U.S. president with the untenable option of retaliating against cities. Asymmetric vulnerability could thus seriously degrade crisis stability by offering up the Minuteman force as a tempting target for MIRVed Soviet ICBMs, with some hope that the United States would be paralyzed in its response.

The perceived immediacy of these threats was, however, buffered for the majority of American elites by the technological lead in MIRV. Ad-ministration officials answered the more extreme position with the argu-ment that the United States could "tolerate a delay in our MIRV deploy-ment without sacrificing any national security interest" because the potential threats against which MIRV was directed could not materialize quickly. The problem in military terms was really to insure that the nec-essary lead time was preserved, meaning that any temporary restraint could not be unwittingly perpetuated should the Soviets fail to recipro-cate.[38]

This relative complacency about short-term military costs did not,

led to unnecessary exacerbation of the arms race in ABM and other systems, and that MIRV was likely to do the same. Richard Harwood and Laurence Stern, "MIRV Seen Adding to 'Mad Momentum,' " *Washington Post*, 22 June 1969, pp. 1, 6. Kahan notes regarding the MIRV program, "a concern that reached great intensity when the Nixon administration entered office . . . that America's qualitative lead might soon be challenged." *Security in the Nuclear Age*, p. 116. There seems to have been little confidence in Washington that the United States could maintain a meaningful advantage in MIRV technologies for more than just a few years.

[37] Nuclear strategists call this scenario "second-strike counterforce"; the idea being that two sides could engage in a counterforce war of attrition with a series of limited strikes against each other's military forces. Nixon's notion of maintaining "flexible options" for employing nuclear weapons under the doctrine of strategic sufficiency encompassed the idea of second-strike counterforce. See Kahan, *Security in the Nuclear Age*, pp. 159–61; and Nixon, *US Foreign Policy For the 1970s: Building for Peace*, pp. 170–73.

[38] See the comments of Congressman Jeffery Cohelan, *Diplomatic and Strategic Impact of Multiple Warhead Missiles*, p. 37.

however, extend to arguments about the possible political consequences of unrequited restraint. At a minimum, unilateral restraint in MIRV promised all the undesirable political repercussions that Kissinger and Nixon foresaw for a similar outcome in ABM. The Joint Chiefs were particularly adamant about the impact of the worsening optical imbalance in *offensive* capabilities, arguing that a "mere appearance of Soviet strategic superiority could have a debilitating effect on our foreign policy."[39] Nixon too expected the Kremlin to make "bolder challenges" against American positions if Soviet leaders thought the United States appeared unwilling to respond to the expanding Soviet nuclear arsenal. To unilaterally restrain the MIRV program while Moscow continued its relentless ICBM deployment program would be a strong indication of American "weakness" that could only incite Soviet adventurism and further sap Washington's negotiating power at SALT. The C,D scenario was thus the least acceptable outcome for U.S. interests, especially from a political perspective.

C,C THE REWARD FOR MUTUAL COOPERATION

The C,C outcome represents a scenario in which both the United States and the Soviet Union do not deploy MIRVs. Although bureaucratic pressures from the military pushed against this outcome because of reluctance to limit American MIRVs, the consensus among top decisionmakers was that a world without MIRV was preferable from the standpoint of American interests to a world in which both sides had the weapon.

Cooperation in MIRV promised major military payoffs in crisis stability and in the possibilities for arms control. Because the evolving "SALT model" envisioned a series of formal agreements with numerical limits on delivery systems to be verified by national technical means, it virtually required constraints on MIRV as a prerequisite. The reason was that land-based ICBMs were of all modern delivery systems the easiest to count and thus the easiest to constrain under SALT. But if either side could deploy vast numbers of warheads on top of a limited arsenal of delivery vehicles, SALT was hardly worth the effort. On the other hand, a world without MIRV was also a world in which a formal SALT treaty could provide useful long-term assurances. If ICBMs were limited to one warhead each, a key goal of SALT—to establish boundaries around potential future threats—would be brought within reach. Banning MIRV would also remove a principal threat to crisis stability in the 1970s. In a world without competent ABM systems and without MIRV, neither side

---

[39] Admiral Thomas Moorer, Chairman of the JCS, in testimony before the Senate Armed Services Committee, *US Military Posture for FY 73*, pp. 505–6.

would have incentive to strike first in a superpower crisis. The promise of MAD would guarantee a robust deterrent for both sides under foreseeable conditions long into the future.

But what if ABM systems were not effectively constrained? Could Washington still be confident of its ability to destroy Soviet cities if it gave up MIRV? In fact, it could. We shall see later that U.S. assessments of the Soviet ABM threat were continuously downgraded during the 1960s, progressively detracting from the perceived need to deploy MIRV as an ABM-buster. At the same time, U.S. defense scientists were developing other ways of penetrating defenses. The conclusions of the 1965 Pen-X study, that "small multiples were the highest confidence, offense conservative, approach to defeating terminal defenses," were no longer dogma in 1969. Alternative penetration techniques—chaff, decoys, and the use of special targeting strategies with "precursor" blasts to disable ABM radars—were thought to be equally efficacious and in some cases less expensive. Because these alternatives did not pose new threats to Soviet forces, they were in all cases less provocative than MIRV.[40]

Giving up MIRV would have also meant sacrificing one method of reducing the consequences of Minuteman vulnerability. But placing many warheads on each missile was certainly not the most attractive or efficient way to deal with the problem. In fact, the Pentagon's 1966 Strat-X study concluded that MIRV was one of the *least* effective responses to ICBM vulnerability. The reasoning was quite simple. MIRV did nothing to enhance the survivability of individual ICBMs. If and when the Soviets deployed their own MIRVs in response, the vulnerability problem would be severely exacerbated and the United States would be worse off than ever. There were other unilateral measures open to Washington that were less likely to escalate the arms race, including the development of mobile land-based missiles, more sophisticated sea-based systems, and superhardening of Minuteman silos. As for bilateral measures, banning MIRV entirely would do more to enhance the survivability of U.S. ICBMs than any other single measure. With intelligence estimates predicting that Soviet ICBM deployments would level off at a number roughly equal to that of the U.S. force, it seemed that the counterforce threat could be kept within predictable bounds so long as each missile carried only one warhead. MIRV, however, would completely change the equation to the ultimate detriment of the United States.

Giving up MIRV would have forced Washington to make increasingly

[40] Quoted by Greenwood, *Making the MIRV*, p. 40. Pen-X was a major 1965 study of various means for defeating defenses against ballistic missiles. The changing consensus on penetration later in the decade is described by Rathjens, *The Future of the Strategic Arms Race*, pp. 17ff. Also see *Third Report of the Defense Science Board Task Force on Penetration*, 15 September 1967, NHP Box 19.

difficult choices about targeting. For some decisionmakers, particularly those concerned with the credibility of extended deterrence, the ability to avoid those choices and cover more targets was the primary argument in favor of MIRV. But it was not an entirely convincing one. Unless the United States could maintain a significant lead in MIRV technologies, the Soviets would be able in just a few years to cover a similar range of targets in the United States. Whatever advantage might accrue to the United States in the interim would be superseded as the Soviets MIRVed. Even according to the "relative vulnerability" logic of Nitze and others, extended deterrence would be no less credible in a world without MIRV than in a world where both sides had MIRV. MIRV, in short, did not get to the root of the ICBM vulnerability problem and did not really address its consequences in a useful way. It would, in fact, make the problem considerably worse within just a few years. Cooperative restraint made good sense from a strictly military and strategic perspective.

Political perspectives cut in the same direction. It is true that MIRV did not become a watershed political issue between the superpowers in the way that ABM did in the 1960s, and as a result it was less tightly linked in the perception of contemporary decisionmakers to the *immediate* prospects for detente. Placing effective limits on offensive systems was, however, recognized to be a necessary step for *maintaining* detente. Cooperation in banning MIRV for this reason promised substantial political payoffs. In addition, it suggested a more constructive role for the U.S. technological edge. Linking constraints on MIRV to Soviet ICBM deployments could establish an important precedent for trades: the U.S. technological lead against the developing Soviet advantage in numbers. Restraining both would be a tremendous boon to the prospects for political detente. And if it could be done without explicit bilateral agreements as the Halperin-Selin proposal had suggested, neither side would have to take the politically difficult step of acknowledging up front that it was sacrificing its traditional strengths for the benefits of superpower cooperation.

D,D THE PUNISHMENT FOR MUTUAL DEFECTION

The D,D outcome represents a scenario in which both sides push forward with testing and deployment of MIRV. All but MIRV's most ardent disciples within the Pentagon recognized that a decision to proceed in this direction would have interactive consequences with Soviet choices, and that the troubling implications of competing deployments would have to be faced. Comparing arguments about American security interests in a world with and without MIRV, the decisionmaking system developed a consensus that viewed mutual defection as a less desirable outcome than cooperative restraint. Despite the continuing reservations of the military, this preference became the basis for future debates about American strategy in MIRV.

Military considerations were in fact the major disincentive to a full-fledged MIRV competition. If Washington were to deploy MIRV, the Soviets could be expected to respond almost immediately by expanding their ongoing missile deployment program from production lines that were already "hot." Within just a few years (estimates ranged from a minimum of two to a maximum of about five), the Soviets would have their own MIRVs and could proceed to retrofit a much larger, modern arsenal of heavy ballistic missiles with the weapon. The Minuteman arsenal would then be at far greater risk than in a world without MIRV. The immediate costs would come in the area of crisis stability. The prospects for continuing cooperation on ABM would also decline as pressures mounted for point defenses to protect land-based missiles. Clearly, a growing MIRV-based counterforce threat could not in the long run co-exist with meaningful arms control on the SALT model.

All of these potential consequences were known to American decision-makers in 1969. This was partly a result of the fact that MIRV had become closely associated with increasingly popular action-reaction explanations for the arms race during the previous few years.[41] Action-reaction logic was particularly compelling when it came to forecasting the consequences of a competition in counterforce. Soon after leaving office as secretary of defense, McNamara stated publicly that because of the Soviet reaction it would provoke, "MIRV potentially is even more destabilizing than the ABM." The call went out from the scientific community as well: George Rathjens wrote in 1969 that "the most serious threat to the present stability is the possibility of the development of systems for delivering several warheads from a single booster." The editors of the *New York Times* opposed MIRV as "an expansion . . . in the American strategic missile forces . . . that the Soviet Union would doubtless match," rendering the Minuteman force more vulnerable than ever to Soviet attack: "the irony is that . . . each SS-9 could carry three five megaton warheads, each of which, with an accuracy of a quarter of a mile, could destroy a Min-

---

[41] While the action-reaction argument had an early and profound influence within ACDA and in limited circles at DoD, by 1969 it had come to constitute an "accepted wisdom" within the mainstream community of defense scientists and other key advisors to the administration. Herbert Scoville, George Rathjens, and George Kistiakowsky were three of the most vocal proponents of this argument. By the turn of the decade, many action-reaction thinkers saw MIRV (and not ABM) as the key strategic issue threatening to undermine hopes of stabilizing the U.S.-Soviet deterrent relationship through arms control. See, for example, Rathjens and Kistiakowsky, "Strategic Arms Limitation."

uteman silo. But . . . American MIRVs . . . would be too small with present accuracies to be used against underground Soviet missiles."[42]

This burst of opposition to MIRV prompted a series of Congressional
hearings in the summer of 1969 that provided MIRV opponents with unprecedented opportunities to bring their arguments to the fore of the policy debate. The tone of the hearings was set with Congressman Bingham's
opening comment that "each increase in the total capability of either nation sets off a counter-reaction, allowing no more than a fleeting gain by
either side." Following on this logic, Congressman Cohelan identified
"the greatest current threat to the U.S. strategic deterrent as the possibility that the Soviets may deploy missiles with multiple warheads capable
of destroying a large fraction of our land-based forces in a first strike."
But the lawmakers' concerns were not limited to the vulnerability of
American missiles. Throughout the hearings, congressmen and administration officials demonstrated an unusual sensitivity to the immediate and
very serious consequences for the Soviet Union of threatening Moscow's
most valued strategic forces with American MIRVs. It was expected that
the Soviets would respond vigorously to this threat, although decisionmakers differed over precisely what form the Soviet response would take.
But even the most ardent supporters of MIRV, including representatives
from the JCS, acknowledged that the Soviets could respond in short order
by deploying a much more threatening MIRVed arsenal of their own. If
that were to happen, the United States would be compelled to respond in
turn with an expensive and complicated restructuring of its strategic arsenal. Arms control under SALT would be rendered obsolete.[43]

Given this grim recognition, the most compelling military argument
that could still be made in favor of a MIRV race was that as the Soviets
caught up in first-generation MIRVs, the United States would have
moved on to a more capable second-generation system, and that a series
of such technological "leapfrogs" could sustain an American advantage
over the long-term. While Washington did hold a lead in MIRV at the
moment, this argument was not very convincing. MIRV was a technology
approaching a plateau: once the warheads achieved a combination of
yield and accuracy sufficient to destroy hardened targets, additional in-
crements in technology would add only marginally to the military utility
of the weapon. It would become more and more difficult for the United
States to "stay ahead" in MIRV. If it were applicable anywhere, the
"leapfrog" argument made more sense for ABM, where technology was

[42] McNamara quoted in "McNamara Offers Missile Curb Plan," *New York Times*, 8
September 1968, pp. 1, 12. Rathjens, *The Future of the Strategic Arms Race*, p. 17; "Moratorium on MIRV," *New York Times*, 12 June 1969, p. 46.

[43] *Diplomatic and Strategic Implications of Multiple Warhead Missiles*, pp. 1–2, 32; also
see pp. 35 ff.

still immature and remained less than fully capable of fulfilling the system's basic mission.

The political costs of mutual defection in MIRV were also expected to be substantial. Although it was ABM and not MIRV that early on became the symbolic test case for arms control cooperation in the 1970s, Nixon, Kissinger, and other key decisionmakers across the spectrum of SALT supporters and skeptics recognized that an unrestricted competition in counterforce weapons could not coexist with a stable arms control regime. Early on in the SALT talks, it became painfully clear that a failure to constrain MIRVs might eventually come to undermine, by extension, the detente relationship of which SALT was an essential part.[44] At the time that the critical decisions for MIRV were being made, the substantial military and political costs of mutual defection were well known among top SALT decisionmakers in Washington.

After the preliminary flight tests of August 1968, the United States faced a series of critical decisions for the future of MIRV. To be sure, the pressure to push forward with MIRV was greater than that behind ABM. But the potential costs of an unrestricted competition in MIRV were expected to be at least as great and perhaps greater than would have been true of defenses. The U.S. preference structure for MIRV came to match an iterated PD with a long shadow of the future. But Washington did not yet have a strong sense of Soviet interests or even preferences in MIRV. Without knowing whether or exactly why a cooperative solution would have strong appeal in Moscow, the challenge for American leaders was to develop a strategy that might elicit cooperation in MIRV.

Strategy Development

The failure of the Halperin-Selin proposal in 1968 did not spell the end of such efforts. Between 1969 and 1971 the Congress and the administration each developed several different options for reciprocal strategies in MIRV, reflecting a continuing broad consensus that a cooperative outcome would be preferable to mutual defection. None of these strategies was fully implemented. To understand why these nascent efforts were deflected, it is first necessary to understand how and why they came about.

Assessing Soviet Interests and Preferences

As was true of ABM, American decisionmakers found it difficult to know how the Soviets defined their interests with regard to MIRV. But unlike

[44] The only real surprise for the future was how quickly this turn of events came about. I consider this at greater length in the following section and in Chapter 7.

the ABM case, Soviet preferences in MIRV were almost equally ambiguous. There were several reasons to suspect that Moscow would prefer a cooperative solution. The first was a logical deduction from what the Americans knew of the Soviets' perspective on quantitative nuclear "superiority." By the late 1960s, most American analysts recognized that the Kennedy administration's early strategic doctrines, coupled with the growth of the U.S. arsenal, probably had provoked real fear in Moscow that the United States was seeking nuclear superiority based on a first-strike capability. Soviet interpretations of the Cuban Missile Crisis would have reinforced pessimistic appraisals of the possible consequences. If nuclear "superiority" could be used for coercion, it made sense for the Soviets to try to avoid additional crises while Moscow remained in an inferior position and to slow down any U.S. programs that might expand the American lead, buying time for a steady move toward parity. A preference to limit MIRV warheads would have been entirely consistent with each of these objectives.[45]

The second reason was the possible vulnerability of Soviet forces to an American MIRV. Because Moscow still lacked a large and reliable sea-based arsenal at the end of the 1960s, the bulk of Soviet strategic forces remained in theory susceptible to preemptive first strike.[46] As the U.S. MIRV program made headway, Moscow must have looked anxiously at its own "window of vulnerability" that it would be unable to close for at least a few years. This would have reinforced preferences for banning or at least postponing the move toward MIRV. At the same time, Soviet leaders must have recognized that this dangerous period would only be temporary. With their large emerging advantage in throw-weight, the Soviets could have looked forward to an edge in counterforce capabilities against U.S. ICBMs once they deployed their own MIRV. But was this presumed "temptation to defect" a significant one? Soviet leaders must have expected that Washington would move in the interim years to reduce or compensate for Minuteman vulnerability. While Soviet scientists

---

[45] Horelick and Rush, *Strategic Power*, pp. 85–105; and Wolfe, *Soviet Power and Europe, 1945–1970*, pp. 85–95. Both discuss Soviet reactions to American strategic policy in the early Kennedy years. While the presumed significance of the nuclear balance in the Cuban crisis has been progressively downgraded by Western historians, the issue here is how the Soviets viewed the question during the late 1960s. There is every reason to believe that at that time Moscow attached considerable importance to the effects of nuclear "inferiority" during the crisis. For a summary, see Kahan, *Security in the Nuclear Age*, pp. 112–14.

[46] It was only in 1968 that the Soviets began deploying the SS-N-6 missile aboard modern, Yankee class submarines; and for several years thereafter, only a small number of these submarines were on patrol at any given time. Before 1968 the sea-based leg of the Soviet triad was made up principally of the SS-N-5, a relatively short-range and inaccurate missile (CEP of 2,800 meters at range 1,200 km) deployed on diesel Golf class and later nuclear Hotel class subs. *Jane's Weapons Systems*, 1969; IISS, *Military Balance 1971–72*.

worked to catch up with the United States in MIRV technology, they could hardly have expected the presumed targets to remain sitting ducks.

For these reasons, Washington might have concluded that Soviet leaders shared PD preferences over foreseeable outcomes in MIRV, with strong incentives to cooperate and a small temptation to defect. If so, a relatively permissive strategy of reciprocity would be most likely to succeed in eliciting cooperation. There were, however, alternative interpretations of possible Soviet interests in limiting MIRV that fell closer to the "Talensky doctrine" logic of the ABM case. That argument, to repeat, was that counterforce had replaced defense as Moscow's favored method of implementing a damage-limitation strategy and that the fundamental goal, to acquire meaningful nuclear superiority over the United States, had not changed. Decisionmakers who favored this interpretation discounted the value of any feedback that pointed to shifts in Moscow's strategic thought and basic conceptions of self-interest in nuclear weapons, and focused instead on the continuing deployment of heavy land-based ICBMs with progressively greater throw-weight and accuracy. But this alternative interpretation of interests did not prima facie rule out a Soviet preference for cooperation in MIRV. According to its logic, a decision to ban MIRV would still relieve Moscow of having to live through a dangerous period where its central deterrent capability might be in doubt. At the same time, Soviet ICBM deployments could continue in the face of a de facto U.S. freeze. The ABM treaty and SALT could go forward; and without believing in a fallacy of the last move, Moscow could envision living 10 years hence in a strategic environment more advantageous to Soviet interests than the alternative.[47] On this assessment of interests the Soviets might have still held PD preferences for MIRV, although they would have done so for very different reasons.

Both interpretations were thus consistent with the idea that the Soviets favored a cooperative solution for MIRV, although each perceived a different set of interests underlying these presumed preferences. This had pivotal consequences for the development of American strategy. If the latter interpretation were closer to the truth, Moscow would be more strongly tempted to exploit American restraint unless the criteria of contingency in American strategy were sufficiently demanding. Time would be a key consideration: to gain cooperation on MIRV and counterforce, Washington would have to prove that attempts at exploitation would be immediately costly to Soviet interests. The former interpretation sug-

[47] The most likely alternative was to enter into open competition with the United States in counterforce. In 1970 or thereabouts, this must have seemed a losing proposition for Moscow, principally because of Washington's short-term advantage in MIRV. While that advantage could have been reversed in time, Soviet leaders could not have foreseen Washington's failure to compensate for the Minuteman vulnerability problem in the interim.

gested that the United States could use its technological lead in MIRV as a buffer and adopt a more permissive strategy of reciprocity. These differing interpretations found expression in two "strands" of MIRV strategy that developed to some degree separately in the legislative and executive branches of the U.S. government.[48]

The Congress and Enhanced Contingent Restraint—1969

Congress's passive acquiescence in the Pentagon's plans for MIRV came to an end late in 1968. During a set of informal staff caucuses that autumn that had been convened to discuss ABM, some Senate staffers argued that the more important issue for the strategic balance and arms control was in fact MIRV. This strategic logic, however, ran counter to bureaucratic and domestic politics. If Congress was going to assert itself for the first time in basic questions of nuclear strategy, MIRV did not seem as propitious an issue as ABM. Grass-roots opposition to ABM was strong and easy to mobilize since defensive systems were highly visible, very expensive, and at best only partially effective. MIRV, in contrast, was essentially "invisible" to the population at large, relatively inexpensive, and technologically competent. All of this made MIRV difficult to criticize except on more sophisticated doctrinal grounds, and this was not easy to do vis-à-vis the general public. Many lawmakers were reluctant to take on the more complex strategic problem of MIRV in part because they saw it as jeopardizing Congress' new-found power in opposing ABM.[49]

Not all of Capitol Hill was thus dissuaded. During the spring of 1969 the influential Republican Senator John Sherman Cooper tried to push Nixon to take up the issue of limiting MIRV as a priority for the administration's "strategic review," which was then being conducted in preparation for SALT.[50] Although Nixon refused to listen to Cooper, he did for political reasons pay greater attention to first-term senator Edward W. Brooke. Nixon and Brooke met in mid-April 1969 to discuss a proposal the senator's staff had put together for a test moratorium on MIRV, un-

[48] These two strands of strategy evolved more or less simultaneously and were closely influenced by one another. I separate them here only to simplify the analysis.

[49] For an account of the staff meetings, see Alton Frye, *A Responsible Congress*, p. 52. A common view was that the upcoming ABM battle was an important enough opportunity that it would be foolish to risk squandering it by trying to do too much too quickly. If Congress "won" on ABM, it would set a precedent for the legislature to play a central role in such decisions that would later allow it to take on MIRV and other more difficult issues.

[50] John W. Finney, "Case Attacks Policy," *New York Times*, 6 June 1969, p. 7. Nixon several times rebuffed both Cooper's and Senator Case's calls for a meeting.

der which the United States would delay further tests for as long as the Soviets refrained from testing any multiple-warhead systems of their own. Brooke's reasoning was that an immediate decision to go ahead with MIRV would be irreversible and fatal to SALT, while a short-term suspension of testing could be used to probe Moscow's interest in mutual restraint without harming American security. Nixon was apparently impressed by the senator's argument and agreed to take the proposal under serious consideration.[51]

Brooke brought this argument to public debate in a speech delivered about a week later in New York. Claiming that MIRV was "the most disturbing breakthrough in strategic weapons since the advent of intercontinental ballistic missiles" and a much more important issue than ABM, Brooke made a public plea for an immediate U.S.-Soviet moratorium on tests of multiple-warhead systems.[52] This sparked new controversy among MIRV skeptics at State and ACDA, MIRV supporters at DoD, and a number of important legislators on Capitol Hill. One immediate reaction in the House was to trump Brooke's position by calling for immediate and unconditional cessation of MIRV tests by the United States. Following this line, Representative Richard McCarthy argued that "the decision as to whether we complete testing of MIRV is the most important of all" and proposed that the United States take on an immediate, unilateral, and unconditional moratorium on MIRV tests prior to SALT. The United States and the Soviet Union could then together "agree not to complete the MIRV tests for the duration of the talks"; and this would lead to a mutual negotiated ban on MIRV.[53] In May, Representative Bingham introduced a draft resolution of a similar character, calling for "immediate deferment of further development and testing by the United States of MIRVs until every effort has been exhausted to reach a mutual MIRV freeze with the Soviets."[54]

[51] Brooke later told Nixon that the Senate believed American "intelligence capabilities can provide a reasonable measure of confidence that we will know whether the Soviet Union continues tests" and that if Moscow did in fact defect, the administration would not be constrained to continue the moratorium unilaterally. From Brooke's letter to Nixon, quoted in Frye, *A Responsible Congress*, p. 55.

[52] Brooke now called for a joint moratorium on testing that would be followed immediately by negotiations with the Soviet Union for a treaty that would severely limit MIRV, ABM, and other weapons systems (particularly counterforce-capable heavy ICBMs) that threatened deterrence stability. "A Choice of Risks: The Dilemmas of National Security," Statement of Senator Edward W. Brooke, American Society of Newspaper Publishers, New York, 24 April 1969, in *Congressional Record*, Senate, 24 April 1969, pp. 10642–44.

[53] *Congressional Record*, House, 15 April 1969, p. 9069.

[54] *Congressional Record*, House, 13 May 1969, p. 12349. The Bingham resolution stated that the test moratorium would ideally be part of "more comprehensive agreements" but in any case "should not be delayed pending the working out of all aspects of such comprehensive agreements."

Neither of these resolutions garnered sufficient support on the Hill or elsewhere to force the hand of the administration. They failed to do so because they were based on inappropriately permissive criteria of contingency. Each resembled a strategy of contingent restraint. Bingham, for example, argued that the United States was in a position of strength on MIRV and could afford to relax its call for reciprocity. Based on his belief that the Soviets were demonstrating a new "non-belligerent attitude" toward the United States, he expected that a unilateral cessation of MIRV tests would be matched by Moscow.[55] Possible U.S. responses, should the Soviets choose not to reciprocate American restraint, were left implicit and subject to later decision. Most American elites, however, could not accept the notion that such an open-ended moratorium without promise of sanctions for noncooperation would induce Soviet restraint. They also feared that a testing moratorium with such a unilateralist "flavor" would in practice *not* be reversed regardless of Soviet actions, or at least not until substantial damage had been done to American security interests. Contingent restraint was thus unacceptable to the vast majority of American decisionmakers.

Alternative strategies based on enhanced contingent restraint were taken more seriously. Senator Brooke and Representative Jeffrey Cohelan introduced comparable resolutions, SR 211 and HR 467, which replaced the idea of a unilateral moratorium with specific terms for a *joint* suspension of multiple-warhead flight tests by the United States and the Soviet Union. SR 211 asked the administration to "refrain from additional flight tests" of MIRV but only for "so long as the Soviet Union does so." Both resolutions also rejected the notion that a MIRV ban could be sustained independent of a more comprehensive strategic arms agreement, and tied the two together in explicit terms.[56]

This approach enlisted the American technological lead in MIRV to enhance the credibility of proposals for a moratorium that would be strictly contingent on Soviet reciprocity. It also called for more attention to verification, with the understanding that dubious activities detected by national means would serve as cause for renewed U.S. MIRV tests. SR 211 would have left the United States with an appropriate and credible response should the Soviets "defect." But it did not pose ultimatums or threaten Moscow with an immediate escalation of the competition. Brooke and Cohelan's strategy of enhanced contingent restraint proved far more acceptable to the Congress: the resolutions garnered 40 cosponsors in the Senate and over 100 in the House.

[55] *Congressional Record*, House, 13 May 1969, p. 12349.

[56] *Congressional Record*, Senate, 17 June 1969, pp. 16148–52. The text of SR 211, from which the quotes are drawn, is on p. 16150.

Concurrently, Brooke pressed his case in private conversations with Kissinger and in a May 23 letter to Nixon. He suggested that the president might make a quiet decision to simply "stretch out" the MIRV test series for several months until the SALT talks began, when the United States could more directly probe Soviet interest in a joint ban. Brooke's proposal rejected more demanding criteria of reciprocity in favor of a strategy of enhanced contingent restraint: he claimed that "each side has a larger interest in persuading the other not to introduce MIRV systems than in deploying MIRV technology of its own," but that "we cannot hope to persuade them [the Soviets] if we insist on proceeding with MIRV."[57] Although Nixon rejected the specifics, his attitude toward Brooke's position was positive overall. In a news conference of June 19, the president referred to Brooke's plan as "very constructive" and suggested that he could in principle support a verifiable, mutual moratorium on MIRV tests in the context of SALT.[58] By the end of June then, both the Congress and the administration were exploring possibilities for a strategy of enhanced contingent restraint in MIRV.

Enhanced contingent restraint was favored by the state of the five variables that influence strategy choice. By 1969, the technological possibilities for MIRV were fully apparent, clarifying a stable set of interests and incentives for U.S. decisionmakers. Technological considerations also, however, indicated few saliencies available as potential focal points for cooperation; and the single most valuable saliency (successful testing) was about to be breached. Sacrificing uncertain short-term advantages for a long-term reduction in the counterforce threat against Minuteman and additional efforts to stabilize the strategic balance were goals consistent with the Nixon administration's strategic theories. And most importantly, American images of the Soviet Union as a competitor had shifted toward the belief that the Kremlin might eschew its temptation to defect and reciprocate American initiatives for cooperative restraint in MIRV. The Halperin-Selin proposal had languished largely because American policymakers expected the Soviet Union to exploit any such demarche. By 1969, in part because of feedback from Soviet behavior on the ABM issue and emerging U.S. conceptions of superpower detente, Washington was in principle cautiously willing to undertake some kind of strategy of reciprocity on MIRV.

The major impediment to enhanced contingent restraint came from the fifth variable, bureaucratic politics. The Pentagon was reluctant to delay MIRV tests, largely because influential military officials were dubious

[57] See Frye, *A Responsible Congress*, pp. 60–61, quoting from a June 1969 letter from Brooke to Nixon.

[58] Robert B. Semple, "Nixon Considers MIRV Test Move," *New York Times*, 20 June 1969, pp. 1, 14.

about the prospects (and in some cases, the desirability) of a MIRV ban.[59] But it is wrong to assume that the Pentagon's opposition spelled a fait accompli. There were many civilian officials at DoD who were far less convinced. The Congress as a whole shared a strong sense that cooperation was more desirable and was considering serious proposals aimed at that outcome. ACDA continued to argue that MIRV lay at the crux of SALT; and although State Department officials questioned this emphasis, most were at least sympathetic to the arguments for MIRV restraint. Nixon and Kissinger showed consistent interest in the possibilities for cooperative restraint, although their interest was always tempered by extreme caution. With this constellation of positions, it is entirely possible that had officials at ACDA, State, DoD, NSC, and a broad spectrum of members of Congress forged a coalition in support of a cogent strategy based on enhanced contingent restraint at this time, they might have gained the support of Nixon and Kissinger and tipped the scales against the Pentagon's opposition.[60]

This battle was essentially fought out during the summer of 1969 in a series of Congressional hearings on the MIRV issue before Foreign Affairs and Foreign Relations subcommittees in the House and the Senate. The most striking feature of these hearings was the way in which widespread support for delaying MIRV cut across the boundaries that divided proponents and opponents of ABM. Nearly all the witnesses testifying before Congressman Clement Zabloski's subcommittee agreed, for example, that a decision to deploy MIRV was at present premature. In the Senate, the mutual moratorium of SR 211 was supported by a broad consensus of defense scientists, extending to opponents (York and Ruina) *and* influential proponents (Dyson and MacDonald) of Safeguard. SR 211 also gained the backing of Senators Gale McGee and Robert Packwood, both of whom favored moving forward with ABM.[61]

[59] See the formal submission of the Office of the Secretary of Defense (OSD) to the House Subcommittee on National Security Policy and Scientific Developments, *Diplomatic and Strategic Impact of Multiple Warhead Missiles*, pp. 284–86. OSD rejected a unilateral moratorium on MIRV tests and also raised serious questions as to the desirability of a mutual moratorium. The major argument against the latter was that Washington would find it politically difficult to resume testing under any conditions once a moratorium was in place; knowing this, the Soviets would be strongly tempted to defect.

[60] This is in contrast to Greenwood, who is much more dubious. *Making the MIRV*, pp. 130–39. The technological determinism within his argument leads to a heavy discount of the strength and sincerity of Washington's interest in possible cooperative outcomes for MIRV.

[61] House hearings are reported in *Diplomatic and Strategic Impact of Multiple Warhead Missiles*, July and August 1969. Senate hearings are reported in *Strategic and Foreign Policy Implications of ABM Systems: Anti-Submarine Warfare, and Multiple Independently Targetable Re-entry Vehicles*, part 3, July 1969.

The arguments against MIRV spread from these hearings and were reported widely in the media. By July 1 the editors of the *Washington Post, Wall Street Journal, New York Times*, and other prominent newspapers had all come out in support of some form of MIRV test moratorium. In late summer, Brooke tried to parlay this momentum by stepping up the pressure on Nixon, Kissinger, Smith, and the secretaries of state and defense. The White House continued to express cautious interest in a mutual moratorium. Smith, as the chief American negotiator and director of ACDA, was firmly committed to pushing a MIRV ban early in the SALT negotiations. And the Pentagon, albeit still reluctant, conceded that on military terms there "were no intrinsic objections to a joint moratorium."[62]

Where did the emerging strategy go off track? A close reading of the summer 1969 hearings reveals major concerns on the part of Pentagon officials about the ability of U.S. intelligence to verify by unilateral means that the Soviets were not conducting MIRV tests clandestinely. John Foster and Assistant Secretary of Defense G. Warren Nutter offered a series of imaginative but still plausible scenarios by which the Soviets might evade American detection and surreptitiously test a multiple-warhead system if they were sufficiently enterprising. Foster even raised the possibility that Moscow might have *already* achieved a MIRV capability in its multiple-warhead tests, because nothing the United States knew could absolutely rule this out.[63] These were not specious arguments. They reflected crucial technical disagreements within the administration and in Congress over whether unilateral monitoring was adequate for enforcing an effective MIRV ban.[64] But they also reflected a deeper, underlying uncertainty about the nature of Soviet interests in MIRV and consequent evaluations of Moscow's temptation to defect. The problem was serious

---

[62] DDR&E John Foster, quoted in Frye, *A Responsible Congress*, pp. 63–64. Foster's position was later seconded by Deputy Secretary of Defense David Packard. Secretary of State Rogers followed by reiterating that the State Department viewed SR 211 as a "helpful" proposal that easily could be made consistent with the administration's interest in a joint moratorium. *New York Times*, 21 August 1969, p. 1.

[63] They suggested, for example, that Soviet scientists could disguise a MIRV test in multiple satellite launches, or test only a single RV in each flight from a MIRV bus. MIRV opponents countered that these were fanciful scenarios that might still be detected by U.S. intelligence. Even if the Soviets could evade surveillance, such tests could not provide sufficient confidence in a MIRV weapon that the Soviets would be apt to deploy it. Frye describes the Pentagon's concerns as "wholly legitimate questions," although he concludes that on balance "there were convincing methods for meeting the verification requirements stressed by the Defense Department." *A Responsible Congress*, p. 62. We shall see, nonetheless, that DoD's concerns were an important factor in derailing efforts at cooperation.

[64] Hedrick Smith, "Nixon's Advisors Divided on Whether to Propose MIRV Test Ban to Soviets," *New York Times*, 20 August 1969, p. 13; Alton Frye, personal communication, February 13, 1989.

enough that the House subcommittee moved to attach a new and critically important condition to its test moratorium proposal. The revised plan urged that the SALT talks take "MIRV *and* MRV as the first order of business and that at the preliminary negotiations we seek to achieve agreement with the Soviet Union to immediately suspend testing of *both* MIRV and MRV weapons."[65]

The decision to include MRV in the test ban was now viewed as a necessary buffer against possibilities arising from Washington's deeper uncertainty over Soviet interests, but politically and strategically it was in principle a nonstarter. A moratorium on testing of all multiple-warhead systems would be patently unacceptable in Moscow for the simple reason that the United States had already *deployed* MRVs on Polaris since 1964, and could hardly call on the Soviets to refrain from even *testing* a comparable system. This dilemma did not go unrecognized by American lawmakers. As a result, neither the House nor Senate resolutions were reported out of committee during the summer of 1969.[66] At least for the moment, Congress's bid for a reciprocal strategy to elicit cooperation in MIRV had been derailed.

The Administration and SALT

The Congress was not, however, the only branch of the government working on this problem. In fact, White House interest in a cooperative solution for MIRV did not begin with Nixon and it was not always reluctant. In the summer of 1968, President Johnson and his top advisors were already weighing various options for an approach to the Soviets on MIRV. They faced determined opposition from the Pentagon. Because the administration's *official, prepared* position for SALT talks did not include a proposal on MIRV, previous histories of MIRV have concluded that Johnson decided not to take on this opposition. But that is not correct.

The president surely recognized that banning MIRV would require him to overcome the stiff resistance of the Pentagon, and that this would be difficult and politically costly to do within formal bureaucratic channels. Johnson chose an alternative route. The president was ready to sidestep the Pentagon and move quickly toward a MIRV ban outside of SALT, before the negotiations officially got underway. According to Dean Rusk,

[65] *Congressional Record*, House Extension of Remarks, 17 November 1969, p. 34513. Emphasis added.

[66] Other reasons for holding up the legislation included continuing reluctance to divert energy and attention from the ABM battle, and the inclination of some legislators to minimize Congressional intrusion on the administration's negotiating posture vis-à-vis the Soviets now that SALT talks seemed imminent.

Johnson had planned to make "a serious effort to grapple with the MIRV problem" when he met Soviet leaders at a summit planned for Leningrad in September 1968. Johnson's favored proposal was for an immediate and mutual ban on all missiles with multiple warheads, and he hoped to conclude such an agreement at the summit as a way of setting SALT off on the right track. Former National Security Advisor Walt Rostow concurs, saying Johnson was "deadly serious" about the plan.[67] But the Leningrad summit never happened. It was canceled—and with it Johnson's planned demarche—when the Soviets invaded Czechoslovakia in August. SALT, and MIRV, were thus bequeathed to the Nixon White House.

The Nixon administration put off wrestling with the Kremlin on strategic arms control until it had reexamined its own preferences and thought through what was known about Soviet positions on the major issues. National Security Study Memorandums 3 and 28 initiated two key studies in the early part of 1969 for this purpose.[68] MIRV received major attention in both. This was due in part to ACDA's insistence that MIRV had reached an urgent point of decision, seconded by Smith's argument that at least a test moratorium was urgently needed to preserve the administration's negotiating options. In June, ACDA officials presented a detailed "stop where we are" proposal for SALT that emphasized MIRV and the advantages of a test moratorium to the United States above all else.[69]

The arguments of MIRV opponents did not go unheeded; but as the top White House decisionmakers struggled to iron out a SALT negotiat-

[67] Dean Rusk, personal communication, August 13, 1989; Walt Rostow, personal communication, October 17, 1989. Rusk reports that "we had in mind making a serious effort to put MIRVs under control," although he notes that "the details of our proposal on MIRVs for that Leningrad negotiation had not been worked out in any detail." See also Michael Gordon, "Past Summit Meetings, Unlike Reagan's, Were for Signing of Key Accords," *New York Times*, 15 November 1988, p. 6; and Thomas Schoenbaum, *Waging Peace and War*, p. 484. According to Schoenbaum, Rusk "optimistically thought there was even a chance for some agreement before the end of the year, during Johnson's term of office." This clashes with Greenwood's assessment that Johnson was not interested in the controversy over MIRV and would not have overruled the Pentagon simply because he perceived the "weight of opinion" in Washington as being against a delay. *Making the MIRV*, pp. 127–28.

[68] Newhouse, *Cold Dawn*, p. 159. The former was a comprehensive review of U.S. military posture and programs; the latter was directed specifically at the state of strategic programs and planning for SALT.

[69] The June 1969 ACDA proposal claimed to "virtually eliminate the potential counterforce threat against the US Minuteman force by . . . improving our confidence that the Soviets were not developing MIRVs or other missile improvements." *A "Stop Where We Are" Proposal for SALT*, ACDA-3356, 11 June 1969, NHP Box 20. Some ACDA officials argued that the administration should begin SALT talks immediately, before finishing its strategic review, specifically for the purpose of getting an agreement on MIRV before the testing program rendered the issue moot. Newhouse, *Cold Dawn*, p. 149.

ing position, the problematic issue of verifying a ban on MIRV quickly emerged as a central sticking point (as it would in the Congress). ACDA, State, and the CIA argued that a test moratorium could be verified by unilateral means, and that the Soviets could not at present deploy an operational MIRV without testing. The Joint Chiefs and some Pentagon civilians disagreed on both points. In April, an interagency MIRV group was established specifically for the purpose of settling this controversy, with Kissinger as chairman. While the panel failed to definitively resolve the issue, it further focused the attention of key decisionmakers, including Nixon and Kissinger, on the problem of MIRV. Interest in a MIRV ban was serious but tinged with caution.[70] When the administration's official position was finally clarified during the summer in a formal OSD statement to the House Subcommittee hearings, it deeply reflected that caution. According to this statement, a mutual test moratorium would be acceptable to the White House only if it were formally agreed upon at SALT in a written accord, and included stringent provisions for verification. Barring that, the U.S. program would go forward without delay.[71] This was a strategy closely resembling contingent threat of escalation.

It was also a very different approach than that favored by the Congress in its evolving strategy for MIRV. The source of this difference lay mostly in the discrepancy between assessments of Soviet interests in MIRV. The legislature's strategy was based on a general perception of Soviet interests that resembled the Garthoff doctrine in the ABM case. The executive's strategy followed from a more pessimistic assessment that viewed Soviet interests as leaving Moscow strongly inclined to exploit U.S. restraint in MIRV. It still made sense to argue that Soviet preferences could support mutual restraint; but eliciting cooperation would require a U.S. strategy with extremely stringent and demanding criteria of reciprocity.

The administration's handling of MIRV at SALT consistently reflected this strategy. In July 1969, Nixon forwarded to ACDA a set of general guidelines for SALT that left open the possibility of a MIRV test moratorium subject to the White House's previously stated conditions. During the next several months there were vague signals from Moscow that the Soviets wished to limit MIRV and might in fact meet those conditions.

[70] See Robert Kleiman, "Nixon Confronts a Momentous Decision on the Hydra-Headed MIRV," *New York Times*, 17 August 1969, sec. 4, p. 2. Hedrick Smith later reported that Nixon had not yet made a final decision but was quite "sympathetic" to Smith's view that a test moratorium would serve both sides' interests. See "Nixon's Advisors Divided on Whether to Propose MIRV Test Ban to Soviets," *New York Times*, 20 August 1969, p. 13. Newhouse discusses the interagency MIRV group set up under Kissinger. *Cold Dawn*, p. 161.

[71] The OSD statement is found in *Diplomatic and Strategic Impact of Multiple Warhead Missiles*, pp. 284–86.

Senator Hubert Humphrey was told by a Soviet academician that the Kremlin saw no obstacle to an early agreement at SALT that would ban multiple-warhead tests. Yuli Vorontsov, at the time Dobrynin's deputy in Washington, hinted that "wiser political forces" in Moscow were battling military officials who wanted MIRV and that the issue could be settled were the United States to offer a reasonable scheme.[72] But these ambiguous signals did not affect the administration's position on the appropriate strategy for MIRV. The United States did nothing to probe the Soviets' position or to elicit greater feedback about Soviet interests in MIRV. When the final negotiating instructions for the first round of SALT reached Smith in November, there was no specific mention of MIRV bans, test moratoriums, or anything else beyond the administration's previous position.[73]

The U.S. side made only tangential mention of MIRV during the first round of talks, and the Soviets neither responded substantively nor raised the issue formally themselves. Kissinger concludes that "the Soviets showed no interest in a MIRV ban," but his account conflicts with those of Smith and Garthoff, both of whom refer to "informal discussions" in which Soviet negotiators indicated their interest in a MIRV ban and their puzzlement that the United States had not brought up the issue.[74] These contacts were not pursued, and American negotiators learned little about Soviet interests that could translate into feedback for resolving uncertainties over the best U.S. strategy for MIRV.

In the meantime, proponents of a more permissive reciprocal strategy for MIRV continued to argue their case. In the winter of 1970, the president's General Advisory Committee on Arms Control and Disarmament under the direction of John McCloy recommended a suspension of MIRV tests; and the Senate followed with a nonbinding resolution urging the president to "immediately suspend deployment of all offensive and defensive weapons," including MIRV.[75] These moves came just as the White House was struggling to put together a negotiating position for round

[72] Alton Frye, personal communication, February 13, 1989; also see Smith, *Doubletalk*, pp. 162–63.

[73] Kissinger, *White House Years*, p. 148; Garthoff, *Detente and Confrontation*, p. 133. Newhouse notes that the White House had put together nine potential bargaining packages, four of which called for a ban on MIRV; but because not one of these could command a consensus among key SALT decisionmakers, none was presented to the Soviets in the first round of talks. *Cold Dawn*, p. 170.

[74] Kissinger, *White House Years*, p. 148; Smith, *Doubletalk*, pp. 165–68; Garthoff, *Detente and Confrontation*, p. 133; Alton Frye, personal communication, February 1989.

[75] See Nixon, *US Foreign Policy for the 1970s: A New Strategy for Peace*, pp. 143–47. Kissinger describes the General Advisory Committee's recommendation for suspension of MIRV tests as having "reflected the prevailing mood" in Washington. *White House Years*, pp. 539–40. The Senate resolution passed 72–6 on April 9.

two of SALT, scheduled to begin in April. On Kissinger's demand, the
various proposals brought up by the bureaucracies were finally distilled
into four discrete options for presentation to the NSC and final decision
on April 8.[76]

Only one of the four (Option C) called for limits on MIRV. This was
the option finally chosen by Kissinger and agreed to by Nixon as the
opening bid for SALT round two. The story behind this selection is somewhat convoluted. Ex post facto, Kissinger describes his plan as being motivated not by a real preference for Option C, but by a bureaucratic finesse cloaking his preference for Option B, which would eliminate the
ban on MIRV. He hoped that after starting with Option C, the United
States could quickly fall back to Option B, which would then be able to
muster nearly unanimous support among the bureaucracies. Kissinger's
"scheme" worked. The Soviets in fact rejected Option C, with the result
that Kissinger claims to have predicted and planned for: the Washington
bureaucracies closed ranks around Option B.[77] This may have been, as
Kissinger implies, a brilliant bureaucratic ploy that finally produced a
consensus in the White House. But what if the Soviets had taken a more
positive position on Option C? Kissinger himself argues that this would
have been "a major step forward" and a "result compatible with our security."[78]

In fact, the Option C proposal was encumbered with a key modification on the MIRV issue that rendered it close to being a nonstarter. As it
was presented to the Soviets, the U.S. plan offered to ban testing and deployment of MIRV but not to ban production. Verification was to be by
on-site inspection. This was troublesome for several reasons. First, it
called for intrusive monitoring procedures, which the Soviets were dead-
set against, and which even the United States would have been hard put
to accept. Second, it would have frozen the Soviets in a position of technological inferiority while leaving a loophole for the United States to produce and stockpile its partially tested MIRV systems without substantial
constraint. The proposal was rejected by the Soviet side more or less out
of hand.

The inclusion of on-site inspection in the U.S. proposal for MIRV is at
first glance rather puzzling. It is important to note that when Option C

[76] Kissinger outlines the four options in detail. Briefly, Option A limited ICBMs and
SLBMs to the current U.S. total, froze bombers, and permitted ABM deployment at the level
then planned for Safeguard (12 sites). Option B further restricted ABM to one site (NCA)
on both sides, or no ABM. Option C added a ban on MIRV. Option D deleted the MIRV
ban, but called for drastic cuts in ballistic missiles to 1,000 total on each side, with ABMs
limited to NCA or zero. *White House Years*, p. 541.

[77] Ibid., pp. 542–45. Garthoff provides an account that is generally consistent with Kissinger's, if somewhat less congratulatory. *Detente and Confrontation*, pp. 135–39.

[78] Kissinger, *White House Years*, p. 544.

was presented to the NSC on April 8, it did *not* require on-site inspection. Of the major agencies involved in the discussions, only the DoD and the JCS registered dissent. Their argument—that verification by national technical means would not be fully adequate—did not cause them to reject Option C but instead led only to a dissenting note attached to the original proposal. The decision to add on-site inspection was made by Nixon and Kissinger, and it was made after the NSC meeting.[79]

Garthoff believes that this unusual story can be explained by DoD's desire to ensure that the Soviets would reject the proposal. Ted Greenwood adds that Nixon and Kissinger "shared the military's reluctance to bargain away the option of deploying MIRV."[80] To repeat the point, it is true that the Joint Chiefs and many Pentagon officials did not favor banning MIRV, but this opposition was not unconditional and in any case was not shared in a wholesale way by the White House. The ability to monitor what the Soviets *could* do in MIRV, and to relate that to American understandings of what they would *want* to do, were still the most crucial issues. The fine details of on-site inspection might have been a new consideration, but the question of how to verify a ban on MIRV flight tests, and more importantly how to understand the relationship between such a ban and MIRV deployment, had been under investigation at the highest technical and political levels for some time.[81]

These studies, as noted earlier, proved inconclusive. The administration could not be entirely certain as to whether Moscow could or more importantly would deploy MIRV clandestinely in the face of a test ban. The root of the problem lay in understanding the sources of what the Soviets perceived as incentives to do so. Uncertainties about monitoring are part and parcel of arms control and most other agreements for international cooperation, and the uncertainties in this case were in *technical* terms rather small. But the significance of those uncertainties was multiplied manyfold by Washington's relative ignorance of Soviet conceptions of self-interest when it came to MIRV. The lack of a consensus in Washington on that score was decisive. Without a set of working hypotheses about the sources of Moscow's incentives to defect, American decisionmakers could not agree about what would be needed to counteract them. The United States did strikingly little to elicit additional feedback that

[79] Garthoff, *Detente and Confrontation*, p. 138; Newhouse, *Cold Dawn*, pp. 179–80; Hedrick Smith, "Panel Urges Concession to Win MIRV Ban," *New York Times*, 29 January 1971, p. 3.

[80] Greenwood, *Making the MIRV*, p. 133; Garthoff, *Detente and Confrontation*, p. 138. Garthoff claims that "technical analysis of verification requirements" could not have been a substantial factor in the decision because an interagency group that was set up specifically to study the details of OSI did not convene until *after* the requirement had been added to the U.S. proposal.

[81] As discussed earlier, Kissinger himself had been involved in these studies. Also see Seymour Hersh, *The Price of Power*, pp. 147–67.

might have clarified the task. When Moscow offered a MIRV proposal of its own, the United States rejected it out of hand without further discussion.[82] The possibility of limiting MIRVs by formal negotiated agreement was not raised again at SALT I.

The administration's final strategy for MIRV was much closer to contingent threat than to enhanced contingent restraint. With extremely stringent criteria of reciprocity and an unrealistic requirement for verification, this strategy had only the barest chance of eliciting cooperation. If it had any effect on Soviet calculations, it probably provoked escalation of the competition.[83] Might a strategy of enhanced contingent restraint have been more successful at this juncture? The technological gap that would have been frozen by a MIRV ban certainly posed a problem, but a comparable assymetry did not block cooperation in ABM. There were various signals outside the negotiations that at least some Soviet decision-makers were willing to work toward a cooperative solution for MIRV, despite the U.S. lead and the problems of verification.[84] The "missed opportunity" for MIRV at this critical juncture lay in the administration's failure to fully probe the potential space for cooperation and put Moscow squarely to the test.

Congress and a Final Attempt

The major impact of the abortive MIRV demarche at SALT was to temporarily silence Congress's efforts on MIRV.[85] There was a backlash,

[82] The Soviet plan called for a ban only on production and deployment of MIRV; it would have permitted continued testing. While this proposal as offered was unacceptable to Washington, the U.S. side made no effort to explore whether the Soviet position was at all flexible.

[83] On-site inspection aside, the Soviets might have readily suspected the U.S. proposal of being disingenuous. By not banning production of MIRVs just at the time that the United States was staged to begin production, the American plan would have left the United States in a position to produce and stockpile MIRV warheads theoretically without limit. From Moscow's perspective, this might have seemed a ploy to achieve offensive "break-out" from a treaty at some point in the future. Garthoff notes, correctly in my view, that the United States could have shown good faith by agreeing to a ban on MIRV production without prejudicing its proposal for on-site inspection of deployments per se. It is certainly possible, as Garthoff says, that the Soviets saw the "loophole of allowing MIRV production as a 'booby-trap' ". *Detente and Confrontation*, pp. 140, 139 n. 34.

[84] Greenwood discusses some of these signals. *Making the MIRV*, p. 134. Garthoff believes that the Soviet decisionmaking elite split on the question, with some leaders wishing to preserve MIRV for the long-term offensive advantage it would offer Moscow against U.S. ICBMs. *Detente and Confrontation*, p. 140. Both accounts concur with Alton Frye's assessment that the Soviets were waiting for the United States to make a sound proposal on MIRV, and that such a proposal *might* have tipped the balance in support of those who favored restraint. Personal communication, February 1989.

[85] Key legislators were reluctant to proceed with Congressional action on MIRV while the administration was involved in talks with the Soviets on precisely this issue, for fear of

however, when in March 1970 the Senate learned that the administration planned to deploy the first group of Minuteman III missiles equipped with MIRV on schedule in several months. The Foreign Relations Subcommittee immediately called hearings to consider a broadened version of SR 211. The twin issues of verifying a test ban and distinguishing MRV from MIRV again took center stage during these hearings and doomed the arguments for a moratorium. When an amended resolution passed as the "sense of the Senate" in April, it did not include any specific reference to MIRV.[86] The first group of MIRVed U.S. ICBMs was deployed, on schedule, in June 1970.

Anti-MIRV forces in Congress tried to continue their struggle by shifting their focus toward efforts to limit the counterforce capabilities of MIRV. This was not an entirely new approach: during 1969 and 1970, Senator Brooke had made several bids to get a commitment from Nixon that the president would work to avoid a U.S.-Soviet counterforce race that would contradict the logic of "strategic sufficiency" and harm U.S. interests. Despite Nixon's reassuring statements to this effect, the Pentagon's program to develop such capabilities was hardly slowed.[87] Similar efforts were rekindled in the summer of 1970 after the first deployment of Minuteman III. One attempt, that would have directed the Pentagon to develop a single-warhead system for Poseidon and Minuteman, failed to pass the Congress.[88] An amendment to the FY 1971 Appropriations Bill that tried to restrict funds for the development of "any MIRV system in which an individual reentry vehicle provides a capability to destroy a hardened target" was withdrawn prior to a vote.[89] While there was sub-

undercutting U.S. bargaining power. Some in Congress expected that the administration would delay any decisive steps on testing for at least as long as the talks on MIRV continued. See Frye, *A Responsible Congress*, pp. 67–68.

[86] See statement of Secretary of the Air Force Robert C. Seamans, Jr., *DoD Authorization for Appropriations for FY 71*, part 2, p. 907; "US Speeds Timetable for MIRV Deployment," *New York Times*, 11 March 1970, p. 1; Senate Subcommittee on Arms Control, International Law and Organzation, *ABM, MIRV, SALT and the Nuclear Arms Race*; and the Senate Committee on Foreign Relations, *Resolution Regarding Suspension of Further Deployment of Offensive and Defensive Nuclear Strategic Weapons Systems*, Report no. 749, 24 March 1970; *Congressional Record*, Senate, 9 April 1970, p. 11062.

[87] See text of Nixon's letter to Brooke, reprinted in *Congressional Record*, Senate, 23 April 1970, p. 12699. Greenwood notes that a stellar inertial guidance mechanism for Poseidon, which would have significantly improved the missile's accuracy, was in fact canceled in FY 1970, but for reasons only tangentially related to Brooke's initiative. *Making the MIRV*, p. 136

[88] *Congressional Record*, Senate, 29 July 1970, p. 26387; and 27 August 1970, pp. 30248–51.

[89] *Congressional Record*, Senate, 27 August 1970, pp. 30253–59. This amendment was notable because it included a specific definition of "counterforce capability" that erred considerably on the side of caution—a combination of warhead yield and accuracy sufficient to generate *one-third* the level of blast overpressure considered necessary to neutralize a hardened silo.

stantial interest in Congress for enacting a *mutual* moratorium on the development of counterforce-capable MIRVs, it was quickly recognized that this could not serve as a saliency for cooperation because the verification techniques to monitor such limits were missing. Even if Washington had wanted to reassure the Soviet Union that U.S. MIRVs did not threaten hardened targets, there was no way it could realistically do so.[90] Other amendments that sought to freeze or limit MIRV deployments on U.S. missiles in 1971 and 1972 were defeated for similar reasons.[91] By the time the first MIRVed Poseidon missiles were declared operational in April 1971, the MIRV case had already ended as a missed opportunity for U.S.-Soviet cooperation.

Strategic Interaction

MIRV appears a puzzle for cooperation theory at first because it fulfills the initial conditions of Axelrod's theory. The puzzle deepens when American decisionmakers develop several different reciprocal strategies for MIRV, some of which resemble enhanced contingent restraint. But that is as far as it went. An evolving process that might have led to cooperation was somehow derailed.

The proximate reason for this missed opportunity was the way in which the American decisionmaking system handled uncertainty about Soviet interests. In MIRV, that uncertainty and consequent uncertainties about capabilities were managed almost entirely by unilateral means. One consequence was that Washington never achieved a consensus on working hypotheses about Soviet interests sufficient to support a strategy of reciprocity. American elites continued to hold disparate beliefs about how the Soviets conceived of their interests in MIRV. These interpretations were irreconcilable without additional feedback. But the United States did not try to elicit more discriminating feedback from Moscow that might have helped to distinguish or to build a consensus between them. Cooperation in MIRV was an interdependent decision, but the Americans knew precious little about underlying Soviet interests.

Without any consensus on working hypotheses, it was extremely difficult for proponents of enhanced contingent restraint to argue their case. These deeper uncertainties entered policymaking through the issue of confidence in technical abilities to monitor current and future Soviet mul-

---

[90] The Special Projects Office and DDR&E did try to develop means for removing cross-range maneuvering capability from the Poseidon bus in a way that would be verifiable to the Soviets, but the effort was dropped after about a year. Greenwood, *Making the MIRV*, p. 136.

[91] Ibid., pp. 135–38; Tammen, *MIRV and the Arms Race*, Chapter 6.

tiple-warhead capabilities. At several key decisional points in the history of U.S. MIRV development and the evolving arms control proposals that were running parallel to it, the uncertainties intervened to accelerate weapons development and throw emerging strategies for restraint off track. American decisionmakers were ultimately unable to forge a consensus on an assessment of Soviet interests sufficient to support a reciprocal strategy for MIRV, as they had done for ABM.

ABM Uncertainties

The link between U.S. MIRV strategy and uncertainties about underlying Soviet interests goes back almost to the beginning of MIRV, when it was first and foremost a means to defeat ABMs. In the late 1950s and early 1960s, U.S. multiple-warhead programs were unusually sensitive to fluctuating levels of uncertainty about what the Soviets were doing in ABM. The first push for multiple warheads came near the end of the 1950s, in response to ambiguous indications that the Soviets might be experimenting with prototype ballistic missile defenses at test ranges in Central Asia.[92] If even a temporary advantage in nuclear capabilities could put vital U.S. interests at risk, as the logic of the Gaither Report claimed, the putative ABM threat had to be taken very seriously. OSD's 1957 Re-entry Body Identification Study did exactly this, and its analysis of means for penetrating defenses gave major impetus to the development and later deployment of the Polaris A-3, the first MRV system.[93]

In 1961, a top Pentagon official told Congress that "the Russians have a large, a very large anti-missile effort and have had for some time."[94] Although the evidence was still equivocal, there were enough signals pointing in that direction during 1961 and 1962 to justify concern. A series of high altitude nuclear tests, conducted with large enhanced X-ray

[92] Freedman, *US Intelligence*, p. 87. These test sites lay beyond the effective range of radar installations in Turkey. This implies that until the first U-2 photos of Sary Shagan were obtained in April 1960 it was probably not possible to say with confidence whether these installations were part of an ABM development program or simply a new type of air defense system.

[93] The November 1957 Gaither Report portrayed the U.S.-Soviet nuclear "balance" as highly unstable and warned that "a temporary technical advance . . . could give either nation the ability to come near to annihilating the other." *Deterrence and Survival in the Nuclear Age* (Gaither Report), pp. 16–17. See also Halperin, "The Gaither Committee and the Policy Process." The Re-entry Body Identification Study is discussed in SIPRI, *The Origins of MIRV*, p. 8.

[94] Richard S. Morse, Assistant Secretary of the Army, testifying before the House Committee on Science and Astronautics, *Research and Development for Defense*, 1961, pp. 70–71.

warheads above the test range at Sary Shagan, suggested that the Soviets might be testing new radars and interceptors for ABM defense. It was also in 1961 that U.S. intelligence detected construction of what appeared to be ABM emplacements around Leningrad. In 1962, the first Galosh installations went up around Moscow. Projections of the number of ABM interceptors the Soviets might deploy in the near term rose to over 8,000. Blusterous Soviet statements about the potency of defenses were properly discounted as propaganda, but they did throw into relief the possible dangers of allowing the Soviet Union to gain an exploitable edge.[95] Assuring that U.S. RVs could penetrate any foreseeable Soviet ABM system became, justifiably, the primary order of the day.

In the midst of these mounting concerns, a 1961 study by the President's Scientific Advisory Committee (PSAC) had come to the troubling conclusion that a single exoatmospheric interceptor armed with an enhanced X-ray warhead could destroy all three RVs of Polaris A-3, rendering it obsolete as a penetration device before it was ever deployed. In 1962, some American analysts began to worry that the Leningrad system's Griffon missile was actually an endoatmospheric interceptor, similar to the U.S. Sprint. If that were so, "light" decoys (because they are sorted out from true RVs when both enter the atmosphere) would also be of no use for penetration. These concerns led directly to a new penetration concept, using a maneuvering bus to launch multiple RVs on widely separated independent trajectories. Setting the stage for MIRV, DDR&E in 1962 reoriented its design parameters for a new ICBM warhead from the "Mark 12 heavy," designed to carry one large weapon, to the "Mark 12 light," which would carry multiple small RVs instead.[96]

New intelligence data collected early in 1963 clarified some of the most troubling uncertainties about Soviet ABMs. It now seemed that the Soviets had stopped the construction around Leningrad and were actually dismantling some of the existing installations. New information led to a reevaluation of the Griffon missile as slow and poorly maneuverable,

[95] See Tad Szulc, "Soviet Test Laid to Defense Goal," *New York Times*, 6 September 1971, p. 3; "US Project Underway," *New York Times*, 24 October 1961, p. 3; "Teller on Soviet Weapons Tests," *New York Times*, 31 October 1961, p. 15. Paul Nitze quotes the early estimates on ABM deployments in Comments, *Foreign Policy* 16 (1974): 82. Khrushchev's comments about Soviet ABMs are quoted in Theodore Shabad, "Khrushchev Says Missile Can Hit a Fly in Space," *New York Times*, 17 July 1962, p. 1; "Excerpts from Premier Khrushchev Address at Peace Conference in Moscow," *New York Times*, 11 July 1962, p. 4.

[96] "Mark 12 Development Plan May Change," *Aviation Week and Space Technology*, 5 November 1962, p. 29. Greenwood discusses the PSAC study. *Making the MIRV*, pp. 97–99.

probably "useless" against ICBM RVs and the Polaris A-3.[97] Construction at Galosh sites around Moscow became sporadic, with long delays that seemed to indicate serious difficulties in design.[98] For most of 1963, it did not appear that the Soviet Union was moving toward rapid deployment of ABM defenses.

This led to a lull in U.S. MIRV development. The Navy's Polaris B-3 program was postponed for at least a year, and the issue of whether a follow-on missile should incorporate MIRV was reopened. The Mark 12 program was at first delayed and later almost canceled.[99] Both actions were closely tied to reduced uncertainty about the Soviet ABM program. If Moscow was not urgently committed to ABM (as now seemed the case), it made good sense for the United States to wait before committing itself to MIRV. And because the bureaucratic forces that would make MIRV so difficult to stop later in the decade had not as yet congealed, this delay might have turned out to have a logic of its own and to last somewhat longer than it did.[100]

The MIRV delay was in fact cut short by a series of new intelligence findings at the end of 1963. Just as it seemed that the Soviets were ready to abandon the Leningrad system, a new set of similar installations was detected along wide arcs in the northern and southern tiers of the Western Soviet Union. With circumstantial evidence and counterfactual arguments about why these new emplacements were probably *not* devoted to air defense, most U.S. analysts concluded that the so-called Tallin Line was the beginning of a new ABM system designed to protect at least the European sectors of the Soviet Union from both ICBMs and SLBMs.[101] In early 1964, new radars and missile emplacements went up around Moscow as well, and tests of an improved high altitude interceptor took

[97] Greenwood, *Making the MIRV*, p. 99; "Soviets Unveil Air Defense Missile in SA-2, SA-3 Family," *Aviation Week and Space Technology*, 18 November 1963, p. 29.

[98] Freedman, *US Intelligence*, p. 88.

[99] Greenwood, *Making the MIRV*, pp. 5–7, 99.

[100] In the context of evolving American strategic theory over the next several years, the delay might even have endured. The burden of proof for a change of policy would have fallen on those who wanted to restart an embryonic program that ran up against the newly identified possibilities for arms control and strategic stability, instead of on those who were trying to slow a program that had already shown technological merit.

[101] See Tammen, *MIRV and the Arms Race*, p. 101. The October 1963 National Intelligence Estimate (NIE), reported to Congress in 1964, concurred: see McNamara, *Military Posture Statement FY 65*, p. 38. Recounting the story of Tallin in 1969, Foster argued that because the deployment sites had been situated along the so-called threat corridors for ICBMs coming over the pole and SLBMs coming north from the Meditteranean and were at a distance from major cities, it was "reasonable to conclude, with the heavy deployment of this new missile system, that it was likely to be an ABM" dedicated to heavy area defense. *Diplomatic and Strategic Impact of Multiple Warhead Systems*, p. 277.

place at Sary Shagan.[102] The baseline assessment of Soviet ABM plans went back to what it had been prior to the 1963 lull.

The actual shock from Tallin was quickly dispelled. Later the same year, CIA analysts downgraded their initial evaluations of Tallin and settled on a revised estimate that if Tallin was indeed a dedicated ABM system, it would not be a very effective one. This confidence was not fully shared by other intelligence agencies, particularly the Defense Intelligence Agency (DIA), and it did not in any case resolve expanded uncertainties about the general Soviet commitment to defense.[103] The apparent inconsistencies in Soviet behavior gave birth to a new argument that perpetuated the impact of Tallin on American beliefs about Soviet interests. If Moscow was willing to dedicate large resources to a relatively primitive system, it was suggested that these installations might be slated for eventual upgrade with new interceptors (the "Tallin upgrade scenario") or might eventually be linked together with Galosh and a set of modern radars to provide a more effective nationwide defense.

These seemingly dramatic changes in the Soviet ABM program were closely linked to a set of key decisions that boosted U.S. MIRV development during 1964. Early in the year, the Mark 12 program was accelerated and reconfigured to include MIRV as its baseline design. The Navy's B-3 warhead, now renamed Poseidon C-3, was made larger and also reoriented toward MIRV. As part of OSD's FY 1966 budget review, a firm decision was made to develop MIRVed front ends for Minuteman and Poseidon. The deployment of both as MIRVed missiles was officially approved by OSD soon thereafter in early 1965.[104] These decisions were tied directly to U.S. concerns about future Soviet defenses. According to DDR&E Foster, MIRV development for "the Poseidon program was started mainly because of the uncertainty of the Tallin threat."[105]

Between 1965 and 1967, new evidence about Soviet ABM programs continued to give impetus to the American MIRV. Construction on Galosh resumed a steady pace and then accelerated in 1966, leading McNamara to predict that the system would reach operational status against

[102] Reported in subsequent testimony before the Preparedness Investigating Subcommittee of the Senate Armed Services Committee by General Earle G. Wheeler, Chairman of the JCS, *Status of US Strategic Power*, part 1, 1968, p. 16.

[103] Freedman, *US Intelligence*, p. 93. The CIA assessments were based on new evaluations of Tallin's mechanical radars, the lack of storage sheds for nuclear warheads near missile installations, and other such signals that together made Tallin look more like an air defense system than an ABM per se. The Air Force, DIA, and Army were less impressed by the evidence and continued to argue that Tallin might in fact be a dedicated ABM.

[104] The Poseidon program was also accelerated to begin deployment one year earlier than had been planned. See testimony of Paul Nitze, then Secretary of the Navy, in *DoD Appropriations for FY 67*, part 1, p. 585.

[105] *Status of US Strategic Power*, 1968, p. 142.

U.S. ICBMs as soon as 1968. Extension of Galosh to cover other major cities was anticipated for the early 1970s.[106] In the context of expanding Galosh deployments, Tallin reemerged as a troublesome issue. In 1966, McNamara informed Congress that "available evidence does not permit a confident judgement [as to whether Tallin was] for defense against ballistic missiles or aerodynamic vehicles or both."[107] Moscow's public stance reinforced Washington's propensity to treat these possibilities as real threats: writings and statements of Soviet military and political elites during this period were almost unanimous in claiming that Soviet territory would effectively be defended from ballistic missiles in the immediate future.[108]

It was precisely during these years that the doctrinal arguments for limiting MIRV, after having been fleshed out by strategic analysts, were gaining attention at the highest levels of the decisionmaking system in Washington. And it was in 1965 that the first serious proposal for limiting MIRV through test restraints was advanced in the Pentagon. But the proponents of these arguments were handicapped by lack of evidence about Soviet interests, and specifically about the Soviets' conception of the relationship between ABM and MIRV. It did not make sense for the United States to delay MIRV on its own, particularly if the Soviets were to push ahead with both offense and defense. Not knowing how Moscow conceived of its interests on that score made it difficult to judge what incentives would be needed to elicit cooperation in MIRV, if that were possible at all. It made it impossible to convince doubters.

Serious reasons to question the depth of Moscow's commitment to defense did not surface again until 1967. At that time, signs of controversy over ABM began to appear in the Soviet press and new intelligence data about the capabilities of Tallin and Galosh confirmed that neither system could provide effective defense against American RVs. Construction of Galosh was sharply curtailed in 1968, and there were no indications of any effort to expand the system to other major cities.[109] New data collected as Tallin Line installations became operational in the spring of 1967 finally confirmed that this system was designed for defense "against high speed aerodynamic vehicles" and not against ballistic missiles.[110]

The years 1968 and 1969 produced further signals of the same kind, that the Soviet ABM threat did not necessitate an immediate concern with

---

[106] McNamara, *Military Posture Statement FY 67*, p. 60; *Military Posture Statement FY 68*, p. 51.

[107] McNamara, *Military Posture Statement FY 67*, p. 60.

[108] See the discussion in Chapter 4 for details.

[109] See Clifford, *Military Posture Statement FY 69*, p. 44. For a dissenting opinion see General Wheeler, *Status of US Strategic Power*, part 1, 1968, p. 16.

[110] See McNamara, *Military Posture Statement FY 69*, p. 62.

penetration. This should have reduced the perceived imperative to proceed with MIRV as an ABM-buster. But the U.S. MIRV program was no longer as responsive to the level of uncertainty about the Soviet ABM threat as it had been in the early 1960s, for two reasons. Bureaucratic momentum that had built up behind MIRV in the interim certainly made the program more resistant to delay at the end of the decade. The more important cause for this change, however, was the shift in doctrinal justification for MIRV away from ABM-buster and toward hard target killer. This was crucial, because uncertainty about the growing counterforce threat from Soviet ICBMs and the underlying interests behind this development was rising dramatically just as similar questions about ABM were being resolved.

Counterforce Uncertainties

The primary strategic rationale for MIRV in the late 1960s was to compensate for and possibly to surpass the capabilities of the Soviets' growing arsenal of modern ICBMs. The fact that Moscow continued its deployment program unabated after reaching numerical parity with the Minuteman force in 1969 confounded American analysts. Why were the Soviets deploying so many ICBMs? And what did this imply for potential cooperation on MIRV?

The roots of this story also go back to the early 1960s. Once the feared "missile gap" was exposed as a chimera and the United States began to deploy Minuteman in hardened silos during 1962, there seemed little immediate danger that American nuclear forces would become vulnerable to preemptive strike. There was also reason to believe that Moscow recognized and accepted this fact. Between 1962 and 1965, Soviet ICBM deployments proceeded at a slow pace, about half as quickly as U.S. projections.[111] The general sentiment among American analysts was that economic and technological constraints in the context of a mild easing of superpower tensions would moderate Soviet aspirations for offensive parity in the short-term, and certainly for anything beyond parity in the longer term. McNamara went further than this in 1965, arguing that although the Soviets could in theory "catch up" in numbers with the U.S. ICBM arsenal by 1970, the slow rate of their deployment program "meant that the Soviets have decided that they have lost the quantitative race."[112]

[111] Freedman, *US Intelligence*, pp. 101–2.

[112] "Is Russia Slowing Down in the Arms Race? Interview with Robert S. McNamara," *US News & World Report*, 12 April 1965, p. 52. The 1963 and 1964 NIEs projected that the Soviets would deploy, at the low end, 400 to 500 missiles by the end of the decade. The

Reassuring public statements aside, there were by 1965 substantive reasons to question this reading of Moscow's interests and intentions. The rate at which the Soviets were constructing new silos rose sharply late in 1964 and again in 1965. Many of these silos were designed for the SS-11, a new small ICBM that offered improvements in performance and reliability over older missiles. Some, however, were dedicated to the SS-9, a much more threatening and extremely large missile with a throw-weight estimated to be almost three times greater than the older SS-7 and SS-8. According to intelligence estimates, it would take only 50 SS-9s with single large warheads to match the gross megatonnage of the entire Minuteman force, while 100 of these missiles alone could fulfill the requirements of "assured destruction" as defined by the Pentagon. Beyond that, the SS-9 had an additional important feature attributed to it by American analysts. Its large throw-weight seemed particularly well-suited to carrying and delivering MIRV warheads with large numbers of RVs against hardened targets. American intelligence agencies thus watched closely to see how the SS-9 deployment proceeded, as a source of feedback about Soviet interests with regard to counterforce. Because the CIA at this time believed that threatening Minuteman was *not* Moscow's principal goal, its estimates projected that SS-9 deployments would level off and that SS-11s would make up the bulk of Soviet ICBM forces by 1970. On similar reasoning, the Defense Department concurred.[113] When Moscow accelerated the deployment of *both* missiles late in 1965, this was interpreted according to the same logic as a bid to achieve parity with the United States sooner rather than later. It was not at that time seen as signaling a Soviet attempt to go beyond that state.[114]

These were sensible arguments so long as the underlying assumptions were correct; that is, if Moscow actually shared Washington's strategic theories about stability and deterrence. But Soviet behavior soon confounded expectations. There was an even more rapid expansion of ICBM deployments in 1966, with emphasis on the SS-9. There was also new evidence that the Soviets were testing an upgraded and more accurate version of the missile. In 1967, Washington revised its intelligence estimates to project that the SS-9 program would reach final deployment at about 200 missiles by the end of the decade.[115] The new data and resulting projections did not clarify the question of Soviet interests; they con-

---

high-end projection was under 700, still significantly below numerical parity with the United States. Freedman, *US Intelligence*, p. 104.

[113] Freedman, *US Intelligence*, p. 109; McNamara, *Military Posture Statement FY 67*, p. 57; Michael Getler, "Arms Control and the SS-9," *Space-Aeronautics* 52, no. 6 (1969).

[114] Freedman, *US Intelligence*, pp. 111–13.

[115] See testimony of David Packard, *Strategic and Foreign Policy Implications of ABM Systems*, 1969, part 1, p. 284.

fused it. While the Soviet arsenal was apparently going to be much larger than was necessary for assured destruction of cities, it was also going to be too small to pose a serious first-strike threat against Minuteman.[116]

For a short period in 1967 and 1968, brewing controversies over what the Soviets' underlying interests actually were downplayed as the SS-9 deployments appeared to be tailing off. But in another instance of changes in feedback carrying more weight than underlying continuities, Washington's intelligence community reacted sharply when the Soviets revived their SS-9 silo construction program in 1968. Estimates for eventual deployment of the missile were quickly raised to between four and six hundred.[117] This ran straight up against the more optimistic interpretations of Soviet interests. It now seemed plausible to argue that Moscow might be reaching for a first-strike threat against Minuteman. But the on-again, off-again SS-9 deployment program was by no means confirming evidence. It was also possible that the Soviets were seeking a partial damage-limitation capability, similar to what some U.S. strategic thinkers favored. Partial damage-limitation capabilities on both sides still would have been consistent with broader cooperative efforts at managing deterrence and certainly with limitations on MIRV.

Even if the Soviets were seeking a first-strike capability, it still made good sense for the United States to try for joint restraint in limiting MIRV.[118] But the two interpretations led to very different arguments about the proper strategy for doing so, specifically regarding whether the Soviets were apt to exploit more permissive strategies of reciprocity. Without more discriminating feedback, U.S. decisionmakers would have found it difficult to forge a working consensus adequate to support a reasonable bid for reciprocal restraint of MIRV at this time. What would have been difficult became nearly impossible as new uncertainties emerged over the issue of a Soviet MIRV.

In 1965, the National Intelligence Estimate for the first time discussed the possible consequences for U.S. strategic forces should the Soviets deploy MIRV. But these were treated principally as long-term projections, because there was as yet no evidence that the Soviets were even close to achieving a multiple-warhead capability of any sort. Over the next two years, Moscow carried out several multiple satellite launchings that did demonstrate some of the prerequisite technology.[119] The press reported

---

[116] Freedman, US Intelligence, pp. 114–15; Status of US Strategic Power, pp. 3, 16–19.

[117] Getler, "Arms Control and the SS-9," p. 43.

[118] It might even have made more sense, given the increasing Soviet advantage in throw-weight and numbers of land-based ICBMs. As noted previously, U.S. decisionmakers recognized that adding MIRV to both sides' arsenals in this scenario would leave the United States at a distinct disadvantage.

[119] Freedman discusses the NIE report and the multiple satellite launches of 1967. US Intelligence, pp. 115–16.

these as possible steps in a dedicated effort to develop MIRV for the SS-9 in the short-term and for its successors.[120] But the DoD did not share in this assessment. As late as 1968, McNamara informed the Congress that the administration had "no evidence of such an effort" to develop MIRV, and that even in the worst case "it would take from four to five years from the start of development for [the Soviets] to attain an operational capability, and we would probably be able to detect the testing of such a system at least two years before that happened."[121]

This relative complacency about the prospects for a Soviet MIRV was severely damaged when Moscow tested a multiple-warhead system in August 1968. The data on these tests pointed to the conclusion that this was only a MRV, comparable in technology to the Polaris A-3. Because it did not appear capable of attacking hardened silos, the SS-9 triplet was viewed by most American analysts as a way of "spreading out" the missile's throw-weight to enhance its efficiency for countervalue strikes. But in the face of the much greater uncertainty about underlying Soviet interests in 1968, disagreements over the meaning and significance of these tests became nearly impossible to settle. The lines of cleavage centered on the question of whether this MRV was a significant step on the technological road to a true MIRV. Secretary of Defense Clifford argued that it "was still too early to assess the ultimate operational configuration" of the system; the most definitive assessment he offered was that "these tests are not incompatible with the ultimate development of a MIRV." DDR&E, with the support of the Air Force, was more pessimistic, arguing that for all practical purposes the triplet warhead was already a MIRV and could threaten Minuteman silos.[122]

When the Nixon administration in 1969 took up the question of limiting MIRVs through SALT, it could not be fully certain as to what the Soviets did or did not already possess in terms of tested technology. Yet it took a decision on this score, or at least a supportable working hypothesis, to determine if a MIRV flight-test ban at this juncture could effectively constrain deployment. The new administration's strategic review failed to reach a consensus on that issue. As if to make matters worse, the level of uncertainty increased further in April (in the midst of the deliberations) when the Soviets began a new series of tests of the triplet warhead at longer range. American analysts were deeply disturbed by the pattern (the so-called footprint) in which the three RVs were dispersed during each of these tests. Secretary of Defense Melvin Laird told Congress that "the area of impact corresponded to a very marked degree to

---

[120] For example, see *Technology Week*, 7 December 1966; *New York Times*, 10 September 1967; and *Aviation Week and Space Technology*, 16 October 1967.

[121] McNamara, quoted in Freedman, *US Intelligence*, pp. 115–16.

[122] Clifford, *Military Posture Statement FY 70*, pp. 79–80.

the various triangles that can be worked out as far as our Minuteman sites are concerned."[123]

Whether or not this was the footprint of a true MIRV, the Soviet tests did resemble triangulation patterns that technicians from the U.S. defense contractor TRW had been working on for some time. The intelligence community again split over how to interpret the significance of these tests: the CIA took a less ominous view, while DDR&E was deeply concerned.[124] When it came to the implications for MIRV limitations, the question was pushed up to the highest SALT decisionmaking level at the White House. For Nixon and Kissinger, the question of whether a MIRV test ban ought to be proposed to Moscow at SALT came to depend on these competing assessments of whether the Soviets could deploy a MIRV system that would threaten Minuteman silos with technology they had *already* tested.

The evidence to that effect was mixed. There were substantial reasons to believe that the SS-9 triplet did not have either the targeting flexibility or the accuracy necessary to attack silos. At the same time, the system was more sophisticated than Polaris A-3 and had guidance capabilities beyond what was needed for a simple MIRV.[125] In short, it did not fit the pattern by which American multiple-warhead systems had evolved. This made it even more difficult to arbitrate between varying interpretations of what the Soviets were trying to do or in fact had already done with regard to MIRV. The special interagency panel that was established under Kissinger to settle this question in the process of planning for SALT failed to do so, as I noted earlier. There was never a consensus on working hypotheses about Soviet interests in MIRV analagous to that which had formed when it came to ABM.[126]

At the last critical juncture for cooperation, proponents of strategies aimed at reciprocal restraint in MIRV were again left without a consensus on working hypotheses that could support their case. They needed to argue that the Soviets had strong motivations to respond to an American demarche on MIRV, but the feedback from Moscow on this score was sparse and equivocal. Given the prevailing level of uncertainty about broader Soviet interests in counterforce, it is not surprising that the administration eventually chose to act on the basis of DDR&E's worst-case assessments of what Moscow could do with its current multiple-warhead

---

[123] Laird, testifying before the Senate Foreign Relations Committee, *Intelligence and the ABM*, 1969, p. 24.

[124] Alton Frye, personal communication, February 13, 1989.

[125] See Freedman, *US Intelligence*, pp. 140–42. Also see *Diplomatic and Strategic Impact of Multiple Warhead Missiles*, pp. 244, 263–65.

[126] Newhouse reports that the panel "reached no conclusions but exhaustively laid out data and identified areas of disagreement." *Cold Dawn*, p. 161.

technology. This was a major reason for the crippling of the administration's proposed reciprocal strategies for cooperation in MIRV.

The same uncertainties and the resulting lack of consensus also checked Congress's concurrent bid for mutual restraint. Setting the stage for the key hearings on the proposed test moratorium in 1969, the *Washington Post* noted that "there are no clear answers to where the Russians stand on MIRV development . . . whether [the SS-9 triplet] were guided warheads (MIRV) or simply gravity bombs, such as the Polaris A-3 . . . is uncertain."[127] These hearings on MIRV, unlike those on ABM, failed to produce a set of working hypotheses that could generate consensus. Administration spokesmen, particularly those from DoD, rejected any delay in the U.S. MIRV program without confronting the arguments against their position. They did not offer definitive claims that the Soviets actually possessed MIRV technology, or that a test moratorium would be ineffectual, but they did not have to. Typical was DDR&E Foster's statement that "the things we do *not* know about this mechanism are completely compatible with MIRV, even though they do not prove MIRV capability." But without more discriminating evidence about underlying Soviet interests, the deep uncertainty reflected in this position would carry the debate. Even Congressman Bingham, a key MIRV opponent and sponsor of the House moratorium proposal, was constrained to admit that given the "considerable differences within the US intelligence community as to precisely what the USSR has been testing, whether it's MRV or MIRV," and his underlying uncertainty about Soviet "trustworthiness," he could not in the final analysis resist the administration's contention that a test moratorium might fail to preserve U.S. security interests in MIRV.[128] "Trustworthiness" in this context simply meant having an ample understanding of why the Soviets were doing what they were in multiple warheads and in counterforce-capable systems more generally. Lacking a consensus on this score, the Congressional bid for reciprocal restraint in MIRV was also derailed.

Could it have been otherwise? As was the case for Tallin, the specific uncertainties about the SS-9 triplet were later resolved. New data from additional Soviet tests during autumn 1969 and winter 1970 confirmed that the system did not, according to Foster, have "the flexibility necessary to target each warhead against a different Minuteman silo."[129] A new TRW study using the data from these tests concluded that the triplet was not a substantial threat to hardened targets, and that the Soviets re-

---

[127] *Washington Post*, 22 June 1969, p. 18.
[128] *Diplomatic and Strategic Impact of Multiple Warhead Missiles*, pp. 14, 27.
[129] *DoD Appropriations for FY 71*, part 1, p. 385.

mained at least several years of development and testing away from the ability to deploy a counterforce-capable MIRV.[130]

This information might have made a marginal difference if it were known in 1969. But by itself it probably would not have been enough to change American strategy. Aiming for a joint test moratorium would certainly have appeared a more viable option for American decisionmakers who already favored this path based on their reading of Soviet interests. But the evidence of late 1969 and 1970 would probably not have been sufficient to support a consensus with decisionmakers holding a more suspicious view of Moscow's underlying counterforce aspirations. Opponents of a MIRV ban would have maintained that the Soviets were strongly inclined to evade a test moratorium and would find some way to do so, go on to deploy MIRV surreptitiously, and leave the United States with the sucker's payoff for unrequited restraint.[131] It is not likely that proponents of enhanced contingent restraint could have won out against this argument in 1970. As it was, they were not even able to generate a consensus on working hypotheses that could logically support a bid for reciprocity. Developing such a consensus needed better evidence of underlying Soviet interests that would have made it seem likely that Moscow would reciprocate American restraint. This kind of evidence was not forthcoming.

The technical problem of distinguishing between MRV and MIRV when it came to counterforce was a real one. But it was not insoluble, as the 1970 evaluation of data from the Soviet triplet tests shows. It was less critical to the outcome of this case than were the underlying uncertainties about Soviet interests. This was the fundamental source of the missed opportunity in MIRV. It did not take very much uncertainty on the MIRV/MRV distinction or the verifiability of a test moratorium to crush bids for cooperation through reciprocity. This is because the U.S. deci-

---

[130] See the report in Michael Getler, "Russian Missile Faulted," *Washington Post*, 17 June 1971, p. 1. According to Getler, technical sources at TRW had "reversed" the conclusions of their earlier report, which in any case had given only "lukewarm" support to the claim that the SS-9 triplet was a MIRV. These conclusions were seconded by the JCS in the Chairman's 1972 report to Congress: "regardless of whether the Soviets were, in fact, working on a MIRV, the Mod-4 (of the SS-9) has thus far failed to demonstrate the achievement of such a capability." Admiral Thomas H. Moorer, *US Military Posture for FY 1973*, pp. 7–8.

[131] Foster in 1969 noted that in theory "the SS-9 triplet might be deployed on the basis of further extensive ground tests and without further flight tests." *Diplomatic and Strategic Impact of Multiple Warhead Missiles*, p. 246. This was a minority view. Most other witnesses agreed that the Soviets could not attain a reasonable level of confidence in their weapon were it to be deployed on this basis. Kissinger shared this belief. In 1972 he argued that testing was the critical issue for MIRV because "without testing, by definition, it is not easy to deploy them. It is, in fact, impossible to deploy them." *Military Implications of the Treaty on the Limitations of Anti-Ballistic Missile Systems and the Interim Agreement on Limitation of Strategic Offensive Arms*, 1972, p. 138.

sionmaking system could not forge or sustain a consensus on working hypotheses about Soviet interests that could explain possible preferences for cooperation at several critical points in the story. Reciprocal strategies for MIRV were derailed, and an evolving process that might have led to a cooperative solution was blocked.

Conclusion

From the standpoint of history and strategic logic, MIRV is an anomalous legacy of U.S.-Soviet arms control. At the birth of SALT, the superpowers failed to limit a weapons system that was known to be directly opposed to basic principles of the nascent arms control regime. MIRV is also a puzzle for cooperation theory. The initial conditions of Axelrod's model were fulfilled in MIRV, leading U.S. decisionmakers to develop several different strategies for reciprocity aimed at eliciting cooperation. But none of these strategies was fully implemented, and MIRV ended as a missed opportunity. Mutual defection in MIRV would soon have severe detrimental consequences for arms control and the superpower relationship more generally.

Would the outcome have been different if the United States had succeeded in putting a strategy of reciprocity in place? There are both historical and strategic reasons to believe that Soviet leaders wished to seriously explore the possibilities of an unMIRVed solution for SALT. But not all strategies of reciprocity would have had equal promise. If Washington had chosen contingent restraint along the lines of certain more permissive Congressional proposals, the Soviets would have been tempted by continuing strong incentives attached to the D,C outcome. It would have made sense for Moscow to move forward with its own multiple-warhead program, probing for the possibility that the United States would not respond to unilateral defection. While Washington's response might in fact have been delayed by domestic politics in the early 1970s (as Kissinger feared), it would have come with considerable vigor just a few years hence. As it was, the consequences of Soviet MIRVing provoked a strong reaction in the late Carter and early Reagan years, a reaction that would have been even more dramatic and hostile had Soviet MIRVing gone forward (even if more slowly) in the face of American restraint. Cooperation would have been a victim here as well.

The United States could have initially chosen a much more demanding strategy for MIRV along the lines of contingent threat of escalation. With its technological lead at the end of the 1960s, Washington could have offered Moscow an explicit and stark choice: either accept a formal treaty trading MIRV for Soviet ICBMs, or face an accelerated MIRV program aimed at placing Soviet strategic forces at risk. There is no reason to believe that Soviet leaders would have accepted the cooperative deal on American terms. While the alternative would have put the Soviet Union in a disadvantageous position for a period of several years, Moscow could have mitigated the consequences by redoubling efforts to expand its ICBM arsenal in the short term, and accelerating its MIRV development program for the longer term. Barring any unforeseen technological "leapfrogs" in the interim, Soviet leaders could then have been confident that in just a few years this escalation of the competition would come to favor themselves. The missed opportunity for cooperation would stand.

Enhanced contingent restraint would have maximized the prospects for cooperation. Washington could have made use of its lead in MIRV technology to reinforce the credibility of a bid for a test moratorium conditional on Soviet reciprocity. If the probability that U.S. restraint was open to exploitation was known to be low, Soviet leaders would have had strong incentives to cooperate. A resulting bilateral moratorium could have evolved into longer-term cooperative restraint. But could the United States actually have adopted such a strategy? The five variables that I use to explain strategy choice mainly favored enhanced contingent restraint. Bureaucratic politics was a major but not a decisive impediment. Powerful bureaucracies opposed the possibilities for a reciprocal strategy, but neither the position of the bureaucracies on the issue nor their power ruled it out. Even Kahan's account of MIRV, the most pessimistic on this score, recognizes that Johnson or Nixon might have struck a deal with the Joint Chiefs by offering a new ballistic missile submarine (SSBN) or advanced manned bomber in place of MIRV. This approach would have made good sense from a variety of perspectives. It would have been more expensive in the short run but considerably cheaper later on. It would have done less damage to the stability of deterrence and would have been more conducive to SALT.[132] In short, because the interests of the bureaucracies could have been met by means other than MIRV, bureaucratic politics does not by itself explain the derailing of American strategies for cooperation.

Cooperation in MIRV depended upon reciprocal strategies. These were undermined not by bureaucratic politics per se but by *uncertainty*. At critical junctures for U.S. decisionmaking on MIRV, uncertainties intervened to deflect the implementation of reciprocal strategies that emerged as part of the process suggested by Axelrod's model. Uncertainty existed about

---

[132] Kahan argues that this deal would have been possible under the condition that "US officials had realized that the acquisition of MIRVs . . . would probably induce the USSR to develop MIRVs with a potential to destroy our own ICBMs." *Security in the Nuclear Age*, p. 138. This chapter shows that the condition was in fact fulfilled long before 1968 or 1969, when Kahan believes that the bureaucratic momentum behind MIRV became irreversible.

more than the immediate issue of Soviet capabilities in multiple-warhead systems; it extended to the deeper issue of basic Soviet conceptions of self-interest in counterforce. Why were the Soviets deploying so many large ICBMs? What kind of multiple-warhead systems were they testing, and why? American decisionmakers could not agree on even provisional answers to these questions that could have supported a strategy of enhanced contingent restraint for MIRV.

They could not agree in part because uncertainty about Soviet capabilities in MIRV was managed through unilateral means. For several critical years after 1965, this meant that the "greater than expected threat," a "projection of Soviet strategic capabilities which assumes the Soviets develop and deploy their forces to a degree we believe is only remotely possible," was the starting point for analyzing U.S. strategic force requirements.[133] The scarce and confusing information that U.S. intelligence could obtain on its own about what the Soviets were actually doing in multiple-warhead systems did not provide sufficient grounds to argue against the default position of the greater than expected threat. By 1969, the United States was poised to respond as if the Soviets were already in possession of a counterforce-capable MIRV system.

Underlying the uncertainty about capabilities, and more important, was a fundamental uncertainty concerning Soviet interests in counterforce that was also managed almost entirely through unilateral means. American decisionmakers held to two kinds of assessments about Soviet interests. Both were consistent with potential cooperative solutions for MIRV, but each prescribed different strategies of reciprocity for eliciting cooperation. Washington could not forge a working consensus between these positions sufficient to support a strategy of reciprocity on MIRV.

Feedback from Soviet behavior that might have helped generate the necessary consensus was inconsistent and ambiguous. The biased way in which U.S. decisionmakers interpreted what little feedback there was made the situation worse. Soviet behavior was increasingly seen in the light of American strategic logic, and changes in specific indicators were emphasized over basic consistencies. Washington showed similar propensities with regard to ABM, but in that case they were accompanied by serious and sustained efforts to elicit more discriminating feedback about Soviet interests. These were efforts to deal with uncertainty about inter-

---

[133] Testimony of Alain Enthoven, *Status of US Strategic Power*, part 1, 1968, pp. 142–43. The development of the greater than expected threat method, and its demise after McNamara left the Pentagon, is described in Enthoven and Smith, *How Much Is Enough*, pp. 178–79; Freedman, *US Intelligence*, pp. 84–86; Newhouse, *Cold Dawn*, p. 72. The greater than expected threat was designed to guide research and development only (not deployment decisions) for "US force plus options" that could be readied for deployment relatively quickly in the unlikely event that the greater than expected threat actually emerged.

ests through *bilateral* means. While not fully successful, they did pay off in a working consensus strong enough to support a strategy of reciprocity for ABM. Why was a similar effort to clarify underlying interests not made on MIRV?

The ambivalence of U.S. strategic doctrine and conceptions of self-interest when it came to counterforce was one reason. But it cannot be the most important reason. American decisionmakers were ambivalent about defenses as well. In the longer term, the picture for U.S. interests in MIRV was actually clearer than it was in ABM, and it was not a pretty one. American decisionmakers had to face conflicting values when it came to pursuing "strategic superiority" through MIRV in the short-term, but there was little ambiguity about how that scenario would impact on American security interests just a few years hence when the Soviets MIRVed as well.

The more important reason is that Washington took as an axiom what was really an unexplored assumption: that the Soviets did not wish to share information on their interests and capabilities in counterforce. What was clear was that there were no formal bilateral institutions in place to facilitate discussions of strategic understandings and conceptions of self-interest in either ABM or MIRV. This was overcome in ABM by making use of informal institutions and contacts to probe the Soviets' understandings of their self-interest and to influence it through meta-strategy. MIRV was a harder problem, from technological, doctrinal, and political perspectives. But it was not so hard as to rule out any possibility of probing or promoting a joint understanding of interests. Neither side engaged the debate at this level. The Soviets did not take on the counter-force issue either with the Americans or among themselves in the visible way that they did for defense. The Americans never pushed them to do so. The notion that both sides might wish to duplicate efforts that were made to clarify interests on defense barely occurred to decisionmakers when they thought about MIRV. As time went on, the underlying uncertainties swelled and a working consensus on Soviet interests became increasingly difficult to construct. Given the deep and expanding uncertainty about interests, it did not take very much uncertainty about the more proximate issues—whether the Soviets had tested MRV or MIRV, and whether they could go on to deploy MIRV in the face of a test moratorium—to send efforts at reciprocity off track.

What was missing from the MIRV case were bilateral institutions for dealing with uncertainty about each side's conceptions of self-interest. In 1968 and 1969, when MIRV reached critical decisional points in the United States, it was too late to build from scratch the kinds of bilateral institutions that would have facilitated clarification of interests adequate to support a consensus on working hypotheses for a reciprocal strategy.

Institutions of this sort were not impossible to foresee. They had developed, mostly informally, in ABM. More formal institutions would emerge over the course of the next few years as a part of SALT. Had either been extant and available to decisionmakers in 1968, that *might* have made a difference for MIRV. Chapter 7 considers this possibility further by examining the nature and potential impact of certain kinds of institutions—those that contribute to joint understandings of how states define their interests in nuclear security issues—as they bear on cooperation theory and U.S.-Soviet arms control.

6

Antisatellite Weapons

SPACE is part of the global commons. When the space age began in the late 1950s, the United States, the Soviet Union, and other states turned their attention to the issue of what rules would govern the use of outer space. Many countries wanted to use space for civilian and commercial applications; and although there were predictable disagreements over the specifics of allocating orbital slots, effective coordination was soon recognized to be a shared interest. The United States and the Soviet Union could even agree on a principle of allocation: because they had the most advanced technologies to exploit the commercial potential of space, "free access" made good sense to both.

Space is also an arena of military competition. Almost as soon as technology made space accessible, the United States and the Soviet Union began to pursue military and security objectives in space much as they have on the earth, on the seas, and in the air. Here their shared interests were much less obvious. Military competition in space from the beginning was a high stakes game: the costs of competing were great and the potential threats involved in falling behind were often perceived as severe. The opportunities have also been immense. In most issues relating to the military use of space, the superpowers acted according to unilateral perceptions of self-interest. They have generally had low regard for the possible interdependence of their respective decisions and have discounted any potential for cooperation. When it comes to military applications, space has mostly been a domain of self-help.

Antisatellite weapons (ASAT) are an important and interesting exception. American and Soviet decisions about whether to develop and deploy antisatellite weapons were not so clearly determined by unilateral preferences on either side. For at least the period between 1960 and 1980, the superpowers treated ASAT as an interdependent game. American and Soviet leaders never signed a treaty that explicitly placed limits on development, deployment, or use of ASATs. Yet there is a history of significant cooperation between the superpowers in ASAT that endured for almost two decades.

Technology played an important role in this because for much of that time technology severely constrained what either side could accomplish with ASATs. But technology by itself does not explain the extent of U.S.-

Soviet cooperation in ASAT or the process by which cooperation came about. As early as 1962, restraint based on political decisions began to extend beyond the limitations of technology. This cooperation arose unexpectedly and under circumstances that were politically and strategically inauspicious. It was sustained at a high level through most of the 1960s while the superpowers competed vigorously in other aspects of the strategic arms race. Although cooperation in ASAT was challenged at the end of the 1960s, it was strongly revitalized in the early 1970s. It began to deteriorate more seriously several years later. By the early 1980s, the story of cooperation in ASAT had gone from "surprising success" to "missed opportunity."

Can Axelrod's model help to explain the growth and decay of cooperation in ASAT? This chapter traces the development of cooperation over a longer historical time frame than the previous two case studies; it thus has a slightly different structure. I begin by discussing the threats and opportunities posed by military missions in space. The things that states can do to respond to threats from space collapse into a dyadic choice between competitive and cooperative options. Like ABM and MIRV, ASAT is a highly competitive response to those threats. From an "objective" standpoint, the United States and the Soviet Union face an interdependent decision in ASAT that takes the form of an iterated game with a long shadow of the future. A similar "objective" assessment of the superpowers' preferences over outcomes in ASAT matches the PD. This suggests the possibilities for a cooperative solution.

At critical junctures for the development of cooperation, U.S. decisionmakers' preferences over outcomes in ASAT came to match these initial conditions. Washington developed different strategies for eliciting cooperation in ASAT at different times, depending in part on the state of the five variables that I use to explain strategy choice. Each of the United States' reciprocal strategies for ASAT rested on a set of working hypotheses about Soviet interests. As in ABM and MIRV, U.S. decisionmakers found it difficult to assess the deeper interests that underlay Moscow's behavior and apparent preferences in ASAT. This complicated the problem of assessing feedback about the impact of American strategy in all three cases. But in ASAT, the hypotheses themselves were of a different character, with different implications for strategies and cooperation. The importance of these hypotheses goes beyond Axelrod's assumptions about preferences and interests, and beyond the bridge principles I developed in the previous chapters.

The story of cooperation in ASAT is different because it begins with Washington's inability to define a stable set of interests underlying its *own* preferences in ASAT. In the 1960s, U.S. decisionmakers looked at ASAT from a position of *radical uncertainty*. Because technology was changing rapidly and in unforeseen ways, weapons scientists, military analysts, and most importantly the key decisionmakers to whom they reported were unable to envision potential "outcome scenarios" in space that would follow from a full-fledged military competition there. On the assumption that the Soviets were in a similar predicament, top decisionmakers first in the Kennedy administration and then under Johnson molded and held together a consensus on a set of working hypotheses about Soviet interests in ASAT. This was sufficient to support a strategy of contingent restraint for ASAT, which led to a tacit cooperation for much of the decade. Cooperation came mostly from strong aversions to competing in an area of radical uncertainty. American decisionmakers believed that both they and their Soviet counterparts were motivated to avoid a competition in ASAT because neither could foresee the impact on their respective interests of a full-fledged arms race in space.

As technological possibilities began to be clarified in the early 1970s, Washington's radical uncertainty gave way to more clearly defined interests and definite preferences over outcomes, whose essential characteristics could now be foreseen. A similar process must have taken place in Moscow. The period between 1972 and 1976 seems to have been the pivotal time in which both sides resolved radical uncertainties about ASAT. They did so entirely separately and in different ways. This was a missed opportunity. Either side might have tried to engage in meta-strategy, to influence the process by which the other was coming to define its self-interest in ASAT. A more conservative approach would have been simply to try to elicit feedback that would have helped decisionmakers understand the other side's interests, without trying to change them. But neither meta-strategy nor any efforts to elicit greater feedback of this kind were tried by either Washington or Moscow.

As a result, when the United States reevaluated its ASAT strategy in 1976 it had only limited information about what the Soviets had done and were doing in ASAT, and almost no understanding of why. The working hypotheses about Soviet interests in ASAT, which had earlier commanded a high level of consensus among U.S. leaders, began to break down. At the same time, new military satellite technologies were making the dangers of unrequited cooperation seem more substantial. American strategy shifted to contingent threat of escalation, and cooperation that had already become tenuous suffered further.

During the early 1980s, cooperation would fall final victim to a change in preferences as U.S. decisionmakers came to favor moving forward with ASAT regardless of what the Soviets chose to do. This did not follow solely from technological change, but was in large part a legacy of earlier cooperation, and particularly of the way in which that cooperation disintegrated. Because the story of the 1980s is not one of PD preferences, I leave it for comment in the final chapter. This chapter ends in 1980 with the argument that ASAT cooperation in the 1960s and early 1970s complicated or even blocked the process by which the superpowers might have adjusted to changes in technology in a coordinated fashion. One legacy of this kind of cooperation was greater competition and diminished security in the future.

Threats and Opportunities in Space

Military Satellites

Why do states build antisatellite weapons? The simple reason is so that they can attack an adversary's satellites. Each superpower's presumptive interest in being able to do that follows from the fact that both have made extensive use of satellites for military missions. Technology has rapidly expanded the range of things that can be done with space-based systems. In 1957 the Soviet Union launched Sputnik, the world's first artificial satellite. By 1963 the United States was operating sophisticated military satellites for photographic reconnaissance, electronic intelligence, early warning of missile attack, detection of nuclear detonation on earth, communications, and navigation. Moscow was not far behind in most of these areas. Once space was opened to military competition, there was no obvious reason why satellites would be treated as any more sacrosanct than aircraft carriers or foreign military bases.

Space-based systems are in general both technologically elegant and highly expensive. But for certain military purposes, satellites turn out to be highly effective and economically viable alternatives to more conventional types of systems. Communications and reconnaissance are good examples. It is easier, more effective and reliable, and probably on balance less expensive to communicate with widespread military forces via satellite than via cable or other means. Satellite reconnaissance is an order of magnitude more effective and efficient for most purposes than "spy" planes and ships. But there is another, more insidious side to the coin of efficiency. If satellites perform basically the same functions as a host of other military support systems, and they perform those functions better, then satellites should presumably be a high-value target for an adversary. This logic has certainly applied to military support systems *not* based in space, including those that carried out some of the functions that satellites later took over. For example, part of the justification for Soviet efforts to deploy advanced antiaircraft systems in the 1950s was to prevent American reconnaissance planes from engaging in what Moscow considered overhead espionage. The Soviet military succeeded in downing the U-2 plane as early as 1960, only several years after its maiden flight. A priori, ASAT would be the next logical step.

Cooperative restraint in ASAT systems would indeed make no sense if satellites were strictly analogous to regular military forces or support systems. Each state's decision about whether or not to develop means of neutralizing or destroying satellites would then be entirely straightforward. But the situation is complicated by the fact that satellites are different. The things that satellites do are not uniformly threatening to an adversary. Some satellite functions act to stabilize the military face-off between the United States and the Soviet Union in ways that benefit *both* sides.

Military analysts often refer to such capabilities as being "benign." Satellite early warning systems are an important example. During the 1950s, U.S. strategic analysts worried deeply about certain scenarios in which mutual fear of surprise attack could lead to an inadvertent war that neither side actually wanted to fight. Reliable early warning systems in space were an essential part of the solution to this problem.[1] Photoreconnaissance satellites also serve the interests of both sides in similar fashion. The information exchange that takes place through photoreconnaissance mostly acts to limit crisis instability by reducing the possibility that pressures to preempt might develop through fear or a mistaken belief that the other side was preparing an imminent attack. Photoreconnaissance is also a central part of the verification capabilities that have made arms control and some degree of arms race stability possible. For straightforward reasons then, each superpower has had strong interests in maintaining and safeguarding its own benign capabilities. What is unusual about satellites is that this interest extends to similar systems that the other side is operating. "Benign" satellites can make deterrence based on the threat of assured retaliation relatively robust and stable, reduce crisis instability and other routes to inadvertent war, and play a facilitative role in arms control—but only if both sides operate them with confidence.[2] The result is a set of shared interests in protecting benign satellites from attack. Since the early 1960s this has been an important reason to avoid a competition in ASAT systems.

These interests are complicated by the fact that not all satellite func-

---

[1] But not the only part; also essential was the development of survivable basing modes for ballistic missiles and more robust command, communication, and control links.

[2] The logic of this argument is most clearly developed by Schelling in *The Strategy of Conflict*, particularly Chapters 9 and 10. If, for example, only one side was able to rely on its early warning systems, the other side would fear a surprise attack and would be pressured to preempt in the event of crisis. Knowing this, the side with early warning systems might in turn have incentives to strike first in anticipation of that "preemption." Extreme crisis instability is the result.

tions are quite so benign. Both sides also use satellites as "force multipliers." Force multipliers provide support to terrestrial military forces, magnifying their effectiveness and military utility. The Soviets, for example, have since 1967 used electronic and radar ocean reconnaissance satellites to locate and track U.S. Navy aircraft carrier battle groups. In the event of war, the information collected by these satellites would presumably be used to guide and support Soviet forces in attacks against the U.S. Navy.[3] Communications satellites can play a similar role for both sides because they allow for more efficient dissemination of information to military combat units in real or near-real time. This kind of information could give one side or the other a decisive military advantage in war.

The distinction between benign satellite functions and those that act as force multipliers is sometimes fuzzy and usually dependent on context. Signals intelligence satellites that are used in peacetime to monitor compliance with arms control agreements can also be used for espionage and to intercept military communications in the course of a war. Photoreconnaissance systems that are accurate enough to aid targeting or to provide information about troop movements can be similarly threatening. If war were to break out, each superpower would obviously have strong incentives to deny these "force multiplier" capabilities to the other. ASATs are one way to do so.

Up to the present, neither superpower has chosen to use satellites in ways that go beyond force multiplication. That is, current satellites (so far as we know) are not equipped with weapons and are not designed for the direct application of force from space. This is largely a reflection of technological constraints. For most military purposes it has until now been easier, less expensive, and more reliable to base weapons on the earth, in the air, and on the seas than in outer space. Some of these technological constraints began to erode in the 1980s and both superpowers began to explore possible missions in which satellites could be used effectively for the direct application of force. American efforts were often highly visible because most were connected with President Reagan's SDI program.[4] For example, U.S. scientists argued that space-based lasers foreseen as part of an advanced BMD system would almost certainly be effective in attacking other satellites as well, and might also be used against military or civilian targets in the air or on the ground.[5] Regardless of the fate of SDI, advancing satellite technology will in the near future

---

[3] Ashton Carter, "The Current and Future Military Uses of Space," in Nye and Schear, *Seeking Stability in Space*, pp. 40–42.

[4] For examples see William J. Broad, "Star Wars Gets Offensive Role," *New York Times*, 27 November 1988, p. 1; and "Military to Ready Laser for Testing as Space Weapon," *New York Times*, 1 January 1989, p. A1.

[5] A good example is Lynch, "Technical Evaluation of Offensive Uses of SDI."

make these and other possibilities for weapons based in space increasingly realistic, and will add to the incentives for deploying ASAT as one possible countermeasure.

Technology and the Threat from Space

Near the end of the 1960s, space technologies began to evolve rapidly in directions that changed the complexion of threats and opportunities in space in important ways. The most significant trend was a gradually accelerating shift in the balance away from satellites having mostly benign functions toward satellites that were at least potentially threatening to the adversary. The changing nature of photoreconnaissance was the most dramatic illustration of this trend. In the late 1960s, U.S. reconnaissance satellites delivered their data by periodically ejecting capsules of exposed film that were then picked up by aircraft or ships. This meant that when a satellite passed over a particular region the data from that pass was not immediately available, because it typically took days and sometimes weeks to recover and process the film.[6] This method was perfectly adequate for monitoring arms control agreements and for other purposes that were not time-urgent. In fact, the delay was in a way fortuitous; it made photoreconnaissance much less of a potential threat because pictures taken days earlier would hardly have been useful for force multiplication against mobile military units in the course of a conflict. Neither side had strong incentives to field a capability to destroy these systems because they would have been largely irrelevant in the event of war.

Technological developments progressively undermined this delicate state of affairs. After experimenting with the electronic transmission of images in the 1970s, the United States sometime in the early 1980s began to operate a new photoreconnaissance system that converts pictures into digital electronic signals that are then radioed to the ground and reconstituted into photos in near-real time.[7] Reconnaissance capabilities of this kind go beyond what is needed for monitoring and are not likely to be seen by the adversary as benign. In the course of a war, real-time photographic data could be used to target and retarget attacks against mobile weapons and other important assets. Early warning satellites are undergoing a similar kind of technological evolution. Older systems could detect that an ICBM had been launched, but were not so discriminating as

---

[6] The Soviets did not use recoverable film capsules until the late 1970s. Earlier, Soviet reconnaissance satellites were launched for extremely short missions and then deliberately returned from orbit to collect the exposed film. Johnson, *The Soviet Year in Space 1983*, p. 10.

[7] Jasani, *Outer Space*, Appendix 1A, pp. 331–43.

to pinpoint the precise silo from which a missile came. New early warning satellites will soon or may already possess such a capability. This kind of information would be tremendously valuable for a nuclear war-fighting strategy where an attacker might attempt to aim follow-on counterforce strikes selectively against silos whose missiles had not as yet been launched. Changes of a similar kind have taken place in the capabilities of communications and navigation satellites as well.[8]

A second effect of technological progress has been to gradually reduce the assymetries that early in the space age characterized U.S. and Soviet dependence upon satellites. The United States early on made greater and more extensive use of military satellites than did the Soviet Union, for reasons of culture, geography, economics, and most importantly technological capabilities. The two sides' programs still differ in some important ways—the United States tends to rely on a smaller number of more sophisticated and expensive multipurpose satellites, while the Soviets have adopted a lower-technology approach by working with a large number of less sophisticated and shorter-lived satellites. But because space offers the same intrinsic opportunities to both states, and because Soviet mission requirements grew in proportion to the development of power-projection capabilities during the 1970s, there has been a striking degree of convergence between the two sides' programs.[9] Military analysts and political decisionmakers continue to disagree as to whether one or the other superpower is in some sense more dependent on satellite systems, or would be more vulnerable to their disruption in wartime. In 1986 the Joint Chiefs argued that "both the United States and the Soviet Union depend on space systems for operational support, the United States more so than the Soviet Union." Secretary of Defense Caspar Weinberger countered this, saying "it is not clear that we depend more heavily. . . . They depend on satellites to a great extent too."[10] All such assessments are based on delicate assumptions and all are extremely dependent on context—the type of war, the kinds of satellites that would come under attack, even the time of year.

What is clear is that the asymmetries that did exist have declined in size

[8] For example, navigation satellites could be used to support final trajectory corrections for reentering nuclear warheads, possibly increasing the accuracy of ballistic missile targeting to within tens of feet. Carter, "The Current and Future Military Uses of Space," p. 48.

[9] For a summary, see Stares, "US and Soviet Military Space Programs." Important differences remain. The Soviets continue to have a higher launch rate and somewhat less sophisticated technology. But both sides now use satellites for the full range of support missions mentioned. And while the Soviets have become progressively more dependent on their space systems, the United States has developed greater redundancy and backup facilities for its systems, mimicking the Soviet approach.

[10] Joint Chiefs of Staff, *Military Posture for FY 87*, p. 81; *DoD Authorization for Appropriations for FY 85*, part 1, p. 87.

and importance over time. After the early 1960s, U.S. decisionmakers rarely acted as if differences in levels of dependence would have a decisive influence in the two sides' calculations of their respective interests in ASAT. Both superpowers were using satellites for important peacetime missions and it was generally accepted that both would attempt to do so for the support of military forces in war. Both sides also would suffer from their disruption. But it has never been obvious that either the United States or the Soviet Union would suffer so much more that there were sizable relative gains to be had from sweeping the sky of satellites. For this reason, ASATs have not been inherently more attractive to one superpower than to the other.

For similar reasons, the threat from space touches both the United States and the Soviet Union in roughly equal proportions. There are two discrete components to this threat. Each side worries that the other's satellites could be used to do damage, or support terrestrial forces that do damage, to its own military forces. Each side also worries about the vulnerability of its own satellites to disruption by an enemy. The second aspect of the threat has been present from the first days of military missions in space, when U.S. decisionmakers feared that Soviet ASATs might destroy space-based systems Washington needed to operate its strategic forces effectively. If space were only being used for benign purposes, the second aspect of the threat would be more important and both sides would favor providing sanctuary to satellites. Avoiding a competition in ASAT would be a relatively simple coordination problem because it would be so clearly a shared interest. But ASAT has never been a game of pure coordination. Both superpowers have always had a substantial interest in being able to deny at least some satellite functions to the adversary should war occur.

Taken together, these conditions produce a "satellite security dilemma" with some interesting properties. In theory, satellites that threaten vital interests are no different than ordinary military systems: each superpower wants to develop means to destroy the other's threatening capabilities and protect its own. But benign satellites are different. Because benign satellites increase the security of both states under a wide variety of conditions, the superpowers share a strong common interest in protecting them. This applies not only to a state's own benign satellites but to those of the adversary as well. A clear illustration of this point is that neither the United States nor the Soviet Union stands to gain by reducing the other superpower's confidence that its early warning systems will function properly and without interference during a superpower crisis. Consider this scenario. If Soviet early warning or communication systems were thought vulnerable to rapid and surprise attack by U.S. ASATs, Moscow might be pressured in the course of a crisis to launch a preemptive attack against the United States while its essential satellite systems were unimpaired. The problem lies in the fact that in a world with ASATs, satellites may be uniquely subject to what military analysts call "use it or lose it" logic.[11] For this reason, the danger of having operational ASATs at the ready goes beyond the possibility that one side would actually strike against the other's satellites. If one side *suspects* that such a strike might be forthcoming, the pressure for it to move first and attack the other side while its own essential satellite capabilities were still intact would rise, perhaps to dangerous levels. Thus the mere existence of a threat to early warning systems could be deeply destabilizing in a crisis.

One solution to the dilemma is obvious: both sides should deploy ASAT systems that are only capable of destroying "threatening" satellites. But this solution is technologically infeasible. The destructive capacity of any currently existing ASAT is limited primarily by the *altitude* to which it can reach. For example, both the United States and the Soviet Union have successfully tested ASATs against targets in low earth orbit, but these weapons would be poorly if at all effective against satellites in geosynchronous orbit. Future ASAT technologies may break this barrier, but the location of the target in space will for the foreseeable future remain the primary determinant of how vulnerable it is. The problem is that benign and threatening satellite functions (to the extent they can be distinguished independent of context) are *not* distributed according to altitude. There are both benign and threatening satellites in low earth and geosynchronous orbits. To further complicate matters, single satellites often incorporate more than one function: the United States, for example, places nuclear explosion detectors and early warning systems aboard a variety of other satellites, including the NAVSTAR GPS navigation satellite.[12] There are no simple answers to the satellite security dilemma.

Managing the Threat: Cooperative and Competitive Responses

The range of measures that states have available to respond to this problem has not fundamentally changed or expanded since the early 1960s, although there have been substantial improvements in the technological

[11] Satellites are large and delicate objects that are easy to identify and target, while hard to defend. What's worse, each side depends on a relatively small number of satellites to provide essential military capabilities. Together, these make space-based early warning networks fragile and tempting targets.

[12] GPS stands for Global Positioning System. NAVSTAR is an advanced navigational system that will provide worldwide access to positioning information of unprecedented accuracy (within 16 meters) at all times and under all weather conditions. The system is scheduled for full deployment early in the 1990s. See Richard W. Blank, "The NAVSTAR Global Positioning System," *Signal* 40 (1986): 73–78. For details on the nuclear detection system being installed on these satellites, see *DoD Authorization for Appropriations for FY 83*, part 7, pp. 4624–25.

efficacy of each. Options in this case, as in ABM and MIRV, collapse in effect into a dyadic choice between cooperative and competitive responses.

The direct response to an emerging set of threats from space is to develop and deploy ASATs. An effective ASAT grants its possessor a self-reliant capability to deny potentially threatening satellite missions by simply destroying the offending system. ASAT could also be used to "protect" one's own satellites through deterrence: a state with an effective ASAT could threaten to retaliate against the other side's satellites if its own were attacked or in any way disrupted. A more subtle attraction of ASAT lies in the general deterrent effect that a sophisticated and cost-effective ASAT system would probably have against the further development and deployment of threatening military satellites. Satellites are expensive and delicate commodities that make tempting targets. If offense dominates defense in space—that is, if it is easier and cheaper to attack satellites than to protect them—the attractiveness of placing military systems in space at all is reduced. Maintaining an advantage in ASAT can thus make space an exceedingly inhospitable environment for the other side. If this general deterrent effect works, it rescues the side with ASAT from having to come up with new, "point by point" countermeasures to respond to each new military satellite system with potentially threatening functions. In addition, ASAT (like MIRV) has had particular appeal for U.S. decisionmakers because of its technological sophistication and elegance in this capacity. American decisionmakers have used each of these rationales to argue in favor of deploying ASAT both as a response to Soviet threats and as a source of unilateral advantage. In theory, ASAT promised to solve a host of strategic problems facing Washington all at once, and to do so in a way that capitalized on America's perceived technological superiority over the Soviet Union.

But ASAT is also a highly *competitive* response to the threat from space. A decision to deploy ASAT places at risk satellite capabilities that are essential to the other side's security, thus exacerbating the security dilemma. Faced, for example, with a threat to communication or navigation satellites, the Soviet Union or the United States would have little choice but to respond. It might do so by "ignoring" the general deterrent effect and engaging in a measure vs. counter-measure race between the offense (ASAT) and defense (satellite). But in a world where it is generally easier to attack satellites than protect them, the more likely response would be to engage in an offensive race for the most competent ASAT.

An ASAT race would be costly to both sides, in dollars (or rubles) and in strategic stability. The economic costs are obvious: an intense competition to make ASATs more effective and satellites more resistant to attack could be fabulously expensive. The strategic stability costs would follow from a decline in confidence that benign satellites would remain invulnerable in the course of a crisis. This decline in confidence would effect both sides; but even if ASAT capabilities were more or less evenly matched, it is not obvious that mutual deterrence would function in space the way it appears to function on earth. Because the balance of interests in space and the relative dependence of the two sides on satellites is unclear, one side might decide that it stood to gain from an exchange of attacks. In certain instances, there might very well be a premium for striking satellites first.[13] Finally, because attacking satellites would be one way to demonstrate a high degree of resolve in a superpower crisis without directly damaging territory or civilian populations, selective attacks leading to a war of attrition against satellites might actually seem an appealing kind of brinkmanship behavior during a crisis.

In sum, there are obvious temptations to seek a unilateral advantage in ASAT. Decisionmakers should prefer the D,C outcome most. But if the advantage of unilateral defection cannot be sustained, the resulting outcome of mutual defection should be much less attractive. The most likely outcome of a full-fledged ASAT race would be a costly and destabilizing competition between offense and defense in space that would on balance damage the security interests of both superpowers in roughly equal proportions.

The *cooperative* response would be to refrain from developing ASAT systems and rely instead on other measures to reduce the impact of the space threat. Mutual deterrence, with both sides holding ASAT systems at the ready, is not the only way to "protect" space-based systems. There is a range of unilateral actions that both superpowers can take to lessen the vulnerability of satellites, and most of these measures do not pose additional threats to the other side. As a first step, some satellites can be placed in higher orbits; others can be given a limited maneuvering capability. Either option renders satellites more difficult to attack with kinetic or directed energy weapon (DEW) ASATs.[14] Almost all space assets can be partially "hardened" against nuclear blast and lasers; and the vital links between satellites and ground stations can be made resistant to jamming and disruption. It is also possible to design redundancy into almost any space-based system by maintaining spare satellites in orbit and on the

---

[13] The primary reason for this, to repeat, is the relatively small number of satellites that would have to be destroyed in order to disable communications, navigation systems, and the like.

[14] The United States in particular has put a great deal of emphasis on deploying satellites in higher-altitude orbits where possible. In the case of photoreconnaissance, where altitude invariably degrades performance, American satellites have been equipped with a variety of warning sensors and decoys, and in some cases have been given a limited ability to maneuver. See Pike, "Anti-Satellite Weapons," p. 13.

ground, ready for rapid launching. Both superpowers have in fact used a mixture of these measures over time to make their satellites less vulnerable to easy attack, what military analysts call "cheap hits."[15]

But unilateral survivability measures have not been sufficiently effective to solve the problem of satellite vulnerability. Survivability measures complicate the job of an attacker; they make the ASAT mission more difficult, but have not made it impossible. On technological grounds, it is generally easier to destroy space platforms than to protect them; neither side has yet developed satellites that would be safe from attack by a determined adversary armed with feasible ASAT capabilities.[16] This makes unilateral cooperation or unrequited restraint in ASAT unattractive from a strictly military perspective. Add to this the presumptive political costs of unrequited restraint in space systems, a highly visible symbol of technological prowess, and it becomes clear that decisionmakers should prefer the C,D outcome least of all.

The alternative is mutual cooperation, which would entail joint restraint in the development and deployment of ASAT systems. Both sides should prefer mutual cooperation to unrequited restraint, but is C,C preferable to D,D? That is, is a world without ASAT clearly more advantageous than a world in which both sides have ASAT? Cooperation can reduce the costs and risks of an ASAT competition, but a world without dedicated ASAT weapons has problems of its own. The first problem is that benign satellites would still not be entirely safe in this world because of what military analysts call "residual" ASAT capabilities. These are other weapons, most obviously ICBMs but also advanced air defense missiles and strategic defense systems, that are not primarily ASAT systems but could in fact be used with some success against satellites. However, the survivability measures that both sides can take on their own would considerably reduce the vulnerability of satellites, particularly those in higher orbits, to such residual capabilities. The likelihood that either side could carry out an effective attack against a hardened and redundant set of satellites, using only "residual" ASAT systems that had not been tested for use against satellites, starts out low and would decline over time to-

[15] For details of what the United States has done in "hardening" satellites against nuclear blast, see Jack Cushman, "AF Seeks Invulnerable Warning Satellites," *Defense Week*, 16 January 1984, p. 12; and Bruce Smith, "New Satellite Systems Designed for Survivability," *Aviation Week and Space Technology*, 8 March 1982, p. 82. On redundancy, see *DoD Appropriations for FY 84*, part 8, p. 503. On resistance to jamming, see *DoD Appropriations for FY 85*, part 5, pp. 437–38. There is obviously less information available about Soviet efforts, although most experts presume that Moscow has taken a similar approach; Nicholas L. Johnson, "C3 in Space: The Soviet Approach," *Signal* 39 (1985): 21.

[16] For a balanced assessment of the extensive technical literature on this subject, see Michael May, "Safeguarding Our Space Assets," in Nye and Schear, *Seeking Stability in Space*, pp. 71–86.

ward insignificance in the face of feasible survivability measures.[17] ASAT arms control is not a perfect solution to the problem of vulnerability simply because satellites are relatively easy to disrupt. But cooperative restraint of ASAT is likely to be a more robust, less expensive, and less risky solution to the problem of protecting satellites than is mutual deterrence when both sides are armed with ASAT.

The more difficult problem in a world without ASAT is the remaining question of what to do about satellites that are *not* benign. If arms control were to establish space as a "safe haven," it becomes possible and tempting to use space more extensively for military support missions and perhaps even for the direct application of force in the future.

ASAT is the most direct but not the only or even necessarily the most effective way to deal with these threats. Because there are important reasons to avoid a competition in ASAT, American decisionmakers have often preferred alternatives. For instance, high political and military officials in the mid-1970s became increasingly concerned about Soviet ocean reconnaissance systems (EORSAT and RORSAT) and the presumptive threat to Navy carrier battle groups. Some civilian analysts saw this as a reason to acquire ASAT; their logic was that if war came the United States would have to destroy ocean reconnaissance satellites in order to protect its Navy. Pentagon officials mostly disagreed. The Navy itself preferred to rely on the alternative approach of "spoofing" Soviet satellites through radar jamming, electronic countermeasures, and deceptive sailing techniques. Similar nonprovocative measures can be employed to reduce the threat posed by other satellite systems.[18] While none is so technically elegant or universally effective as ASAT, all avoid the escalatory, expensive, and destabilizing effects of a full-fledged offense-defense race in space. If the opportunity costs of ASAT cooperation can be controlled by making benign satellites more survivable and reducing the impact of threatening satellites in this fashion, the superpowers should prefer cooperation and mutual restraint to a full-fledged competition in ASAT.

In sum, an objective assessment of preferences leads to the argument that ASAT should be viewed as a mixed-motive game matching the conditions of the PD. The general considerations that made ABM and MIRV iterated games with long shadows of the future also apply with at least equal strength to ASAT. From an objective perspective then, ASAT fulfills

[17] See Carter, "Satellites and Anti-Satellites."

[18] I discuss the controversy over satellite ocean reconnaissance later in this chapter. Combining nonprovocative countermeasures is under most circumstances likely to be more complex and expensive than relying *solely* on ASAT. But the latter is probably not a realistic option. If both sides have ASAT and expect mutual deterrence of attacks against satellites to hold in the course of a war, each would still have to take steps to reduce the exposure of its terrestrial forces to observation and targeting from space.

the initial conditions for cooperation under Axelrod's model. From a subjective standpoint, we shall see that decisionmakers have not always shared these assessments. But at critical decisional points for ASAT in the 1960s and 1970s, U.S. policymakers did come to see the ASAT issue as an iterated PD game with a long shadow of the future. In accordance with the expectations of the model they went on to develop reciprocal strategies aimed at eliciting cooperation from the Soviet Union.

ASAT in the 1960s

The story of ASAT starts most clearly with America's reaction to the successful launch of the world's first artificial satellite, Sputnik I, in 1957. Although U.S. scientists were engaged in extensive research and development in space technology relevant to both satellites and antisatellite weapons for at least the prior decade, the acceleration of U.S. space programs in the wake of Sputnik was truly massive.[19] Sputnik, of course, was more than just a political signal that the Soviet Union had achieved new status as a first-rate scientific and technological rival to the United States. Sputnik also created a new military problem, with the immediate possibility that the superpowers' security competition was about to be extended to outer space. A series of equally impressive technological achievements by the Soviet space program during the next several years underscored that possibility, even as Washington was entering the space age on its own. In 1959, Soviet spacecraft impacted on the moon and sent back pictures of its far side; in 1961, a Soviet astronaut was carried into orbit ahead of an American. None of these missions were "military" ones in a traditional sense, but the military potential of space was lost on no one. In 1961, the Secretary of the Air Force warned the Congress that "every advance in technology which contributes to man's ability to move in space also contributes to military capabilities in space."[20]

As the ICBM race began in earnest during the late 1950s, there was little reason to believe that the competition would end with weapons that merely traveled *through* space. Despite popular appeals for the peaceful and cooperative exploitation of humanity's "common heritage," both superpowers were tempted and to some degree compelled to predict and plan for a full-scale arms race in space. For Washington at least, it seemed that space would be the new and possibly decisive military frontier. The Air Force claimed that "leadership in space vehicle development could

[19] For a detailed history, see McDougall, *The Heavens and the Earth*.
[20] Steinberg, *Satellite Reconnaissance*, p. 29; *1961 Hearings on Military Posture*, p. 1080. The general military potential of space had of course been recognized long before this.

confer decisive national power"; others argued that "the country that controls the moon will control the earth."[21] These were extreme views, but there was a strong consensus that space had now emerged as a critical arena of superpower competition and that the Cold War itself might well be decided in space. In consequence, the overwhelming sense among American decisionmakers at the end of the 1950s was that an arms race in space had become inevitable.

It was not at all agreed, however, that an "inevitable" arms race in space was undesirable from the U.S. perspective. Some political decision-makers and many military officials in Washington looked forward to this new phase of superpower competition; they argued that despite the un-deniable Soviet headstart, anything that focused the rivalry on advanced technology would turn out in the long run to be profoundly advantageous to the United States. The services quickly became enthusiastic proponents of imaginative space weapons—from orbiting bombers to space-based defenses against ballistic missiles—as well as more feasible satellite sys-tems for reconnaissance, communication, and navigation. In this view, the "coming age of space combat" played directly to the strengths of the United States.[22] So long as the competition in space was thought to be like an iterated game, there was reason to believe that the United States with its inherent advantages in technology would eventually come out on top.

Not all Americans agreed, however, that the arms race in space would be like an iterated game. Many feared the possibility of a military fait accompli where the first side that conquered space would attain a per-manent and decisive advantage. According to the popular rendition of this argument, known as the Panama Hypothesis, the United States risked being denied any access to space by expanding Soviet satellite and ASAT capabilities.[23] If that were true, Washington had to respond without hes-itation and immediately stake its claim in space. There were "strategic areas in space vital to future scientific, military, and commercial pro-grams—which must be occupied by the United States lest their use be forever denied us through prior occupation by unfriendly powers."[24]

Continuing Soviet achievements in space made these dire predictions seem uncomfortably realistic. In 1961, Moscow successfully launched a probe to Venus from an orbiting spacecraft, suggesting steps toward a capability to direct weapons from space at other space targets or even directly at the earth. Also in late 1961, Moscow terminated the nuclear

---

[21] *Space and National Security*, "Talking Papers," AFXPD-LR, 1 November 1960, NHP Box 11; York, *Race to Oblivion*, p. 124.

[22] For the Army and Air Force's plans, see Steinberg, *Satellite Reconnaissance*, p. 6; Kil-lian, *Sputnik, Scientists, and Eisenhower*.

[23] Steinberg, *Satellite Reconnaissance*, p. 5.

[24] *Astronautics*, June 1961, p. 36.

test ban moratorium with a series of large atmospheric weapons tests, certain characteristics of which indicated a role in either ABM or ASAT development. In August 1962 the Soviets achieved a close rendezvous of two manned spacecraft (Vostok 3 and 4), which seemed to some American scientists further evidence that the Soviet military was aiming for a near-term capability to destroy U.S. satellites by whatever means it could. More pessimistic Pentagon officials claimed that Soviet space vehicles might already possess the capability to intercept and destroy American satellites at will.[25]

Given what was known about Soviet conceptions of self-interest in space at this time, American decisionmakers had to take a worst-case view of these possibilities. Before Sputnik, Moscow had long held to the principle that national sovereignty should govern the use of airspace, particularly when it came to reconnaissance and other military support missions.[26] In rejecting Eisenhower's 1955 Open Skies proposal, Khrushchev made clear that the Soviet government viewed reconnaissance as espionage and would take whatever steps it could to prevent such spying. In May 1960, less than four years after its maiden flight, the advanced U-2 spy plane was shot down by a Soviet surface-to-air missile (SAM). There was every reason to believe that Moscow's response to American reconnaissance satellites would be similarly brisk, limited only by the more difficult technological challenge of shooting down satellites. And while the Soviets worked at denying space access to the Americans, they also seemed determined to make use of space themselves for their own military purposes. In a comment that was widely reported in the U.S. media in 1961, the chief of the Soviet strategic rocket forces Marshal Sergei Biriuzov announced "it has now become possible, at a command from earth, to launch rockets from a satellite at any desired time, at any point," directed presumably against other space targets or even at the earth.[27] While this was generally dismissed as propagandistic blustering by responsible officials in Washington, Biriuzov's remarks underscored the military and political dangers of complacence in the face of a growing and technologically competent Soviet space program.

Washington's response was not long in coming. In 1958, just as the United States approved its first programs to deploy early warning and

[25] See Walter R. Dornberger, "Arms in Space: Something Else to Worry About," *US News & World Report*, 9 October 1961, p. 76; Sorensen, *Kennedy*, p. 699; *Science*, 24 August 1962; *1962 Hearings on Military Posture and HR 9751*, p. 3766.

[26] John Lewis Gaddis, "The Evolution of a Satellite Reconnaissance Regime," in George, Farley, and Dallin, *US-Soviet Security Cooperation*, p. 355.

[27] Radio Broadcast of February 25, 1963, cited by Steinberg, *Satellite Reconnaissance*, p. 74. For the Soviet response to Open Skies, see Eisenhower, *Waging Peace*, p. 521; and Rostow, *Open Skies*, pp. 63–64, 79–85.

reconnaissance satellites, the Pentagon's new Advanced Research Projects Agency was tasked to develop Weapons Systems 1621, the SAINT satellite inspection system. SAINT was to be the first building block in a dedicated long-term ASAT program. But the services were not willing to wait for SAINT; in the short term, the Army and the Air Force each proposed adaptations and upgrades of current weapons systems so as to give them some capability against satellites quickly.[28] Science advisor George Kistiakowsky was a prominent opponent of these proposals: he argued that the United States could not deter Soviet ASAT attacks by possessing an ASAT of its own. Eisenhower was sympathetic to Kistiakowsky's objections because he too suspected that the U.S. ASAT venture would spur greater Soviet efforts; but the president also saw little choice but to proceed.[29] By the end of 1960, U.S. reconnaissance satellites were proving their value and the Soviet threats against them were becoming increasingly worrisome. *Aviation Week* predicted that Moscow would have the technology to disrupt U.S. satellites as soon as 1963.[30] The surest way to protect satellites, it seemed, was through deterrence; and the most promising deterrent was an equal threat to attack Soviet space assets if Moscow were to interfere with ours.

The adequacy of the American space effort was an important issue in the 1960 presidential campaign. As a candidate, Kennedy seemed particularly concerned; and after he warned that "if the Soviets control space they can control the earth," the Army and the Air Force redoubled their efforts to secure funding for more ambitious ASAT programs.[31] After taking office in 1961, the new president responded by adding $1.5 billion to Eisenhower's budget for space.[32] At the same time, concern over the Soviet program grew more urgent. In 1962, McNamara argued that the United States needed immediately to "develop a system for . . . the final destruction of unfriendly satellites," while *Aviation Week* warned that any further delay in exploiting "the military applications of space technology at this late date could be fatal."[33]

During its first two years, the Kennedy administration reshuffled the U.S. military space program to prioritize systems that promised to lead

[28] *NASA Authorization for FY 60*, pp. 646–55.

[29] Kistiakowsky, *A Scientist at the White House*, p. 334. York basically concurs with Kistiakowsky's assessment of Eisenhower's position; see York, *Race to Oblivion*, p. 131.

[30] *Aviation Week and Space Technology*, 14 November 1960, p. 26.

[31] Kennedy quoted in John Logsdon, *The Decision to Go to the Moon*, p. 76. For the response of the services, see Stares, *The Militarization of Space*, pp. 72–73.

[32] Steinberg, *Satellite Reconnaissance*, p. 72.

[33] *1962 Hearings on Military Posture and HR 9751*, p. 3179; *Aviation Week and Space Technology*, 25 June 1962, p. 21.

to quick deployment of an operational ASAT.[34] In May 1962, McNamara reversed previous decisions and approved the development of a modified Nike Zeus missile for use in an ASAT role. Originally Project Mudflap, the Nike Zeus upgrade was later renamed Program 505. Later that year, the Air Force was given the go-ahead for its ADO-40 proposal, an ASAT system based on a modified Thor booster that promised a greater capability in range and altitude than 505. Later renamed Project 437, the Air Force system was slated for deployment by early 1964.[35] These decisions were taken with full knowledge of the severe technological limitations on both of these systems; but the purpose was simply to provide some "quick-fix" ASAT capability as rapidly as possible.[36] By the end of 1962 the stage had been set for a full-scale arms race in space and both superpowers had pronounced themselves ready and able to proceed with the competition.

Interdependent Decisions and Contingent Restraint

The expected ASAT race did not occur. During the last half of 1962, the Kennedy administration undertook a detailed reexamination of the American space program that produced a distinct change in Washington's conceptions of self-interest and in the foundations of its overall strategy for ASAT. This new assessment would set the tone of American space policy for at least the next decade.

The most visible change in Washington's view centered on sharply revised estimates of the *immediacy* of the Soviet space threat. DoD analysts now reported that "the Soviets were not forging ahead with military space work" to the degree that they had previously feared. The Vostok "rendezvous" was reinterpreted as an indication of how *far* Soviet technology remained from producing a militarily effective ASAT (the two spacecraft actually only passed within several miles of each other). The possibilities for using satellites as launch platforms for weaponry in the

[34] As part of this plan, Kennedy rejected Air Force requests to add a satellite kill capability to Project SAINT and cut the budget for this program early in 1962. Plagued by technical difficulties and cost overruns, SAINT did not promise to produce a militarily useful capability in a reasonable amount of time.

[35] Stares, *The Militarization of Space*, pp. 117–25.

[36] Projects 437 and 505 were designed as direct-ascent interceptors to be launched from fixed bases on Pacific islands: this meant that the United States would have to wait for an offending satellite to pass almost directly over the base in order to attack it. Both systems also used nuclear warheads as a kill mechanism. The general risk of provoking nuclear war notwithstanding, U.S. decisionmakers now knew as a result of weapons tests that nuclear explosions in space would probably disrupt many satellites (including friendly ones) over an extremely large area.

near term were downplayed, as were current Soviet capabilities for the extensive command and control systems that would be necessary to make effective use of the military potential of space.[37] According to Washington's revised interpretation, the state of space technology actually made a fait accompli much *less* likely in the foreseeable future.

If space competition were more like an iterated game, this opened up new possibilities either for long-term exploitation of the U.S. technological edge or for limiting the race through mutual restraint. This was a critical juncture for U.S. military space policy, and the Kennedy administration could have gone in either direction. It chose to explore the latter possibility, although at the time of the decision there were almost no indications of parallel interest in Moscow.

Official statements from Washington underwent a dramatic shift in tone beginning in the summer of 1962, to stress a new American commitment to seek mutual restraint in space. In Congressional testimony that June, DDR&E Harold Brown and Deputy Secretary of Defense Roswell Gilpatric signaled the new line by drastically downplaying the immediate military importance of ASAT systems. Instead of demanding more resources for ASAT technology that could be deployed in the short term, the Pentagon officials now argued for a long-term or "building block approach in this area" that would be limited to a kind of technological "insurance" should conditions change in the future.[38] Gilpatric later expanded on the new approach, announcing that "the U.S. believes that it is highly desirable for its own security and for the security of the world that the arms race should not be expanded into outer space and we are seeking in every feasible way to achieve that purpose." President Kennedy echoed the message, claiming that "space can be explored and mastered without feeding the fires of war." Washington also brought its new line to the United Nations, where Ambassador Albert Gore argued that "it is especially important that we do everything now that can be done to avoid an arms race in outer space," and announced that the United States would do nothing to prejudice that outcome.[39]

Washington's new approach to space was clearly at odds with previous beliefs that an arms race in space was inevitable or deeply advantageous to American security interests. At the same time, none of these statements implied that the United States was willing to hold back its own program indefinitely without some signal of reciprocal interest from Moscow.

[37] *Science*, 6 July 1962, p. 23; Steinberg, *Satellite Reconnaissance*, p. 80.

[38] This was in sharp contrast particularly to Gilpatric's previous position that the DoD would press forward with ASAT and other military missions in space in the short term. See *NASA Authorization for FY 63*, p. 343.

[39] *Congressional Record*, 21 September 1962, pp. 7007–9; *New York Times*, 13 September 1962; *Documents on Disarmament*, 1962, p. 1123.

While not demanding any specific negotiations or formal treaty procedures, Washington's spokesmen made clear that the expressed U.S. willingness to refrain from hostile activities in space was contingent on a Soviet response. Gilpatric stressed that "we will of course take such steps as are necessary to defend ourselves if the Soviet Union forces us to do so." Kennedy reminded his listeners that he "did not say that we should go unprotected against the hostile misuse of space." Gore announced that the United States would slow its military efforts in space only so long as the Soviets would do likewise and themselves "refrain from taking steps that would extend the arms race into outer space."[40]

The new approach went beyond political rhetoric. Over the next several years, the administration's revised attitude acted as a significant political constraint on U.S. ASAT development programs, which had been given programmatic and budgetary boosts earlier in the decade. The change was reflected in general terms in McNamara's 1963 Posture Statement, which conspicuously downplayed the importance of "space defense systems" for the near term. In December 1962, DoD effectively canceled Air Force Project SAINT.[41] Technological difficulties with the system were an important reason for its demise. Advances in other technologies that could be used to gain information about satellites, particularly ground-based electro-optical systems, also reduced the need for SAINT as an orbital satellite inspection system. But SAINT, as the Air Force expected and hoped, could have been reoriented as a dedicated ASAT system by incorporating a kill mechanism. While it made sense for the Air Force to expect this in 1961, it was no longer consistent with Washington's revised space policy at the end of 1962. SAINT was canceled, at least in part, because of basic changes in the administration's beliefs about military uses of space, ASAT, and the possibilities for mutual restraint.[42]

These changed beliefs affected other ASAT-relevant programs as well.

[40] See note 39 above.

[41] J. W. Finney, "Pentagon Drops a Satellite Goal," *New York Times*, 4 December 1962, p. 5. This was officially announced as a decision to "reorient" the program, but as all future tests were postponed indefinitely and not rescheduled, it was in effect a decision to cancel SAINT.

[42] Stares disagrees, citing technology as the principal reason for SAINT's demise; but contemporary sources, including Finney's article cited above, emphasize political factors behind the decision. Stares, *The Militarization of Space*, pp. 116–17. Steinberg reports several interviews with Air Force officials responsible for SAINT indicating that "a fear of escalation of military conflict and arms competition in space was a primary reason for the demise of SAINT." *Satellite Reconnaissance*, p. 84. Viewing the cancellation of SAINT in the context of decisions about other ASAT systems taken at approximately the same time also weakens the technological determinist argument, since some of the alternatives were more promising than SAINT.

Funds for the Air Force's Blue Gemini program, a *manned* satellite inspection system that was supposed to be SAINT's successor, were cut along with other manned programs that had ASAT potential in the FY 1964 budget.[43] The two most important systems with short-term ASAT potential, Projects 505 and 437, were continued but only within sharply limited bounds. Project 505 showed a mixed record in initial tests during 1962 and 1963. It was declared operational that summer, but only a single interceptor missile was actually deployed. In 1964, McNamara dropped the "ready requirement" for 505 and the system was essentially put into mothballs.[44]

The decision to phase out 505 entirely was made in 1966. Technology was again an important reason: apart from its limited range, 505 used a nuclear warhead as its kill mechanism, which meant that its use would have jeopardized an uncertain number of satellites other than the target, and widely disrupted communications on earth. The cancellation of 505 did not, however, signal the end of the U.S. ASAT program. Project 505 was dropped in part because its Air Force rival, Project 437, was at least marginally more promising. Project 437 underwent successful testing in 1964 and was declared operational in June of that year. It had a more extensive capability, to launch two missiles against satellites at a range of 1,500 nautical miles and an altitude of 200. The critical limitation of 437 was that it too relied on a megaton-range nuclear warhead. By the end of 1964, 437 as well was no longer being treated as the high-priority program it was supposed to have been.[45] When President Johnson spoke about the system that year, he was at pains to stress its operational limitations and the moderate level of American commitment to it. This was reflected in DoD's budget for FY 1965: as funds were redirected away from many development programs and toward ready forces for Southeast Asia, the burden of cuts fell disproportionately on 437.[46]

The general lack of enthusiasm for 437 was also in part a reflection of technology, but technology explains least well the fate of 437's successors. As early as 1963, DoD had begun to investigate several promising *nonnuclear* modifications and follow-on projects to 437. The first of these was 437 X (later renamed 437 AP), an advanced satellite inspection system.[47] The more important modification was 437 Y, a program to de-

[43] "Satellite Inspection Proposals Asked," *Aviation Week and Space Technology*, 3 June 1963, p. 33.

[44] Bell Laboratories and McDonnell Douglas personnel carried out several additional tests of the system in 1965 and 1966. Stares, *The Militarization of Space*, p. 119.

[45] Ibid., pp. 120–22.

[46] *Aviation Week and Space Technology*, 21 September 1964, p. 21; Stares, *The Militarization of Space*, pp. 124–25.

[47] Project 437 AP was tested several times between 1965 and 1967, but it is unclear

velop a nonnuclear ASAT warhead with precise terminal guidance for use atop 437's Thor booster as well as other missiles. Later redubbed Program 922, this technologically promising system was given low priority by the Pentagon and received only limited funding. DoD let contracts for the program in 1965 and called for an initial testing date before 1969. But 922 never got off the ground. The meager $20 million allocation for 922 in the FY 1968 budget was slashed by half, and the program was entirely canceled later that year.[48]

Both technology and economics were important constraints on U.S. ASAT programs during the 1960s, yet they do not fully explain what the United States chose *not* to do in ASAT during this period. Technological determinism is a weak argument here because ASAT technology was imperfect, not impossible. It is always risky to invest in imperfect technologies, but it is also an opportunity for exerting comparative advantage. Certainly, the United States chose to try to exploit a similar comparative advantage in the technologically imperfect MIRV and ABM programs at about the same time, as well as in military and civilian space programs *other* than ASAT. For example, Washington throughout the decade devoted substantial technological and economic resources to the development of tracking facilities and sensor systems for identifying objects in space.[49] The growing war in Southeast Asia meant that money was tight all around, but neither research and development for new satellite systems nor funding for the manned space program that led to the Apollo moon landing in 1969 suffered deeply from economic constraints.[50]

A similar commitment of economic, technological, and political resources could have been brought to bear on ASAT, but it was not. While both the Kennedy and Johnson administrations kept a moderate program of research and development alive, at no time did either push the deployment of a militarily significant ASAT weapon in the short or medium term. Instead, the United States consistently sought to engage the Soviet Union in a tacit cooperative arrangement for mutual restraint. American strategy for doing that came to closely resemble contingent restraint.

---

whether it ever achieved operational status. See Stares, *The Militarization of Space*, pp. 125–26. Project 437 AP was more sophisticated than SAINT, but it suffered from the same lack of a convincing mission rationale or other military justification.

[48] *Aviation Week and Space Technology*, 22 March 1965, p. 13; Stares, *The Militarization of Space*, p. 129.

[49] Stares, *The Militarization of Space*, pp. 131–34.

[50] Between 1966 and 1969, U.S. funds for the manned space program more than tripled, from about $150 million to over $500 million. Spending for military satellites also increased dramatically over this period. "Space defense," in contrast, languished, with less than $17 million funding as late as 1969. For most of the 1960s, space defense accounted for a fraction of a percent of the entire space budget. Figures from *NASA Authorization Hearings*, FY 1961–71.

Without making specific threats or ultimatums, Washington signaled that it would not push forward with ASAT unless compelled to do so by Soviet actions. The United States held on to only a minimal and militarily insignificant ASAT program. Proposals to move forward with technologically feasible concepts for a nonnuclear ASAT were rejected or postponed. At best, the American space defense programs of the 1960s served as a quiet reminder to Moscow that the United States could and would compete in ASAT if the Soviets chose to move in this direction.[51] If they did not, then a tacit mutual restraint could be observed without the necessity of negotiations or formal treaties. Both sides would maintain maximum freedom for exploring and exploiting the possibilities of space, but neither would build ASAT systems to disrupt the other's efforts.

Explaining the Shift

There are several puzzles here. The first concerns Washington's abrupt about-face in 1962. The United States began its military foray into space with a unilateral attitude focused on American security interests, but quickly came to recognize ASAT as an interdependent decision. This shift came several years before similar shifts in ABM and MIRV. It came before the new arms control theories of the early 1960s, which were so important in the history of the previous two cases, had established a strong and broad consensus within the American decisionmaking elite. It came in an area that epitomized the American technological advantage. And it came without any evidence of compatible Soviet interests in restraint, or even signals that Moscow was ready to acknowledge the interdependent nature of the decision to proceed with a full-fledged arms race in space. The second puzzle is that while facing a Soviet Union by all indications committed to destroying American satellites as soon as it had the technology

[51] For a different interpretation, see Raymond Garthoff's review of George, Farley, and Dallin, *US-Soviet Security Cooperation*, in *Science*, 16 September 1988, pp. 1517–18; and "ASAT Arms Control Still Possible," *Bulletin of the Atomic Scientists*, August–September 1984, p. 30. Garthoff believes that U.S. ASAT programs actually provoked the Soviets toward developing and testing an ASAT of their own, which they presumably would not have otherwise done. He cites a 1966 article in the confidential journal *Military Thought* in which a Soviet colonel expressed a concern about the current significance of the "ASAT problem." His concern, however, was primarily with regard to American reconnaissance satellites and the need for a Soviet ASAT to combat them, *not* with American ASATs per se. It was not until 1972, several years after the Soviets tested their own ASAT, that Soviet military writers expressed worries about the American ASAT program. This calls into doubt Garthoff's conclusion that "the Soviet military saw the American ASAT program as proceeding on full steam" during the 1960s.

to do so, the United States chose a highly permissive strategy of reciprocity, contingent restraint, in an attempt to elicit cooperation.

The third puzzle is that it seems to have had a positive effect. The Soviet Union, which had been pressing its opposition to reconnaissance satellites in public and private channels and most dramatically in the UN General Assembly, dropped its objections in September 1963.[52] This shift in Moscow's attitude was certainly prompted in part by the fact that the Soviets were now operating their own reconnaissance satellites, but the shift in American strategy was at least a permissive and most probably a contributing factor.[53] Further changes in the tenor of U.S.-Soviet interaction on space issues seemed to substantiate the effect. In October 1963 the superpowers joined forces to support Resolution 1884 of the UN General Assembly, which called upon all states to refrain from placing in space "nuclear weapons or any other weapons of mass destruction."[54] This resolution formed the basis for the Outer Space Treaty of 1967. Although neither of these accords specifically addressed ASAT, both incorporated and emphasized shared expectations of restraint; because the 1967 treaty stated that "ownership of objects launched into Outer Space . . . is not affected by their presence in outer space," it implicitly proscribed interference with another country's satellites. Although the Joint Chiefs objected to the lack of verification procedures behind the Outer Space Treaty, the White House stood firmly in support and the Senate ratified it by unanimous vote.[55] This reflected a widespread assessment among American elites that the United States and Soviet Union had, through tacit cooperation, successfully avoided the dangerous arms race in space that both sides had expected in the early 1960s.

The move to ASAT cooperation began with the change in American conceptions of self-interest in space around 1962. Technological possibilities and constraints played a key role in that change. Washington quickly discovered the value of photoreconnaissance for its own purposes, as Discoverer and its successors proved highly effective and valuable sources of

---

[52] See *Documents on Disarmament*, 1962, pp. 871–72, 1131; for the text of the Soviet draft General Assembly resolution see Jenks, *Space Law*, pp. 317–19.

[53] Contemporary American decisionmakers certainly thought so. Gaddis notes other possible explanations for the shift in Soviet attitudes, with some evidence for each. "Evolution of a Satellite Reconnaissance Regime," pp. 358–59. But expectations of ASAT restraint were a necessary prerequisite in any case: tacit cooperation on satellite reconnaissance would have been ruled out by a full-fledged competition in ASAT.

[54] *Yearbook of the United Nations*, 1965, pp. 101–2, 133–34.

[55] The Outer Space Treaty was forged principally between the United States and the Soviet Union and later submitted to the UN General Assembly for accession by other states. For the text of the treaty, see *Arms Control and Disarmament Agreements*, p. 52; for ratification hearings before the Senate Committee on Foreign Relations, see *Treaty on Outer Space*, 1967, p. 94.

information during peacetime and in the midst of crises. But while reconnaissance and certain other military support missions could be carried out with great effectiveness from space, the potential for placing cost-effective and controllable weapons in space was far less certain. During the next few years, both superpowers weighed options to place nuclear weapons in orbit; the United States unilaterally rejected this choice and it seems that the Soviets did too, albeit after a partial test series of a FOBS.[56] So long as there were no pressing reasons for either side to station hostile military systems in space and there were considerable benefits to be had from photoreconnaissance, creating a sanctuary for satellites made good sense from a unilateral American perspective.

One way to create that sanctuary would have been to try to "seize the high ground" in space, as some Americans wished to do at the end of the 1950s. But the competitive approach looked far less attractive after the Kennedy administration's broad reevaluation of American space policy. Technology mattered here too, but the principal impact of technology came through a change in perceptions of the shadow of the future. American decisionmakers were glad to "discover" that the Panama Hypothesis was wrong; but the same technological constraints that ruled out a fait accompli in space for the Soviets in effect did the same for the Americans. Competition in space was going to be an iterated game. If Washington were to choose the competitive route, it would have to be prepared for a continuing struggle and confident of its ability to stay a step ahead of the Soviets in space.

Generally, most American elites believed that a competition in high-technology weapons did play directly to the strengths of the United States. In ABM and particularly in MIRV, this was an important factor motivating the minority of decisionmakers who preferred competition. But similar beliefs did not have the same impact on the range of U.S. preferences for ASAT. The reason is that the uncertainties about competing in ASAT were of a fundamentally different character.

Decisionmakers in ABM and MIRV faced a situation characterized by moderate uncertainty, as I defined it in Chapter 3. By the mid-1960s, the technological possibilities for both kinds of systems were clear within a range of approximation. Strategic planners could envision what a future

---

[56] FOBS stands for fractional orbital bombardment system. The United States never developed FOBS because it judged orbiting bombs to be dangerous and not cost-effective regardless of what the Soviets did. When the Soviets tested a FOBS in 1966 and 1967, the United States reacted calmly. McNamara argued against reconsidering DoD's 1965 decision not to develop a comparable weapon, and downplayed the significance of the Soviet "challenge." Moscow soon stopped testing the system and so far as can be known did not deploy it; apparently, the Soviets came to similar conclusions regarding its cost and effectiveness. See *DoD Appropriations for FY 69*, part 1, p. 252.

world would look like with or without these weapons, and it was possible to estimate the costs, risks, and potential benefits of competition. But the uncertainties in space were different in kind. Even the outlines of the possible consequences following from a full-fledged competition in space were as yet impossible to foresee in the early 1960s. Technology was one reason: without knowing what basic conceptual breakthroughs might yet emerge in space research, military planners could not offer much help to political decisionmakers struggling to clarify national interests and goals. They could not estimate the level of resources that would have to be committed to space under various scenarios. Because interests and goals remained so poorly defined, space was viewed by many American elites as an entirely new and unique area of national security competition. Decisionmakers questioned whether precedents and analogies from previous military experience on land or even on the high seas would be applicable to space. The potential costs and benefits of competition could not be predicted or even effectively estimated, because it was assumed that some crucial parts of the "equations" had not as yet been foreseen. This was *radical uncertainty*, and it had markedly different effects from the moderate uncertainty that affected decisionmaking for ABM and MIRV.

The first effect was on the way in which the American decisionmaking system reformulated its own preferences for ASAT. Once the fear of a fait accompli in space was gone, the short-term incentives to grasp some unilateral advantage (so important in MIRV) looked fundamentally less convincing in ASAT. The burden of proof fell on those who believed that an arms race in space would favor the United States, because no one could make convincing claims about what the advantages would be. Vague arguments about possible benefits did not stand up to the incalculable risks of competition. Arms racing in space came to be viewed as a potential "sinkhole" for technology and money. American decisionmakers were reluctant to set off on this uncharted course, at least until they had a better conceptual understanding of how future possibilities might impact on American interests. The shift in U.S. preferences toward cooperation was due partly to the obvious benefits of safeguarding photoreconnaissance, but a general aversion to the unknown hazards of competition was at least as important.

Radical uncertainty also affected the way in which U.S. decisionmakers thought about Soviet interests and preferences in ASAT. Forging a consensus on this score adequate to support a strategy of reciprocity, at least during the 1960s, turned out to be a surprisingly easy task. The working hypotheses about Soviet interests in ASAT were based, however, on a foundation very different from that which would support U.S. strategy for ABM.

In ABM, there was substantial communication and feedback from the

Soviets about their evolving interests, ambiguities in that information notwithstanding. In ASAT there was very little such information. When Washington made its first serious bids for cooperation around 1962, Moscow had not shown signs of either compatible interests or corresponding preferences. And although the United States went to some lengths to establish legitimacy under international law for its satellite reconnaissance program and to avoid obvious public provocations of the Kremlin with it, the Americans did not engage in an active meta-strategic campaign to ferret out and explore possibilities for influencing Moscow's conceptions of self-interest in this area.

How, then, were U.S. leaders able to develop working hypotheses about Soviet interests and forge a consensus around them? Radical uncertainty played a critical role. American decisionmakers seem to have assumed that the same radical uncertainties affecting their own conceptions of self-interest were weighing on Moscow, and that the Soviets' public recalcitrance and apparent preferences did not reflect deeply held interests. On this assumption, Soviet leaders would be as anxious as the Americans were to avoid deep involvement in a competition whose promises and costs they could not even roughly foresee. This working hypothesis was strongly reflected in the new public approach of the Kennedy administration during 1962 and 1963. When Moscow responded positively, shifting its position and quietly accepting satellite photoreconnaissance without controversy or fanfare in the waning months of 1963, the assumptions and resultant hypothesis were taken to have been at least partially substantiated. The Kennedy administration moved forward on a wager that this quiet acceptance superseded Moscow's previous unyielding rhetoric and signaled the beginning of a fundamental shift in Soviet conceptions of self-interest in space.

Other changes in Soviet behavior, particularly the Kremlin's new eagerness in 1963 to "reach agreement with the United States Government to ban the placing into orbit of objects with nuclear weapons on board," were interpreted along the same lines.[57] McNamara and his deputies championed the argument that the informal approach of offering "tacit deals" for mutual restraint met success because Soviet interests in space so nearly matched those of the Americans.[58] Their case was strengthened in the eyes of many by the dramatic success of negotiations leading to the

[57] See the address to the UN General Assembly of Soviet Foreign Minister Andrei Gromyko, in *Documents on Disarmament*, 1963, pp. 522–23.

[58] Stares, *The Militarization of Space*, pp. 85–87. American beliefs about Soviet conceptions of interest in space at that time are reflected in the fact that the United States was ready to engage in an arms control agreement with Moscow that did not include stringent verification procedures. This was an unprecedented and politically difficult step in the early 1960s.

Limited Test Ban Treaty (which, among other things, prohibited nuclear explosions in outer space) during the summer of 1963.[59] By the end of that year, the working hypotheses that would support American strategy in ASAT for at least the next decade were essentially in place.

Given PD preferences and a set of working hypotheses about Soviet interests compatible with a cooperative solution, we expect to see U.S. leaders develop strategies of reciprocity aimed at achieving mutual restraint in ASAT. What is surprising, given the tenuous nature of the foundation on which those hypotheses were constructed, is that U.S. leaders would have put in place and sustained a highly permissive strategy of contingent restraint. The explanation for this lies in the five additional factors that influence strategy choice. Contingent restraint was favored by the relative stability of currently understood interests and incentives in space. Photoreconnaissance was the most important of these. Although the United States was first to recognize the value of photoreconnaissance for purely self-interested reasons, almost as soon as they deployed comparable systems it became clear that the Soviets recognized similar benefits. The possibility of *joint* interests in photoreconnaissance (to facilitate arms control verification, crisis management, and the like) played no essential role in this. On a strictly unilateral basis, both Washington and Moscow found that they had much to gain from Discoverer and Kosmos.[60] And because the technology had not yet shown its more dangerous side, both states had relatively little to lose. As long as interests and incentives in photoreconnaissance remained stable, temptations to deploy ASAT in the short term were reduced to the point where contingent restraint appeared a viable strategy.

The nature of saliencies in space had a more equivocal impact on strategy. There was one concrete saliency that must have been unambiguous for both sides: as Albert Gore put it, "it should be easier to agree now not

[59] In July 1963, the same month that Khrushchev first admitted that the Soviets were themselves using photoreconnaissance satellites, Moscow also suddenly dropped its long-standing opposition to negotiating a limited (as opposed to a comprehensive) test ban. Henry Tanner, "Test-Ban Envoys Arrive in Moscow amid Rising Hope," *New York Times*, 15 July 1963, pp. 1, 10.

[60] The USSR deployed its first Kosmos photoreconnaissance satellite in April 1962, about two years after the United States deployed Discoverer and just prior to the Kennedy administration's reappraisal of its strategy for space. The first public signal of unilateral Soviet interests in photoreconnaissance came 15 months later, when Khrushchev boasted to Belgian Foreign Minister Paul Henri Spaak about the capabilities of Soviet satellites. In the interim, the Soviets had launched as many as nine reconnaissance satellites. Klass, *Secret Sentries in Space*, pp. 120–26. Both Stares and Gaddis suggest that satellite photos might have proven unexpectedly useful to the Soviets, particularly for collecting intelligence on China. Gaddis, "Evolution of a Satellite Reconnaissance Regime," pp. 358–59; Stares, *The Militarization of Space*, p. 238.

to arm a part of the environment that has never been armed than later to agree to disarm parts that have been armed."[61] If there was only one saliency in space and it was about to be breached, strategies with more stringent criteria of reciprocity would be favored. But Gore's view, although popular in Washington, did not tell the whole story. There were likely to be other important saliencies in space that would emerge as technological possibilities were clarified and radical uncertainty was resolved. Even in the early 1960s, some military analysts suggested that it might be possible to protect space assets in geosynchronous orbit from ASAT systems threatening satellites at lower altitudes.[62] If there were going to be many saliencies in space, a more permissive strategy of reciprocity might make better sense early on in the race.

The general political environment also cut both ways. In 1962, predominant American images of the Soviet Union as a competitor could only favor extremely stringent forms of reciprocity in the high-stakes arena of military space. But changing American beliefs about the nature of the U.S.-Soviet competition and specifically about the role of technology in it pushed in the other direction. Moscow's dramatic demonstration of its technical proficiency in space dispelled any illusions that the United States could easily outpace Soviet science; Washington's technological edge was obviously not so commanding that it could dominate the competition. American technology could, however, serve as a "buffer" that would allow the United States to adopt a less urgent attitude toward Soviet achievements. Taken together, these views on technology were at least conducive to a permissive strategy of reciprocity that was more strongly favored for other reasons.

Several important reasons came from the new strategic thought of the early 1960s, which had a crucial impact on American strategy for ASAT several years before similar effects were felt on other weapons systems. In a general sense, space seemed to many Americans the ideal place to start applying some of the ideas that were raised by the new arms control theories. Growing sensitivity to the security dilemma and to action-reaction spirals as important causes of the arms race focused many decisionmakers' attention on space as a new arena where the inadvertent excesses and

[61] From a speech by Albert Gore, U.S. representative to the First Committee of the UN General Assembly, December 3, 1962; reprinted in *Documents on Disarmament*, 1962, vol. 2, pp. 1119–24.

[62] This was part of the rationale behind the U.S. drive to station its communication satellites in higher orbits as quickly as possible. Of course, this saliency turned out to be less important in the long run for reasons discussed earlier. But it was a reasonable expectation in the early 1960s, particularly when the possibility of replacing kinetic ASAT weapons with lasers or other DEW systems had not yet been seriously foreseen.

mistakes of the past might be avoided.[63] McNamara's 1963 Posture Statement reflects the impact of this logic: "as the arms race continues and the weapons multiply and become more swift and deadly . . . more armaments whether offensive or defensive cannot solve this dilemma. Mutual deterrence underscores the need for a renewed effort to find some way, if not to eliminate these deadly weapons completely, then at least to slow down or halt their further accumulation."[64]

Some specific implications of strategic theory also favored permissive strategies of reciprocity for ASAT. The new emphasis on undesirable consequences for both sides of "reciprocal fear of surprise attack," to borrow Schelling's phrase, logically implied that both should favor invulnerable early warning systems based in space. And if strategic stability in the coming age of parity was going to rest on MAD and a mutual threat of second-strike retaliation, it made sense to protect satellites that were nearly essential to that balance. Strategic theory also opened up a whole new range of limited arms control agreements that both superpowers might find attractive; and it made sense to protect the satellites that would be needed to monitor such agreements. This was the *joint* side of interests in photoreconnaissance; it was apparent to the Americans early on and seemed to have had some influence on Soviet thought as well, even prior to 1963.[65]

Finally, the array of bureaucratic politics around ASAT in the 1960s was such that a strategy of contingent restraint could be implemented without a crippling amount of opposition. Once the ASAT mission was taken out of the Army's purview (with the cancellation of Project 505) and placed in the custody of the Air Force, organizational interests declined in importance. The Air Force was never an enthusiastic proponent of ASAT during the 1960s: following tradition, its major interest in space lay in the possibilities for a manned military space program. And after a short spurt of attention in the aftermath of Sputnik, the outlook for this interest was bleak.[66] Also important was the high level of attention that

---

[63] See Schlesinger, *A Thousand Days*, pp. 502–4.

[64] *1963 Hearings on Military Posture*, p. 307.

[65] Publicly, the Soviets demurred; but in private, informal conversations as early as 1960, a Soviet spokesman had acknowledged that the notion of "spying" on nuclear forces had a somewhat different connotation than traditional forms of military espionage. See Rostow, *Open Skies*, pp. 82–83.

[66] Stares provides a detailed account of the bureaucratic politics surrounding ASAT in the 1960s. Apart from its primary interests in tactical and strategic air power, the Air Force had other reasons to be less than zealous about ASAT. It had little incentive to use its own money to "defend" the space assets of other services. And because it had strong organizational and budgetary reasons to support continuing expansion of the military satellite program, a world without ASAT was a world in which it could happily live and even prosper. *The Militarization of Space*, Chapters 3–5.

was given to space in the White House during most of the 1960s. President Kennedy had a special personal interest in this issue; his leadership in taking on the political risks of a permissive reciprocal approach for American space policy was an important force behind the shift in U.S. strategy in 1962.[67] Johnson followed in a similar vein, accepting de facto responsibility for the 1967 Outer Space Treaty and other space arms control proposals that lacked convincing verification procedures. In both cases, the continued involvement of the president discouraged any dissatisfied bureaucratic actors from undermining or even deeply challenging contingent restraint.[68]

Cooperation under Radical Uncertainty

Radical uncertainty was a key factor shaping Washington's reevaluation of interests in space and specifically in ASAT around 1962. It was also important in the development of working hypotheses about Soviet interests that could support a highly permissive strategy of reciprocity for pursuing cooperation. Those hypotheses were subjected to some rudimentary tests, which the Soviets mostly passed. Satellite photoreconnaissance and the several treaties banning nuclear weapons in outer space were the most important of these. When Moscow proved itself willing to accept and even to promote these measures, U.S. decisionmakers interpreted this as confirmation of the working hypotheses about Soviet interests that underlay their strategy.

These were at best only partial tests of the hypotheses, and they were usually recognized as such. But because the United States had little information from any other source to work with, American decisionmakers gave great credence to the results. There were alternative explanations for each apparent signal of changing Soviet preferences, the simplest being that the Soviets had merely recognized that it would serve larger purposes

[67] Garthoff explains how Kennedy overcame a great deal of bureaucratic resistance to the idea of tacit deals or declaratory bans without verification procedures. "Banning the Bomb in Outer Space."

[68] The Joint Chiefs were consistently the most dubious. In a representative statement, they urged caution in the negotiations leading up to the Outer Space Treaty: "the Joint Chiefs of Staff believe that a serious disadvantage could arise in the future if the treaty resulted in an adverse influence on the conduct of the US military space effort. The idea that the potential USSR threat in space had been reduced by this treaty could lead to a diminution of the US military exploitation of space." Stares, *The Militarization of Space*, p. 101; quoting from a Memorandum for the Secretary of Defense from the Joint Chiefs of Staff, JCSM-838–65, 23 November 1965. Although General Wheeler (Chairman of the Joint Chiefs) expressed continuing concerns when the treaty came up for ratification, he reported that on balance the Joint Chiefs "had no military objections to it." *Treaty on Outer Space*, p. 84.

to "agree" to "refrain" from doing what they were unable to do in space with current technology. Did Moscow's newly cooperative attitude reflect a deeper set of interests, that it would not be to their advantage to try? American decisionmakers discounted discrepant signals that might have pointed in the other direction, particularly the Soviet FOBS tests and the growing statements of concern from Soviet leaders and military officers about the U.S. military satellite program.[69] In effect, U.S. strategy came to be based on a weakly buttressed set of working hypotheses about Soviet interests that were able to command sufficient consensus primarily because of the effects of radical uncertainty. Reinforcement came when contingent restraint contributed to tacit cooperation, which American decisionmakers viewed against the background of their earlier expectations as a surprising and important success.

But did the lack of any challenge to satellites in the 1960s actually represent a convergence of two states' self-interest in an embryonic cooperative deal for space? Washington never made a serious attempt to find out. The same hypotheses that supported the U.S. demarche for cooperation while Soviet leaders remained publicly recalcitrant later inhibited Washington from going further, to seek out better feedback about Soviet conceptions of self-interest in space. American decisionmakers made assumptions about the sources of changed Soviet preferences but shied away from testing them more rigorously or even trying to explore them with Moscow. As the decade progressed and cooperation seemed to hold, there were still no attempts to forge a shared consensual knowledge about interests in space, or even to understand how each side might be developing or revising conceptions of self-interest on its own. There were several reasons for this apparent neglect, among them technological arrogance and some continuing ambiguity regarding American interests in space.

But the most important reason was the perceived success of cooperation itself. As long as both sides appeared to respect a tacit deal for mutual restraint, there seemed little reason to work toward a deeper understanding of the nature of their shared interests. There was even some sense in Washington that it would be positively undesirable to do so. A joint attempt to clarify evolving interests would have forced both Washington and Moscow to recognize difficult trade-offs, most importantly those between military satellite capabilities and ASAT. These were trade-offs that neither state was yet ready to face. But the path that was taken postponed

[69] Raymond Garthoff, personal communication, November 1988; Garthoff, "ASAT Arms Control: Still Possible," provides several examples drawn from the Soviet journal *Military Thought* and elsewhere.

this problem into the indefinite future, in effect leaving both superpowers to "solve" it on their own.

Tacit cooperation rested on that choice, but its success contributed to an illusory sense of stability in a set of shared interests. Conceptions of self-interest in the two capitals, highly sensitive to changing technologies, were bound to come under pressure as radical uncertainties began to resolve themselves at the end of the decade. In the 1970s, conceptions of self-interest did shift in response. But because radical uncertainty was resolved unilaterally in Washington and Moscow, the two sides' interests shifted at different rates and in very different directions. The Americans, at least, failed to recognize what was happening to the foundation of interests that had lain behind cooperation. In this sense, cooperation as it evolved during the 1960s set the stage for its own deterioration and a turn toward competition in the next decade.

ASAT in the 1970s

Two important challenges to ASAT cooperation emerged at the end of the 1960s. New technologies made both challenges feasible, but it was a series of political decisions that brought them into being. The first challenge came from the increasing use of satellites for military support missions by both the United States and the Soviet Union. This trend began to expand rapidly at the end of the 1960s, and with the use of new technologies resulted in a blurring of the distinction between benign and threatening satellites that had been reasonably clear earlier in the decade. Concern over this problem and its many implications grew slowly and unevenly in Washington. White House and National Security Council officials, for example, became more concerned about Soviet efforts in satellite ocean reconnaissance; while the Navy, confident of its ability to protect its ships with passive countermeasures, hastened to reassure them that an ASAT was not needed for this purpose.[70] The more widely held

[70] The Soviets launched their first EORSAT, a passive receiver of electronic transmissions from ships, in December 1967. Sometime in the early 1970s they added RORSAT systems, which track targets with an active radar. These two systems are designed to operate in tandem, since the countermeasures that a naval vessel can use to evade detection by one system generally increase the probability of detection by the other. Tandem operation started in 1974, but the Soviets have had serious technical problems with the RORSAT in particular, and have rarely (only twice in the 1980s) had a fully functioning constellation of ocean reconnaissance systems on station. See "Soviets Push Ocean Surveillance," *Aviation Week and Space Technology*, 10 September 1973, pp. 12–13; Stares, *Space and National Security*, pp. 22–23. It is difficult to find Navy officials arguing in favor of ASAT as a countermeasure for ocean reconnaissance. The Navy has consistently held to the position that it can suc-

concern was with Moscow's increasing use of "tactical" photoreconnaissance satellites, launched and recovered on short notice specifically for the purpose of monitoring military force deployments in tense regions. Moscow first made extensive use of these systems during crises on the Sino-Soviet and Indo-Pakistani borders in 1969 and 1971. The problem grew in scope and political significance during the 1973 Yom Kippur War, when U.S. intelligence reports indicated that the Soviets had shared important photoreconnaissance data with the Egyptians while the Americans denied comparable information to the Israelis. Moscow's decision to share this data, a decision assumed by Americans to have been taken at the highest levels of the Soviet leadership, directly "violated" what some in Washington thought to be a part of the tacit superpower deal on space, not to provide such information to client states involved in hostilities.[71]

The second challenge was more immediate, more dramatic, and potentially more serious. It came in a series of Soviet space tests that began at the end of 1968. On October 19 and 20 of that year, the Soviets launched two satellites into co-orbital tracks. Within several hours, the second satellite passed close to the first. It then exploded in space. The United States observed what seemed to be a repeat performance on November 1. Without question, the Soviets were testing some kind of satellite defense, inspection, or destruction system; but it was not clear which. The Pentagon hesitated to make a decision until early 1970, when its analysts concluded that the Soviets had "successfully tested a hunter-killer satellite that can seek out and destroy other orbiting spacecraft." Tests of the system continued irregularly through 1971. In December 1971, a low altitude interception test took place over the northern latitudes, and the explosion in space lit up the nighttime sky over Sweden for a moment. As the media reported it, "the Russians had demonstrated their ability to place hunter killer spacecraft in the vicinity of targets with orbits characteristic of electronic ferrets, meteorological and navigation satellites and photoreconnaissance."[72] It seemed, for all intents and purposes, that the tacit deal for ASAT cooperation had been broken.

---

cessfully counter the threat by spoofing, jamming, and otherwise deceiving these satellites through nondestructive means.

[71] Jasani, *Outer Space*, p. 105; *Soviet Space Programs 1971–75*, Staff Report of the Senate Committee on Aeronautical and Space Sciences, vol. 1 (1976) pp. 466–73. Also see Baker, *The Shape of Wars to Come*, pp. 77–79. In his autobiography, Sadat specifically denied these allegations. *In Search of Identity*, p. 260. Heikal's account is equivocal. *The Road to Ramadan*, p. 241.

[72] G. E. Perry, "Russian Hunter-Killer Satellite Experiments," *Royal Air Force Quarterly* 17 (1977): 333. For a contemporary report, see "Soviet Target Shots in Space May be Anti-Satellite Arms," *International Herald Tribune*, 5–6 April 1969, p. 3. For a report of the Pentagon's assessment, see "Launching the Killer Cosmos," *Newsweek*, 16 February 1970,

The political and military significance of that conclusion was not so immediately clear. Spectacular displays notwithstanding, the Soviet ASAT was technologically primitive and would be seriously limited in any military operations. The most serious limitation was its "co-orbital" method of interception: instead of ascending directly to destroy a target, the Soviet ASAT maneuvered into an orbit that intersected the target's orbit after several trips around the earth. Even the most sophisticated co-orbital interceptor can only attack a satellite when the target's ground track runs close to the launch point of the weapon, which occurs at most twice a day for satellites in low earth orbit (LEO). This meant that the Soviets would have to wait an average of six hours to launch an attack against a given satellite. And since there were known to be only two launch facilities capable of handling the ASAT system and its massive, delicate, liquid fueled booster, the potential threat added up to a maximum launch rate of several interceptors per day under the best of circumstances. What's more, American military analysts agreed that the Soviet ASAT could only threaten satellites in low earth orbit; satellites outside LEO remained essentially invulnerable.[73]

Technical constraints on the weapon aside, Johnson administration officials saw the Soviet decision to test an ASAT in such blatant fashion as a serious challenge to cooperation. The political decisions that lay behind this overt challenge were viewed as fundamentally more important than the military significance of the emerging capability. The Soviet venture in ASAT could not be dismissed as FOBS had been several years earlier, in part because of the highly interdependent nature of the ASAT problem, but also because of the political weight that ASAT cooperation had come to bear in the interim.

American responses to the Soviet challenge would continue to reflect that legacy through most of the 1970s. The Soviet ASAT underwent two long series of flight tests, first between 1968 and 1971, and again between 1976 and 1978. The "objective" challenge, the ASAT weapon itself, was essentially the same in the early and the latter part of the decade. But the U.S. response in the two cases was markedly different. In the first instance, the Nixon administration reacted mildly to the Soviet challenge. It chose to maintain a permissive strategy of reciprocity that was aimed at revitalizing cooperation. About five years later, the Ford administration reacted sharply and within a short period of time revised American

---

p. 17. Johnson provides a summary of the testing program. *The Soviet Year in Space 1982*, p. 26.

[73] Office of Technology Assessment, *Anti-satellite Weapons, Countermeasures, and Arms Control*, OTA-ISC-281, 1985; U.S. Department of Defense, *Soviet Military Power*, 1985, pp. 55–56; Garwin, Gottfried, and Hafner, "Anti-satellite Weapons," *Scientific American* 250 (1984): 45–49.

strategy in ASAT quite radically. The new strategy, which would be taken up and pressed forward by the Carter administration, was contingent threat of escalation. These decisions marked a critical juncture for cooperation in space. As in the case of the decisions made in the early 1960s, the decisions of the 1970s were influenced but not determined by technology or the objective characteristics of the threat. Why then did U.S. strategy shift so dramatically?

1970: The First Reconsideration

The Nixon administration was forced to confront the Soviet ASAT challenge almost immediately upon entering office.[74] Its immediate response to the Soviet space interception tests was extremely circumspect; on several occasions in 1969 and 1970, Pentagon spokesmen refused to confirm or deny public media speculation about an evolving ASAT threat.[75] Preoccupied with other strategic weapons issues and with the Vietnam War, the administration seemed content to "wait and see" if the Soviet tests represented a serious commitment to moving forward with ASAT. Moscow, in any case, did not appear to be forcing the issue: the Pentagon found no evidence of any Soviet ASAT tests conducted during 1969 and for much of 1970. When this lull came to an end with two reported tests in October 1970, Kissinger immediately requested that OSD produce a study of the motivations and consequences of the Soviet challenge and possible U.S. responses.[76]

Kissinger's mandate prompted the formation of an interagency study group under Pentagon scientist Manfred Eimer that was originally tasked to produce a quick study of the ASAT question for consideration by the White House. But despite a rapid succession of several ASAT tests in the winter of 1971, any sense of urgency in the NSC's concerns seemed to dissipate once the problem had been sent out for study, and the Eimer

[74] An early study of the U.S. space program by a Presidential Space Task Group set up in February 1969, emphasized the cost-effective use of space for military support missions and questioned the value of manned military space efforts. ASAT does not seem to have been directly addressed. Levine, *The Future of the US Space Program*, pp. 123–26. "Nixon's Task Group Preparing a Vital Space Policy Report," *Space/Astronautics* 51, no. 6 (1969): 28–31.

[75] For example, see the testimony of Secretary of the Air Force Robert Seamans in *DoD Appropriations for FY 71*, part 1, pp. 662–63. DDR&E John Foster in early 1970 acknowledged that the Soviets were testing what appeared to be a primitive ASAT, but argued that it posed no serious threat to U.S. interests. Ibid., part 6, p. 88.

[76] Johnson, *The Soviet Year in Space 1983*, p. 39.

Group (as it came to be called) did not produce a final report until 1973.[77] That report gave a moderate assessment of the Soviet ASAT's capabilities, stressing the serious limitations of its co-orbital interception method. The Eimer Group judged the military benefits of having this primitive weapon operational to be small or even insignificant. In fact, the technology the Soviets had apparently chosen seemed so poorly suited for most military applications that Pentagon analysts were confounded in their attempt to understand the logic behind Moscow's decision to test it. The Eimer Group could not in the end reach consensus on a "specific target" or even an "identifiable reason" for the Soviet ASAT. On this basis, the group finally concluded that the Soviet ASAT tests should *not* be interpreted as the first manifestation of a serious effort to develop a militarily significant threat against American space assets.

This left the critical question of why the Soviets chose to provoke the United States with these tests, and in so doing jeopardize a tacit cooperation that at least the Americans thought to be valuable. There were several potential explanations. It was possible that the "tacit deal" over photoreconnaissance had been an illusion, and that Moscow's apparent acceptance of this deal was simply a means of buying time for developing technology for countermeasures. It was also possible that the Soviets still hoped to deploy offensive weapons in space, and that the Panama Hypothesis remained alive. The ASAT could also have been a preliminary response to developments in U.S. military satellite capabilities that the Soviets feared would eventually pose direct threats to their security interests. Finally, some members of the Eimer Group continued to suspect that Moscow's ASAT was an "unintentional" product of internal politics; a program pushed forward by the military that had somehow evaded scrutiny by political leaders.

These diverse interpretations resolved, roughly, into two competing schools. Either the Soviets were cautiously testing U.S. interests and commitment by offering a limited challenge to ASAT cooperation; or they simply did not share American conceptions of the benefits of mutual restraint in space and were trying to exploit the United States for a unilateral advantage. There was very little concrete evidence to distinguish between these competing arguments in the early 1970s. But in light of the continuing perception of a high-stakes game in space, beliefs about the potential American technological edge, and the lack of any convincing feedback from the Soviets about their interests in cooperation, there would have been strong reasons to act on the basis of a worst-case sce-

---

[77] Eimer was at this time Assistant Director for Intelligence at DDR&E. The following is based on Stares, *The Militarization of Space*, pp. 162–64, who bases his account on a confidential interview with a former DoD official.

nario. Forced to respond to an explicit Soviet challenge, the latter interpretation would have provided decisionmakers the most obvious guidance for at least a short-term, prudent American policy response.

The Eimer Group, however, came down squarely in favor of the first interpretation, seeing in the Soviet decision at most a limited "probe" of American restraint in ASAT. It did so for two related reasons. The first had to do with the vestiges of radical uncertainty that continued to influence American conceptions of self-interest in ASAT. The question marks of technological possibilities had not yet been fully resolved to the point where U.S. decisionmakers had a clear picture of alternative futures in space. It was hard to see how the same uncertainties, which were thought to be affecting Soviet leaders' calculations in a similar fashion, could have been very much less troubling in Moscow.

Second and more important was the legacy of cooperation in the 1960s. Tacit cooperation for the United States rested on the assumption that the Soviets shared Washington's view of how to manage radical uncertainty, preferring a "no ASAT" deal that left both sides free to deploy more sophisticated military satellites. The apparent success of this deal cemented the underlying assumption in Washington. When the deal was challenged, American decisionmakers held on to previous assumptions about Soviet interests and viewed the challenge almost entirely in this light. Other possible interpretations, such as the notion that Soviet actions were intended as a signal of concern and a hedge against the more gradual developments in potentially threatening military satellite technology, were heavily discounted. So was the possibility that Moscow had been committed all along to competing in space, as soon as it was technologically "ready."

Tacit cooperation as it had evolved in the 1960s was a critical factor that encouraged this discounting. It did so in the following way. The U.S. bid to restrain an emerging arms race in space succeeded in the early part of the decade, but it did not slow technological change. As technological possibilities in space became increasingly clear, the radical uncertainty that had underlain cooperation was gradually resolved, in the Soviet Union as well as in the United States. As the process unfolded and radical uncertainty evolved into moderate uncertainty in both capitals, decisionmakers would have begun to foresee and evaluate potential future strategic environments in space and develop clearer preferences over alternative outcomes.

But in large part due to the early and dramatic success of cooperation, neither side sought to explore how the other's conceptions of self-interest in space might be changing toward the end of the 1960s. Cooperation actually inhibited any impulse to do so, because it contributed to an artificial sense of stability among "common" U.S.-Soviet conceptions of interest in space that may never have been fully shared, even in the early 1960s. This effect maintained itself in the face of gradual changes in the character of military satellites, and despite the direct challenge of Soviet ASAT tests at the end of the decade. Even after the Soviet test series came to an end in 1971, Washington made no concerted effort to elicit more discriminating feedback about Soviet interests or to forge a new consensual knowledge about space in tandem with the Soviets. Tacit cooperation and the expectation that it would be revitalized blocked the impulse to do either. But that expectation was based on a set of working hypotheses about Soviet interests that were only weakly supported by evidence when they were formulated several years earlier and had not been subjected to demanding reexamination since. Put simply, the working hypotheses that formed the foundation of a highly permissive strategy of reciprocity in the 1960s were never directly tested or even discussed with the Soviets in the way that analogous assumptions about ABM were. The early apparent success of cooperation in the ASAT case was a critical reason why.

To 1976: Enhanced Contingent Restraint

The Eimer Group's conclusions set the tone for a mild U.S. response to the Soviet ASAT. The overall recommendation of the study was that Washington should do what it could to discourage an ASAT race and aim instead at rescuing cooperation in space. As a partial step, it proposed that the United States implement an assortment of satellite survivability measures to reduce the vulnerability of American space assets without posing any new threats to Soviet security. At the same time, the Eimer Group explicitly rejected the notion that the United States should respond with a new ASAT program of its own. In accordance with the prevailing assessment of the motives behind Moscow's challenge, a serious U.S. effort to develop and deploy new and more sophisticated ASATs did not seem necessary; in fact, it could have the unwanted effect of actually stimulating the Soviets to develop a more militarily significant weapon of their own. In any case, there was serious concern about moving into a world where both sides had deployed even rudimentary ASATs, due to fears that mutual deterrence might not work in space quite so well as on earth.[78]

[78] Stares, *The Militarization of Space*, p. 164. The concept of mutual deterrence in space was deemed weaker in part because the Americans at this time saw themselves as somewhat more dependent on space assets than the Soviet Union. But the primary argument was that satellites, being important and vulnerable strategic assets that could be attacked without directly causing loss of life, might seem tempting targets for demonstrations of resolve in a superpower crisis.

Cooperation and mutual restraint in ASAT was still clearly seen as serving U.S. interests. But the Soviet challenge could not just be written off, because it did seem to indicate that Moscow was motivated to pursue a unilateral advantage in ASAT if the United States would permit it. The Soviet decision was finally explained as a test of American resolve, a limited "probe" to determine if U.S. restraint in ASAT was in fact contingent on Soviet actions. On that logic, a somewhat more demanding strategy of reciprocity seemed necessary to revitalize cooperation.

The Nixon administration's policy for military space came to closely follow this logic. There was an immediate surge of support for satellite survivability measures, despite worsening budgetary pressures and only lukewarm interest on the part of the Air Force. As part of this program, the FY 1972 "Aerospace Defense Program" included new funds for developing and deploying "survivable satellite" technologies and for designing onboard sensors to provide warning of attempted attacks. In ASAT, the Pentagon was directed to take some steps to reduce lead time for a possible deployment, but proposals for moving forward with an "off-the-shelf" ASAT in the short term were rejected. Greater emphasis was put on a long-term program to explore new technologies, most importantly terminal homing warheads with nonnuclear kill mechanisms. None of these programs went beyond the research and development stage, and there was no push to bring any of the new technologies to deployment in the near term.[79]

Between 1970 and 1973, the Nixon administration's strategy for ASAT thus moved progressively toward enhanced contingent restraint as it brought in new measures to emphasize the credibility of the U.S. commitment to respond to Soviet actions in space if and when that became necessary. Implementing enhanced contingent restraint, however, was not always a straightforward problem. The Pentagon faced a difficult choice in this regard when it came to the fate of Project 437, the Air Force's nuclear-tipped ASAT still deployed and active in the Eastern Pacific. Project 437 had become much less important as a potential stepping stone toward more useful ASAT systems once the development of nonnuclear modifications for it were canceled in the late 1960s; and in 1970 Project

[79] *DoD Appropriations for FY 72*, part 6, pp. 275–76. The Air Force was lukewarm on satellite survivability for several reasons. Most importantly, it did not see the Soviet ASAT as a serious short-term threat. In that case, "hardening" satellites against attack just added new weight and new costs to the already difficult technical problems of satellite design. There was also fear that the money going to satellite survivability would reduce the resources available for the satellite programs themselves, which were already under considerable fiscal stress. For additional details on ASAT, see Stares, *The Militarization of Space*, p. 203. Project Spike, another proposed ASAT with nonnuclear kill that was a favorite of some Air Force officials, was carried through preliminary design in 1971 and 1972. It was later blocked at the development stage when its funding was deleted from the FY 1973 budget.

437 was placed on "standby" status with a lag time to operational readiness of 30 days.[80] After a single exercise to practice reactivation of the
system in November 1971, subsequent tests were canceled. The Air Force
generally had little enthusiasm for 437 and wanted to hasten its demise.
But 437 remained the only active ASAT system then available to the
United States, and to cancel it outright at this juncture seemed to many
American decisionmakers an inappropriate signal.[81] Project 437 was not
allowed to die the quiet death that it otherwise might have. During the
summer of 1972, a hurricane seriously damaged 437's data-processing
and launch facilities. After two concerted efforts to reconstitute the system, it came back on line in March 1973. Repairs eventually ran to a cost
of about $24 million, an unusually large sum to spend on a weapon of
marginal military utility that was already slated to be phased out in the
next two years. To be sure, 437 was not the only reason to rebuild the
facilities on Johnston Island.[82] But as part of the administration's strategy
of enhanced contingent restraint, it did play a role as a visible signal of
Washington's resolve to compete in ASAT should Soviet actions demand
it.[83]

Moscow did not demand it. In fact, several developments in the early
1970s seemed to corroborate Washington's assessment of the Soviet
ASAT as only a limited probe. The first bit of evidence came when Moscow stopped its ASAT tests abruptly in the fall of 1971, without any indication of follow-on efforts. That same fall, the Soviets agreed to two
small treaties in the context of SALT (Agreement to Reduce the Risks of
Outbreak of Nuclear War and the "Hot Line Modernization" Pact) that
implicitly banned interference with certain space assets.[84]

[80] Garthoff, "ASAT Arms Control," p. 30. Garthoff believes that this was not known in
Moscow as late as 1972, when a *Military Thought* article referred to both the Nike-Zeus
ASAT (the long-extinct Project 505) and the Thor ASAT (Project 437) as "active means of
American ASAT." See Major General M. Cherednichenko, "Scientific-Technical Progress in
the Development of Weapons and Military Technology," *Military Thought* no. 4 (1972) [I
thank Ted Hopf for translation].

[81] This was not true of the Air Defense Command, which seemed to favor the continuation of 437 for mostly parochial reasons. See Stares, *The Militarization of Space*, pp. 201–
2.

[82] Stares notes that these facilities were also slated for various ABM tests and for the
National Nuclear Test Readiness Program, held in abeyance after the signing of the Limited
Test Ban Treaty. Ibid., p. 202.

[83] Garthoff disagrees. Referring to the 1972 *Military Thought* article cited above, he argues that U.S. ASAT programs "inadvertently triggered" the Soviet ASAT testing program.
This cannot be true of the decisions about Project 437 in the 1970s. Garthoff mistakenly
writes that the 1972 article appeared "just as the Soviet ASAT testing program was being
gotten under way"; the first test series of the Soviet ASAT actually began in the late 1960s
and *ended* in 1972. *Science*, 16 September 1988, p. 1518.

[84] The Risks of Nuclear War agreement commits both sides to rapid consultation in the
event of any disruption in early warning systems. The Hot Line pact provides for a link

ASAT was never placed directly on the table for negotiation or even serious discussion at SALT I.[85] But the sense that a tacit agreement on ASAT had been revitalized underlay important aspects of the talks and was instrumental to the outcome. The United States proceeded on the assumption that because of overlapping technologies, it would have been difficult to effectively ban ABM for the long term if both sides were left free to pursue ASAT. More immediately, the central verification provisions of SALT relied heavily on space assets and particularly on photoreconnaissance satellites. When Moscow agreed to a codified principle of "non-interference with national technical means of verification" within the treaties, this was interpreted by Washington's strategic community as explicit acceptance of each side's legitimate right to operate these satellites essentially unhindered. On this logic, since photoreconnaissance satellites (always based in low earth orbit) seemed the most likely imputed "target" of the Soviet ASAT, it was reasonable to see Moscow's acceptance of this provision as confirmation that the Soviets had de facto signed on to a revitalized deal for mutual restraint in ASAT.

The same working hypotheses about Soviet interests that underlay cooperation in the 1960s, and logically consequent assumptions about the success of American strategy for ASAT in the early 1970s, continued to guide U.S. military space policy for the next several years as a result. Between FY 1972 and FY 1976, the Posture Statements of the secretary of defense did not even mention the existence of a Soviet ASAT. The Pentagon was similarly restrained when it came to the question of an American ASAT. The only serious program that might have led to a new ASAT system in the medium term (Project Spike) was cut out of the FY 1973 budget and effectively canceled thereafter. Even the surge of interest in satellite survivability measures diminished; funding for these programs was barely maintained between FY 1972 and FY 1976.[86]

These decisions about the U.S. military space program were not always taken as part of a carefully and consciously orchestrated strategy for ASAT restraint. The Nixon administration's priorities in defense policy and in Soviet policy were usually elsewhere; budgetary constraints and the improving political environment of detente were other general reasons not to set off on a high-technology, high-risk competition in a new

---

between the Soviet Molniya and American Intelsat satellites to supplement ground-based hot line communications, and calls for measures "to insure the continuation and reliable operation of the communications circuits and systems of terminals" (Article 2).

[85] Garthoff reports that neither side "even raised the matter." *Detente and Confrontation*, p. 189.

[86] See *Military Posture Statements* of the Secretary of Defense for FY 1972–76. For details on Project Spike, a direct-ascent nonnuclear ASAT proposed by the Air Defense Command in 1971, see Stares, *The Militarization of Space*, pp. 202–3.

set of strategic weapons systems. But the same conditions did not stop the United States from competing in other areas (such as MIRV) and would not have held back ASAT if Washington's assessment of Soviet interests in space had been otherwise. The difference was that observed changes in Soviet behavior, specifically the halting of ASAT tests and the accession to several treaties with indirect commitments on ASAT, were interpreted to reinforce the working hypotheses about Soviet interests in space that had been passed down from the success of tacit cooperation in the 1960s. If a strategy of enhanced contingent restraint based on those hypotheses appeared to gain success in revitalizing tacit cooperation on ASAT, the burden of proof in Washington lay with those who wanted to change it. Until the middle of 1975, almost no one did.[87]

1975–1977: The Second Reconsideration

Soon after Nixon's resignation in 1974, the Ford administration called for another broad reassessment of U.S. policy for military space. This led, by steps, to an important change in American strategy that culminated in 1977 with Ford's decision to accelerate development and testing that would lead to near-term deployment of a highly sophisticated ASAT system based on state-of-the-art miniature homing vehicle (MHV) technology. This decision was remarkable because the Soviet ASAT threat in 1977 was essentially the same in military and technical terms as it had been at the start of the decade. It was also remarkable because the majority of the American strategic community and top decisionmakers, including the president, continued to favor a cooperative solution of mutual restraint in ASAT. But Washington's strategy for eliciting cooperation shifted dramatically. By the end of 1977 the United States was committed to the development of the MHV ASAT interceptor and its deployment in the early 1980s should the Soviets not agree to some formal arrangement for mutual restraint in the interim. This was a strategy of contingent threat of escalation. How did it come about?

The change in American strategy began with the reevaluation of military space policy in 1975, which was prompted mainly by the change of administration. Ford's national security team early on set up a number of

---

[87] The DoD in particular maintained a relaxed attitude toward ASAT during this period. Foster told the Congress in 1972 that "it has never been clear to us that we ought to go out and develop an [ASAT] system." Part of the reason for this was that DoD wanted to maintain space as a sanctuary for its own military satellites, but concern about similar uses of space by the Soviet Union remained low. Until 1975 at least, DoD consistently favored a low-level program for ASAT R & D, coupled with moderate efforts to decrease the vulnerability of American satellites. *DoD Appropriations for FY 73*, part 4, p. 813.

specialized panels to assess the state of science and technology and its impact on the military balance. Space programs were an important focus of discussion, but not primarily because of the Soviets' earlier ASAT challenge. More important was a growing sense among top political decisionmakers that recent technological developments in space systems warranted a broad new appraisal of what was now and would soon become possible to do with military systems in space.[88] This reflected the fact that radical uncertainty, which previously had such an important influence on U.S. decisionmaking, was now largely resolved into more conventional, moderate uncertainty; and U.S. interests and incentives in space were quickly becoming more focused and clear.[89] So, by implication, were the trade-offs between costs and benefits within possible future scenarios of cooperation and competition in ASAT.

One important consequence was the new surge of interest and concern about the expanding use of satellite systems for crisis monitoring and other tactical military purposes by both sides. In 1974 the NSC commissioned a new panel specifically for the purpose of looking at the growing role of space-based assets in supporting military forces in regional conflicts and local wars. Expanding beyond its mandate, the Slichter Panel (chaired by Charles Slichter of the University of Chicago) came to address in broader terms the threat of disruption of U.S. satellites by a Soviet ASAT. The panel came to the disturbing conclusion that the United States was potentially quite vulnerable to such attacks because the military had become highly dependent for many of its most important missions on satellites that were "largely defenseless and extremely soft to countermeasures." This prompted enough concern at the White House to commission a follow-on study under the direction of Solomon Buchsbaum, a former chairman of the Defense Science Board, aimed specifically at the problem of satellite vulnerability and the closely related ASAT question.[90]

The Defense Department was also growing more concerned with the relative U.S. and Soviet positions in military space, but officials here did

---

[88] Another important impetus behind the broad reassessment of military technology issues was a widely held belief that the quality of scientific and technical advice to the president had suffered following Nixon's decision to disband PSAC. Kissinger and Deputy National Security Advisor Brent Scowcroft were the officials responsible for final approval of each panel's findings.

[89] Andrei Kokoshin reports that a similar set of reconsiderations took place in the Kremlin at about the same time. According to Kokoshin, military officials newly optimistic about the technological possibilities for space-based BMD and other weapons systems in space managed to gain a serious hearing before the Politburo. Their arguments were eventually but not easily defeated by a majority of scientists who held to a more guarded assessment of current technologies. Personal communication, January 1990.

[90] Stares, *The Militarization of Space*, pp. 168–69, drawing from confidential interviews with NSC staff officials.

not share the sense of urgency about satellite vulnerability that was beginning to creep into the assessments made in the executive branch. Pentagon analysts paid more attention to the rapid growth of the *Soviet* military satellite program: in addition to improving its ocean reconnaissance, photoreconnaissance, and communication systems, Moscow was now seen to be making use of geodetic satellites for improving the accuracy of its ICBMs. DoD spokesmen also made much of the fact that the aggregate number of Soviet satellite launches had bypassed the number of American launches after 1971 and was continuing to grow rapidly.[91] While this high launch rate mostly reflected the less sophisticated technology of Moscow's shorter-lived satellite systems, it also seemed to signal a substantial and still growing Soviet commitment to the use of space for military purposes.

The Soviet ASAT, on the other hand, was not a priority issue at DoD, at least until Moscow resumed testing its co-orbital interceptor in February 1976. This is not to say that ASAT dropped off the map before 1976: as early as 1973 some Pentagon officials were sounding warnings about possible applications of Soviet efforts in high-energy lasers to ASAT.[92] This concern was temporarily piqued by a series of "blinding" incidents that occurred in the fall of 1975, when sensors aboard three U.S. satellites were illuminated by radiation emanating from an unidentified source in the western part of the Soviet Union. Following an investigation that by all accounts did not provide fully satisfactory answers to all the outstanding questions, the Pentagon concluded that the cause had been a fire in a Siberian gas pipeline and *not* a deliberate test of some exotic antisatellite laser.[93] The Soviet ASAT "threat" quickly returned to a position of relative obscurity at the Pentagon.

The military's relatively sanguine attitude reflected a continuing sense at DoD and among the services that the Soviet ASAT, dormant since 1971, was neither a serious threat to U.S. satellites nor a first step in a larger Soviet plan to move in that direction, and thus did not necessitate any dramatic American response. Accordingly, the secretary's Military Posture Statement for FY 1976 included only a brief account of Soviet space activities and requested only minimal increases in funding for "space defense research," aimed principally at reducing the vulnerability of U.S. satellites. The FY 1977 Posture Statement was similarly re-

[91] "Geodetic Launches and Soviet Targeting," *Aviation Week and Space Technology*, 7 June 1976, pp. 23–24; *NASA Authorization for FY 83*, pp. 75–76.

[92] *Aviation Week and Space Technology*, 6 August 1973, p. 9; "High Energy Laser Weapons," *Science News*, 3 July 1976, p. 12.

[93] Philip Klass, "Anti-satellite Laser Use Suspected," *Aviation Week and Space Technology*, 8 December 1975, pp. 12–13; "DoD Continues Satellite Blinding Investigation," *Aviation Week and Space Technology*, 5 January 1976, p. 18.

strained: while noting increased U.S. dependence on military satellites, it asked only for about $43 million to be budgeted for space defense programs limited to "continuing R and D efforts to develop technologies for detecting, tracking, and identifying objects out to geo-stationary orbits, and for enhancing the survivability of satellite systems." There was no mention of ASAT at all.[94] The Air Force, still the natural bureaucratic "home" for ASAT, remained similarly ambivalent. As late as the start of 1976, neither the Pentagon nor the services were arguing the case that the United States ought to move forward with ASAT, either for bargaining purposes or for actual deployment.

The major catalyst for U.S. policy came again from the executive branch, in the wake of what seemed a dramatic reversal by the Soviet Union. Without any warning or prior signal that such a move was imminent, the Soviets on February 16, 1976, resumed tests of their co-orbital ASAT interceptor. This prompted a flurry of activity in Washington. The White House immediately directed the Buchsbaum panel to produce an interim report for the president with an assessment of the Soviet weapon and possible American responses. From a military and technical standpoint there was very little new to say. So far as U.S. analysts could tell, the Soviet interceptor was essentially the same device that had been tested five years earlier, with only two detectable differences. The first was that the Soviets were now seen to be experimenting with a passive infrared sensor system to help the ASAT zero-in on its target, to replace the active radar sensor they had previously used as a terminal homing mechanism. This was potentially important because the infrared sensor, harder to counter or spoof, would have improved the military performance of the Soviet weapon. Unfortunately for the Soviets, however, all the tests with the new sensor mechanism ended in failure. The second difference was in the operational status of the system's launching facilities at Tyuratam, which had been upgraded (at what would have been considerable expense) so as to reduce the lag time from alert to launch to 90 minutes or less.[95]

These improvements were of marginal military significance. The Soviet ASAT was still laboring under the limitations imposed by its co-orbital

[94] Secretary of Defense Donald H. Rumsfeld, *Military Posture Statement FY 77*, January 1976, p. 93. It was later revealed that the United States had had a small nonnuclear ASAT research program underway in secret since 1974, but that the level of funding had been inadequate to support the development even of a prototype before the mid-1980s. Norman Kempster, "New US Satellite Killer Project is Revealed," *Los Angeles Times*, 31 March 1977, p. 3.

[95] Johnson, *The Soviet Year in Space 1983*, p. 39; Meyer, "Soviet Military Programmes and the New 'High Ground,' " p. 212; "Satellite Killers," *Aviation Week and Space Technology*, 21 June 1976, p. 13.

method of interception. Most American satellites remained outside of its reach; and those that were in low earth orbits had been rendered somewhat less vulnerable to "cheap hits" by satellite survivability measures put into place in the interim. But these military considerations played less of a role in the American response than they had after the first series of tests earlier in the decade. The new test series was seen in Washington as a dramatic reversal of Soviet policy on ASAT, and was taken to be more important for what it indicated about Moscow's commitment to the ASAT mission in general.

The Soviet decision to resume ASAT testing early in 1976, as the SALT II negotiations were entering a critical phase and the detente relationship was under increasing pressure, made it difficult to view ASAT as a low-priority program for the Kremlin. It also made it difficult to explain ASAT as a favored program of the Soviet military that had somehow escaped political oversight by the top leadership; or as a limited probe aimed at testing the American commitment to contingent restraint. That commitment had already been tested in 1971, and U.S. decisionmakers at the time believed that Nixon's response had passed the test and produced a revitalized cooperative deal. But just a few years hence there seemed a new seriousness of purpose in the Soviet ASAT program. In 1976, for example, the Soviets tested their ASAT at least four times. Most troubling to American analysts was one particular test that took place in conjunction with a coordinated military exercise for large-scale nuclear war, including simulated strategic bombing raids and launches of ICBMs.[96] This seriousness of purpose was difficult to reconcile with the working hypotheses about Soviet interests that underlay American strategy for ASAT. Another interpretation, that Moscow did not share U.S. understandings about the advantages of cooperative restraint in ASAT and had developed a different set of preferences, began to look like a viable alternative. In a series of comments on the renewed Soviet challenge, Defense Department spokesmen began to reflect this weakening of the consensus about the sources and consequences of Soviet interests. For example, Pentagon official Malcolm Currie in October 1976 publicly stated that "the Soviets have developed and tested a potential war-fighting antisatellite capability . . . and seized the initiative in an area which we hoped would be left untapped. They have opened the specter of space as a new dimension for warfare, with all that this implies."[97]

In the White House and particularly in the NSC, where doubts about

[96] This was revealed in a CIA document discussed by Stares (*The Militarization of Space*, pp. 144–45) and reported on in "Russia's Killer Satellites," *Foreign Report*, 14 January 1981, p. 2.

[97] From a speech to the Air Force Association reported in *Aviation Week and Space Technology*, 8 November 1976, p. 13.

the continuing compatibility of Soviet and American conceptions of self-interest in space had been growing for several years, the 1976 tests put American policy on ASAT to its most severe test. In the short term, however, the administration stuck by the current strategy of enhanced contingent restraint. After receiving the interim report from the Buchsbaum panel, President Ford in the fall of 1976 issued a National Security Decision Memorandum (NSDM-333) that called for an immediate and substantial increase in funding for satellite survivability measures. But he did not order any change or acceleration in U.S. ASAT research and development programs in the short term. The White House hedged the issue by arguing that any change in strategy or even in emphasis within the U.S. ASAT program would have to await further studies by the Buchsbaum panel and by a newly established Defense Science Board Panel.[98]

The final report of the Buchsbaum panel was issued in December 1976. It reiterated earlier warnings about the vulnerability of American space assets and called for quick action on a number of additional measures to diminish that vulnerability. The report recognized that satellite survivability measures could complicate the job of an attacker but that such efforts by themselves could not protect American satellites if the Soviets were to push forward in a determined way with ASAT. Should the United States develop its own ASAT in response? The final report of the Buchsbaum panel explicitly rejected this option. The arguments were essentially the same as those made by the Eimer Group after the first series of Soviet tests about five years before. There was no specific military rationale for a U.S. ASAT; and any argument that the United States could deter attacks against its own satellites by holding the Soviets' less valuable and more easily replaceable space systems at risk was still a weak reed. Instead, the best solution from Washington's perspective would be to negotiate a highly constraining arms control agreement to severely limit or ban ASAT systems on both sides.[99]

The arguments of the Eimer and Buchsbaum studies, and the resulting assessments of American preferences in ASAT, were nearly indistinguishable. But the policy prescriptions of the two reports differed in an important way. The new emphasis in 1976 on achieving a *formal, negotiated* agreement for ASAT restraint was a significant addition, with major consequences for cooperation. Military and arms control analysts in Washington quickly recognized the daunting technological problems that would encumber effective verification of any agreement that might be

---

[98] Stares, *The Militarization of Space*, p. 170. NSDM-333 also established a new system program office at the Space and Missile Systems Organization within the Air Force to coordinate efforts on satellite survivability.

[99] Ibid.

reached.[100] There were also serious political obstacles, not least of which was that a treaty acceptable to Washington would presumably ask the Soviets to dismantle their own field-tested interceptor without an obvious quid pro quo from the United States. Still, the abrupt resumption of Soviet ASAT tests, interpreted in Washington as the second "breaking" of the ASAT deal, made a return to tacit cooperation seem untenable. Cooperation remained the principal goal of U.S. strategy, but cooperation would now have to be enshrined in a comprehensive formal agreement prohibiting ASAT deployments and severely restricting relevant research and development programs. It was clear to all those involved in working out the details that this was going to be very hard to engineer.

The objective of reaching a formal agreement placed extraordinary new demands on the U.S. strategy for achieving cooperation, just as the working hypotheses about Soviet interests that had supported relatively permissive strategies of reciprocity up till then were deteriorating. There were no obvious contenders to replace those hypotheses, in large part because the United States had done little to explore how Soviet conceptions of self-interest in space were changing in the interim. With so little understanding of Moscow's interests, and now with great uncertainty even of Moscow's preferences in ASAT, it was becoming extremely difficult to maintain a consensus around working hypotheses sufficient to support a reciprocal strategy for ASAT. By the end of 1976, U.S. decision-making for ASAT had reached a critical juncture.

The Ford administration took the first step toward a new American strategy. Late in 1976 the NSC staff answered the final report of the Buchsbaum panel with a list of policy options for the president, one of which was to proceed with immediate development and deployment of a U.S. ASAT. Ford himself was uncertain, and he appears to have been swayed toward delay by continuing opposition from DoD.[101] In the midst of these discussions, the Soviets tested their ASAT once again on December 27. This event seems to have played a critical role in finally breaking

---

[100] ASAT verification was known to be far more demanding, in principle, than verification of limits on ICBMs. The basic reason was that while a few "extra" undetected ICBMs would not make a significant difference in the military balance, a few ASATs might, because the United States in particular was thought to be so dependent on a relatively small number of military satellites.

[101] The Military Posture Statement for FY 1978 noted both the increasing threats from Soviet military satellites and the threat posed to U.S. satellites by Moscow's ASAT; according to Secretary of Defense Donald Rumsfeld, "space [which] has thus far been a relative sanctuary may not remain so indefinitely." But the report did not call for a U.S. ASAT program in response. Instead, it noted that U.S. policy for managing the threat would focus on "significantly increased US space defense R and D and procurement programs to provide for an improved capability . . . in ground and space based satellite surveillance systems and satellite survivability programs." *Military Posture Statement FY 78*, pp. 137–38.

the hold of the old working hypotheses on at least the president's decisions for U.S. ASAT strategy. As another test of the co-orbital system, it was no different than any of the previous tests; in fact, it ended in failure after two revolutions.[102] But it prompted the Ford administration's single most important decision for U.S. space policy. In the wake of the test, the White House issued another National Security Decision Memorandum (NSDM-345) that called for the Defense Department to immediately develop an operational ASAT system based on the advanced MHV technology.[103] Taken during the last days of his tenure in office, Ford's decision was not closely linked either to arms control proposals or to new and more satisfying arguments about how U.S. ASATs might deter or compensate for attacks on American satellites. But the decision would be picked up by the incoming Carter administration and developed into a new comprehensive strategy for ASAT, contingent threat of escalation.

ASAT in the Late 1970s

As each of his predecessors had done, President Carter on entering office ordered a thorough review of American military space policy, under the auspices of the NSC. Over the course of the next 18 months, Ford's decision on ASAT would be incorporated into what White House officials called a two-track policy for space. Track 1 called for immediate development and possible near-term deployment of an operational, high-technology ASAT weapon, while Track 2 involved a serious effort to engage the Soviet Union in bilateral negotiations aimed at limiting such deployments on both sides by formal treaty. This was a strategy of contingent threat of escalation. It is important to note that Washington's preferences in ASAT had *not* changed: the principal goal of American strategy remained a cooperative solution of mutual restraint. Official statements from the White House and the DoD continued to stress the benefits of that outcome for both sides, while warning of the dangers of unbridled competition. Shortly after entering office, Carter set the tone in a suggestion to Soviet leaders that the two sides begin a new arms control relationship by agreeing "to forego the opportunity to destroy observation satellites."[104] Secretary of Defense Harold Brown followed up with an

---

[102] Johnson, *The Soviet Year in Space 1983*, p. 39.

[103] For an account of NSDM-345 see Hafner, "Averting a Brobdingnagian Skeet Shoot," pp. 50–51.

[104] See the transcripts of press conferences of President Carter and Secretary of State Cyrus Vance on March 9 and 30, 1977, reprinted in Labrie, *SALT Handbook*, pp. 423, 429. Although the space policy review had barely begun at the time, the administration followed this up with an immediate and direct demarche to the Soviets. When Secretary of State Cyrus

explicit statement of the administration's preferences in testimony before Congress: while defending the decision to accelerate the MHV program, he argued that "the preferable situation, even though we would be foregoing the ability to knock out some Soviet military capabilities, would be for neither country to have an ability to knock out the other's satellites."[105] The administration later formalized these preferences in a Presidential Directive on National Space Policy, PD-37. This document described the U.S. ASAT program as a "response to Soviet activities in this area" and noted that "by exercising mutual restraint, the two countries have an opportunity at this early juncture to stop an unhealthy arms competition." Mutual restraint, however, was no longer to be a tacit arrangement. PD-37 expressed a clear demand for "verifiable comprehensive limits on antisatellite capabilities," while warning that "in the absence of such an agreement, the United States will vigorously pursue development of its own capabilities."[106]

While PD preferences remained, U.S. strategy for achieving a cooperative outcome had changed in important ways. Instead of relying on an implicit threat to do what was necessary in ASAT, the United States had now committed itself to near-term deployment of a sophisticated ASAT weapon that would push the competition upward toward a higher technological plane. That outcome could still be avoided, and top U.S. officials went to some lengths to remind the Soviets that Washington in fact still deeply preferred to avoid it. Cooperation, however, would now depend upon the Soviets' acceptance of explicit concessions, leading to a formal agreement in the immediate future. The Pentagon, which had earlier been recalcitrant on ASAT, was brought on board behind this new approach. The FY 1979 Posture Statement was the first to make explicit mention of U.S. ASAT programs, although it noted that these remained "for the present short of operational or space testing." The rationale for U.S. ASAT efforts was based on a continued preference "for both sides to join in on an effective and adequately verifiable ban on ASAT," but noted that "in the absence of negotiated controls our program seeks a balance of operational capabilities for the 1980s."[107] By operational capabilities, the United States now meant an ASAT system designed for specific mili-

---

Vance traveled to Moscow later in March with a set of proposed "deep cuts" in strategic weapons, he also carried a set of options on ASAT arms control.

[105] *DoD Appropriations for FY 79*, part 2, p. 826.

[106] "Description of a Presidential Directive on National Space Policy," White House Press Release, 20 June 1978. PD-37, the outcome of a long-term, multiagency review of American policy for military space that began in March 1977, can be seen as a nearly definitive statement of American preferences for ASAT. For details, see Craig Couvalt, "Unified Policy on Space," *Aviation Week and Space Technology*, 2 January 1978, pp. 14–15.

[107] *Military Posture Statement FY 79*, p. 125.

tary missions that was an order of magnitude more sophisticated than any American system developed or conceived during the 1960s and early 1970s, and the contemporary Soviet weapon as well.

The MHV ASAT was designed to exploit to full advantage the American technological edge. Instead of relying on the co-orbital method of interception and requiring a massive booster for launch, the American ASAT, only 30 centimeters in diameter and 15 kilograms in weight, would sit on top of a short-range attack missile carried under the wing of an F-15 fighter. The ASAT would be launched from the F-15 directly at the target satellite, use passive infrared sensors to affect final course corrections, and collide with the target at high speed, destroying it without any explosive charge.[108] These technical details made a tremendous difference in the military significance of the weapon. With its direct ascent method of interception, the MHV could destroy a target satellite minutes after being launched, instead of the several hours involved in co-orbital interception. With a large stockpile of this compact and easily managed weapon on hand, and with its flexible launching system, the United States could presumably threaten to attack a large number of Soviet satellites within a short period of time, something the Soviet interceptor clearly could not do. The decision to build the MHV was a decision to do more than simply "match" Soviet capabilities in ASAT; it was a definite escalation of the level of technological competition in ASAT.

It is important to recognize that the MHV was not the only thing the United States could reasonably have done in ASAT at this juncture; while advancing technology made the MHV feasible, neither politics nor technology made the decision to proceed with its rapid development inevitable. The MHV was not yet a bureaucratic darling: neither the DoD nor the Air Force was in 1977 or 1978 a major proponent of this expensive and unconventional system, and neither was anxious to make the substantial commitment of resources and attention to the program that the White House demanded.[109] There were also viable technological alternatives to the MHV. The most interesting option, first proposed by an interagency ASAT working group under Walter Slocombe, was a ground launched co-orbital interceptor designed to disable satellites with a

[108] Craig Couvalt, "Antisatellite Weapon Design Advances," *Aviation Week and Space Technology*, 16 June 1980, pp. 243–47.

[109] In part, this reflected continued ambivalence in the Pentagon about ASAT in general. Stares discusses several reasons for this, including lack of enthusiasm for an untraditional mission and remaining hopes of many Pentagon officials of avoiding an expensive competition between ASATs and satellite survivability measures. Probably the most important reason for the military's ambivalence was the projected expense of the MHV relative to other programs that officials believed were more important, in a time of tight military budgets. *The Militarization of Space*, pp. 172–78.

shower of metal pellets. Because this system could have been built with "off-the-shelf" technologies, it promised to provide an operational ASAT capability in just a few years at much lower cost than the MHV.[110] It also offered the option of postponing a decisive technological escalation of the competition, which might have been an attractive feature had U.S. decisionmakers remained committed to the earlier strategy of enhanced contingent restraint. Put simply, the pellet ASAT would have provided a near-term capability matching but not exceeding the Soviet ASAT, with the implied threat that the United States could do more if necessary. This could have been supplemented by putting greater resources into satellite survivability measures and maintaining research funds for the MHV as a long-term option. The combination would have been a potentially viable strategy of enhanced contingent restraint, but the United States decisively rejected this option. The pellet ASAT was barely funded after FY 1978. Other alternatives for ASAT, such as reactivating Program 922, were similarly rejected. Some additional money did go toward improving the survivability of satellites. But the clear emphasis of the rapidly expanding "space defense" program in Pentagon budgets for FY 1978 and thereafter was the MHV ASAT.[111] By the end of 1978 the new U.S. strategy—contingent threat of escalation linked to demands for a formal negotiated treaty on ASAT—was firmly in place.

Explaining Contingent Threat of Escalation

The new strategy was founded on a revised set of working hypotheses about Soviet interests that had gained a consensus, but only a tenuous one, in Washington during 1978. That consensus emerged as part of the administration's large-scale review of military space policy that was carried out by a series of interagency study groups reporting to a high-level review committee under the NSC. The deliberations of Slocombe's ASAT working group as reported by Stares are of particular interest here.[112] Participants in this study group from State, DoD, CIA, JCS, and ACDA all agreed that cooperation was still the United States' preferred outcome

[110] Slocombe was at this time Deputy Assistant Secretary for International Security Affairs in DoD. For a description of the pellet ASAT program, see *FY 1979 Arms Control Impact Statements*, p. 102.

[111] The pellet ASAT program was kept alive only as a backup to the MHV should the latter prove impractical. It received less than $10 million in development funds between FY 1978 and 1980. Funding for satellite survivability measures jumped to $19 million in FY 1978 and remained relatively constant in real dollars through FY 1981. Funding for the MHV increased by stages from $20.9 million in FY 1978 to $82.5 million three years later. Stares, *The Militarization of Space*, pp. 209–10.

[112] Ibid., pp. 182–84.

for ASAT. They also agreed that the principal purpose of the MHV was
to provide stronger incentives pushing the Soviet Union toward a negotiated agreement for mutual restraint. This rested on a shared prior assumption that the Soviet leadership in fact maintained substantial interests in cooperation that were similar to those of the United States and
could thus be ferreted out given appropriate incentives.

That assumption was not entirely new in form, having been carried
over from the 1960s and early 1970s. But it now had a very different
content. Because the foundation of American conceptions of self-interest
in space had changed in the interim, basic assumptions about the nature
of Soviet interests in cooperation were similarly modified. This led to the
development of a new consensus on working hypotheses quite different
from those of the earlier period.

The previous consensus had pictured the Soviet leadership as highly
motivated to pursue cooperation as a result of radical uncertainty. The
new consensus was built around a different set of working hypotheses in
which radical uncertainty played much less of a role. This reflected
changes in how American decisionmakers conceived of U.S. self-interest—it was not based on any new information about Soviet thought per
se. As technological possibilities for both ASAT and military satellite systems became increasingly clear to the American side, radical uncertainty
no longer dominated the formation of preferences within the U.S. decisionmaking system. The pivotal assumptions behind the new working hypotheses were that Soviet leaders were also formulating more precise conceptions of self-interest based on a fuller understanding of the risks and
benefits of cooperation in space, and that this process mirrored the one
taking place in Washington.

The new working hypotheses about emerging Soviet interests rested on
three pillars. The first was a negative one, the continuing deficit of information due to lack of communication about interests in space that I previously called a legacy of 1960s cooperation. The second and more important pillar was the nature of the evolution in American conceptions of
self-interest in space that was taking place in the late 1970s. These
changes followed from technological improvements that were rapidly
transforming what had been possibilities for military satellite systems into
realities. The United States deployed its first ocean reconnaissance system
in 1976, providing valuable real-time information on the movements of
Soviet naval forces. New and much more sophisticated signals intelligence satellites for eavesdropping on military communications, weapons-
test telemetry, and radar signals were deployed soon thereafter under the
secret Rhyolite program. Synthetic aperture radars potentially useful for

locating submerged submarines, aircraft, and even cruise missiles, were also tested in space for the first time in 1978.[113]

The immediate impact of this technological outburst was to blur further the distinction between benign and threatening satellites and to shift the overall balance of space systems heavily toward the latter. This rendered the trade-offs involved in maintaining space as a sanctuary even more complex. The United States needed confidence that its new satellite systems would be safe from Soviet attack, but it also worried about giving Moscow license to deploy its own military satellites at will. With continued reasons to deplore the instabilities that were likely in a world where both sides had ASAT, the stakes of cooperation and competition in space had become higher and more nearly balanced. From the American perspective, the temptation to defect and possible penalties for exploited restraint in ASAT had become much greater than either had been when interests were dominated by radical uncertainty. If a comparable assessment of interests was now coming to guide Soviet decisionmaking, where similar (if perhaps less dramatic) technological advances were thought to be at hand, it made sense for the United States to pursue a more tightly defined strategy of reciprocity to get to cooperation.[114]

The logical slippage in this argument was not in the notion that radical uncertainty was declining in importance in Moscow. It was in the companion assumption that as radical uncertainty declined it was being replaced with an assessment of interests comparable to that taking hold in the United States. With no communication and little concrete feedback to examine, American decisionmakers continued to suffer a strong tendency to interpret Soviet behavior according to criteria drawn from American conceptions of self-interest. It was here that the third pillar, the Soviets' decision to resume testing their ASAT weapon in 1976, intervened. Moscow carried out several tests of its ASAT during 1977, just as the Carter administration's policy review was in full swing. At about the same time, a series of articles in *Aviation Week* reported on expanding Soviet research efforts in particle beams and lasers. Pentagon analysts continued to view the co-orbital interceptor as a primitive weapon of little military

[113] On ocean reconnaissance see *DoD Authorization for Appropriations for FY 85*, part 8, p. 3890. On signals intelligence see Richard Burt, "US Plans New Way to Check Soviet Missile Tests," *New York Times*, 29 June 1979, p. 3; and Richelson, *The US Intelligence Community*, pp. 120–23. On synthetic aperture radars and other new detection technologies see *DoD Authorization for Appropriations for FY 85*, part 7, pp. 3413–14; and "Rockwell Tests Model of Teal Ruby System," *Aviation Week and Space Technology*, 23 January 1984, p. 52.

[114] For a summary of what is known about comparable Soviet developments in the 1970s, see Johnson, *The Soviet Year in Space 1981*; and Meyer, "Soviet Military Programmes and the New 'High Ground.' "

import. They also agreed that the Soviets were not even close to operational deployment of weapons based on other technologies, and that in any case ASAT would not be the principal application for directed-energy weapons (DEW) research.[115] Still, the resumption of testing and further evidence of Soviet interest in technologies that could have been adapted to attacking satellites reinforced American beliefs that with the reduction in radical uncertainty, the Soviets had lost much of their strongest motivation for cooperative restraint. The new consensus rested on working hypotheses that saw Soviet decisionmakers as still interested in cooperation, but much more highly motivated to exploit U.S. restraint and pursue a unilateral advantage in ASAT if possible. For reasons that I will discuss shortly, the new consensus was not so firmly established within the U.S. decisionmaking system. But to the extent that it did hold sway for several years at the end of the 1970s, this consensus pointed strongly toward a new strategy for the United States that would incorporate much more demanding criteria of reciprocity. Changes in the five additional variables that affect strategy development reinforced that tendency.

The rate of change of interests and incentives relating to space was clearly most important. Radical uncertainty was now much less a factor, at least in American calculations. It had become clear that the offense would have the immediate advantage in space, and that it was possible to build ASATs threatening to even hardened satellites in low earth orbit and probably, in time, to those in geosynchronous orbit as well.[116] It was equally clear that both sides could build sophisticated military satellites with force support capabilities unheard of in the 1960s. With these rapid advances in military satellites at hand, U.S. decisionmakers were not quite certain of their own willingness to accept any constraints on deployments in space. Nor were they sure that the Soviets would be similarly interested.[117] The problem was complicated still more by the blurring of any remaining saliency between benign and threatening satellite functions. If some form of ASAT restraint were still possible in this increasingly high-

[115] Clarence Robinson, "Soviets Push for Beam Weapon," *Aviation Week and Space Technology*, 2 May 1977, pp. 16–23; "Soviets Test Beam Technologies in Space," *Aviation Week and Space Technology*, 13 November 1978, p. 14. For Pentagon responses, see Stares, *The Militarization of Space*, p. 192.

[116] For a summary discussion, see Carter, "Satellites and Anti-Satellites."

[117] The Soviets were at this time known to be concentrating on reconnaissance and particularly EORSAT and RORSAT working in tandem. Emerging technologies for a new generation of American satellites promised even more impressive capabilities in real-time photoreconnaissance, tactical communications, electronic intelligence, and navigational positioning systems that might offer improvements up to 300% in the firepower efficiency of conventional artillery. Office of Technology Assessment, *Anti-Satellite Weapons, Countermeasures, and Arms Control*, pp. 33ff.; Jasani, *Outer Space*, pp. 132–33, 178, 331–43.

stakes contest, only a strategy with extremely demanding criteria of reciprocity seemed adequate to overcome the new pressures to compete.

Changes in the image of the Soviet Union as an adversary supported this reasoning. Detente, as experienced in the United States, had already done much to undermine elite perceptions of the Soviet leadership as generally favorable toward superpower cooperation. Nixon and Kissinger's conception of an organic linkage between mutual restraint of the military contest and the broader U.S.-Soviet political relationship had not borne itself out in Soviet behavior. It seemed instead that Moscow was apt to exploit U.S. restraint when possible and press for an advantage, in developing countries' civil wars, in the nuclear balance, and elsewhere.[118] Cooperation in areas of mutual interest might still be possible, but encouraging cooperation now seemed to require strong measures aimed at discouraging inherent Soviet tendencies to seek unilateral advantage. This translated almost directly into arguments about "bargaining from strength" and similar versions of strict reciprocity that found easy application in the high-stakes arena of military space.

Developments in strategic theory also pointed toward establishing a "position of strength" in ASAT, although not necessarily with the goal of eliciting cooperative restraint. Support for an American ASAT flowed logically from the arguments of increasingly influential "conservative" political elites and strategic thinkers who were questioning the viability of the current state of nuclear deterrence.[119] The basic thrust of their analysis was that rough parity and the threat of MAD might not be sufficient to deter the Soviet Union from challenging the most vital interests of the United States, and certainly was not sufficient to deter less central challenges. While the more radical versions of the argument failed to convince most decisionmakers, modifications of American nuclear doctrine starting in the mid-1970s did reflect the impact of these claims with changing notions about the relationship between parity and deterrence. The mainstream still rejected efforts to return the United States to a position of meaningful strategic superiority, seeing that as unattainable and probably undesirable in any case. But a renewed effort to develop forces and doc-

[118] That is, both the central nuclear balance and the "theater balance" in Europe. It was in 1977 that Soviet deployments of a new intermediate-range missile in Europe, the SS-20, first attracted public attention in the West following Helmut Schmidt's important speech to the IISS in London. See the 1977 Alastair Buchan Memorial Lectures, *Survival*, January–February 1978; and the discussion by Lawrence T. Caldwell, "Soviet Policy on Nuclear Weapons and Arms Control," in Dan Caldwell, *Soviet International Behavior and U.S. Policy Options*.

[119] See, for example, the publications of the Committee on the Present Danger; the influential article by Pipes, "Why the Soviet Union Thinks It Could Fight and Win a Nuclear War"; and the writings of Colin Gray during this period, especially *The Future of Land-Based Missile Forces* and *The Geopolitics of the Nuclear Era*.

trines keyed to nuclear war-fighting seemed a sensible and practical if not a necessary alternative, given Soviet doctrine and capabilities that were clearly pushing in this direction. For political and economic reasons, official Washington was skeptical of the U.S. ability to match Soviet efforts in a quantitative race for war-fighting forces. American technology, however, was the natural compensation; and space remained the premier arena for capitalizing on the technological edge. Even if it lacked a clear mission against current Soviet targets or a convincing rationale as to how it could bolster deterrence, the MHV ASAT seemed to fit the bill.[120]

Finally, contingent threat of escalation answered the concerns of a growing number of bureaucratic players whose interest in the ASAT mission had grown. The "two-track" strategy met the president's and the State Department's strong desire for an arms control solution in space, while offering the Pentagon a vigorous research and development program for a high-technology ASAT. There was no inherent contradiction between the two tracks. Both sides of the debate acted on the presumption that the prospect of an advanced U.S. ASAT capability would give the Soviet Union needed incentives to cooperate, and that an appropriate arms control deal could be worked out and sustained. Both sides also agreed that if cooperation faltered, it would serve U.S. interests to have a high-technology ASAT weapon, much more capable than the Soviet device, immediately operational.[121] Contingent threat of escalation met each of these objectives.

The Failure of Contingent Threat

Each of these additional factors reinforced tendencies toward a strategy of contingent threat that were already present in the new working hy-

---

[120] Carter administration officials rarely addressed either of these points directly because they viewed the MHV program principally as an inducement for a cooperative solution wherein the weapon would never actually be deployed. Deputy Undersecretary of Defense Seymour Zeiberg explicitly doubted the argument about deterrence, testifying that "the idea of tit-for-tat with satellites to my mind does not make sense." *DoD Authorization for Appropriations for FY 80*, part 6, p. 3027. When a harder-line position came to guide American ASAT policy in the next administration, both rationales were made explicit; but the logic behind the arguments was still frail. See *White House Fact Sheet Outlining US Space Policy*, 4 July 1982; *Military Posture Statement FY 84*, pp. 226–27; and my analysis in Weber and Drell, "Attempts to Regulate Military Activities in Space," in George, Farley, and Dallin, *US-Soviet Security Cooperation*, pp. 412–24.

[121] See Stares' report of the deliberations of the interagency ASAT Working Group during 1977 and 1978 in *The Militarization of Space*, p. 183; and DDR&E William Perry's testimony regarding the Working Group's report to the president in *DoD Appropriations for FY 79*, part 3, pp. 726–27.

potheses about Soviet interests. But they did not provide or point to any further evidence that would bolster the hypotheses themselves; and the consensus behind those hypotheses remained frail. The reason for this is that while U.S. leaders now saw their Soviet counterparts as more highly motivated to compete in ASAT than they had earlier thought, they did not fully understand why and could barely agree on potential explanations. Almost all the proposed explanations drew heavily from the evolving American conception of self-interest in space, and all were hard to square with the observable data about Soviet behavior.

Why did Moscow decide to resume flight tests of an already proven ASAT weapon when the system's technological limitations were such that its performance could not be significantly improved through further testing? One way to explain this decision was as a limited probe, a low-cost and low-risk test of the contingency of American restraint; but the United States had already responded to a similar probe at the start of the decade. Alternatively, the ASAT could have been part of a dedicated effort to gain a militarily significant capability against American satellites; but in that case, why hold on to the primitive co-orbital method of interception? If Soviet technology could do no better, it made even less sense to provoke the United States toward competing in an area where American technology could prove decisive. A third possibility was that Soviet leaders perceived a serious and growing threat from American military satellites that they did not believe they could redress on their own, given their technological disadvantage. In that case the ASAT test series might have represented a signal of concern, a message about how the Soviets were coming to view the relationship between continuing restraint in ASAT and the lack of any corresponding constraints on military satellites. But this third explanation does not seem to have been given serious consideration in Washington.[122] In fact, no explanation gained sufficient support to reinforce the new working hypotheses about Soviet interests and strengthen the fragile consensus around them.

Why not? The answer lies in the way in which conceptions of self-interest were evolving in the two capitals. Radical uncertainty was being resolved in Washington and probably in Moscow as well. But more accurate understandings of the technological possibilities in space were not being matched by a growth in common understanding about the consequences for self-interest. Unlike the case in ABM, in ASAT there had been no effort to forge common conceptions of self-interest or even to explore how each side's unilateral conceptions might be changing. This was a

---

[122] This is not necessarily a claim for the validity of the third possibility (or, for that matter, the others); nor is it a claim for intentionality of the message. My point is simply that this was a reasonable interpretation of Soviet behavior that could have been explored and put to tests had it been considered in depth.

harmful consequence of the success of earlier cooperation, which left each side to develop its own consensual knowledge for interpreting self-interest in space as technology advanced. Technological change made cooperation vulnerable in the late 1970s, but it did not dictate its demise. Cooperation decayed toward failure because of the strategy of contingent threat of escalation and the weak consensus of working hypotheses on which it was based.

The history of the two-track strategy reflects the importance of both in explaining the failure. Track 1, the MHV program, got off to a much quicker start than the second track of negotiations. The prime contract for the MHV development program was let in the fall of 1977.[123] During the next several months, the Pentagon carried out several studies to define in more specific terms the technical and operational requirements for a viable system that could be deployed before the end of the decade. By May 1978 the Joint Chiefs had completed preliminary studies of military missions for the MHV, which resulted in a prioritized target list of Soviet satellites. That summer, Air Force proposals to further accelerate the program and bring forward its initial operational date were approved. Despite several technological glitches in the development program, it looked as if the MHV might very well be ready for flight tests early in the 1980s.[124]

Track 2, the bid for a negotiated solution, fell far behind as the process of putting together a U.S. negotiating position ran into difficulties. That process did not really begin in a serious way until September 1977, when President Carter first responded to the ASAT working group's evaluation of different arms control options by indicating his preference for a comprehensive agreement that would ban ASAT testing and deployment.[125] In early 1978 the NSC established a new ASAT working group for the purpose of developing the specifics of a negotiating position on this basis.

Controversy soon erupted over two issues.[126] The first was simply the initial problem of defining what should be included in a formal agreement on ASAT. While the Soviet co-orbital interceptor and the American MHV were clearly "dedicated" ASATs, other weapons systems like the Galosh ABM, ICBMs, and even advanced air-defense missiles could be given a rudimentary capability to attack satellites. How important were these "residual" ASAT capabilities? From the perspective of the various bu-

[123] George C. Wilson, "Air Force Begins Development of Satellite Killer," *Washington Post*, 23 September 1977, pp. 1, 4.

[124] *DoD Authorization for Appropriations for FY 80*, part 1, pp. 3020, 3037; *DoD Appropriations for FY 80*, part 1, p. 692.

[125] See *DoD Appropriations for FY 79*, part 3, pp. 726–27.

[126] For accounts, see Stares, *The Militarization of Space*, pp. 192–95; and "Killer Talks," *Aviation Week and Space Technology*, 28 November 1977, p. 13.

reaucratic players in Washington, the answer to that question turned mostly on differing assessments of how strongly committed the Soviets were to being able to destroy American satellites. The DoD now took a worst-case view of the problem, while representatives from State and ACDA were more sanguine. A second disagreement surfaced over the question of verification. Pentagon officials were dubious about whether limits on even the dedicated Soviet ASAT could be effectively monitored; State and ACDA representatives countered with the argument that any undetected violations could at most amount to a small stockpile of weapons that would be left untested, unreliable, and insignificant from a military standpoint. Again, resolving the verification issue depended mostly on assessments of Soviet interests: would Moscow see itself as having anything to gain by secretly stockpiling its ASAT interceptor? These two specific questions coalesced in what became a sharp disagreement about basic questions of substance for a cooperative solution that would serve U.S. interests in ASAT. From its perspective the Pentagon doubted both the desirability and feasibility of a comprehensive ban on ASATs and pushed for the United States to seek a "noninterference/no hostile act" agreement, with rules of the road for space not unlike those for the high seas. The State Department and ACDA continued to favor an entirely different kind of cooperative solution, a comprehensive ban on testing and deployment of dedicated ASATs.

There were surprising omissions in both of these proposals.[127] The most important was a glaring neglect of the subject of military satellites. This was in part a result of Washington's own ambivalence about accepting limitations on its military satellite program, but it was also a result of the fact that the United States knew little about how developing Soviet interests on this score related to ASAT. This was a legacy of cooperation under radical uncertainty in the 1960s, which had gone forward with almost no bilateral exploration of each side's conceptions of self-interest in space. In the late 1970s, cooperation could no longer rest on radical uncertainty. A necessary condition for a new cooperative deal would have been a common conception of interests when it came to the relationship between ASATs and the military satellites that were their presumptive targets, or at least a more detailed understanding of how each side conceived of that relationship on its own. The negotiations themselves would soon show that no such common interest or shared understandings had

---

[127] For example, neither party to the debate considered the problem of how Moscow could be expected to verify limits on the U.S. ASAT once it was tested. Because the size and mode of operation of the MHV would make it relatively easy to stockpile or deploy surreptitiously, it could be much more threatening than the Soviet system (which would have been hard to "hide" in significant numbers) under an arms control regime severely limiting deployment.

developed during the 1970s. In fact, the talks would show that the lack of communication had left both sides further apart than either had realized. When the issue was finally brought out for joint consideration at the end of the decade, it was essentially too late. With the new strategy of contingent threat of escalation, the United States had set severe time restrictions for the two sides to gain a joint understanding of their respective interests that might have supported a new cooperative solution based on something other than radical uncertainty. This was a de facto ultimatum that could not be met as the MHV program rushed toward deployment.

The U.S.-Soviet ASAT negotiations, in fact, did not even begin until June 1978. The American delegation arrived in Helsinki for the first round of talks without specific negotiating instructions, a result of continuing disagreements in Washington about the broadest questions of what kind of ASAT agreement would be desirable.[128] The Soviet delegation offered little explicit information about Moscow's interests on this score, but two conspicuous bits of feedback that were probably closely connected did emerge. The first was that the Soviets suspended their ASAT test series in May, just prior to the start of the talks, in what seemed an effort to demonstrate a continuing serious preference for a cooperative solution in ASAT. In the course of the negotiations, the Soviet delegation then emphasized Moscow's particular concern about possible military applications of the U.S. space shuttle. In private discussions, Soviet negotiators tied the shuttle issue directly to the ASAT test moratorium, linking both to Moscow's broader concerns about military satellites. This dovetailed with a series of discussions that had taken place between Soviet Ambassador Dobrynin and Secretary of State Vance earlier that spring in which Dobrynin had emphasized the importance of dealing with the shuttle and other potentially threatening space systems early in the course of the talks.[129]

These presumptive signals had little impact on American decisionmaking in the short term. The test moratorium was obviously discounted because of previous experience with the temporary suspension of the Soviets' ASAT test program after 1971. The apparent lack of attention to the signals of concern over offensive military capabilities in space is more difficult to explain. The Soviet delegation, judged by the American negotiators to be poorly prepared for serious talks on most of the relevant questions, had shown consistent attention to a single issue that was related less directly to ASAT per se than to the broader problem of expand-

[128] Stares, *The Militarization of Space*, p. 196.

[129] "Soviets Said to Agree on Satellite Talks," *New York Times*, 1 April 1978, p. 1; "Soviets See Shuttle as Killer Satellite," *Aviation Week and Space Technology*, 17 April 1978, p. 17; "Antisatellite Move," *Aviation Week and Space Technology*, 21 August 1978, p. 11.

ing military missions in space. The U.S. delegation did not respond substantively at first because it had explicit instructions to the effect that the shuttle was a nonnegotiable item and its operations were off-limits for discussion.[130] The first round of talks closed without tangible progress, and a second round was convened at Bern the following January. During this round, the Soviet team appeared better prepared to engage in serious and detailed "negotiations seeking concrete results," as Moscow now labeled the talks. The two sides did hold substantive discussions of various possible deals on ASAT at this time, but the issue of the space shuttle and its potential military applications blocked substantive progress. At the same time, the United States refused to join the Soviets' unilateral ASAT test moratorium on the grounds that Moscow had refused to consider dismantling its already tested ASAT weapon.[131]

It was only in the aftermath of the second round of talks that Washington hammered out a specific and concrete proposal to be presented at the talks. This called for a short-term no-use agreement in conjunction with a testing moratorium to be followed by agreement to ban the possession of dedicated ASAT weapons entirely.[132] The U.S. proposal sidestepped the issue of offensive military capabilities in space; but precisely that issue continued to bedevil the negotiations. At the third round of talks, held between April and June 1979 in Vienna, the two sides did make substantial progress toward a joint draft treaty on "no use" of ASAT weapons, but Moscow's concerns about the space shuttle remained a major sticking point and an impediment to going further toward a more comprehensive agreement. The Soviets raised the issue of military satellites directly when they demanded an escape clause even in the no-use agreement, reserving the right to attack satellites whose "hostile or pernicious acts" infringed upon national sovereignty. This was a forceful signal of how Moscow had come to view the relationship between military satellites and ASAT, but its significance was apparently lost on the Americans, who again refused to take the issue under serious consideration.[133]

Why was the issue of military satellite capabilities left outside the negotiating track of U.S. strategy for ASAT? Part of the explanation lies in unilateral conceptions of interest: most importantly, an innate resistance

---

[130] Stares, *The Militarization of Space*, p. 197.

[131] See Donald Hafner, "Arms Control Measures for Anti-Satellite Weapons," *International Security* (Winter 1980–81): 56–59; National Academy of Sciences, *Nuclear Arms Control*, p. 162.

[132] "Antisatellite Talks," *Aviation Week and Space Technology*, 23 April 1979, p. 15.

[133] Stares, drawing from Walter Slocombe's account, reports that "some Western observers interpreted this to be part of the long standing Soviet desire to curb the potential use of direct broadcasting satellites for propaganda purposes." *The Militarization of Space*, p. 199. It is doubtful that Moscow's concerns were so limited.

to limiting high-technology weapons where the United States was believed to have an edge. This resistance was strong throughout official Washington and particularly within the Pentagon, but it did not by itself determine U.S. preferences for ASAT: the allure of state-of-the-art space systems still had to be balanced against the need to protect whatever satellites the Pentagon was going to deploy against disruption or attack by a Soviet ASAT. The legacy of earlier cooperation in space was a crucial factor influencing how that balance was perceived and acted upon. Through the end of the 1970s, U.S. decisionmakers resisted opening the Pandora's box of issues surrounding the "legitimacy" of satellite reconnaissance and other military missions in space. Those questions had been effectively dealt with by putting them aside quietly in the 1960s. Cooperation had apparently been sustained amid the challenges of the 1970s through similar tacit means. An essential part of the tacit deal that led to ASAT cooperation under radical uncertainty was precisely that each side would be left on its own when it came to military satellites.

Technological evolution meant that by the end of the 1970s the ASAT and military satellite issues were no longer separable in this way. Both superpowers were faced with the challenge of bringing them together. The fundamental problem with the 1960s deal was that it left the United States and the Soviet Union to develop new consensual knowledge and conceptions of self-interest in space that could accomplish this entirely on their own. The apparent success of revitalized cooperation in the early 1970s reinforced this effect, which stood in the way of common efforts to define joint interests in a rapidly changing technological environment. This effect maintained itself even as the two sides met to negotiate a treaty in 1978. The foundation of previous cooperation had deteriorated in the interim years, and nothing had arisen to replace it. Cooperation under radical uncertainty impeded any impulse toward meta-strategy, so that neither side tried to influence the process by which conceptions of self-interest were changing on the other. Cooperation even inhibited communication between the two sides, which at a minimum would have spawned greater understanding of how the two states were developing new conceptions of interests in space on their own.

The boundaries imposed by earlier cooperation were not really broken until the end of the 1970s negotiations, and even then they were only partially breached. The process of exploring interests that lay behind each side's evolving preferences in ASAT began extremely late, proceeded with reluctance on both sides, and never got very far. Time was running out on the ASAT talks; a fourth round originally scheduled for fall 1979 was put off for several months as the Carter administration chose to concentrate its resources on the domestic struggle for SALT II. Meanwhile, the MHV "track" of the U.S. strategy of contingent threat of escalation proceeded apace.[134] The ASAT talks finally fell victim to the rupture in U.S.-Soviet relations after the invasion of Afghanistan, ending Track 2 of the U.S. strategy for ASAT. As if to underscore the demise of prospects for cooperation, the Soviets resumed testing their ASAT in April of 1980.

Conclusion

Was ASAT cooperation a victim only of unfortunate circumstance? Arguments to that effect from some closely involved U.S. officials seem hard to accept.[135] Whether or not a no-use accord could have been signed in the absence of the Afghanistan invasion, a more extensive agreement with limits on ASAT testing and deployment or even rules of the road for space was hardly conceivable. The technical details specifying what kinds of limits would be desirable and verifiable within more far-reaching agreements had not been fully worked out, even in the United States. To the end of the negotiations, the CIA, DoD, and ACDA each had their own criteria for effective monitoring of proposals on ASAT systems; and an interagency group set up to reconcile their positions failed in its task. When it came to defining rules of the road that would offer some protection to satellites while not unacceptably regulating "legitimate" satellite missions, the disputes ran even deeper.[136]

These controversies, again, reflected technological constraints and trade-offs that would have been difficult to manage regardless. But the essence of the disagreements continued to flow from differing assessments of Soviet interests in ASAT. For the more optimistic coalition, which believed that the Soviet leadership shared central interests in cooperation with the United States, comprehensive limits (even if imperfectly verifiable) made excellent sense. For the more pessimistic coalition, which saw

[134] By the spring of 1979, the Pentagon had already begun detailed planning for the first flight tests of the MHV. "Avco Wins USAF Award for Antisatellite Targets," *Aviation Week and Space Technology*, 25 June 1979, p. 23.

[135] Draft texts for no-use pacts that were developed during the third round of negotiations have not been made public, but Raymond Garthoff reports that the two sides were rather close to agreement on the details. *Detente and Confrontation*, p. 760. Herbert York, a principal on the negotiating team, was also relatively optimistic, although he stressed that many difficult problems remained to be solved. The most important, not surprisingly, were Soviet objections to the space shuttle and the issue of protecting satellites belonging to third parties (such as China or NATO states). Personal communication, June 1987.

[136] Robert Toth, "US-Soviet Talks Seen Soon on Anti-Satellite Arms Ban," *Los Angeles Times*, 5 November 1977, p. 1; Stares, *The Militarization of Space*, p. 195. For summaries and assessments of the arguments see Michael May, "Safeguarding Our Space Assets," and Donald L. Hafner, "Negotiating Restraints on Anti-Satellite Weapons: Options and Impact," in Nye and Schear, *Seeking Stability in Space*.

the Soviet Union as highly motivated to pursue a unilateral advantage in ASAT as part of its overall political approach to superpower relations or specifically to support its nuclear war-fighting doctrines, the limits to ASAT cooperation were set by the very strictest standards of verification.[137] What was missing from both arguments was any attempt to deal directly with the problem of military satellites and its linkage to ASAT. Without a serious effort to explore Soviet understandings of this linkage, it is difficult to see how a cooperative solution taking suitable account of Soviet interests could have been fashioned. For this reason alone, it is hard to see how cooperation could have been revitalized at the end of the 1970s.

There were proximate and underlying reasons for the deterioration of ASAT cooperation at the end of the 1970s. The proximate reason was the strategy of contingent threat of escalation. This strategy bet on the incentives from a highly competitive move in ASAT to elicit cooperation in the form of a formal, negotiated solution within a short period of time. While the MHV program forged ahead, Washington's efforts to define goals for a cooperative solution in a complex and rapidly changing strategic environment lagged behind. The negotiating track was simply outpaced by the weapons development track. It is true that the race was cut short by a spurious event, the invasion of Afghanistan. But it is doubtful whether more time would have made a difference in the outcome, given the relative rate of progress along the two tracks.

Is this a necessary property of strategies of contingent threat? In general, perhaps not—I leave that for discussion in the final chapter. But in the case of ASAT strategy in the 1970s, it was. This points toward the underlying reason for the failure of cooperation—the legacy of cooperation in the 1960s. The mid-1970s was the pivotal time in which both sides resolved radical uncertainties about ASAT. But because they were bound to the legacy of 1960s cooperation, they did so entirely separately and in different ways. The crucial missed opportunities came in the mid-1970s when the two sides began to define, entirely for themselves, how they would balance their interests in ASAT cooperation against the emerging possibilities of military satellites that were no longer predominantly benign. Neither meta-strategy nor any efforts simply to elicit greater feedback about the other side's evolving interests were given serious attention.

There were difficult technical and political trade-offs to be made in ASAT, perhaps even more difficult than those in ABM or MIRV. But the

---

[137] State and ACDA were the principal members of the former coalition, while DoD and the CIA formed the core of the latter. The NSC remained divided through the end of the Carter administration. Stares, *The Militarization of Space*, p. 199.

fact that each superpower was left to make those trade-offs entirely on its own and with almost no knowledge about how the other superpower was doing the same, virtually guaranteed a lack of common ground. If the two sides had gone through the process of defining their interests jointly, or had communicated earlier than they did about their evolving conceptions, it is possible that the outcome might still have been the same, because they might have found no common interests to be gained. But that is doubtful, for reasons that I also discuss in Chapter 7.

The MHV system itself was not ready for preliminary flight tests until 1984. But ASAT cooperation essentially came to an end with the failure of the two-track strategy at the end of the 1970s. The missed opportunity for cooperation was then sealed through a more radical shift in American interests and subsequent preferences in the early 1980s, which took ASAT outside the realm of the PD game entirely for U.S. decisionmakers.[138] This shift also bore the mark of the legacy of previous cooperation. I leave its rationale and consequences for discussion in the concluding chapter.

[138] For a detailed discussion, see Weber and Drell, "Attempts to Regulate Military Activities in Space," pp. 412–26. Until late 1985, U.S. ASAT policy was one of unconditional defection, reflecting a shift in preferences such that the United States would compete in ASAT regardless of Soviet actions. At the end of 1985, the MHV testing program was blocked by a funding moratorium imposed by the Congress. Despite vehement opposition by the Reagan administration, the Congress renewed its action each year until 1988, when the Air Force abandoned the MHV for lack of flight tests. Soon thereafter, new high-technology ASAT systems using other kinetic kill mechanisms and high energy lasers were brought forward to replace it. See "FY 1989 Aerospace Budgets: Major Weapons System Funding," *Aviation Week and Space Technology*, 29 February 1988, p. 21; "US Air Force Will Expand Exotic ASAT Technology," *Aviation Week and Space Technology*, 25 April 1988, p. 27; and "Pentagon Preparing to Restart Anti-Satellite Program in January," *Aviation Week and Space Technology*, 14 November 1988, p. 33.

7

Conclusion

Nuclear Weapons, Interdependence, and Cooperation

COOPERATION is a response to interdependence. But it is not the only possible response. States may choose instead to eschew the potential benefits of cooperation and accept only what they can achieve relying on their own resources. Many disincentives to cooperation have their roots in the anarchic structure of international politics. For two powerful states with divergent political interests and ideologies, the disincentives are magnified. And if there are not strong perceptions of interdependence between such states, cooperation becomes nearly a non sequitur. This is not just a theoretical point. National leaders, as Robert Jervis notes, have often been only dimly aware of the conditions and consequences of security interdependence.[1] If the leaders of the United States and the USSR believed that they could assure their state's security by acting on their own, they would certainly have preferred to do so instead of relying even marginally on the cooperation of a powerful and distrusted adversary.

In a world without nuclear weapons, security autarky or something very close to it might have been a real option for the superpowers. But in this world, nuclear weapons and the resulting vulnerability of both sides' homelands to almost instantaneous destruction virtually erased that option from the minds of decisionmakers on both sides.[2] The effect was never absolute. Political and military elites in Moscow held on to the rhetoric of security autarky for some time, even after the Soviet state's behavior had changed in ways that reflected a deeper perception of interdepen-

---

[1] Jervis, "Realism, Game Theory, and Cooperation." George Downs, David M. Rocke, and Randolph Siverson argue similarly that states sometimes choose to build defensive weapons rather than offensive ones, but they rarely do so in order to alleviate the security dilemma. They do so because decisionmakers think they can get more unilateral security per dollar spent, without thinking about the impact on the other side. "Thus, the British adopted a policy of building picket ships and fortifying the coast during their naval race with France in 1859–61 without giving any particular thought to how the French would respond, or what impact it would have on their arms race." Downs, Rocke, and Siverson, "Arms Races and Cooperation," in Oye, *Cooperation under Anarchy*, p. 124.

[2] I have argued elsewhere that this should be seen as a historically and contextually bounded belief only, not as an objective condition that necessarily reflects reality. I also explore the implications of an alternative set of beliefs that may be equally supportable in "Cooperation and Interdependence."

dence. American decisionmakers and the American public alike were always ambivalent about interdependence, for reasons of history, culture, and technological conceit. But the leaders of both superpowers have at least since the late 1960s paid serious attention to the way in which unilateral efforts to enhance their own state's security through the development and deployment of strategic weapons systems would affect the calculations of the other. Cooperation has not always been the result; in fact, cooperation has been rare. But the point is that choices about MIRV, ASAT, ABM, and other strategic weapons systems were treated as interdependent decisions, where neither state could by its own actions assure a preferred outcome. This is the realm of game theory. And it is the essence of the problem that this book has tried to solve. Why and how have the United States and the Soviet Union achieved cooperative agreements with the goal of enhancing security in certain strategic weapons issues, but not in others?

To answer this question, I began with a simple model of cooperation in the PD borrowed from Axelrod. I developed a means for elaborating this formal model and applying it to a set of historical cases. There were four steps: bridging game-theoretic concepts to empirical indicators, adding additional concepts, focusing on the key intervening variable of strategy, and exploring the causal paths through which strategies affect the "evolution" of cooperation. I used this expanded model to examine three cases that shared initial conditions for cooperation but varied in outcome. This chapter reviews and expands upon the results. I begin with some comments about game theory and the study of international cooperation. From there, I consider the sources and consequences of strategy in U.S.-Soviet arms control. I go on to discuss how the additional concepts that I added to the model help to explain the evolution of cooperation. This leads to a broader argument in which I differentiate the concept of cooperation and consider its implications for arms control and superpower relations in general. I conclude with a set of prescriptions for the future that seem to me more important than ever as the possibilities for U.S.-Soviet cooperation appear to expand over the coming years.

Game Theory and International Cooperation

Formal game models are mathematical abstractions. In the tradition of rational choice arguments, game theory builds models of strategic interaction between idealized actors who try to maximize exogenously-determined preferences in light of the constraints of interdependence. It is a straightforward problem to demonstrate the internal validity of an abstract-deductive game model, but to demonstrate its external validity is more complex. Does formal theory have anything useful to say about the real world? The burden of proof lies not with empirical evidence to "disprove" the formal theory. It lies with the formal theory to prove its relevance to real-world events.[3]

Game theory is not by itself an empirical theory of how real-world "actors"—be they states, firms, or individuals—actually behave. It is an information generator. Game theory illuminates the structural constraints and the resulting logic of interdependent decision that actors face. It highlights certain variables and causal pathways that may be important in the real world. The PD model, for example, starts from starkly realist assumptions, but it offers more discriminating arguments about international discord than does realism. The PD demonstrates that mutual defection is not always the result of sharply conflicting interests, but sometimes of "missed opportunities" in mixed-motive games where both sides would have done better had they been able to cooperate. Realism tends to lump both into one. Demonstrating the external validity of the PD model means harnessing this greater differential power into a theory of international cooperation that does more than a simple realist theory can.

I did this by using Axelrod's simple theory of cooperation in the PD as a heuristic, and expanding it through direct contact with historical evidence. My original rationale for choosing an empirical methodology, which I discussed in Chapters 1 and 3, withstood the test of three case studies. Axelrod's theory did not by itself explain the outcomes in ABM, MIRV, and ASAT. What it did was identify an important causal path to cooperation that was operating in some form in each case. Historical process tracing shows that the putative causal chains linking independent and dependent variables in the deductive model have analogues in the world of U.S.-Soviet arms control. But to fill in the workings of the causal path and discover why it does not always lead to cooperation, I had to go beyond game theory's simplistic notions about strategy.

Formal theorists understand that an "optimal" strategy depends upon an actor's expectations of the opponent's behavior and on assessments of the kind of environment in which the game takes place. But the formal, deductive algorithms that they introduce to "capture" the processes by which these expectations and assessments are formed are characterizations that have no claim to external validity.[4] By posing general questions

---

[3] I agree with Bueno de Mesquita's argument that the internal validity of a deductive theory depends only upon the logic of the theory itself. Bueno de Mesquita points out that there are potentially an infinite number of such deductive statements. Empirical evidence sorts out which of these are relevant to real-world events (externally valid) and which are trivial. It follows that the burden of proof lies with the formal theory to demonstrate that it is indeed relevant. Bueno de Mesquita, *The War Trap*, Chapter 1, especially pp. 8–11.

[4] In theory, these formalizations could be tested for external validity in their own right.

directly to the cases, I examined how at least one decisionmaking system actually developed expectations, made assessments, and formulated, implemented, and modified strategies of reciprocity. This led to several new findings—for example, how U.S. decisionmakers developed working hypotheses about Soviet interests, emphasized change over consistency in feedback related to those hypotheses, and underwent brief periods of openness to change interspersed among much longer stretches of stasis. It is hard to see how these findings would have come out of a primarily formal analysis.

Formal theorists will probably object to what I have done, and particularly to my claim that the maximum power of game theory in international politics lies in its use as a heuristic to guide case-study research. First, there is the matter of parsimony. Second, and more important, there is the notion that all of the problems and inadequacies I have pointed to are *in principle* soluble within the formal approach. The argument is that these problems are not yet solved by formal theory but there is nothing inherent in the methodology to say they could not be solved. I do not dispute either point. My claim is a weaker one but also more realistic. Formal theory by its nature *discourages* attention to these problems. It does that because of the current weakness of its tools to handle them. Much of what can be done in principle is rarely even attempted in practice. More progress is needed in both traditions, and both should proceed. But for the present I believe we can learn more about the way the world works, admittedly at some price in parsimony and obvious generalizability, through an approach that gives primary attention to history.

Structural Possibilities, Strategies, and Cooperation

Axelrod's *The Evolution of Cooperation* contains an intriguing argument about the structural possibilities for cooperation under anarchy. Self-interested actors caught in a stark world of the PD without central authority, institutions, or the ability to communicate, *can* cooperate if certain restrictive conditions are met. This does not mean that they *must* cooperate or that they *will* cooperate.[5] Will the structural potential for cooperation be realized? In the game-theoretic model, this depends upon the introduction and propagation of the TFT strategy. But TFT does not

---

In reality, this is rarely done; and that is not, I believe, a coincidence or an oversight. The nature and content of many of these algorithms, Baye's Theorem included, make them inherently difficult to test.

[5] To reiterate an important point: Axelrod's conditions are not sufficient conditions for cooperation. They may not even be necessary conditions, if other routes to cooperation besides the one he has identified exist.

translate directly into real-world behavior. States can employ different types of strategies based on reciprocity that are broadly consistent with TFT. Similarly, states develop, implement, and change strategies in a more complex way than do game-theoretic actors.

Three cases from U.S.-Soviet arms control that fulfilled the initial structural conditions for cooperation produced three different outcomes. Why? The central hypothesis of this book is that differences among strategies of reciprocity could explain this variance. Enhanced contingent restraint emerged as the strategy most likely to promote cooperation, while contingent restraint and contingent threat of escalation were more likely to lead, by different paths, to missed opportunities.

This argument has limitations. The focus on structural constants and on strategy as a variable sets fairly restrictive boundaries on what can be explained. The argument also has a certain "static" quality to it because it takes cooperation or discord (i.e., the outcome) as a discrete endpoint for analysis. The next step will be to relax the boundaries and move toward a more dynamic analysis of cooperation. To get to that point, I review the findings on two critical questions that emerged from Chapter 3: why do states choose the strategies they do, and how do different strategies of reciprocity affect the prospects for cooperation?

Strategies of Reciprocity

At critical points in each of the three cases, U.S. decisionmakers developed strategies of reciprocity aimed at eliciting cooperation. These strategies rested first of all on Axelrod's preconditions: PD preferences among outcomes in what was seen as an iterated game with a long shadow of the future. But they also rested, in each case, on a set of working hypotheses about Soviet interests. It was not enough to regard Soviet preferences, which were often relatively easy to observe, as a basis for pursuing cooperation. Without a consensus on working hypotheses about Soviet interests to explain those apparent preferences, the U.S. decisionmaking elite could not agree on an appropriate strategy of reciprocity. In MIRV, no such consensus was reached and several proposed strategies of reciprocity were sent off track. In ABM and ASAT, a consensus on working hypotheses about Soviet interests did develop, albeit by different routes.

These working hypotheses served several purposes. They reinforced decisions to seek cooperation; they influenced the type of strategy that was chosen to achieve it; and most importantly, they defined what kind of information decisionmakers would seek out as feedback and how they would evaluate it. In ABM, U.S. decisionmakers focused their attention on indicators drawn directly from the logic of the working hypotheses, and they weighted the importance of change in those indicators much more heavily than underlying consistencies. In ASAT, the nature and logic of the working hypotheses blocked deeper exploration of Soviet interests in the closely linked area of military satellites and inhibited the evolution of the space regime.

In neither case, however, did the working hypotheses substantially evolve: once established, they were extremely resistant to change. Feedback that seemed discrepant was either assimilated to the logic of those hypotheses or discounted entirely for long periods of time. When change came, it was paroxysmal and drastic. In the interim, strategies of reciprocity that were developed beneath those hypotheses were insulated from change. The strategies took on a degree of autonomy that reflected the institutionalization of working hypotheses about Soviet interests in Washington's decisionmaking system.

Working hypotheses about Soviet interests did not by themselves determine what kind of strategy American decisionmakers chose. To explain that choice, I proposed five additional variables that are most important at the critical decisional points. The first concerned *interests and incentives* and the rate at which decisionmakers perceived both to be changing. When technology outran the bounds of consensual knowledge and radical uncertainty prevailed, U.S. decisionmakers were more likely to favor permissive strategies of reciprocity. This effect was most pronounced in ASAT during the 1960s, but it also had an impact on MIRV in the early part of that decade. At later stages of each case, as uncertainties resolved toward a moderate level, strategies moved progressively toward more stringent forms of reciprocity. In ABM, where in the late 1960s technology and consensual knowledge joined to produce relatively clear understandings of the costs and benefits of alternative outcomes, enhanced contingent restraint was sustained. These strategies were in fact aimed at different kinds of cooperative outcomes. Under radical uncertainty, permissive forms of reciprocity were intended to shut off broad areas of competition on the basis of strong aversions, with less concern for relative gains. The more stringent forms of reciprocity aimed at circumscribed arrangements with carefully balanced trade-offs between the two sides.

The second variable was the issue of *saliencies*. More permissive forms of reciprocity rested on beliefs that the two sides recognized or could be made to recognize the same saliencies as significant focal points for cooperation. In MIRV, no such saliencies were available, and attempts to "construct" a saliency between multiple warheads that were not independently targetable and those that were foundered on the details of verification. In ABM, there were a number of potential saliencies conspicuous to both sides for much the same reasons, and this favored a strategy of enhanced contingent restraint. In ASAT, American decisionmakers came to favor more stringent forms of reciprocity as saliencies were overcome one by one. This was a result not only of the decline in numbers, but also of a growing belief that Soviet leaders did not recognize the same saliencies in space for the same reasons as did the United States.

The third variable was the *general political environment*, which I divided into images of the Soviet Union as an adversary and images of the superpower competition. The former, even when strongly negative, had a surprisingly small effect on American strategy. Attempts to cooperate were based more on a reading of Soviet interests and preferences in a particular weapons system than on a broad-based assessment of what kind of a state the Soviet Union was. Thus, beliefs that the Soviet Union was ideologically committed to full-fledged struggle for hegemony did not preclude the pursuit of cooperation with permissive strategies of reciprocity, as in ASAT during the early 1960s. When beliefs began to change during the early years of detente, and many American leaders accepted the notion that the Soviet Union sought a broad, constructive political relationship with many potential positive-sum sectors and that mutual restraint in the military realm would facilitate political cooperation, this favored permissive strategies of reciprocity but did not in the end influence the United States to risk cooperation in the looming problem of MIRV.[6] Strategies of reciprocity were also to a considerable extent insulated from negative images of equilibrium in the superpower competition. When U.S. decisionmakers suspected that relative gains for one side might cumulate and threaten the maintenance of the balance of power, American strategy tended strongly toward contingent threat of escalation, as in ASAT prior to 1962 and after 1976. But even highly pessimistic beliefs about the volatility of the superpower balance did not rule out efforts to cooperate in limited sectors. And when equilibrium was thought to be more robust, U.S. decisionmakers were ready to discount the importance of small relative gains, to assume that Moscow was motivated to do the same, and to favor relatively permissive strategies of reciprocity.

The fourth variable was *strategic theory*. When American decisionmakers judged that the two sides' strategic theories were essentially congruent on the significance of a particular weapons system for strategic stability, they were apt to choose relatively permissive strategies of reciprocity. The surprise was that the sources of the assumption of congru-

---

[6] Of course, all the usual caveats apply to my description of the beliefs of the American decisionmaking elite, which was both divided and uncertain in these assessments during each of these periods. Yet in spite of important disagreements on these issues, Washington was able to support strategies of reciprocity in ASAT and ABM when a consensus on working hypotheses about Soviet interests was attained. Beliefs about interests were transcendent.

ence barely mattered for the effect. In ABM, beliefs about congruence were based on relatively extensive communication and feedback; in ASAT, similar beliefs were based on the most scant data about Soviet interests; but the effect was basically the same. When strategic theories were thought to be discrepant, this in itself did not stop attempts to cooperate but it did push American strategy toward greater stringency. Beliefs about the role of technology in the nuclear balance acted generally to moderate both of these influences for most of the 1960s and 1970s. In ABM and in the early phase of ASAT, American decisionmakers treated the U.S. technological edge as a "buffer"; but they did so with prudence, believing that the advantage could be squandered if too much reliance were placed on it or if the Soviets were given too much time to respond. It was also the American lead in MIRV technology that allowed Halperin, Brooke, and other supporters of MIRV restraint to push forward strategies of enhanced contingent restraint for this system. It was not until the latter half of the 1970s that technology was treated as a means of imposing "unbearable" costs on the Soviets that would either force cooperation or leave the United States in a position of unilateral advantage—the essence of a strategy of contingent threat.

The fifth variable was *bureaucratic politics*. The parochial interests and demands of government bureaucracies, the military, and public pressure often tugged in different directions at American strategy, and frequently in directions that key decisionmakers did not favor. For this reason, MIRV and ABM have sometimes been seen as quintessential stories of bureaucratic politics influencing foreign policy. But while bureaucratic politics set constraints for American strategy and was particularly troublesome for the more permissive variants of reciprocity, it was almost never the limiting or decisive factor in the choice of strategies. In MIRV, President Johnson recognized the opposition of the Pentagon to cooperation—and designed a diplomatic maneuver around it. The final decision to proceed with MIRV did not reflect parochial preferences so much as a shared assessment of what the United States had to do. In ABM, the executive branch fought the Congress and the public successfully, both prior to 1968 when it wanted to go slower than the rest, and after that time when it wanted to go faster. In ASAT, President Kennedy stepped out ahead in taking on the political risks of tacit mutual restraint in a high-technology, high-stakes arena. President Ford later pushed a reluctant Air Force to develop the MHV ASAT; and when the Air Force developed a greater parochial interest in the system toward the end of the decade, President Carter threatened to stop it through negotiations. Only in late 1985 was the Congress able to block the Reagan administration's ASAT strategy with an amendment restricting funds for continued testing of the MHV.[7] What stood out in bureaucratic politics was the essential leading role of the president and his surprising ability in most cases to implement strategies despite the many constraints.

Strategy and Outcomes

In Chapter 3, I divided strategies of reciprocity in arms control into three ideal types—contingent restraint, enhanced contingent restraint, and contingent threat of escalation. Chapters 4, 5, and 6 traced the processes through which each influenced the prospects for cooperation. In ABM, Johnson's early strategy of contingent restraint drew little positive response from the Soviets. After late 1967, the United States adopted and sustained a more demanding strategy of enhanced contingent restraint. Safeguard in particular provided an infrastructure and foundation for reciprocating Soviet defection in the medium to long term, while not provoking escalation in the short term. The Nixon administration shepherded this program through a reluctant Congress while at the same time resisting the services' interests in moving more rapidly to heavy defense. Linked with careful communication and a coordinated approach to negotiations, this strategy played an important part in the "surprising success" of the ABM treaty. In MIRV, proposed reciprocal strategies that came closest to being implemented were in conception similar to enhanced contingent restraint; but because these strategies were never given a serious chance, the relationship with outcomes cannot be evaluated fairly. In ASAT, a U.S. strategy of contingent restraint that was adopted under conditions of radical uncertainty in the early 1960s contributed to a tacit cooperation for much of that decade. When Moscow challenged cooperation at the end of the decade, Washington responded by modifying its strategy toward enhanced contingent restraint; and in the context of resolving uncertainties, ASAT cooperation was for a period of time revitalized. The shift to a strategy of contingent threat of escalation in the mid-1970s coincided with a sharp deterioration of cooperation. As the MHV deployment "track" progressively outran the negotiating track, what was left of cooperative restraint in space seemed poised on the brink of dissolution by 1980.

What can we conclude? With such a small number of cases, a static, correlational analysis of the relationship between strategies and outcomes is absurd.[8] What is interesting and possible to do is to trace the impact

---

[7] I discuss the history and future of this imposed moratorium in a few pages.

[8] It should be apparent from my discussion in Chapter 3 that I doubt this problem can be solved simply by adding more cases. Until we better understand the details of the processes that link independent to dependent variables I would remain extremely dubious of any at-

each ideal type strategy has on the operation of reciprocity en route to cooperation. Contingent restraint with its highly permissive criteria of reciprocity does not work in U.S.-Soviet arms control under most conditions. Its major failing is that it offers an excess of temptation for the adversary to "probe" for the possibility that the state's restraint is not actually contingent on reciprocity but is de facto unconditional or irreversible. If the adversary chooses to engage in such probes, the side employing contingent restraint, slow to respond at first, is likely to react dramatically when a critical decisional point is reached. Perceptions that concessions have been exploited will reinforce bad-faith images of the opponent and complicate attempts to revive cooperation. The adversary for its part may be confounded by the sudden vehemence of the state's paroxysmal reaction to what were thought to be low-risk probes. Unless there is sufficient time and strong channels of communication to bring understandings of intentions and expectations back into line, mutual defection is the most likely result.

This story bodes poorly for the potential utility of strategies like GRIT, Charles Osgood's prescription for achieving arms control and reducing international tensions through bold initiatives that resemble strategies of contingent restraint. It also bodes poorly for the long-term stability and political implications of tacit cooperation under radical uncertainty, at least when it is reached through strategies of contingent restraint as it was in the ASAT case.

Contingent threat of escalation is also inappropriate for most U.S.-Soviet arms control problems, although the sources of failure here are different. Contingent threat tends to provoke competitive responses in the short term and produce feuding cycles from which it is difficult to disengage. Demanding specific actions on the part of an adversary to forestall defection leaves insufficient room for assymetries, particularly when the two sides' force structures start from different baselines. It also ignores the problems of domestic politics and the issue of time when it comes to influencing a state to change strategic weapons policies. When such demands call for reversing actions that the adversary is currently taking or has taken, contingent threat may engage concerns about reputation and paradoxically increase the perceived costs of cooperating. Contingent threat of escalation may be more successful in relationships where the power distribution is radically skewed between the actors, but it is not likely to succeed over the long term in the U.S.-Soviet nuclear relationship.

Enhanced contingent restraint is the most promising strategy of reci-

tempt to draw conclusions with even very large numbers of cases (and I doubt that very large numbers of appropriate cases exist).

procity for achieving cooperation in U.S.-Soviet arms control. Enhanced contingent restraint is based on permissive criteria of reciprocity, and it invites exchange of roughly equivalent concessions to take place over a period of time. It does not demand precise terms of reciprocity or specific concessions that the adversary must fulfill, and it maintains flexibility with regard to the window of time in which some response must arrive. It does not commit the state to specific actions in response to defection, but it does provide adequate preparation for measures that aim at a rough compensation and not at escalating the competition or pursuing advantage.

These are obviously general criteria for a strategy that at some point must touch the complex realities of U.S.-Soviet arms control. They are ultimately unsatisfying. Later, I will allay some of the problem by developing specific arguments about how enhanced contingent restraint can be brought to bear on some and perhaps many arms control issues. But my dissatisfaction has deeper roots than simply the lack of immediate applications to policy. It stems more from the static nature of the analysis on the last few pages. Focusing on structural constants, strategies, and cooperation has run straight up against the limitations of a static analysis that takes cooperation or discord as a discrete outcome. There are reasons to stretch beyond this focus and move toward a more dynamic perspective.

Equifinality is the most important of those reasons.[9] There are multiple sources of failure in international cooperation. A static model driven by game theory tends to treat these as distinct and separate routes to the same outcome, and then to consider that outcome as if it were a single discrete event. But this is ultimately deficient. Cooperation in U.S.-Soviet arms control is not what physicists call a "singularity": time and history do not stop and begin anew after the "outcome" of a case. Antecedent conditions do not dissolve at critical junctures. Just as there are different causal routes to failure, so are there different sequelae. The route by which the two states arrive at an outcome matters, because it influences the subsequent trajectory of U.S.-Soviet cooperation over time. It was for this reason, which I can now state clearly from a slightly different perspective, that I was driven in Chapter 3 to add new concepts to the game-theoretic model, concepts that could stretch its dynamic nature past the preliminary step of making a single-shot PD into an iterated game. Axelrod's formalization of cooperation in a game of many rounds was the first step. Looking at the relationship between interests, consensual knowledge, and learning in U.S.-Soviet arms control is the next.

[9] Equifinality is a term used in general systems theory to refer to a system in which there is more than one causal "route" to a similar endpoint or outcome.

The Dynamic Nature of Cooperation

Sources of Preferences

Consistent with a game-theoretic approach, I began by defining preferences as an actor's comparative evaluation of alternative potential outcomes. It is a common critique of game theory that it does not deal with the sources of preferences; but the critique is misplaced, because game theory does not profess to deal with the sources but only with the strategic consequences of preferences as they are given in a particular environment. That said, the game-theoretic approach will falter if preferences are volatile or if strategic interaction is heavily influenced by factors other than the structure of the environment.[10] Both of these are present in U.S.-Soviet arms control cooperation.

This leads to two pivotal issues about preferences. The first is simply how a state, in this case the United States, defines its own preference structure for a particular weapons system. Using the notion of argument-based choice, I pictured the emergence of preferences as an active and creative process of evaluation and comparison of contending arguments in a political realm, not as an economistic derivative of static utilities. This begs the question of where the arguments come from. The obvious answer is that decisionmakers compare arguments about how alternative outcome scenarios will fit within their conceptions of self-interest. It is those broader conceptions of interest that set the terms of argument and the standards for comparison among them. Preferences cannot exist on their own, but only in relation to interests.

What are the conditions of that relationship? International relations theory has gone through several phases in answering that question. For Hans Morgenthau, the relationship between state interests and preferences in an issue as central as nuclear security would have been unproblematic, at least from an analytic standpoint. Regime theory and related arguments later improved upon classical realism's peculiarly static conception by adding the notion that bounded rationality, long-term time perspectives, linkages among issues and complex value trade-offs, and even international institutions could intervene between the "basic causal variables" of power and state interests, and by extension between interests and preferences.[11]

---

[10] The same could be said of all theories drawn from the rational choice tradition.

[11] This characterizes the more expansive tradition of regime theory, which goes beyond an austere economistic view of regimes as institutions that only reduce transaction costs for deals between self-interested states. Regime theorists, as noted in Chapter 2, remain divided over whether the larger effects some of them ascribe to regimes are felt to any substantial degree in security issues.

The concept of consensual knowledge takes this argument one step further. It implies that state interests are sensitive to an interpretive framework of ideas and theories about cause-effect and ends-means relationships that are often poorly tested but are widely accepted by the relevant actors. Consensual knowledge, as I understand the concept to have been used until now, does not dissolve into a social construction of reality. In most cases, empirical data does talk back to the theories; for example, the failure of import substitution for Third World nations eventually led to a change in consensual knowledge about development strategies among international financial institutions and their client states. But consensual knowledge in nuclear security issues must be different. History has never spoken clearly to theories about the relationship between nuclear weapons and power in international politics; and it has not spoken at all to the central question of what deters attack by one nuclear state upon another.[12] How, then, do decisionmakers in Washington and Moscow define their interests and by extension their preferences about a particular strategic weapons system? They must depend on untested and possibly untestable theories that generate a set of alternative potential futures for the strategic environment and provide the criteria for evaluating and comparing those futures. Consensual knowledge provides operational definitions of interests that go beyond the very general goal of enhancing security, and it defines the relationship between interests and preferences in a particular weapons system. It must play a particularly important role in U.S.-Soviet arms control cooperation; but because consensual knowledge in nuclear security issues is fundamentally different than its analogue in political economy, that role is likely to be unique. I will return to this important issue in a moment.

The second pivotal issue about preferences is the question of how one state evaluates the preferences of the other. In the model of the iterated game, states learn about each other's preferences by watching their behavior and extrapolating from it.[13] Central security issues between rival superpowers in a bipolar world are the strongest possible set of cases for this kind of argument. But the evidence of ABM, MIRV, and ASAT is not supportive. Preferences were often relatively transparent and stable for stretches of time in each case, but the patterns of reciprocity that we observed were highly irregular, bearing no obvious relation to preferences. The apparent significance of the timing of events and particularly of unexpected "shocks" (such as the Soviet test of a MRV system in the sum-

---

[12] Joseph Nye makes a similar observation, emphasizing the deductive and counterfactual nature of the arguments that make up "strategic consensual knowledge." "Nuclear Learning and US-Soviet Security Regimes."

[13] For an application, see Downes, Rocke, and Siverson, "Arms Races and Cooperation," p. 145.

mer of 1968, the on-again off-again Soviet ICBM deployment program during the SALT talks, and the resumption of ASAT tests in 1976) also confounds the argument. If extrapolation from past behavior explains these findings, it is certainly not linear extrapolation; and if extrapolation follows some more complex algorithm, that algorithm is not likely to be "discovered" by deduction.

I argued instead that American decisionmakers used these events, as well as other pieces of feedback, to construct working hypotheses about the deeper Soviet conceptions of self-interest that could explain Soviet preferences. These working hypotheses were critical in decisions to pursue cooperation and in the choice of strategy; and by this route they also had an important impact on the outcome and its sequelae. How were these working hypotheses formed, and how and why did they change? Empirically, I discovered several patterns and biases that were nearly consistent in how the U.S. decisionmaking system selected and made use of feedback. First, decisionmakers stressed the importance of observed *changes* in patterns of Soviet behavior, even when the changes were of marginal significance and came on top of more fundamental and long-standing elements of *consistency*. For example, when the Soviets either slowed or sped up the rate of construction on Galosh, or when an ASAT test series was begun or completed, this had a particularly large impact on American assessments of Soviet interests.[14] American decisionmakers also attached considerable weight to the content and tone of Soviet writings and political statements as communication about Soviet interests, particularly when the messages were seen as changing. In several instances, Americans actively sought out such low-cost forms of reassurance that their working hypotheses about Soviet interests were fundamentally sound.[15]

A third interesting pattern was the way in which American decisionmakers worked to construct partial "tests" of alternative interpretations of Soviet interests. Although the tests were imperfect at best, the United States in many cases made a direct effort to offer Soviet leaders concrete opportunities to engage in more convincing reassurance by communicating to them that certain key actions or indicators would be treated as

[14] This finding will not surprise cognitive pyschologists, who encounter a similar pattern in decisionmaking by individuals, but it is notable to see the pattern reproduced in a complex decisionmaking system that is designed in part to avoid the impact of such individual decisional pathologies.

[15] This may seem more of a puzzle to cognitive psychologists. Distilling the experimental results, Deborah Larson notes that individuals tend to evaluate such actions on the basis of two factors: consistency, and cost to the party taking the action. See Larson, "Order under Anarchy." Much of the communication treated as relevant feedback by American decisionmakers was neither costly to Soviet leaders nor particularly consistent.

tests. The "results" of these tests were then given more weight than their due. For example, a test of Soviet interests in ASAT during the early 1970s was built up around Moscow's moratorium on flight testing of its interceptor and several small agreements with tangential relationship to ASAT. When the Soviets halted flight tests and signed on to the accords, Washington took this as evidence that its working hypotheses were correct and that American strategy based on those hypotheses had achieved success in revitalizing cooperation.

Each of these patterns reflected an underlying tendency to evaluate feedback from the Soviet Union according to criteria derived from the logic of American consensual knowledge. In most instances, there was a strong bias toward assuming convergence on the essential elements of that body of theories. When the Americans developed a set of interests for ASAT in the early 1960s, they were willing to engage the Soviets in cooperation on the basis of assumptions that Moscow shared a similar complexion of interests drawn from the same logic of radical uncertainty. When Johnson, McNamara, and their predecessors in the scientific community found Soviet elites resistant to their strategic arguments about defenses, they tried to influence Soviet conceptions of self-interest and were later inclined to believe that they had succeeded. And when it was suspected that Soviet interests might point in a direction different from those of the United States, as under the Talensky doctrine interpretation in ABM or in the later years of ASAT, the United States continued to seek cooperation (albeit with more demanding strategies of reciprocity) on terms drawn from the logic of American consensual knowledge.

Consensual Knowledge and Learning

Static preferences and mechanistic concepts of strategic interaction fail to explain irregular patterns of reciprocity or success and failure in U.S.-Soviet arms control cooperation. To take the next step and push strategic interaction past game theory's view requires understanding how states' strategies change. In Chapter 3, I defined learning as a redefinition of conceptions of interest that in turn drives a change in strategy. Such redefinition could take place in two ways. The United States, as an example of the first way, could simply undergo a change in consensual knowledge—that would be a primary cause. Second, U.S. decisionmakers could agree on a different set of working hypotheses about Soviet interests. Either route would prompt a change in strategy; but the sources and methods of both are at first glance puzzling. Why should consensual knowledge that is not subject to falsification ever change? Why should working hypotheses based in part on that consensual knowledge and in part on feedback that decisionmakers tend to assess in ways that reinforce it change? Answering these questions requires going back to look at what is unique about consensual knowledge in strategic nuclear issues, and the consequences for learning.

The first and most obvious characteristic of consensual knowledge in strategic nuclear issues is its highly abstract and deductive nature and its insulation from evidence. Most of the central ideas are products of abstract, counterfactual arguments divorced from reality. The theories that are built on those ideas are for the most part not subject to falsification. For individual decisionmakers, this is a source of chronic uncertainty. For a complex political decisionmaking system, it is a source of chronic controversy. Domestic constituencies will continuously challenge the consensual knowledge that guides the state's actions, on both intellectual and political grounds. They are right to do so. At any given moment there are alternative and equally plausible theories available that could support a very different consensual knowledge and a very different policy agenda. Complicating the political arguments is the fact that decisionmakers may come to suspect that some of those alternative theories have actually been adopted by the other superpower and lie behind its behavior.

This should in fact be expected in strategic nuclear issues because of a second special characteristic. The sources of innovation in this area have been almost entirely confined within national boundaries. Put differently, new ideas about strategic nuclear issues have until now been formulated either in the United States or in the USSR. International institutions have rarely if ever played a creative role. Instead, they have functioned mostly as imperfect conduits, as weak links between decisionmaking systems on the two sides that continued to develop and adopt strategic consensual knowledge almost exclusively on their own.[16] Given two states with radically different strategic and military traditions, cultures, and domestic decisionmaking systems for defense, it is no surprise that they were likely to develop different ideas about nuclear weapons. And although we know less about how certain ideas were "selected" as the bases for consensual knowledge, it is also not surprising if the "products" were different in the two superpowers.[17]

[16] There is an obvious and important contrast with international institutions in political economy and elsewhere. The International Monetary Fund and World Bank, for example, have frequently played creative roles in formulating consensual knowledge, in addition to propagating it among states. Ernst Haas and others have examined the role of transnational "epistemic communities" made up of scientists or "technocrats" that are both sources and conduits for new ideas in these and many other issues as well. For an example see Peter Haas, "Do Regimes Matter?"

[17] For an argument about possible "selection mechanisms," see my "Interactive Learning in US-Soviet Arms Control," in Breslauer and Tetlock, *Learning in US and Soviet Foreign*

Both of these characteristics help explain why consensual knowledge in nuclear security issues has been volatile and unstable, despite the fact that contending alternatives are not falsified. Still, neither instability nor volatility has prevented cooperation at particular moments, and if we slice into the evolution of cooperation at a given point in time with a static analysis we barely notice the consequences. From a dynamic perspective, the picture looks very different.

The U.S. decisionmaking system did not learn smoothly or in a patterned way from the international environment. Neither did the Soviet Union's. Instead, learning has been lumpy or discontinuous.[18] Both sides appear to have undergone "critical learning periods," or windows of time in which decisionmaking systems demonstrated an unusual degree of plasticity. These lasted only for short and delimited periods of time. While a state was in a critical learning period, external influences and shocks played an inordinately large role in altering consensual knowledge and working hypotheses about the other side's interests.[19] But once the latter were established during these periods, both were then resistant to change, and so were the strategies that were based upon them. The ASAT story provides a particularly clear example of the United States in a critical learning period around 1976 and 1977, and there were similar periods for both ABM and MIRV.

From a dynamic perspective, critical learning periods are the most important junctures in the evolution of cooperation. Conceptions of interest and national strategies that are established during these periods send reciprocity off on one trajectory or another. Critical learning periods do not determine outcomes; but they powerfully constrain and direct the subsequent processes of interaction that do. Because the prospects for cooperation are so sensitive to what happens during these windows, a full dynamic theory of cooperation must explain critical learning periods in great detail. What causes a critical learning period to occur? How long can it last? What determines its end point and result? And what is the legacy of that result: is the outcome stable or self-reinforcing, or predisposed toward conditions that will engender another critical learning period soon thereafter?

The rest of this chapter examines some of the implications of this "critical juncture" approach toward cooperation, without pretending to an-

---

Policy. I owe a great debt to conversations with Emmanuel Adler and to his written work for stimulating my thought on this subject.

[18] See Nye, "Nuclear Learning"; Coit D. Blacker, "Soviet Strategic Arms Control Policy 1969–1989," in Breslauer and Tetlock, *Learning in US and Soviet Foreign Policy*; and Holloway, *The Soviet Union and the Arms Race*, Chapters 2, 3, 5.

[19] At all other times, plasticity is much reduced; and feedback that appears objectively to be of equal magnitude has little or no impact upon conceptions of interest or strategies.

swer these questions.[20] But before I continue it is important to comment on why the kind of pattern reflected in critical junctures confounds most contemporary approaches to international relations. It does this because theories about state learning have so far been wedded to one or another variant of the concept of equilibrium.[21] According to this view, states learn by responding in some fashion to changes in the environment so as to bring conceptions of interest back into line with external events. Equilibrium may never be reached, but the "system," made up of the state and its environment, always tends in that direction.

It does this because the equilibrium model admits only one source of dynamism, only one engine that drives learning. The environment changes; the learning entity does not. This is most clear in the rational unitary actor archetype of game theory, but it is also true in the cybernetic model of complex decisionmaking organizations. In cybernetics the environment changes but the receptor itself does not—it simply responds in a passive way. That is, its receptive field, threshold, and repertoire of possible responses are all fixed, at least in the short term. The picture of state learning that comes out of this model is one where instability is exceptional and the system tends naturally toward stability, even if it never reaches that state.

But what if there is more than one source of dynamism in the system? What if the learning entity is not a passive responder to changes in the environment, even in the short term? Push past the cybernetic model and the picture changes. The decisionmaking system, the receptor, is not passive. It is modulated. It constructs tests of its working hypotheses and actively elicits feedback from the environment. Its receptive field, sensitivity, and repertoire change as consensual knowledge changes. Now place the modulated receptor in an environment that is itself changing rapidly as a result of technology and the actions of another state that is a similarly complicated decisionmaking entity. If the rate of change in the environment is constantly greater than the rate of change in the state's conceptions of self-interest, the latter will not catch up to or even approach the former. The system will not tend toward equilibrium. Instead, it will be

[20] The notion of "critical junctures" is a familiar one in macrohistorical and sociological research. For a recent application to state/labor movement politics in 20th-century Latin American regimes, see Collier and Collier, *Shaping the Political Arena*.

[21] This concept comes in two forms. The simpler equilibrium notion pictures a complex system as always tending to approach a stable state: the effects of small changes are damped over time and balance tends to be restored. In the more complex "punctuated equilibrium" models, instability does occur but it is a temporary and isolated phenomenon. It comes in rare spurts and is an abnormal state; systems then tend toward a new equilibrium. Most arguments about learning in international relations are built on one or the other foundation. See Gould, "Is a New and General Theory of Evolution Emerging?"; and for an application, Krasner, "Sovereignty: An Institutional Perspective."

driven progressively further *away* from equilibrium. In that case, even the most sophisticated equilibrium-based approaches will not succeed in explaining paroxysms in state learning, and by implication similar patterns in the evolution of cooperation.

What can explain these patterns? There are models in the natural sciences, particularly in modern physics, that explore the behavior of systems that are driven away from equilibrium by multiple sources of dynamism. These systems typically exhibit regularities, but of a nonlinear kind. Some resemble cycles, in which the system oscillates unpredictably between two or more points. All exhibit "critical periods," which are sharply delimited windows of time during which small shocks can dramatically change the direction of evolution and send the system off on one trajectory rather than another. The possibilities at those critical periods are broad but not infinite: future paths are constrained by the state of the system when it reaches the critical period and, importantly, by the path it took to get to that point.[22] This is not yet an explanation of critical learning periods, irregular patterns of reciprocity in U.S.-Soviet arms control, or the paroxysms of cooperation in it. But there are ideas here that may eventually help to answer some of the puzzles that have been raised in my attempt to push toward a more dynamic analysis. In what follows I will focus on observable consequences in the world of arms control, but I ask that the reader keep these ideas and their possible significance in mind for future research. The most important implications that we can talk about now are the historical consequences for arms control cooperation of state learning that is volatile, discontinuous, and unsynchronized between the two sides that are trying to cooperate.

Path-Dependent Cooperation

Slicing into the evolution of cooperation at a given moment, time $= t$, defeats the logic of explaining a system that does not tend toward equilibrium. Cooperation in U.S.-Soviet arms control is path-dependent. By this I mean simply that outcomes reflect the processes and particularly the strategies taken to get there. Cooperation or noncooperation is not a singularity; history does not begin anew after the ABM Treaty or the tacit agreement on ASAT restraint around 1963. The evolution of cooperation after each point, what I prefer to call its "trajectory," in turn reflects the route that was taken to get to each critical juncture and the logic by which

[22] See Prigogine, *From Being to Becoming*, especially the discussion of transitions during critical periods on p. 147; also, Prigogine and Stengers, *Order Out of Chaos*; and Thompson and Stewart, *Nonlinear Dynamics and Chaos*.

it was resolved. In each case, there were special features to that route and to that logic that are not a part of the game-theoretic model.

Radical Uncertainty and ASAT Sequelae

Game-theoretic preferences are based on expected utility calculations for different potential outcomes. States' preferences in arms control reflect the decisionmaking systems' comparative evaluation of alternative potential futures for the strategic environment. In most cases, the uncertainties attached to those potential futures are *moderate*, as I defined the term in Chapter 3. Technological possibilities fall within the purview of current consensual knowledge, and it is possible to make estimates of the costs and benefits in different scenarios. Rarely, rapid technological change gives birth to possibilities that cannot be evaluated and whose potential consequences are impossible to foresee with current consensual knowledge. Under *radical* uncertainty, decisionmakers find themselves unable to envision what the strategic environment will look like if certain technical innovations go forward. ABM and ASAT show that cooperation is possible in either world. The strategies of reciprocity and the consequent route to that outcome in each world were, however, quite different. So were the sequelae of agreement. Cooperation achieved under radical uncertainty is not the same as cooperation achieved under moderate uncertainty.

Radical uncertainty about ASAT and the working hypothesis that Soviet leaders shared in it favored U.S. decisions to adopt a highly permissive strategy of reciprocity for ASAT in the early 1960s. The result was cooperation that rescued the superpowers from a contest that would have involved massive costs without foreseeable benefits. At the same time, cooperation left both sides free to explore the technological possibilities in military satellites and to develop new conceptions of self-interest in space as those possibilities became more clear. Because the tacit deal avoided this issue, each side developed those new conceptions entirely on its own. This was not simply an innocuous formula to buy time or to postpone the challenge of solving harder problems. Chapter 6 showed that the legacy of cooperation under radical uncertainty did more than just leave the sources of innovation within national boundaries.[23] It actually inhibited exploration of how each superpower was developing new consensual knowledge on its own to guide the inevitable trade-offs that

---

[23] The innovations I am speaking of here refer to ideas about interests—the foundations of new consensual knowledge, as discussed above—not *technological* innovation per se.

both would eventually have to make between ASAT restraint and the attractions of military satellites.

When radical uncertainty began to resolve, the United States and the Soviet Union each faced the problem of balancing these interests, but they did so separately and in different ways. Maintaining cooperation past this point would have required finding new common ground between the two sides' conceptions of self-interest. But the space regime was not set up to do this. In fact, the legacy of cooperation as it developed in the 1960s actively hindered such efforts. The boundaries imposed by cooperation under radical uncertainty were broken late in the process of deterioration and even then were only partially breached. The result was a sharp turn toward competition at the end of the Carter administration that would culminate in a change of U.S. preferences in the early 1980s.

The Reagan administration's review of military space policy, begun in the summer of 1981, charted a new course for American ASAT strategy that was the first product of this underlying change in preferences. Rhetoric about cooperation in the peaceful use of space aside, the United States was now committed to unilateral pursuit of military advantage in space regardless of what the Soviets did. Because cooperative restraint had no part to play in serving the new conception of American interests, ASAT was no longer a PD. The MHV program was no longer viewed as a part of contingent threat of escalation, designed to give Soviet leaders greater incentive to cooperate. It was recast as a priority weapons program with specific military missions, to be brought to deployment as quickly as possible. The United States also committed itself to rapid development of follow-on ASAT weapons with even more sophisticated technologies that could threaten Soviet satellites in geosynchronous orbit in the near future.[24]

The dynamic of deteriorating cooperation that had begun in the 1970s accelerated. The Soviets renewed tests of their ASAT weapon in 1981 and 1982. The Pentagon responded with a worst-case assessment of the current Soviet ASAT and a series of dire warnings about Soviet research in DEW ASATs, which it claimed could lead to the deployment of a laser

---

[24] In a sharp departure from Carter administration statements, the Reagan White House in 1982 proclaimed as official policy that "the United States will proceed with development of an anti-satellite (ASAT capability) *with operational deployment as a goal.*" *White House Fact Sheet Outlining US Space Policy,* 4 July 1982 (my emphasis). DDR&E Richard De-Lauer later testified before a Senate Foreign Relations Committee subcommittee that "the US ASAT program is not a bargaining chip and never was." *Arms Control and the Militarization of Space,* 20 September 1982, p. 27. In 1984 he informed the House Armed Services Committee that the Pentagon had been tasked to focus on possibilities for "a follow-on system with additional capabilities to place a wider range of Soviet satellite vehicles at risk." "Anti-Satellite Weapon Research Is Pressed," *Washington Post,* 28 February 1984, p. 3. For the official Pentagon position, see *Military Posture Statement FY 84,* pp. 226–27.

ASAT in the early 1990s.[25] When the new Soviet leader Yuri Andropov announced a temporary moratorium on ASAT tests in August 1983 and invited the United States to respond, Washington rejected the Soviet demarche out of hand. Moscow followed up by submitting a draft treaty to the United Nations that would ban the testing and deployment of new antisatellite systems, but the United States flatly refused to enter into any negotiations on this basis.[26] Instead, the White House pushed the Pentagon to accelerate the MHV testing program through 1985.[27] By the end of that year, cooperation in space had reached its nadir.

The process by which cooperation unraveled continued to reflect the logic of its evolution from a strategy of contingent restraint under radical uncertainty. The United States, initially slow to react to Soviet probing, revised its strategy in paroxysms, and the Soviets were confounded by the vehemence of the response. Perceptions that concessions had been ignored or exploited for reasons that neither side understood reinforced bad-faith images of the opponent in both capitals. Consensual knowledge about U.S. interests in space underwent a radical shift in the early 1980s, producing a new set of preferences for ASAT that left no room for cooperation. The ASAT experience was not the only reason for this shift—President Reagan's dedication to a strategic defense initiative (SDI), among other things, reinforced it—but the legacy of cooperation in space was part of what lay behind that specific commitment.[28] Both SDI and

[25] The Soviet ASAT tested in 1981 and 1982 was, again, the same co-orbital interceptor essentially unimproved since 1968. As in the mid-1970s test series, all tests involving the passive infrared sensor system failed. Johnson, *The Soviet Year in Space 1983*, p. 39; Department of Defense, *Soviet Military Power*, 1983, p. 67. DoD's concern about imminent Soviet DEW capabilities was not unanimously shared; see my discussion in Weber and Drell, "Attempts to Regulate Military Activities in Space," p. 414.

[26] "Andropov Urges Ban on Weapons to Attack Satellites," *Washington Post*, 19 August 1983, p. 1. The text of the Soviet draft treaty is reprinted in Office of Technology Assessment, *Anti-satellite Weapons, Countermeasures, and Arms Control*, pp. 145–46. Under the pressure of impending elections, President Reagan nominally agreed to meet with the Soviets in the summer of 1984 to discuss "feasible negotiating approaches" for ASAT, but only as part of comprehensive talks that also dealt with intermediate-range and strategic forces. As the Soviets had earlier walked out of the INF talks and refused to set a resumption date for START in response to the deployment of American cruise missiles and Pershing II in Europe, this condition for negotiations on ASAT was a nonstarter. "US Says It Weighs Kremlin's Motives in New Arms Offer," *New York Times*, 1 July 1984, p. 1; "US Agreed to Talk about Space Arms without Clear Plan," *New York Times*, 3 July 1984, p. 1.

[27] Weber and Drell, "Attempts to Regulate Military Activities in Space," pp. 416–17.

[28] The technical demands of a near-perfect strategic defense focused SDI, at least during its early stages, on space-based defensive systems. ASAT was intertwined with this endeavor, because to deploy SDI platforms in space would require that the United States gain control of that arena. It was also intertwined because scientists on both sides recognized that satellites were much easier targets than ballistic missiles and that the first fruits of SDI would probably be better ASAT weapons.

ASAT were important parts of a new and broad emphasis on exploiting the U.S. technological edge as a way of redressing the effects of past cooperation that American decisionmakers now felt had been one-sided in favor of the Soviet Union. Military space seemed the ideal place to compensate for the abuses of detente.

Bureaucratic politics intruded on the Reagan administration's ASAT policies. After a first attempt in 1984 that was turned back by a massive White House lobbying effort, the Congress in 1985 voted to ban additional tests of the MHV unless the Soviets tested their ASAT.[29] Because this bill passed again in 1986 and 1987, and the Soviets did not test, the MHV program was left in a state of suspended animation. Facing tighter budgets at the end of the 1980s, the Air Force in February 1988 asked that the moribund MHV program be canceled; and it was in fact deleted from the FY 1989 budget.[30] At the start of 1988 the United States no longer had an active dedicated ASAT program and the Soviets had not tested their co-orbital interceptor for about five years.

Does this mean that cooperation had been reestablished? Not at all. Only the shape of U.S. policy and not its basic substance was affected by these events; conceptions of interests and preferences had not changed. The Congressionally imposed test ban applied to the MHV program only. With its cancellation in 1988 the Pentagon redirected its attention to other ASAT activities. In March 1988 the Air Force began work on a new ground-based kinetic-kill interceptor system using ERIS technology.[31] About $50 million was budgeted in 1988 and again in 1989 for research and development of several ground-based laser systems designed to attack satellites. In November 1988 the Pentagon announced that it would begin development of a new sea-based ASAT interceptor for use by the Navy.[32] The following month, Defense Secretary Frank Carlucci disclosed a plan to upgrade an existing high-energy laser system in the New Mexico desert so that it could be tested against satellites in the near fu-

[29] The 1984 bill passed the House but was rejected by the Senate. "Anti-satellite Tests Backed, with Condition," *Washington Post*, 13 June 1984, p. A9. The 1985 bill is reported in *Congressional Record*, House, H12035, 16 December 1985, p. 8097; and the Pentagon's extremely negative reaction in *Military Posture Statement FY 86*, p. 215.

[30] "USAF Budget Cuts SICBM Program," *Aviation Week and Space Technology*, 22 February 1988, p. 15; "Major Weapons System Funding," *Aviation Week and Space Technology*, 29 February 1988, p. 21.

[31] "USAF Studies Ground-Based ASAT Systems to Replace F-15 Missile," *Aviation Week and Space Technology*, 7 March 1988, p. 21. ERIS is Exo-atmospheric Re-entry Interceptor Subsystem, a long-range missile designed as part of SDI that is conceptually similar to the Spartan missile that was part of the Safeguard ABM in the early 1970s.

[32] "Pentagon Planning to Restart Anti-Satellite Program in January," *Aviation Week and Space Technology*, 14 November 1988, pp. 33–34.

ture.[33] The explicit goal of this multifaceted effort is to provide the information and experience needed to make a decision in 1991 or soon thereafter on how best to proceed with directed-energy ASATs. The Bush administration early on committed itself to maintaining this goal.[34]

Will the current ASAT "lull" perpetuate itself? We should worry that it will not, even if the general deceleration of the U.S.-Soviet military competition that began at the end of the 1980s continues through the early 1990s. The current lull in ASAT reflects the legacy of earlier cooperation. It is not founded on common interests or shared understandings of how the two sides' interests in space differ. I will return to this point when I differentiate the concept of cooperation in a few pages.

Institutions and ABM Sequelae

Cooperation is not always the product of radical uncertainty. In Axelrod's game-theoretic world, cooperation can evolve under anarchy among self-interested actors in the PD who know precisely what their interests and preferences are. "Under anarchy," in the first few chapters of Axelrod's book, means in the absence of institutions. In the second half of his book, and in the world of superpower arms control, cooperation breeds and is in turn affected by institutions (be they weak or strong) that develop in and around it. For regime theorists, institutions facilitate cooperation, either in a "rational guise" (by reducing transaction and information-search costs and making specific reciprocity easier) or a "reflective guise" (by affecting conceptions of self-interest and making diffuse reciprocity easier).[35] The path to cooperation in ABM started close to Axelrod's stark game-theoretic world but became dotted with institutions along the way. Conversely, the path to cooperation in MIRV was blocked

---

[33] "ASAT Tests to Be Conducted with Upgraded Miracl Laser," *Aviation Week and Space Technology*, 19 December 1988, pp. 29–30; William J. Broad, "Military to Ready Laser for Testing as Space Weapon," *New York Times*, 1 January 1989, pp. 1, 20.

[34] "Star Wars Shield Called Only Partial," *New York Times*, 27 January 1989.

[35] Keohane, "International Institutions." In the conclusion to *Cooperation under Anarchy*, Keohane and Axelrod tend toward a minimal view drawn from game theory, seeing institutions as facilitating the operation of certain strategies given predetermined preferences. Institutions are then an alternative to power for dealing with pitfalls of reciprocity. Robert Keohane and Robert Axelrod, "Achieving Cooperation under Anarchy," in Oye, *Cooperation under Anarchy*, pp. 249–51. Jervis takes a wider view of institutions in the case of the Concert of Europe, arguing that extensive and regular communication between elites led to changed estimates of the behavior of other states through better understandings of the interests behind those behaviors. This may have in turn driven some redefinition of states' conceptions of self-interest, at least for a period of time. Robert Jervis, "From Balance to Concert," in Oye, *Cooperation under Anarchy*, pp. 73–76.

by the deficiencies of institutions. What are the consequences for the trajectory of cooperation?

The more limited "rational" view, which sees institutions as collectively rational and functional additions to a game-theoretic environment that facilitate the operation of strategies given predetermined preferences, offers a simple perspective. Because of the technical characteristics of ABM, it was easy to develop institutions that could make noncompliance clear and otherwise reduce the costs of sanctioning. In MIRV, technological limits on verification meant that neither side was willing to accept the intrusions and constraints that similar institutions would have required. Cooperation succeeds in ABM and fails in MIRV at time $= t$ in 1972. But this is again only a static explanation. Even in the ABM case of institutional "success," it says little about why one set of "functional" institutions came into being and not another, or about the consequences of that fact for the trajectory of cooperation past time $= t$.

The institutional legacy of SALT did more than just alter transaction costs. This is not surprising. Given the significance of ideas in defining interests in the strategic nuclear environment and the unusual nature of those ideas and resulting consensual knowledge, any international institutions that do develop in this area are likely to have a disproportionate impact on state learning and changes in conceptions of self-interest. The particular institutional structure that developed along the road to the ABM Treaty and its companion agreements helped make cooperation possible in 1972. But from a dynamic perspective, the institutions of SALT did not reinforce the cooperative solution of which they were a part and may in fact have helped to undermine it.

SALT's peculiar institutional framework began its evolution in the middle and late 1960s, when American elites came to the belief that fundamental differences between U.S. and Soviet understandings of nuclear weapons, deterrence, and stability would make it impossible to capitalize on newly recognized possibilities for mutually beneficial, cooperative arms control. Meta-strategic efforts to influence Soviet conceptions of self-interest grew into a network of formal and informal institutions where U.S. and Soviet elites debated their respective ideas about consensual knowledge in the nuclear realm. The SALT negotiating forum and its offspring, notably the Standing Consultative Commission (SCC), were formal institutions through which such ideas were occasionally exchanged. But these kinds of institutions, in terms of the broader "reflective" agenda of what institutions can do, were always extremely weak. For most of the 1970s the semiofficial and informal contacts (mostly between scientists and strategists on the two sides) were stilted and rarely affected policy debates, at least in Washington. The SALT negotiations did not do much better, even in the view of optimists like Ambassador

Smith.[36] And the SCC in practice was mostly limited to doing what institutions in the "rational guise" do, reducing transaction and information costs by dealing with instrumental issues of compliance. Despite its mandate to do so, the SCC rarely reached out to explore broader questions of how interests might be changing on the two sides and how that might affect the trajectory of cooperation.[37]

The SALT "regime" was weak at the international level. But it was not so weak domestically, at least not in the realm of ideas. Norms and principles that were thought to be derived from an international regime became embedded in the domestic decisionmaking systems of both superpowers. There were some visible manifestations of this in Washington and Moscow: in both capitals the decisionmaking system for defense underwent changes that reflected a set of ideas about what SALT was—the norms and principles of a putative international regime.[38] But the domestic "reflections" were not the same on the two sides. This was a result of more than just the fact that the U.S. and Soviet decisionmaking systems started off as very different "mirrors" and therefore reflected the same norms and principles in different ways. In fact, the two states incorporated different norms and principles. They had very different ideas about

[36] Pessimists like William Van Cleave argued that "exchange of views on strategic matters fell far short of expectations . . . and little was learned about the Soviet Union's nuclear objectives or military doctrine." *International Negotiations*, Hearings before the Subcommittee on National Security and International Operations of the Senate Committee on Governmental Affairs, July 25, 1972, pt. 7, p. 201. Smith and many others would differ with the intensity of Van Cleave's view but not with its basic thrust. The level of uncertainty about fundamental Soviet interests in arms control that was reflected even in the immediate aftermath of the May summit and during the ABM treaty ratification hearings speaks to Van Cleave's basic point.

[37] Graybeal and Krepon, "Making Better Use of the Standing Consultative Commission," describe the mandate of the SCC and tell something of its deliberative processes. They note that its broad charter includes discussions of strategic doctrine, new technological possibilities, and alternative views of interests, but that in practice "the SCC has concerned itself primarily with implementation and compliance questions for the SALT accords" (p. 185). See also Buchheim and Caldwell, *The US-USSR Standing Consultative Commission.*

[38] Institutional changes were most evident on the U.S. side: the enhanced visibility and influence of ACDA, the increasing leverage of the Congress, the greater voice of scientists, civilian analysts, and arms control advocates both inside and outside of government, as well as new procedures such as requirements to file arms control impact statements, to name a few. Most Soviet scholars agree that SALT had a substantial effect on Moscow's defense decisionmaking system as well, although the formal institutional manifestations of that effect are harder to see. At a minimum, SALT broadened the scope of input for many decisions outside the bounds of the professional military and very senior political figures, to include scientists, specialists on U.S.-Soviet relations, and a small cadre of civilian analysts. See Condoleeza Rice, "SALT and the Search for a Security Regime," in George, Farley, and Dallin, *US-Soviet Security Cooperation*, pp. 298–300; and Stephen Meyer, "Civilian and Military Influence in Managing the Arms Race in the USSR," in Art et al., *Reorganizing America's Defense.*

what the essence of the SALT deal was and its foundation in consensual knowledge.[39] What's more, neither side understood what SALT meant for the other, and the regime's weak international institutions did little to correct for this. Instead, decisionmakers proceeded as if U.S. and Soviet ideas about nuclear weapons and deterrence were the same in their essentials or at the very least compatible.

Although this permitted the superpowers to achieve a kind of cooperation in the short run, it was damaging to the prospects for cooperation over the longer term. Several elements of immediate post-SALT history stand out. In the wake of the May Summit, the United States accelerated development programs for several key strategic weapons systems, including the Trident SSBN, the B-1 bomber, the MX missile, and various cruise missile projects.[40] The Soviets continued their own massive program to develop and deploy new and imposing counterforce-capable ICBMs quickly. In the summer of 1973, Moscow began testing what was unambiguously a MIRV device aboard two new experimental missiles, the SS-17 and the massive SS-18. At the same time, the Soviets were known to have under development two additional ICBMs, a new submarine and SLBM, and a modern bomber that would come to be known as the Backfire. The pace and scope of the Soviet program confounded American analysts; but the most disturbing thing was the almost single-minded focus on counterforce.[41] Suffice it to say, without recounting the rancorous middle and late 1970s debates in Washington over what this meant, that Americans progressively lost confidence in the working hypotheses about Soviet interests that had underlain SALT. New hypotheses were brought

[39] This is by now a standard assessment, although it obviously was not so in 1972. I link this to a broader analysis of detente in "Realism, Detente, and Nuclear Weapons," pp. 66–77.

[40] This was not just a response to parochial demands for compensation from the Pentagon. It reflected a broader and growing uncertainty in Washington over the nature of the Soviet interests that led to SALT I. See *Report by the Senate Foreign Relations Committee on the Treaty on the Limitation of Anti-ballistic Missile Systems*, July 1972; *Military Implications of the Treaty on the Limitation of Anti-Ballistic Missile Systems and the Interim Agreement on Limitation of Strategic Offensive Arms*, July 1972. Kissinger captures this sense quite well when he describes his feeling at a midnight press conference in Moscow on May 27, 1972, just after the treaty was signed, that SALT would be "either a turning point or another impulse to the superpower arms race, either an augury of a more peaceful international order or a pause before a new set of crises." *White House Years*, p. 1244.

[41] Freedman, *US Intelligence*, p. 170. The United States never came close to giving up its own commitments in this area, but the emphasis on MIRV technologies combining yield and accuracy aimed at hard target kill capability was downgraded for several years after 1972. Several programs, including a stellar inertial guidance system for Poseidon and an advanced ballistic reentry system, were canceled over Pentagon objections. See the testimony of DDR&E John Foster in *ABM, MIRV, SALT, and the Nuclear Arms Race*, p. 509.

forward to do battle in the arena of American domestic politics.[42] The weak international institutions of SALT remained inadequate channels to explore these alternative explanations of Soviet behavior. This debate was never settled in Washington and it continues to this day. By the end of the 1970s, what was clear was that each side had gone off in its own direction and that those directions were incompatible, at least for the moment. Neither side's political elites or strategic thinkers understood why.[43] Arms control cooperation was the victim and it remained so, at least until a new leader came to power in Moscow and changed the equations dramatically.

Even if *preferences* with regard to ABM did overlap at time $= t$ in 1972, there was no inherent reason to believe that preferences would do the same in other nuclear issues or even in ABM at time $= t + 1$. If overlapping preferences were derived from different underlying interests, technological and political changes were bound to send those preferences off in different directions. The SALT regime did not drive them back together. If anything, the strong domestic reflections of a weak international regime probably inhibited learning by each state as it might have gone on individually. The regime certainly did very little to provide a source of innovation in ideas outside national boundaries. It did not provide appropriate forums for the sharing of nationally generated ideas that might have led to joint learning or common understanding of differences. The regime did not reduce the volatility and instability of consensual knowledge on each side; in fact, it may have exacerbated it. Both sides held on to expectations derived from their own conceptions of the norms and principles of SALT about how the other side would behave and about how cooperation would contribute to their interests. Those expectations were dramatically disappointed. This did great harm to superpower relations starting in the mid-1970s and was certainly one of the most important reasons for the demise of detente.

This was in no sense inevitable, as a stark realist account might have it. The institutions of SALT were neither "optimal" nor over-determined by

[42] A prominent new school of interpretation argued that Soviet military thought had indeed been reconceptualized in the late 1960s, but not in the direction that proponents of the Garthoff doctrine believed. On this logic, the Soviets were doing everything they could to reinforce "nuclear paralysis" at the central level and to slice away at the credibility of extended deterrence, so as to increase the probability that a war in Europe might be fought out with conventional weapons (where Moscow had a considerable advantage). For an exposition of the argument, see MccGwire, *Military Objectives in Soviet Foreign Policy*, pp. 242ff. There were other competing interpretations that also fit with observed Soviet preferences; see, for example, Gelman, *The Brezhnev Politburo and the Decline of Detente*.

[43] Blacker, "Soviet Strategic Arms Control Policy 1969–1989," reports signs of profound confusion on the Soviet side that began to surface around 1977 and continued into the Gorbachev era.

objective constraints; they were the products of historical contingency and most importantly of particular conjunctions between ideas that were also not "absolute." The first real experiment with superpower arms control cooperation might have turned out differently had the institutions that developed around it been different. At the same time, there would have been multiple sources of failures and missed opportunities as well as surprising successes for arms control in any institutional environment. To repeat my earlier point, equifinality and path dependence confound a static analysis as well as a first-order dynamic analysis of an iterated game. The history of U.S.-Soviet arms control continues to affect the trajectory of cooperation today and will do so in the future. How do we understand path dependency if it means that the trajectory of cooperation past the point of any "outcome" reflects the logic taken to get there? One way to further capture this logic is to differentiate the concept of cooperation on the basis of the kinds of interests that cooperative outcomes reflect.

Differentiating Cooperation

In game theory, cooperation can happen when actors' preferences "overlap." Typically, we think of overlapping preferences as coming from a foundation of *common interests*. Common interests depend on at least partially shared consensual knowledge. In this view, two states (or individuals or firms) try to cooperate because they have identical or at least compatible images of the goals to be achieved and the resultant environment that cooperation is expected to help produce. Game theory illustrates many of the reasons why cooperation based on common interests is hard to achieve in an anarchic environment. But when the impediments are overcome, as they sometimes are, cooperation based on common interests is likely to be relatively stable. Without doubt, exogenous shocks from technology or unrelated political events can lead to changes in states' definitions of self-interest and undermine this kind of cooperation. But barring such shocks, cooperation based on common interests will provide benefits to both sides that confirm their expectations about what cooperation was supposed to achieve. When shocks do hit, the states will try to limit their detrimental impact and retain the valued benefits of cooperation by making mutually acceptable adjustments. Diffuse reciprocity may be the best way to do this; and each "success" may reinforce the strength of the underlying common interests.

Common interests are not the only way for preferences to overlap. Cooperation can also come about on the basis of *complementary interests*. States with complementary interests do not share consensual knowledge and do not have identical visions of the goals to be achieved through cooperation. Instead, they have preferences that are only congruent and short-term objectives in a particular weapons system that look to be the same but only at a given moment in history. Complementary interests may well explain some of the volatility in U.S.-Soviet arms control cooperation. For example, Moscow and Washington each wanted to limit ABMs in 1972. But the interests that lay beneath these congruent preferences may have been very different on the two sides. They did not agree on longer-term goals, nor did they hold a shared image of how cooperation would impact upon the future strategic environment. Their preferences overlapped, but this may have been simply an artifact, a chance result of how deeper conceptions of interests that were not the same became engaged in a special set of political and technological circumstances.

Cooperation on the basis of complementary interests is prone to be a wasting asset.[44] Two states arrive at a cooperative outcome from different "starting points" of different interests and they agree to cooperate for different reasons. They are brought into a new relationship by a unique set of historical circumstances. Those circumstances are likely to be ephemeral. When they dissipate, there is no longer any basis for cooperation and the agreement is likely to break down. It may break down even sooner, because cooperation on the basis of complementary interests is likely to be vulnerable to exogenous shocks. If neither side gets the benefits it expected from cooperation with a distrusted adversary, no one will work very hard to save it.

In the abstract, cooperation based on complementary interests might be viewed as a way of "buying time" and avoiding a descent into competition long enough to develop a more stable foundation of common interests. In practice, this has not been the pattern in U.S.-Soviet arms control. ASAT may be the premier example. ASAT cooperation made no provisions for developing shared consensual knowledge and common interests; in fact, cooperation depended precisely on avoiding this. The resulting trajectory of cooperation is instructive.

The breakdown of cooperation based on complementary interests tends to have unexpectedly severe consequences for future efforts and for superpower relations generally. Decisionmakers on each side are inclined to suspect that their counterparts have dealt with them in bad faith and that their trust (however minimal) has been betrayed. Perceptions of exploitation lead to changes in the image of the adversary that make cooperation in generic terms look extremely unattractive. In that case, a pow-

---

[44] For a different view, see Wolfe, *The SALT Experience*, pp. 250–51, who argues that arms control cooperation can be sustained on the basis of short-term benefits outweighing costs while bypassing underlying differences of purpose.

erful state with unprecedented capabilities to provide for its own security is almost certain to choose self-help, even if it is a nonoptimal solution to the security problem.[45] It is important to keep in mind that this is not necessarily because the failure of cooperation damages the stability of the nuclear balance in any significant way. Instead, it is the result of contradicted expectations about precisely what cooperation was supposed to achieve, and the political recriminations that follow. That leaves a possible gap, a route for sustaining cooperation that has not been explored. But before I explore it I want to comment on the more direct route to sustainable cooperation, through common interests.

I see three potential ways to lay the groundwork for cooperation through common interests. The first would be for two states to simply start with common interests. That did not happen in U.S.-Soviet arms control for all the obvious reasons: differences in history, culture, ideology, security environment, and so on. The second would be for a natural convergence to take place, bringing two states with initially discrepant consensual knowledge to nearly shared meanings and common interests over time. While some natural convergence seems to have taken place in U.S.-Soviet arms control, the odds are stacked against this route as well. The original divergence among the two sides' beliefs about nuclear weapons was extremely wide. The experience of cooperation over the last decades has not brought them much closer, in part because of the nature of consensual knowledge in strategic nuclear issues and in part due to some of the detrimental legacy of cooperation itself. Bipolarity has not favored convergence or the "mimicking of successful product lines" as it does in the ideal world of the economic market, because there has been no event to distinguish between success and failure.[46] There has been no nuclear war, no failure of deterrence; the apparent robustness of nuclear security means that there is very little pressure to converge. What's more, there are any number of pressures to retain beliefs, ranging from individual cognitive factors to organizational factors and finally to the natural self-help dynamic among powerful states. We should not expect this pattern

[45] Cooperation based on complementary interests may work more effectively as a way of buying time in other issue areas and in multilateral forums, particularly when agreements are aimed only at avoiding shared aversions. Felicia Wong has pointed out to me that a similar pattern may be seen in the story of cooperation among G-7 governments and major corporate lenders in incremental rescheduling of Mexico's debt during the 1980s, which in effect was limited to avoiding the shared aversion of default and financial catastrophe. But as noted in Chapter 1, most of what can be done to avoid the shared aversion of nuclear war the superpowers can do on their own, albeit at greater cost. When agreements go beyond shared aversions, as they must to make arms control worth the trouble, cooperation based on complementary interests gets harder to sustain.

[46] For the classic statement of oligopoly theory on this point, see Fellner, *Competition among the Few*, especially pp. 3–50.

to change very much in the 1990s, even with dramatically reduced tensions in U.S.-Soviet relations. Whatever mild pressure there is that favors natural convergence is bound to be at least matched and probably overcome by new challenges from technological possibilities that will emerge at a more rapid pace in the future.

The final way to reach cooperation on the basis of common interests would be to force convergence through meta-strategy. The prospects here are also doubtful, because meta-strategy has to overcome all the impediments to natural convergence and others as well. Meta-strategy has had to rely on weak tools of verbal and logical persuasion to pit abstract and mostly unfalsifiable arguments against each other in poorly institutionalized channels of communication between two distrustful states. The lessons of history and particularly of the ABM case are again instructive. American decisionmakers found that it was extremely difficult to evaluate the success or failure of efforts at meta-strategy.[47] They also discovered that there was considerable potential for miscues, with the "target" state taking away unintended or inappropriate lessons. Efforts that failed or were suspected to have failed, for whatever reason, were costly later on. Decisionmakers on both sides were inclined to suspect that they had been deceived, that meta-strategy had been aimed at manipulating their behavior in directions that would benefit the manipulator. This helped to fuel sharp turns from cooperation to competition in U.S.-Soviet arms control and in superpower relations more generally, leaving an unhappy legacy not likely to be erased merely by time or even by the expansion of detente in the 1990s.

If forging cooperation based on common interests is not a practicable alternative for U.S.-Soviet arms control, are there ways in which cooperation based on complementary interests can be sustained? Political economists ask an analogous question when they analyze the prospects for extensive and stable trade relations between states with very different domestic economic systems. The U.S.-Japanese relationship is a good example. Stephen Krasner makes the convincing argument that diffuse reciprocity (which concentrates on setting up equitable procedures, the "level playing field") will not produce equitable outcomes in trade between two states with very different domestic structures, because the same rules will lead to discrepant and often incompatible domestic patterns of behavior. He recommends specific reciprocity, by which he means

---

[47] See my discussion in Chapter 4. Uncertainties about the interests that lay behind Moscow's acceptance of the ABM Treaty in 1972 expanded as the decade progressed. The bitter arguments that took place in Washington during the 1980s about Soviet compliance with the treaty were partly a consequence of those uncertainties. For a striking example, see Duffy, *Compliance and the Future of Arms Control.*

sector-specific trade deals focused directly on outcomes that each side finds acceptable on their own terms.[48]

Could a similar approach succeed in U.S.-Soviet arms control? I think not, for theoretical and historical reasons. Defenders of SALT rarely found the agreements' "sector-specific benefits" to be a powerful argument against SALT opponents in Washington. While better outcomes in trade and particularly in any single commodity are easy to quantify, the benefits from specific quantitative deals on different kinds of nuclear delivery systems are open to diverse interpretation. It is also hard to keep sector-specific nuclear deals apart; there is too much inherent linkage between issues. Even the most isolated deal, like the 1987 INF agreement, was closely tied to other strategic issues and could not be treated on its own. In trade, a series of sector-specific agreements, each acceptable on its own terms, might add up to a trade "regime" that was acceptable overall. The same might not be true in arms control. In any case, specific reciprocity in U.S.-Japanese trade has not had convincing success. New issues arise faster than sector-specific deals can be cut, and agreements often obsolesce quickly with changes in technology and market conditions. The same impediments are likely to be even more troubling in U.S.-Soviet arms control.

What is left? Is it possible to achieve and sustain arms control cooperation based on complementary interests in any other way? I believe that it is, because of certain unique characteristics of the nuclear balance that are not reproduced in trade or most other issue areas. The nuclear world is a world of multiple equilibria: there is more than one solution to the problem of deterrence and stability. There may in fact be many solutions, an embarrassment of equilibria. And there is no a priori reason to believe that any particular solution is better than another; *or that the two sides necessarily have to choose the same one.* The United States and the Soviet Union chose different solutions in the early 1970s, each based on its own consensual knowledge. This did not lead to a failure of deterrence. There were other, equally plausible solutions that were not tried. For example, an arms control arrangement that explicitly left both sides free to build as many accurate offensive weapons as they wished might have been equally stable to the SALT I deal, so long as both states moved to insure the invulnerability of essential retaliatory capabilities and command and control facilities.[49] To repeat the point, the ideas and institutions of SALT

---

[48] Krasner, "A Trade Strategy for the United States"; idem, *Assymetries in Japanese-American Trade*. Stretching the analogy, the Structural Impediments Initiative negotiations, which were begun in 1989 with the goal of forcing some degree of convergence between U.S. and Japanese economic "cultures," could be thought of as analogous to meta-strategy in arms control.

[49] These are things each state could have done on its own, if at some expense. The Soviets

were in no sense historical absolutes or an optimal solution to the nuclear security problem.

What overcame the evolution of cooperation under SALT was not asymmetric outcomes in numbers of weapons systems per se. It was not even fundamentally a problem of strategic instabilities. The basic problem, as I noted earlier, was contradicted expectations derived from divergent understandings about what the future of the strategic environment would look like and how arms control cooperation would contribute to it. Cooperation failed in MIRV because no attempt was made to reconcile those expectations and understandings. It succeeded in ASAT at the supposed price of postponing reconciliations into the future, but the real price turned out to be avoiding them entirely and cooperation suffered as a result. It succeeded in ABM because decisionmakers bet that a reconciliation had in fact been achieved in the form of common interests. Subsequent actions by both superpowers that damaged the odds behind that bet played a large part in the demise of detente in the 1970s and severely complicated the possibilities for arms control cooperation in the future.

One solution to the problem stands out in relief from this story. Gaining cooperation on the basis of common interests through diffuse reciprocity seems unlikely; sustaining cooperation on the basis of complementary interests through specific reciprocity seems equally unlikely. The solution must lie elsewhere. I propose achieving cooperation on the basis of complementary interests through something akin to diffuse reciprocity.

It is the unique characteristic of multiple solutions to the nuclear security problem that creates this potential resolution. The nuclear world permits differential effects: in other words, it is possible for each side to choose its own solution based on its own conception of self-interest and to sustain cooperation on that basis. But this is possible only if both sides understand and accept those conceptions of interest in a way that permits decisionmakers to comprehend the significance of the other state's actions and predict how it is likely to behave in the future. The central point is that the United States and Soviet Union need *not* share the same consensual knowledge to sustain cooperation through this route. What they must share is a joint understanding of each other's consensual knowledge and resultant expectations about the future of the strategic environment. This is a different solution than any thus far tried in U.S.-Soviet relations. Is it possible to conquer the history of SALT and explore it?

---

went partly in this direction by moving toward mobile ICBMS, while the United States demurred. The Soviets essentially solved the "window of vulnerability" problem on their own. In contrast, Washington's efforts to enlist Moscow's help in solving its Minuteman vulnerability problem have probably been the single largest proximal cause of dissension in the arms control relationship for the past 20 years, and it is likely to continue to be a problem in the 1990s. For further discussion, see my "Cooperation and Interdependence."

Arms Control, Cooperation, and the Future of U.S.-Soviet Relations

The year 1989 was one of great change in U.S.-Soviet relations. While arms control was not an important cause of that change it may well be a beneficiary. Both U.S. and Soviet leaders now seem to accept that there are new opportunities and unprecedented economic and political incentives to capitalize on them. But the experience of the last 20 years should put a damper on enthusiasm. There is no reason to suspect that the legacy of SALT has been overcome. The several routes by which cooperation can fail remain, as does the potential for arms control failures to damage political aspects of U.S.-Soviet relations. The point may seem banal, but it is important to remember that arms control cooperation should contribute to positive developments in security and overall U.S.-Soviet relations. Otherwise, both states would be better off taking care of their security needs entirely on their own.

There is real potential for arms control cooperation to suffer another cycle of volatility, with detrimental consequences for the broader range of U.S.-Soviet relations. The several sources of volatility discussed earlier in this chapter are still in place. There are already specific weapons systems on the agenda that could turn out to be new missed opportunities of substantial importance. For example, what will the United States and later the Soviets do with nuclear-tipped SLCMs? What will be the future of land-based mobile ICBMs, with multiple or single warheads? Neither side seems to have clearly defined its own interests with regard to these weapons, and there is no reason to suspect that they will come to the same conclusions. Institutional mechanisms for developing shared expectations about the future of the strategic environment under these conditions remain weak. Paradoxically, the massive changes in Europe that took place in 1990 may soon make this problem worse. What in the short run looks like a positive sea-change in the security environment in Europe may in a few years look much less positive as new problems arise. U.S. and Soviet leaders will continue to worry about security in Europe but may again find themselves with very different understandings and expectations, and only the weakest means to reconcile them.

Even if political relations continue to improve in Europe, the problem of discrepant understandings is likely to intensify in the future. One of the effects of increasingly rapid technological change is that the gap between what is feasible and the subset of technological possibilities that states actually embody in their military forces will grow. At least in the West, commercial technology now leads military technology in many important sectors. This means that there will be a host of new technological possibilities for weapons systems, a greater proportion of which will remain unexplored and undeveloped. States will have to worry about which technologies other states have chosen to work with and why. At best, the stage is set for cooperation under radical uncertainty. SALT failed to handle less difficult challenges of the same sort in the 1970s. SALT institutions inhibited learning by each state, did not provide an adequate forum for the sides to explore each other's understanding of interests, and did not beget any sources of innovation outside national boundaries. The result was a series of misunderstandings, disappointed expectations, and "partial deals" that barely evolved. This legacy does not bode well for the future.

In the last section, I argued that arms control cooperation could develop more effectively through a different route than that which was institutionalized under SALT. The solution I proposed might be labeled "expected diversity." The basic notion was that nuclear security did not depend upon the two sides sharing the same conceptions of self-interest. Convergence of consensual knowledge is unlikely but it is also unnecessary. Because the nuclear security problem is one of multiple equilibria, it is possible for the sides to choose different solutions and sustain cooperation on that basis, so long as they understand the logic of the other side's solution and the behavior it entails. This might reduce the scope of attempts to cooperate in U.S.-Soviet arms control, but that is less important than what "expected diversity" could do to ameliorate the cycles of volatility that have so far plagued the effort.

In practical terms, there would be two facets to reorienting arms control cooperation on this basis. The first would be to establish a knowledge-based international regime, a set of institutions designed to educate decisionmakers on each side about the conceptions of self-interest in nuclear weapons held by the other. The second would be to change domestic institutions so that each state could more effectively implement strategies of enhanced contingent restraint, to capitalize on the possibilities for cooperation that would be opened up by the first.

A "Knowledge"-Based Regime: Joint Strategic Research

Instead of focusing efforts on reducing the numbers of specific weapons systems, the United States and Soviet Union should begin an extensive program of joint research in the most basic issues of strategic theory. Joint strategic research should be the primary agenda for arms control, and it should take place within an ongoing dialogue involving high-level military and civilian officials. The principal objective would be to render each side's conceptions of self-interest in nuclear security issues more transparent to the other. The practical goal would be to develop symmetrical expectations about each side's future behavior, based on shared understandings about what is and is not the same in the two sides' consensual knowledge about nuclear weapons.[50]

The purpose of joint strategic research would be to reduce the sources of volatility in U.S.-Soviet arms control cooperation. One way in which a knowledge-based regime might do that would be to insure that the working hypotheses about interests that support attempts to gain cooperation in specific cases are closer to being correct. The trajectory of any cooperative deals would then tend not to undermine but instead to reinforce those working hypotheses, because expectations about how cooperation will contribute to change in the strategic environment would come closer to being fulfilled. Cooperation would rest on joint understandings about what each side was giving up, what each was likely to do in the future, and most importantly, why. The scope of arms control would probably decline in the short run, but agreements that were achieved would probably be more stable.

In the longer run, a regime based on joint strategic research could more effectively deal with the consequences for cooperation of rapid technological change. Opportunities like ABM, a story of cooperation that was achieved under moderate uncertainty and sustained for a relatively long period of time, will be less common in the future. Instead, the future is

---

[50] There have in fact been a few semiofficial channels where something like joint strategic research has been taking place for some time: in addition to groups like International Pugwash and the Dartmouth Task Force on Arms Control, the U.S. and Soviet Academies of Sciences in 1981 established a standing Committee on International Security and Arms Control that has focused to some degree on very basic questions of strategic thought and the impact of new technological possibilities on it. Wolfgang K. H. Panofsky, "The Activities of CISAC" (Manuscript; Stanford, Calif. March 3, 1989). At the official level in the United States at least, there has generally been little enthusiasm for ongoing dialogue; interest has mostly been confined to short-term and temporary contacts seen as potentially useful for exploring a limited set of issues relating to particular weapons systems. Military officials have been extremely reluctant to engage in any such contacts until quite recently. In 1988, Secretary of Defense Frank Carlucci and Soviet Minister of Defense Dmitri T. Yazov met twice for the express purpose of discussing "the substance of USSR and US military doctrines" in nuclear and other issues. Admiral William Crowe, Jr., and Marshal Sergei Akhromeyev, Chairman of the JCS and Chief of the General Staff respectively, followed with an exchange of visits in July 1988 and June 1989. In January 1990, U.S. and Soviet military chiefs met (along with top military officials from nations involved in the ongoing Conference on Security and Cooperation in Europe) in Vienna to continue a "closed door seminar" on military doctrine. John Cushman, "Carlucci Says Soviet Talks Built Bridge," *New York Times*, 18 March 1988, p. 1; Michael Gordon, "Soviets Are Still Stockpiling Ammunition, US Reports," *New York Times*, 11 January 1990, p. A9; Alan Riding, "Military Chiefs of East and West Meet to Discuss Europe's Security," *New York Times*, 17 January 1990, p. 1. For a discussion of earlier military-to-military contacts and some of the difficult political issues involved, see Campbell, "The Soldier's Summit."

likely to be made up of more ASAT-like stories of radical uncertainty. Joint investigation into the strategic implications of emerging technological possibilities and the opportunities for limiting undesirable effects might encourage new agreements that would block off certain areas while permitting both sides to go forward in others. This kind of agreement could be stable if two conditions were met. First, each side would have to know better than they have in the past precisely what the other understood the terms of the deal to be. Second, substantive linkages to other issues, such as the tie between ASAT and military satellites, could not be passed over, postponed indefinitely, or assigned to each side to deal with on the basis of its own strategic logic, opaque to the other side. Joint strategic research could foster both conditions.

Joint strategic research is the logical institutional structure to support a regime of cooperation through expected diversity. But it is also possible that this institution and its regime could itself evolve over time. I noted earlier that the sources of innovation in U.S.-Soviet arms control, new ideas about cooperation, have until now been confined within national boundaries. Under SALT, that had a number of harmful results: it led to a weak international regime with strong domestic reflections that fostered cooperation on the basis of complementary interests and may have inhibited learning. In the short term, the purpose of joint strategic research would be to conquer that legacy. It would facilitate communication about ideas and conceptions of self-interest, and enhance transparency about the learning processes of the two states, without necessarily trying to bring them into congruence.

Yet such congruency might well be an unintended consequence. Until now the United States and the Soviet Union have undergone critical learning periods—during which conceptions of self-interest in nuclear security shifted dramatically—at different times and with different results. I traced some of this asynchrony to the unusual characteristics of consensual knowledge in the nuclear realm. An institution that focused attention directly on that consensual knowledge might not abolish critical learning periods (after all, we don't yet fully understand what causes them) but it might make each side more aware of their existence and timing. The possibilities for at least partial convergence of consensual knowledge during such windows would then seem to increase. It is also possible that institutions for joint strategic research would serve a *creative* function in and of themselves, developing new ideas and acting as a source of innovation outside the national boundaries of the two states. If that were to occur in arms control while the learning processes of the two sides were becoming more nearly synchronized, it is at least possible that cooperation could evolve from a foundation of expected diversity to one of shared meanings over time. It is possible, but cooperation should not and need not depend on it in the short term.

Enhanced Contingent Restraint

Joint strategic research could establish a foundation for sustained cooperation in U.S.-Soviet arms control, but the two sides would still have to reach agreement on specific weapons systems and technologies. Many of the emerging challenges will probably resemble PD games, where both sides will have substantial incentives to defect and pursue some unilateral advantage. I have shown that cooperation is possible in this kind of arms control game where the initial conditions of Axelrod's model are met, but that it is by no means inevitable. Strategy is a critical variable that intervenes between structural possibilities and successful cooperation. As an ideal type, enhanced contingent restraint is the most effective means to promote cooperation in U.S.-Soviet arms control.

The key element in enhanced contingent restraint is that which makes it "enhanced": a set of visibly credible options that a state can use to respond to defections or to limited probes by the other side, without undermining possibilities for returning to mutual restraint. The point is to demonstrate that a decision not to move forward with a particular weapons system is in fact conditional on reciprocal restraint from the other side and that the state playing the strategy is "unexploitable." From a practical standpoint, this is not always easy to do. There are some specific steps that the United States, at least, could take to make it easier.

The most direct way to establish a strategy of enhanced contingent restraint is to develop the necessary infrastructure that would facilitate future decisions to compensate for defection. In ABM, the early phases of Safeguard did precisely this; another example is the "JCS safeguards" that President Kennedy set up in conjunction with the Limited Test Ban Treaty of 1963.[51] In the future it will be necessary to take other steps of this kind, some of which are likely to be expensive. In seeking further limitations on mobile land-based ICBMs, for example, it would serve the United States to maintain an infrastructure of production facilities for a viable system that could be brought on line relatively quickly. Short-term investments in demonstrating the conditional nature of restraint will re-

---

[51] In addition to continuing a vigorous underground testing program for nuclear warheads, the United States made special provisions to maintain aircraft and other facilities that could be used for a resumption of atmospheric tests on relatively short notice. George Bunn (former chief counsel to ACDA), personal communication, June 1988. See also *Military Implications of the Proposed Limited Test Ban Treaty: An Interim Report*, pp. 16–24.

pay themselves by obviating the need to pay the much more expensive costs of missed opportunities for cooperation later on.

The current Pentagon weapons procurement system is a major obstacle to policies based on this kind of reasoning. Generally speaking, that system treats the defense acquisition process as a pipeline: it is thought to function best when research and development goes in at one end and weapons come out the other. The measure of success for any program is whether fully deployed weapons systems actually materialize; a program that does not proceed to deployment is considered a failure (as is the program officer who was in charge of it). Institutional changes could counteract some of these tendencies. For example, career incentives for program managers could be restructured so that rewards are less focused on bringing systems through to deployment. Funding for research and development, which in the late 1980s frequently suffered disproportionately at the hands of Pentagon budget cutters, could be given a much higher priority (particularly if the time-urgency of threats continues to decline). This could help solve an important dilemma facing major defense contractors, which currently fund with their own resources much of the research and development costs for new weapons systems up through the prototype stage, with the expectation that costs will be recouped when the weapon goes into production. If many weapons are going to be brought up through the system and then put on hold *prior* to the production stage, that funding mechanism will have to be revamped.[52] The Pentagon will have to pay to maintain research and development capabilities and most importantly a production infrastructure as well, to support the credibility of enhanced contingent restraint over the long term.

Domestic politics and the diverse demands of the Washington bureaucracies are further obstacles. Still, there are reasons to believe that both can be handled effectively by a strong president. To forge and sustain a public consensus to support this kind of strategy, with its high instrumental costs, will require consistent and confident leadership that can explain to diverse audiences why we must spend money in support of cooperative restraint. The three case studies in this book, and the more recent history of U.S.-Soviet arms control, suggest that this is not at all impossible. Bureaucratic politics remain a formidable challenge, but it may now be somewhat easier to manage in practice than it was in the 1970s. The pivotal issue here is *consistency*: the effectiveness of any contingent strategy can be severely degraded by conflicting signals. The experience of the last decades will help here, as will the dramatically increased level of transparency in U.S.-Soviet relations. Experience and transparency together mean better communication, and it is less likely that an isolated, discrep-

---

[52] I am indebted to Richard Wagner for many of the ideas presented here.

ant signal from a bureaucratic player on one side would in the future set off a "worst-case scenario" response in the other. International institutions for joint strategic research can play an important role here as well. If the Soviets understand the interests that lie behind American strategy, communication will be that much less tenuous. The prospects for cooperation will increase accordingly.

There are several different ways to think about the problem of cooperation between states. My goal in this book was to force a formal model of cooperation in the PD to confront a set of historical cases from U.S.-Soviet arms control, and to expand the model so that it could explain why these two states have sometimes been able to achieve cooperation under the most difficult circumstances. By developing a more elaborate model I have also underscored the limits of its own applicability. The prospects for cooperation in the U.S.-Soviet nuclear security relationship are less extensive than what might have been suggested by Axelrod's intriguing "solution" to the problem of cooperation in the PD. Even in a world of robust nuclear parity, the United States and the Soviet Union will each retain principal responsibility for their own security. Yet within that world there is space for cooperation, and some of that space has not yet been explored.

References

Books

Allen, Jonathan, ed. *March 4: Scientists, Students, and Society*. Cambridge: MIT Press, 1970.

Arrow, Kenneth. *Social Choice and Individual Values*. New York: Wiley, 1963.

Art, Robert J., and Waltz, Kenneth N., eds. *The Use of Force: International Politics and Foreign Policy*. Boston: Little, Brown, 1971.

Art, Robert J.; Davis, Vincent; and Huntington, Samuel P., eds. *Reorganizing America's Defense: Leadership in War and Peace*. Washington, D.C.: Pergammon-Brassey's, 1985.

Axelrod, Robert. *The Evolution of Cooperation*. New York: Basic Books, 1984.

Bacharach, Samuel B., and Lawler, Edward J. *Bargaining: Power, Tactics, and Outcomes*. San Francisco: Jossey-Bass, 1981.

Baker, David. *The Shape of Wars to Come*. New York: Stein and Day, 1982.

Ball, D. *Politics and Force Levels: The Strategic Missile Program of the Kennedy Administration*. Berkeley: University of California Press, 1980.

Berman, R. P., and Baker, J. C. *Soviet Strategic Forces: Requirements and Responses*. Washington, D.C.: Brookings, 1982.

Betts, Richard K. *Nuclear Blackmail and Nuclear Balance*. Washington, D.C.: Brookings, 1987.

Blacker, Coit, and Duffy, Gloria, eds. *International Arms Control: Issues and Agreements*. Stanford, Calif.: Stanford University Press, 1985.

Blalock, Hubert M., and Blalock, Ann B., eds. *Methodology in Social Research*. New York: McGraw-Hill, 1968.

Bilder, Richard B. *Managing the Risks of International Agreement*. Madison: University of Wisconsin Press, 1981.

Brams, Steven. *Superpower Games*. New Haven: Yale University Press, 1985.

Brennan, Donald G., ed. *Arms Control, Disarmament, and National Security*. New York: G. Braziller, 1961.

Breslauer, George, and Tetlock, Phillip, eds. *Learning in US and Soviet Foreign Policy*. Boulder, Colo.: Westview, forthcoming.

Bruner, Jerome S.; Goodnow, Jacqueline S.; and Austin, George A. *A Study of Thinking*. New York: Wiley, 1956.

Bueno de Mesquita, Bruce. *The War Trap*. New Haven: Yale University Press, 1981.

Bull, Hedley. *The Control of the Arms Race: Disarmament and Arms Control in the Missile Age*. London: Weidenfeld and Nicholson, 1961.

Caldwell, Dan. *American-Soviet Relations from 1947 to the Nixon-Kissinger Grand Design*. Westport, Conn.: Greenwood, 1981.

Caldwell, Dan, ed. *Soviet International Behavior and U.S. Policy Options.* Lexington, Mass.: Lexington, 1985.

Carter, Ashton B., and Schwartz, David N. *Ballistic Missile Defense.* Washington, D.C.: Brookings, 1984.

Cohen, Raymond. *International Politics: The Rules of the Game.* London: Longman, 1981.

Collier, Ruth Berins, and Collier, David. *Shaping the Political Arena: Critical Junctures, the Labor Movement, and Regime Dynamics in Latin America.* Princeton: Princeton University Press, forthcoming.

Craig, Gordon A., and George, Alexander L. *Force and Statecraft: Diplomatic Problems of Our Time.* New York: Oxford University Press, 1983.

Deane, Michael J. *The Role of Strategic Defense in Soviet Strategy.* Miami: Current Affairs Press for the Advanced International Studies Institute, University of Miami, 1980.

Duffy, Gloria, ed. *Compliance and the Future of Arms Control.* Cambridge, Mass.: Ballinger, 1988.

Eisenhower, Dwight David. *Waging Peace 1956–61: The White House Years.* Garden City, N.Y.: Doubleday, 1965.

Enthoven, Alan, and Smith, K. Wayne. *How Much Is Enough? Shaping the Defense Program 1961–1969.* New York: Harper and Row, 1971.

Fellner, William. *Competition among the Few: Oligopoly and Similar Market Structures.* New York: Knopf, 1949.

Freedman, Lawrence. *US Intelligence and the Soviet Strategic Threat.* London: Macmillan, 1977.

———. *The Evolution of Nuclear Strategy.* New York: St. Martin's, 1981.

Frye, Alton. *A Responsible Congress: The Politics of National Security.* New York: McGraw Hill, 1975.

Gaddis, John Lewis. *Strategies of Containment: A Critical Appraisal of Postwar American National Security Policy.* New York: Oxford University Press, 1982.

Garthoff, Raymond L. *Detente and Confrontation: American-Soviet Relations from Nixon to Reagan.* Washington, D.C.: Brookings, 1985.

Gelman, Harry. *The Brezhnev Politburo and the Decline of Detente.* Ithaca, N.Y.: Cornell University Press, 1984.

George, Alexander L. *Managing US-Soviet Rivalry: Problems of Crisis Prevention.* Boulder, Colo.: Westview, 1983.

George, Alexander L., and Smoke, Richard. *Deterrence in American Foreign Policy: Theory and Practice.* New York: Columbia University Press, 1974.

George, Alexander L.; Farley, Philip J.; and Dallin, Alexander, eds. *US-Soviet Security Cooperation: Achievements, Failures, Lessons.* New York: Oxford University Press, 1988.

Gergen, Kenneth J.; Greenberg, Martin; and Wills, Richard H. *Social Exchange: Advances in Theory and Research.* New York: Plenum, 1980.

Giffen, Colonel Robert B. *US Space System Survivability: Strategic Alternatives for the 1990s.* National Security Affairs Monograph Series 82–4. Washington, D.C.: National Defense University Press, 1984.

Gilpin, Robert. *American Scientists and Nuclear Weapons Policy*. Princeton: Princeton University Press, 1962.

———. *War and Change in World Politics*. Cambridge: Cambridge University Press, 1981.

Goulding, Phil G. *Confirm or Deny: Informing the People on National Security*. New York: Harper and Row, 1970.

Gray, Colin S. *The Future of Land-Based Missile Forces*. Adelphi Paper No. 140. London: International Institute for Strategic Studies, 1977.

Gray, Colin S. *The Geopolitics of the Nuclear Era: Heartland, Rimland, and the Technological Revolution*. New York: Crane, Russak, 1977.

Greenwood, Ted. *Making the MIRV: A Study of Defense Decision Making*. Cambridge, Mass.: Ballinger, 1975.

Haas, Ernst B. *When Knowledge Is Power*. Berkeley: University of California Press, 1990.

Halperin, Morton. *Bureaucratic Politics and Foreign Policy*. Washington, D.C.: Brookings, 1974.

Hardin, Russell. *Collective Action*. Baltimore: Johns Hopkins University Press, 1982.

Harsanyi, John C. *Rational Behavoir and Bargaining Equilibrium in Games and Social Situations*. New York: Cambridge University Press, 1977.

Heikal, Mohamed. *The Road to Ramadan*. New York: Quadrangle/New York Times Book Co., 1975.

Hempel, Carl G. *Philosophy of Natural Science*. Englewood Cliffs, N.J.: Prentice-Hall, 1966.

Hersh, Seymour. *The Price of Power: Kissinger in the Nixon White House*. New York: Summit Books, 1983.

Holbraad, Carsten. *The Concert of Europe*. London: Longman, 1970.

Holloway, David. *The Soviet Union and the Arms Race*. New Haven: Yale University Press, 1983.

Holsti, Ole R.; Siverson, Randolph M.; and George, Alexander L., eds. *Change in the International System*. Boulder, Colo.: Westview, 1980.

Horelick, Arnold, and Rush, Myron. *Strategic Power and Soviet Foreign Policy*. Chicago: University of Chicago Press, 1966.

Ikle, Fred. *How Nations Negotiate*. New York: Praeger, 1967.

International Institute for Strategic Studies. *The Military Balance*. London: IISS (various years).

Jane's Weapons Systems. Boston: Science Books International (various years).

Jasani, Bhupendra, ed. *Outer Space: A New Dimension of the Arms Race*. London: Taylor and Francis, 1982.

Jayne, Edward Randolph. *The ABM Debate: Strategic Defense and National Security*. Cambridge: MIT Center for International Studies, 1969.

Jenks, C. Wilfred. *Space Law*. New York: Praeger, 1965.

Johnson, Lyndon B. *The Vantage Point*. New York: Holt, Rinehart, and Winston, 1971.

Johnson, Nicholas. *The Soviet Year in Space*. Boulder, Colo.: Teledyne Brown Engineering (various years).

Kahan, Jerome H. *Limited Agreements and Long Term Stability: A Positive View toward SALT.* Washington, D.C.: Brookings, 1972.

———. *Security in the Nuclear Age: Developing US Strategic Arms Policy.* Washington, D.C.: Brookings, 1975.

Kahneman, D.; Slovic, P.; and Tversky, A., eds. *Judgement under Uncertainty: Heuristics and Biases.* New York: Cambridge University Press, 1982.

Kaplan, Lawrence S. *The United States and NATO: The Formative Years.* Lexington: University Press of Kentucky, 1984.

———. *NATO and the United States: The Enduring Alliance.* Boston: Twayne, 1988.

Keohane, Robert O. *After Hegemony: Cooperation and Discord in the World Political Economy.* Princeton: Princeton University Press, 1984.

Killian, J. R. *Sputnik, Scientists, and Eisenhower.* Cambridge: MIT Press, 1977.

Kissinger, Henry. *White House Years.* Boston: Little, Brown, 1979.

Kistiakowsky, George. *A Scientist at the White House: The Private Diary of President Eisenhower's Special Assistant for Science and Technology.* Cambridge: Harvard University Press, 1976.

Klass, P. *Secret Sentries in Space.* New York: Random House, 1970.

Krasner, Stephen. *Assymetries in Japanese-American Trade: The Case for Specific Reciprocity.* Policy Paper in International Affairs no. 32. Berkeley: Institute for International Studies, 1987.

Krasner, Stephen, ed. *International Regimes.* Ithaca, N.Y.: Cornell University Press, 1983.

Krass, Allan S. *Verification: How Much Is Enough?* Stockholm: Stockholm International Peace Research Institute, 1985.

Labrie, Roger P., ed. *SALT Handbook: Key Documents and Issues.* Washington, D.C.: American Enterprise Institute, 1979.

Lapp, Ralph. *Arms Beyond Doubt: The Tyranny of Weapons Technology.* New York: Cowles, 1970.

Lauren, Paul Gordon, ed. *Diplomacy: New Approaches in History, Theory, and Policy.* New York: Free Press, 1979.

Levine, Arthur. *The Future of the US Space Program.* New York: Praeger, 1975.

Logsdon, John. *The Decision to Go to the Moon: Project Apollo and the National Interest.* Cambridge: MIT Press, 1970.

Long, Franklyn A., and Rathjens, George, eds. *Arms, Defense Policy, and Arms Control.* New York: Norton, 1976.

Long, Franklyn A.; Hafner, Donald; and Boutwell, Jeffrey, eds. *Weapons in Space.* New York: Norton, 1986.

Luce, R. Duncan, and Raiffa, Howard. *Games and Decisions.* New York: Wiley, 1957.

MccGwire, Michael. *Military Objectives in Soviet Foreign Policy.* Washington, D.C.: Brookings, 1987.

McDougall, Walter A. *The Heavens and the Earth: A Political History of the Space Age.* New York: Basic Books, 1985.

McNamara, Robert S. *The Essence of Security: Reflections in Office.* New York: Harper and Row, 1968.

Myers, Kenneth A., and Simes, Dmitri. *Soviet Decision Making, Strategic Policy, and SALT*. Washington, D.C.: Center for Strategic and International Studies, 1974.

National Academy of Sciences, Committee on International Security and Arms Control. *Nuclear Arms Control: Background and Issues*. Washington, D.C.: National Academy Press, 1985.

Newhouse, John. *Cold Dawn: The Story of SALT*. New York: Holt, Rinehart, and Winston, 1973.

Newsom, David D. *Private Diplomacy with the Soviet Union*. Lanham, Md.: University Press of America, 1987.

Nixon, Richard M. *R.N.: The Memoirs of Richard Nixon*. New York: Grosset and Dunlap, 1978.

Nye, Joseph S., and Schear, James A., eds. *Seeking Stability in Space: Anti-Satellite Weapons and the Evolving Space Regime*. Lanham, Md.: University Press of America, 1987.

Ordeshook, Peter C. *Game Theory and Political Theory*. Cambridge: Cambridge University Press, 1986.

Oye, Kenneth A., ed. *Cooperation under Anarchy*. Princeton: Princeton University Press, 1986.

Oye, Kenneth A.; Lieber, Robert J.; and Rothchild, Donald, eds. *Eagle Defiant: United States Foreign Policy in the 1980s*. Boston: Little, Brown, 1983.

Parrott, Bruce. *The Soviet Union and Ballistic Missile Defense*. Boulder, Colo.: Westview, 1987.

Pickering, Andrew. *Constructing Quarks: A Sociological History of Particle Physics*. Chicago: University of Chicago Press, 1984.

Posen, Barry R. *The Sources of Military Doctrine*. Ithaca, N.Y.: Cornell University Press, 1984.

Potter, William, ed. *SALT and Verification*. Boulder, Colo.: Westview, 1980.

Prados, John. *The Soviet Estimate: US Intelligence Analysis and the Russian Military Strength*. New York: Dial, 1982.

Prigogine, Ilya. *From Being to Becoming: Time and Complexity in the Physical Sciences*. San Francisco: Freeman, 1980.

Prigogine, Ilya, and Stengers, Isabelle. *Order Out of Chaos: Man's New Dialogue with Nature*. Boulder, Colo.: Random House for New Science Library, 1984.

Rathjens, George W. *The Future of the Strategic Arms Race: Options for the 1970s*. New York: Carnegie Endowment for International Peace, 1969.

Richelson, Jeffrey. *The US Intelligence Community*. Cambridge, Mass.: Ballinger, 1985.

Rostow, W. W. *The Diffusion of Power: An Essay in Recent History*. New York: MacMillan, 1972.

———. *Open Skies: Eisenhower's Proposal of July 21, 1955*. Austin: University of Texas Press, 1982.

Sadat, Anwar. *In Search of Identity: An Autobiography*. New York: Harper and Row, 1978.

Sagan, Scott. *Moving Targets: Nuclear Strategy and National Security*. Princeton: Princeton University Press, 1989.

Schell, Jonathan. *The Fate of the Earth*. New York: Knopf, 1982.

————. *The Abolition*. New York: Knopf, 1984.

Schelling, Thomas C. *The Strategy of Conflict*. London: Oxford University Press, 1960.

Schelling, Thomas C., and Halperin, Morton. *Strategy and Arms Control*. Washington, D.C.: Pergamon-Brassey's, 1965.

Schlesinger, Arthur M., Jr. *A Thousand Days*. Boston: Houghton Mifflin, 1965.

Schoenbaum, Thomas. *Waging Peace and War: Dean Rusk in the Truman, Kennedy, and Johnson Years*. New York: Simon and Schuster, 1988.

Seaborg, Glenn T. *Kennedy, Khrushchev, and the Test Ban*. Berkeley: University of California Press, 1983.

Shevchenko, Arkady N. *Breaking with Moscow*. New York: Knopf, 1985.

Sloss, Leon, and Davis, M. Scott. *A Game for High Stakes: Lessons Learned in Negotiating with the Soviet Union*. Cambridge, Mass.: Ballinger, 1986.

Smith, Gerard. *Doubletalk: The Story of SALT I*. New York: Doubleday, 1980.

Snyder, Glenn H., and Diesing, Paul. *Conflict among Nations: Bargaining, Decisionmaking, and System Structure in International Crises*. Princeton: Princeton University Press, 1977.

Sorensen, Theodore C. *Kennedy*. New York: Harper and Row, 1965.

Stares, Paul B. *The Militarization of Space: US Policy 1945–85*. Ithaca, N.Y.: Cornell University Press, 1985.

————. *Space and National Security*. Washington, D.C.: Brookings, 1987.

Steinberg, Gerald M. *Satellite Reconnaissance: The Role of Informal Bargaining*. New York: Praeger, 1983.

Steinbruner, John D. *The Cybernetic Theory of Decision: New Dimensions of Political Analysis*. Princeton: Princeton University Press, 1974.

Stern, Paul; Axelrod, Robert; Jervis, Robert; and Radner, Roy. *Perspectives on Deterrence*. New York: Oxford University Press, 1989.

Sturm, Thomas A. *The USAF Scientific Advisory Board: Its First Twenty Years 1944–64*. Washington, D.C.: USAF Historical Division Liaison Office, 1967.

Talbott, Strobe. *Endgame: The Inside Story of SALT II*. New York: Harper and Row, 1979.

————. *Master of the Game: Paul Nitze and the Nuclear Peace*. New York: Knopf, 1988.

Tammen, Ronald. *MIRV and the Arms Race: An Interpretation of Defense Strategy*. New York: Praeger, 1973.

Taylor, Michael. *Anarchy and Cooperation*. New York: Wiley, 1976.

Tetlock, Philip; Husbands, Jo L.; Jervis, Robert; Stern, Paul; and Tilly, Charles, eds. *Behavior, Society, and Nuclear War*, Vol 1. New York: Oxford University Press, 1989. Vol 2, forthcoming.

Thompson, J.M.T., and Stewart, H. B. *Nonlinear Dynamics and Chaos*. New York: Wiley, 1986.

Ury, William. *Beyond the Hotline*. Boston: Houghton Mifflin, 1985.

Von Neumann, John, and Morgenstern, Oscar. *Theory of Games and Economic Behavior*. Princeton: Princeton University Press, 1944.

Walt, Stephen. *The Origins of Alliances.* Ithaca, N.Y.: Cornell University Press, 1987.

Waltz, Kenneth N. *Man, State, and War: A Theoretical Analysis.* New York: Columbia University Press, 1959.

———. *Theory of International Politics.* Reading, Mass.: Addison-Wesley, 1979.

Weihmiller, Gordon R., and Doder, Dusko. *US-Soviet Summits: An Account of East-West Diplomacy at the Top.* Washington, D.C.: Institute for the Study of Diplomacy, 1986.

Wiesner, Jerome. *Where Science and Politics Meet.* New York: McGraw-Hill, 1965.

Wolfe, Thomas W. *Soviet Strategy at the Crossroads.* Cambridge: Harvard University Press, 1964.

———. *Soviet Power and Europe, 1945–1970.* Baltimore: Johns Hopkins University Press, 1970.

———. *The SALT Experience: Its Impact on US and Soviet Strategic Policy and Decision Making.* Cambridge, Mass.: Ballinger, 1979.

Yanarella, Ernest J. *The Missile Defense Controversy: Strategy, Technology, and Politics, 1955–1972.* Lexington: University Press of Kentucky, 1977.

York, Herbert. *Race to Oblivion.* New York: Simon and Schuster, 1970.

Zoller, Elisabeth. *Peacetime Unilateral Remedies.* Dobbs Ferry, N.Y.: Transnational Publishers, 1984.

Zumwalt, Elmo R. *On Watch: A Memoir.* New York: New York Times Book Co., 1976.

Articles and Papers

In addition to the articles listed, I have made extensive use of articles from contemporary newspapers and periodicals, including but not limited to the following: *Aerospace Daily, Air Force Magazine, Astronautics, Aviation Week and Space Technology, Boston Globe, Bulletin of the Atomic Scientists, Defense Week, Foreign Affairs, Foreign Broadcast Information Service Daily Reports, Foreign Policy, Fortune Magazine, International Affairs, International Herald Tribune, Izvestia, Life, Los Angeles Times, Military Thought, Newsweek Magazine, New York Times, Pravda, Science, Science News, Signal, Space/Aeronautics, Technology Week, Time Magazine, US News & World Report, Washington Post, Wall Street Journal.*

Achen, Christopher. "When Is a State with Bureaucratic Politics Representable as a Unitary Rational Actor?" Manuscript, 1989.

Adams, Benson D. "McNamara's ABM Policy 1961–1967," *Orbis* 12 (Spring 1968).

Alexander, A. "Decision Making in Soviet Weapons Procurement." Adelphi Paper no. 147, International Institute for Strategic Studies, Winter 1978–79.

Axelrod, Robert. "Effective Choice in the Prisoner's Dilemma." *Journal of Conflict Resolution* 24 (March 1980).

Beer, Francis A. "Games and Metaphors." *Journal of Conflict Resolution* 30 (March 1986).

Buchheim, Robert W., and Caldwell, Dan. "The US-USSR Standing Consultative

Commission: Description and Appraisal." Working Paper no. 2, Center for Foreign Policy Development, Brown University, May 1983.

Campbell, Kurt M. "The Soldier's Summit." *Foreign Policy* 75 (Summer 1989).

Carter, Ashton B. "Satellites and Anti-Satellites: The Limits of the Possible." *International Security* 10 (Spring 1986).

Crawford, Vincent P. "Dynamic Games and Dynamic Contract Theory." *Journal of Conflict Resolution* 29 (June 1985).

Gaddis, John Lewis. "The Long Peace." *International Security* 10 (Spring 1986).

Gardner, R. N. "Cooperation in Outer Space." *Foreign Affairs* 41 (January 1963).

Garthoff, Raymond. "SALT I: An Evaluation." *World Politics* 31 (October 1978).

———. "Banning the Bomb in Outer Space." *International Security* 5 (Winter 1980–81).

———. "ASAT Arms Control: Still Possible." *Bulletin of the Atomic Scientists* 40 (August/September 1984).

Garwin, Richard L.; Gottfried, Kurt; and Hafner, Donald. "Anti-satellite Weapons." *Scientific American* 250 (June 1984).

Gould, Stephen Jay. "Is a New and General Theory of Evolution Emerging?" *Paleobiology* 6 (Winter 1980).

Gouldner, Alvin. "The Norm of Reciprocity." *American Sociological Review* 25 (April 1960).

Gowa, Joanne. "Anarchy, Egoism, and Third Images: *The Evolution of Cooperation* and International Relations." *International Organization* 40 (Winter 1986).

Graybeal, Sidney N., and Goure, Daniel. "Soviet Ballistic Missile Defense Objectives: Past, Present, and Future." In *U.S. Arms Control Objectives and the Implications for Ballistic Missile Defense*, Proceedings of a Symposium at the Center for Science and International Affairs, Harvard University, November 1–2, 1979. Boston: Puritan Press, 1980.

Graybeal, Sidney N., and Krepon, Michael. "Making Better Use of the Standing Consultative Commission." *International Security* 9 (Fall 1985).

Greenwood, Ted. "Reconnaissance and Arms Control." *Scientific American* 228 (February 1973).

Grieco, Joseph M. "Anarchy and the Limits of Cooperation: A Realist Critique of the Newest Liberal Institutionalism." *International Organization* 42 (Summer 1988).

Haas, Ernst B. "Why Collaborate? Issue-Linkage and International Regimes." *World Politics* 32 (Spring 1980).

Haas, Peter M. "Do Regimes Matter? Epistemic Communities and Mediterranean Polution Control." *International Organization* 43 (Summer 1989).

Hafner, Donald. "Averting a Brobdingnagian Skeet Shoot: Arms Control Measures for Anti-satellite Weapons." *International Security* 5 (Winter 1980–81).

Halperin, Morton. "The Gaither Committee and the Policy Process." *World Politics* 13 (April 1961).

———. "The Decision to Deploy the ABM: Bureaucratic and Domestic Politics in the Johnson Administration." *World Politics* 25 (October 1972).

Jervis, Robert. "Cooperation under the Security Dilemma." *World Politics* 30 (January 1978).

———. "Realism, Game Theory, and Cooperation." *World Politics* 40 (April 1988).

Keohane, Robert. "Reciprocity in International Relations." *International Organization* 40 (Winter 1986).

———. "International Institutions: Two Approaches." *International Studies Quarterly* 32 (December 1988).

Krasner, Stephen. "Sovereignty: An Institutional Perspective." *Comparative Political Studies* 21 (April 1988).

———. "A Trade Strategy for the United States." *Ethics and International Affairs*, 1988.

Kreps, David M.; Milgrom, Paul; Roberts, John; and Wilson, Robert. "Rational Cooperation in the Finitely Repeated Prisoner's Dilemma." *Journal of Economic Theory* 27 (August 1982).

Kurth, James. "A Widening Gyre: The Logic of American Weapons Procurement." *Public Policy* 19 (Summer 1971).

Larson, Deborah Welch. "Game Theory and the Psychology of Reciprocity." Manuscript, Columbia University, July 1986.

———. "Crisis Prevention and the Austrian State Treaty." *International Organization* 41 (Winter 1987).

———. "Order under Anarchy: The Emergence of Convention in US-Soviet Relations." Paper delivered at the American Political Science Association convention, September 1989.

Lebow, Richard Ned, and Stein, Janice G. "Rational Deterrence Theory: I Think Therefore I Deter." *World Politics* 41 (January 1989).

Lipson, Charles. "International Cooperation in Economic and Security Affairs." *World Politics* 36 (July 1984).

Lynch, Harvey. "Technical Evaluation of Offensive Uses of SDI." Working Paper of the Center for International Security and Arms Control, Stanford University, 1987.

Machina, Mark. "Choice under Uncertainty: Problems Solved and Unsolved." *Economic Perspectives* 1 (Summer 1987).

March, James G., and Olsen, Johan P. "The New Institutionalism: Organizational Factors in Political Life." *American Political Science Review* 78 (September 1984).

McNamara, Robert S. "Defense Fantasy Come True: In an Exclusive Interview Secretary McNamara Explains in Full the Logic behind the ABM System." *Life*, September 29, 1967.

Meyer, Stephen. "Soviet Military Programmes and the New 'High Ground.'" *Survival* 25 (September–October 1983).

Miller, Steven. "Politics over Promise." *International Security* 8 (Spring 1984).

Moe, Terry M. "On the Scientific Status of Rational Models." *American Journal of Political Science* 23 (February 1979).

Molander, Per. "The Optimal Level of Generosity in a Selfish, Uncertain Environment." *Journal of Conflict Resolution* 29 (December 1985).

Morgan, Patrick. "Arms Control in International Politics: Some Theoretical Reflections." Working Paper no. 48, Center for International and Strategic Affairs, 1985.

Nye, Joseph. "Nuclear Learning and US-Soviet Security Regimes." *International Organization* 41 (Summer 1987).

Osgood, Charles E. "Suggestions for Winning the Real War with Communism." *Journal of Conflict Resolution* 3 (December 1959).

Pike, John. "Anti-Satellite Weapons." Federation of American Scientists Public Interest Report no. 36, 1983.

Pipes, Richard. "Why the Soviet Union Thinks It Could Fight and Win a Nuclear War." *Commentary* 64 (July 1977).

Rathjens, George, and Kistiakowsky, G. B. "Strategic Arms Limitation." *Proceedings of the Nineteenth Pugwash Conference in Science and World Affairs*, October 22–27, 1969.

Richelson, Jeffrey T. "PD-59, NSDD-13, and the Reagan Strategic Modernization Program." *Journal of Strategic Studies* 6 (June 1983).

Rosenberg, David Allen. "The Origins of Overkill: Nuclear Weapons and American Strategy 1945–1960." *International Security* 7 (Spring 1983).

Rothstein, Robert. "Consensual Knowledge and International Collaboration." *International Organization* 38 (Autumn 1984).

Schelling, Thomas C. "What Is Game Theory?" In *Contemporary Political Analysis*, edited by James C. Charlesworth. New York: Free Press, 1967.

———. "A Framework for the Evaluation of Arms Control Proposals." *Daedalus* 104 (Summer 1975).

Simon, Herbert A. "Human Nature in Politics: The Dialogue of Psychology with Political Science." *American Political Science Review* 79 (June 1985).

Stares, Paul. "US and Soviet Military Space Programs." *Daedalus* 114 (Spring 1985).

Stockholm International Peace Research Institute. *The Origins of MIRV*. SIPRI Research Report no. 9, August 1973.

Tversky, Amos, and Kahneman, Daniel. "Rational Choice and the Framing of Decisions." *Journal of Business* 59 (October 1986).

Wagner, R. Harrison. "The Theory of Games and the Problem of International Cooperation." *American Political Science Review* 77 (June 1983).

Weber, Steve. "Realism, Detente, and Nuclear Weapons." *International Organization* 44 (Winter 1990).

———. "Cooperation and Interdependence." *Daedalus* 120 (Winter 1991).

Wiesner, Jerome. "Comprehensive Arms Limitation Systems." *Daedalus* 89 (Fall 1960).

York, Herbert. "ABM, MIRV, and the Arms Race." *Science* 169 (July 1970).

———. "Multiple Warhead Missiles." *Scientific American* 229 (November 1973).

Public Documents

In addition to the documents listed here, I made use of several short memos cited in the footnotes. Nuclear History Project (NHP) documents are identified by their NHP Box number.

ABM, MIRV, SALT and the Nuclear Arms Race. Senate. Committee on Foreign Relations. Subcommittee on Arms Control, International Law and Organization. 91st Cong., 2d sess., 1970.

Allocation of Resources in the Soviet Union and China. Congress. Joint Economic Committee. Subcommittee on Priorities and Economy in Government. 94th Cong., 1st sess., 1975.

Anti-satellite Weapons, Countermeasures, and Arms Control. Office of Technology Assessment. OTA-ISC-281. Washington, D.C.: GPO, 1985.

Arms Control and Disarmament Agreements: Texts and Histories of Agreements. Department of State. Arms Control and Disarmament Agency, 1980.

Arms Control and the Militarization of Space. Senate. Committee on Foreign Relations. Subcommittee on Arms Control, Oceans, International Operations and Environment. 97th Cong., 2d sess., 1982.

Arms Control Impact Statements. Department of State. Arms Control and Disarmament Agency. Submitted to the Senate Committee on Foreign Relations. Various years.

Arms Control Implications of Current Defense Budget. Senate. Committee on Foreign Relations. Subcommittee on Arms Control, International Law and Organization. 92d Cong., 1st sess., 1971.

Authorizations for Military Procurement. House. Armed Services Committee. Annual.

Background Paper for NATO Ministerial Meeting in Luxembourg, 13–15 June 1967. Department of Defense. NHP Box 17.

Ballistic Missile Defense. Report of the Defense Science Board Task Force, 15 September 1966. NHP Box 16.

Congressional Record.

Department of Defense Appropriations. House. Committee on Appropriations. Subcommittee on DoD Appropriations. Annual.

Department of Defense Authorization for Appropriations. Senate. Committee on Armed Services. Annual.

Deterrence and Survival in the Nuclear Age (Gaither Report). Scientific Advisory Board. Security Resources Panel. Washington, D.C., 1957. Declassified January 1973.

Diplomatic and Strategic Impact of Multiple Warhead Missiles. House. Committee on Foreign Affairs. Subcommittee on National Security Policy and Scientific Developments. 91st Cong., 1st sess., 1969.

Documents on Disarmament. Department of State. Arms Control and Disarmament Agency. Various years.

Draft Presidential Memorandum on Strategic Offensive and Defensive Forces. Department of Defense, 9 January 1969. NHP Box 17.

The Economics of National Priorities. Congress. Joint Economic Committee. 92nd Cong., 1st sess., 1971.

Hearings on Military Posture. House. Armed Services Committee. 87th Cong., 1961–62; 88th Cong., 2d sess., 1964.

Intelligence and the ABM. Senate. Committee on Foreign Relations. 91st Cong., 1st sess., 1969.

International Negotiations. Senate. Committee on Governmental Affairs. Subcommittee on National Security and International Operations. 92d Cong., 2d sess., 1972.

Memorandum for Mr. Bundy, on meeting with Secretary McNamara on the DoD FY 1967 Budget, 9 November 1965. Spurgeon Keeny. NHP Box 18.

Memorandum for the President, FY 67–71 Strategic Offensive and Defensive Forces. Robert S. McNamara, Secretary of Defense, 1 November 1965. NHP Box 19.

Memorandum on Minuteman, Polaris, and Poseidon. Department of Defense 1967 Budget, 8 November 1965. NHP Box 19.

Military Implications of the Proposed Limited Test Ban Treaty: An Interim Report. Senate. Committee on Armed Services. Preparedness Investigating Subcommittee, 88th Cong., 1st sess., 1963.

Military Implications of the Treaty on the Limitations of Anti-Ballistic Missile Systems and the Interim Agreement on Limitation of Strategic Offensive Arms. Senate. Committee on Armed Services. 92d Cong., 2d sess., 1972.

NASA Authorization Hearings, 1960–77. Senate. Committee on Aeronautical and Space Sciences.

NASA Authorization Hearings, 1978–87. Senate. Committee on Commerce, Science, and Transportation. Subcommittee on Science, Technology, and Space.

Report by the Senate Foreign Relations Committee on the Treaty on the Limitation of Anti-ballistic Missile Systems. Senate. Committee on Foreign Relations. *Strategic Arms Limitations Agreements* Hearings. 92d Cong., 2d sess., July 1972.

Research and Development for Defense. House. Committee on Science and Astronautics. 87th Cong., 1st sess., 1961.

Scope, Magnitude, and Implications of the United States Antiballistic Missile Program. Congress. Joint Committee on Atomic Energy. 90th Cong., 1st sess., 1967.

Soviet Military Power. Department of Defense. Various years.

Soviet Space Programs (1966–70) and (1971–75). Senate. Committee on Aeronautical and Space Sciences. Staff Reports.

Space and National Security. Air Force "Talking Papers," AFXPD-LR, 1 November 1960. NHP Box 11.

Space Law: Selected Basic Documents. Senate. Committee on Commerce, Science, and Transportation, 1978.

Statement of the Secretary of Defense on the Five Year Defense Program and Annual Defense Budget. Secretary of Defense. Annual.

Status of US Antisatellite Program. General Accounting Office. Report to the Honorable George E. Brown, Jr. GAO/NSIAD-85-104, June 1985.

Status of US Strategic Power. Senate. Committee on Armed Services. Preparedness Investigating Subcommittee. 90th Cong., 2d sess., 1968.

A "Stop Where We Are" Proposal for SALT. Department of State. Arms Control and Disarmament Agency. ACDA-3356, 11 June 1969. NHP Box 20.

Strategic and Foreign Policy Implications of ABM Systems. Senate. Committee on Foreign Relations. Subcommittee on International Organization and Disarmament. 91st Cong., 1st sess., 1969.

Strategic Arms Limitations Agreements. Senate. Committee on Foreign Relations. 92d Cong., 2d sess., 1972.

Third Report of the Defense Science Board Task Force on Penetration. Defense Science Board, 15 September 1967. NHP Box 19.

Treaty on Outer Space. Senate. Committee on Foreign Relations. 90th Cong., 1st sess., 1967.

United States Armament and Disarmament Problems. Senate. Committee on Foreign Relations. Subcommittee on Disarmament. 90th Cong., 1st sess., 1967.

US Foreign Policy for the 1970s: A New Strategy for Peace. Richard M. Nixon, 1970.

US Foreign Policy for the 1970s: Building for Peace. Richard M. Nixon, 1971.

United States Military Posture. Joint Chiefs of Staff. Annual.

US Tactical Air Power Program. Senate. Committee on Armed Services. Preparedness Investigating Subcommittee. 90th Cong., 2d sess., 1968.

US-USSR Strategic Policies. Senate. Committee on Foreign Relations. Subcommittee on Arms Control, International Law and Organization. 93d Cong., 2d sess., 1974.

Weekly Compilation of Presidential Documents.

White House Fact Sheet Outlining US Space Policy, 4 July 1982.

Yearbook of the United Nations. United Nations. Various years.

Index

ABM (Antiballistic Missile Systems), cooperation in, 143–46; hard site vs. area defense, 98n; scenario for mutual cooperation in, 106–9; scenario for mutual defection in, 109–11; scenario for temptation to defect, 103–4; scenario for unrequited cooperation, 104–5
—U.S.: and bureaucratic politics, 135–36; and Congress, 128–30; decision point for, 98–100; deployment as dyadic choice, 99–100, 102–3; deployment options in, 63–64; and detente, 107–8; early research in, 86–87; early preferences in, 95–96; and early strategic theory, 87; public opposition to, 103
—Soviet: actions during negotiations, 133, 138–39, 140–41; early research in, 90; Galosh, 91, 96, 105n
ABM strategy (U.S.), contingent restraint as, 111–13; and feedback, 133–34, 144, 146; enhanced contingent restraint as, 113–19, 119–23; and working hypotheses, 118, 138–39
Achen, Christopher, 21n
adaptation, 79–80
anarchy, 7, 8n
argument-based choice, 68
arms control, 3–4; and bureaucratic politics, 20–21; and game theory, 17–23; international environment of, 19–20; relative vs. absolute gains in, 22–23; states as dominant actors in, 20
arms control theory, 25–28; classical, 25; and mixed-motive games, 26; and preferences, 25
arms races, action-reaction model of, 167
Arrow, Kenneth, 69
auxiliary theories, 60; as bridge principles, 61
ASAT (Antisatellite Systems), arms race in, 214–15; as competitive response, 214; and crisis instability, 213–15; evolution of self-interest in, 263–66; formal cooperation in, 252–53, 264–69; legacy of

cooperation in, 242–43, 268; and moderate uncertainty, 248; and radical uncertainty, 205–6, 230–31, 235–37, 242–43, 291–92; residual systems, 216; as prisoner's dilemma, 204–5, 215–18; and SALT I; tacit cooperation in, 223–24; verification of, 265
—U.S.: and the armed services, 249–50; bureaucratic politics and, 262; desire for cooperation in, 223–24; enemy image and, 261; interests in, 258–60; preferences in, 206, 212, 219; and strategic theory, 233–34, 261–62
—Soviet: interests in, 259; preferences in, 206, 212; tests of, 238–39, 250–51, 259, 263
ASAT strategy (U.S.), contingent restraint, 226, 232–33; contingent threat of escalation, 240, 247, 254–57, 260–62, 270; enhanced contingent restraint, 244, 252; and feedback, 236; shift in, 227–28; two-track, 254, 264; and working hypotheses, 205, 230–31, 235–36, 243, 247, 251, 253–54, 258–60
autarky, 272
Axelrod, Robert, 4–5, 10–11, 35–40, 43–45

bridge principles, 15, 59–65; as part of specific research project, 61–62
Brooke, Edward W., 173–75, 177, 185
Buchsbaum Panel, 248, 250, 252
Bueno de Mesquita, Bruce, 274n
bureaucratic politics, 20–21, 28, 78–79, 279–80, 311–12

Carter administration, and ASAT, 240, 254, 264
case study structure: historical background, 65–66; payoff analysis, 66–70; strategy development, 71–79
Clifford, Clark, 155–56
common interests, 7–8; and cooperation, 300, 302